Dividing Lines

PRINCETON STUDIES IN AMERICAN POLITICS:
HISTORICAL, INTERNATIONAL, AND COMPARATIVE
PERSPECTIVES

SERIES EDITORS
Ira Katznelson, Martin Shefter, Theda Skocpol

A list of titles
in this series appears
at the back of
the book

Dividing Lines

THE POLITICS OF IMMIGRATION
CONTROL IN AMERICA

Daniel J. Tichenor

PRINCETON UNIVERSITY PRESS

PRINCETON AND OXFORD

Published by Princeton University Press, 41 William Street, Princeton, New Jersey 08540
In the United Kingdom: Princeton University Press, 3 Market Place, Woodstock,
Oxfordshire OX20 1SY

Library of Congress Cataloging-in-Publication Data

Tichenor, Daniel J., 1966–
Dividing lines : the politics of immigration control in America / Daniel J. Tichenor.
p. cm. — (Princeton studies in American politics)
Includes bibliographical references and index.

1. United States—Emigration and immigration—Government policy—History.
I. Title. II. Series.

JV6483 .T494   2002
325.73—dc21   2001036870

British Library Cataloging-in-Publication Data is available

This book has been composed in Galliard

Printed on acid-free paper. ∞

www.pup.princeton.edu

Printed in the United States of America

10 9 8 7 6 5 4 3 2 1

ISBN-13: 978-0-691-08805-1

ISBN-10: 0-691-08805-5

FOR MY PARENTS, RUTH AND JAY

who taught me to love politics, books, and strangers, and for my wife, Elaine, and children, Natalie and Eric, who stole my heart

Contents

Tables and Figures

Figures

Acknowledgments

OVER THE LONG journey that led to *Dividing Lines*, I have received more support from family, friends, teachers, colleagues, and students than I can adequately recount. James Hollifield got me started on this project, pushing me early on to think about questions of immigration and membership that I am still working out. Lawrence Fuchs offered not only expertise and constructive criticism in the initial stages of my research, but he also let me borrow his home and his impressive personal collection of official papers and immigration works. Deborah Stone offered incisive suggestions on the earliest version of the manuscript. My greatest intellectual debts are to two scholars who inspired me as a graduate student and who continue to give invaluable support and advice: Sidney Milkis and R. Shep Melnick. At crucial stages of this project, Shep provided encouragement, practical wisdom, and penetrating feedback. Sid was my dissertation supervisor, and his attentiveness to this study and to my professional well-being has been an enormous godsend. His passion for reconnecting history and political science and his ideas about democracy and American political development richly inform the analysis that follows.

In the course of my research, I received gracious archival assistance from the staffs of the American Jewish Historical Society, the John F. Kennedy Presidential Library, the Library of Congress, the National Archives, and other institutions. I am profoundly grateful to the more than one hundred former and current government officials, lobbyists, and other policy "insiders" who granted interviews and provided me access to transcripts of House and Senate committee markups as well as to organizational and personal papers. Each of these interviewees was promised anonymity, but their powerful insights and colorful oral histories enliven my account of contemporary immigration politics.

My students at Rutgers University persistently enlighten and energize me; two of them, Frederick Strasser and Abraham Strasser, provided superb research assistance and are destined for seats on the federal bench. Many of my Rutgers colleagues regularly offer engaging discussion and support, or simply remind me why I got into the academic business in the first place. Special thanks are owed to Dennis Bathory, Richard Lau, Susan Lawrence, Richard Lehne, Milton Heumann, Michael Paris, Gerald Pomper, and Wilson Carey McWilliams for their encouragement.

A number of colleagues at other institutions read all or part of the manuscript and offered wonderful guidance on how to enhance this work. They include Gary Freeman, Desmond King, Robert Lieberman, Eileen McDonagh, James Morone, Carol Nackenoff, Andrew Polsky, Rogers Smith, and several anonymous reviewers. I have benefited over the years from the generosity of several academic mensches: Earlham professors Stephen Heiney, Robert M. Johnstone, and Maria Chan Morgan, as well as Martha Derthick, Martin Levin, Susan Moller Okin, Peter Skerry, and Marc Landy.

Generous financial support for this work was provided by an Abba Schwartz Fellowship from the John F. Kennedy Presidential Library, a Governmental Studies Fellowship from the Brookings Institution, as well as Gordon and Sachar Fellowships from Brandeis University.

It has been a pleasure working with my editor, Chuck Myers, of Princeton University Press. I am also grateful to the series editors, Ira Katznelson, Martin Shefter, and Theda Skocpol.

In significant respects, this is a deeply personal book. I grew up hearing stories from my paternal grandfather and great-aunt about the structural barriers they encountered trying to rescue Hungarian Jewish family members during the late 1930s; few of them survived the Holocaust. My maternal grandparents were German immigrants to the United States who took on the unsettling demands of an adopted country to leave behind poverty of the old; theirs is a story, however clichéd, that can be told by every generation of American immigrants. For all of my grandparents' love, struggles, and success, eugenicists not withstanding, I am thankful. I am especially grateful to my parents, Ruth and Jay Tichenor, my sister Kristin and her family, and my mother-in-law, Delores Replogle, who give me moral support and unconditional love. My spirited children Natalie and Eric provide a constant supply of hugs, giggles, howls, and crayon-covered walls that remind me that book writing is a distraction from this world's true blessings. I am most grateful to my wife, Elaine Replogle, whose love, passion, intellect, and always more robust sense of justice and community at once soothes and challenges me.

Dividing Lines

CHAPTER ONE

Introduction

THIS STUDY IS an inquiry into the politics of American immigration control over more than two centuries. The revered historian Oscar Handlin once observed that any adequate treatment of "the course and effects of immigration" on our country "involved no less a task than to set down the whole history of the United States."[1] Fortunately, my purposes here are much more modest. Few of the leaders of the early republic could have guessed how profoundly immigration would influence U.S. national development. Yet almost every subsequent generation has readily understood the capacity of newcomers to dramatically alter the American society that received them. Each has had at its disposal ample evidence that the demographic transformations introduced by robust immigration often translate into important economic, social, and political change. Given these high stakes, it is little wonder that U.S. policies governing immigrant admissions and rights have been the object of significant political struggle throughout American history. My chief aim in this volume is to provide a fresh analytic account of these pivotal struggles, of the immigration policies that prevailed, and of the recurrent and emergent processes that shaped both over time—processes not easily revealed in the short time horizons of most contemporary social science research. It is a story of contested change in a country celebrated and reviled for its political inertia.

Nations define themselves through the official selection and control of foreigners seeking permanent residence on their soil.[2] Immigration policy involves not only regulating the size and diversity of the population, but also the privileging of certain visions of nationhood, social order, and international engagement. For Americans who have traditionally disagreed over whether theirs is truly "a nation of immigrants," to borrow the memorable phrase of John F. Kennedy (or more precisely, that of his ghostwriter), these regulatory decisions have been especially difficult.[3] In nearly every era of U.S. history, there has been fierce debate on the economic, social, cultural, and national security consequences of new immigration. Whereas native-born citizens and leaders tend to mythologize their sojourner past (the slave trade is conveniently excised from this iconography), they have often clashed over whether the latest arrivals compare favorably with those who came before.

For all of the conflict that this issue has inspired in American national politics, it is striking how many of these struggles have culminated in dramatic policy innovations that set distinctive regulatory patterns for extended periods of U.S. history. Table 1.1 helps capture the scope of historical policy change by providing an overview of major federal immigration legislation since the Gilded Age. Later chapters also highlight significant judicial and administrative policy activism during the same periods. Figure 1.1 presents a picture of the changing shape of legal immigration to the United States since the 1820s (when official immigration statistics were first kept). The development of federal immigration policy reflects important patterns and variations over time, including long-term shifts between restricting and expanding immigration opportunities. Save for the fleeting Alien and Sedition Acts, the national government embraced an essentially laissez-faire approach to immigration for many decades after the founding.[4] Immigration reforms of the late-nineteenth century brought both sweeping Chinese exclusion policies and limited screening of other immigrant groups; entry for most white European newcomers remained unfettered at the close of the Gilded Age. During the Progressive Era and the 1920s, immigration opponents fought successfully for increasingly draconian restrictions targeted at southern and eastern Europeans as well as nonwhites. The result was a fiercely restrictionist policy regime based on national origins quotas and racial exclusions that endured well after the Second World War. During the 1960s, national origins quotas were dismantled in favor of a new preference system that reserved most annual visas for immigrants with family connections to U.S. citizens and permanent residents. In subsequent years, economic uneasiness and unprecedented levels of Asian, Latin American, and Caribbean immigration contributed to a surge of popular anti-immigrant views in the country. Nevertheless, national policymakers adopted several major reforms in recent decades that significantly expanded immigrant admissions and rights. Although many scholars point to a "new nativism" emerging in American politics during the past decade,[5] the policy impact of modern restrictionists has been remarkably meager.

The central puzzle to be addressed in this book is how and why these decidedly expansive and restrictive policy regimes have emerged from American immigration politics over time. That is, how do we explain why the U.S. national state has been quite receptive to immigrants during long stretches of its history, while it has pursued decisive restrictions on the number and characteristics of newcomers in other periods? More generally, why have certain ideas, social interests, and political actors triumphed over others in periodic struggles over immigration policy in U.S. history? These are the questions I attempt to parse in the pages that follow. I do so by analyzing national immigration policymaking *across* American political development. To truly understand the broad patterns

TABLE 1.1
Overview of Major U.S. Immigration Legislation

Historical Period	Legislation/Year	Major Provisions
Gilded Age	Immigration Act (1875)	Bars prostitutes and criminals
	Chinese Exclusion Act (1882)	Makes Chinese laborers inadmissible
	Immigration Act (1882)	Bars convicts, "lunatics," "idiots," and those "likely to become a public charge" and establishes head tax on immigrants
	Contract Labor Act (1885)	Prohibits contract labor admissions
	Chinese Exclusion Act (1888)	Extends Chinese exclusion
	Immigration Act (1891)	Creates federal immigration bureaucracy; authorizes deportation of illegal aliens
Progressive Era and 1920s	Immigration Act (1903)	Bars polygamists and "anarchists"
	Gentlemen's Agreement (1907)	Severely limits Japanese immigration
	Immigration Act (1907)	Creates Dillingham Commission; increases head tax; creates new exclusion categories
	Immigration Act (1917)	Imposes literacy test for admission; bars virtually all Asians from entry
	National Quota Law (1921)	Limits immigration of each nationality to 3% of the number of foreign-born of that nationality living in the U.S. in 1910
	National Origins Act (1924)	Sets annual quotas for each nationality at 2% of the number of persons of that nationality in the U.S. as determined by the 1890 census.
	National Quota Law (1929)	Apportions annual quotas of 1924 for each country according to each nationality's percentage of 1920 census
New Deal and World War II Years	Immigration Act (1940)	INS transferred from Labor to Justice Department as national security measure

TABLE 1.1 (*cont.*)

Historical Period	Legislation/Year	Major Provisions
	Bracero Program (1943)	Bilateral agreements with Mexico, British Honduras, Barbados, and Jamaica provide for guestworkers
	Act of December 17 (1943)	Repeals Chinese exclusion in favor of meager quotas
The 1940s and 1950s	War Brides Act (1945)	Allows for immigration of foreign-born spouses and children of U.S. military personnel
	Displaced Persons Act (1948)	Facilitates admission of European refugees
	Internal Security Act (1950)	Expands grounds for both exclusion and deportation; establishes alien registry
	Immigration and Naturalization Act (1952)	Reaffirms national origins quota system; adds new grounds for exclusion based on political activities, ideology, and sexual preference
	Refugee Relief Act (1953)	Grants permanent residence to 214,000 European refugees
	Refugee-Escapee Act (1957)	Grants special status to refugees fleeing communist regimes
The 1960s and 1970s	Cuban Refugee Act (1960)	Begins Cuban Refugee Program
	Refugee Assistance Act (1963)	Extends cash, medical, and educational support to refugees
	Bracero Reauthorization (1964)	Terminates Bracero Program
	Hart-Celler Act (1965)	Dismantles national origins quotas; begins seven-category preference system with an emphasis on family reunification
	Indochina Refugee Act (1975)	Begins Indochinese resettlement program
	INA Amendments (1976)	Sets per country limits (20K) for both the Eastern and Western Hemispheres
	Indochinese Refugee Act (1977)	Admits 174,988 refugees from Indochina

TABLE 1.1 (*cont.*)

Historical Period	Legislation/Year	Major Provisions
	INA Amendments (1978)	Establishes worldwide ceiling of 290,000 on annual immigrant admissions
The 1980s and 1990s	Refugee Act (1980)	Adopts UN definition of "refugee"; expands annual refugee admissions
	Immigration Reform and Control Act (1986)	Grants amnesty/permanent residence to 3 million undocumented aliens; imposes watered-down employer sanctions; establishes immigrant antidiscrimination agency in Justice Dept.; initiates special agricultural worker program
	Immigration Act (1990)	Increases annual immigration cap to 675,000; reaffirms family reunification preferences but adds employment-based and "diversity" visas
	Personal Responsibility Act (1996)	Limits immigrant access of noncitizens to public welfare benefits
	Illegal Immigration Reform and Individual Responsibility Act (1996)	Strengthens border enforcement and employer sanctions; expedites the deportation process; establishes exceptions for noncitizen access to public benefits

and transformations of this crucial policy area requires a long-term historical perspective that may illuminate causal processes often obscured by short time-frames.

This study places special emphasis on the powerful interactions between political institutions, ideological traditions, and organized social interests that have received scant attention in prevailing society-centered theories of the immigration policy process. As the noted sociologist and immigration scholar Alejandro Portes recently noted, there is a glaring absence of "systematic theoretical analysis of both the external pressures impinging on the state and the internal dynamics of the legislative and admistrative bodies [and other governing institutions] dealing with immigration."[6] This book attempts to redress some of these important gaps. American immigration control over time can be explained as much by changes in how public policy is formulated and implemented—and more

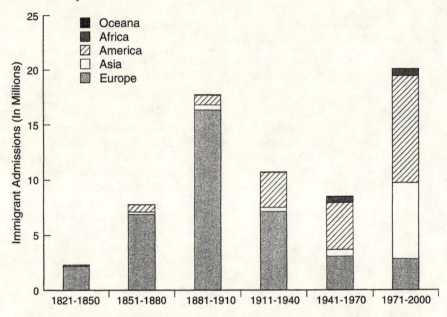

Fig. 1.1.   U.S. Immigration by Region of Origin, 1820–2000 (Source: *INS Statistical Yearbook, 2001* [Washington, DC: Government Printing Office, 2001])

generally by how politics is organized in the United States—as by economic, social, and cultural forces. Like other recent works of historical institutionalism, this volume attempts to offer new insights about state-society relations and the possibilities of policy innovation in an American polity replete with structural veto-points and a political culture hostile to centralized state authority.[7]

While my chief purpose is to explain policy patterns and variations, two additional concerns inform my investigation of immigration control across U.S. political development. First, I also hope to highlight the capacity of both restrictive and expansive immigration policies to transform the American political landscape. John Kingdon has recently joined Seymour Martin Lipset in arguing that early immigration helped send the United States along a particular developmental pathway;[8] yet we should bear in mind that subsequent waves of immigration—especially in large volumes and from new sources—have had the potential to be disruptive forces that may unsettle existing orders and possibly encourage political turning points. In this vein, policies that advance "new" immigration introduce demographic shifts in the American population that may alter other facets of U.S. political life. As we shall see, new immigrants have proven capable of influencing the electoral calculations of party leaders and individual candidates, recasting how established interest groups define their policy goals, building new ethnic organizations to influence government actions, and even contributing directly to shifts in social science expertise with relevance to policymakers. Likewise, policies designed to restrict new immigration, although usually intended to preserve the socioeconomic and political status quo, have in fact routinely entailed the creation of new state structures and powers to enhance federal government regulation of aliens both at and within its borders. Government efforts to harness the disruptive force of immigration, however illusory as a goal, thus have produced significant national state-building in U.S. political history.

A second related concern of this book is to consider what immigration policymaking in American political development reveals about how different generations of government officials have interpreted the demands of liberal democracy and political community in the United States. Whether the product of what Rogers Smith views as contending traditions of liberal democracy and ascriptive inequality or what Ira Katznelson identifies as a liberal tradition whose "principled thinness" leaves it "vulnerable to illiberal temptations," exclusionary visions of ethnic, racial, and religious hierarchy have found more than fleeting expression in government efforts to regulate immigrant admissions.[9] Yet a rich variety of other ideological commitments also have influenced national immigration policy, including official decisions to advance expansive opportunities for alien admissions at times of popular animus toward aliens. Whereas commentators from A. Lawrence Lowell to Peter Brimelow have insisted that immigration controls reflect "the need for homogeneity in a democracy," others, from Jane Addams to Hubert Humphrey, have countered that "American democracy has no genealogy."[10] Immigration policymaking over the long haul unveils a powerful rivalry of liberal, republican, and inegalitarian traditions in American political history, one that belies the hegemonic liberal consensus or solidifying "American Creed" described by scholars from Louis Hartz to Samuel Huntington.[11] But whereas many studies have examined these respective traditions in isolation of one another, this work explores the political and institutional processes that have influenced competition between these ideological streams and have translated them into concrete policies.

Chapter 2 provides a theoretical foundation for understanding immigration policymaking in American political development. I begin with a critique of various theories of public policy and American politics that attach special causal importance in the policy process to either economic conditions, the power of social interests, shared national values, public opinion, or electoral realignments. Each of these rubrics has some merit as an explanatory variable, but none adequately accounts for the evolution of American immigration policies. I advance instead a historical-institutionalist view that examines how the political activities of government officials and social groups are "conditioned" by distinct institutional and ideological orderings of the national state and political party systems.[12] As such, I hope to address what Richard McCormick calls the "politics-policy puzzle": the significant but oft-neglected connections between broad changes in the national polity and policy formulation in American history.[13]

The analytical framework I present in chapter 2 places special emphasis on four interlocking processes that illuminate key patterns and transformations of U.S. immigration policy across American political history. First, I argue that the exceptional fragmentation of power in the American governmental system has long unleashed an institutional dynamism that presents social groups and other policy activists with changing structural opportunities and constraints to pursue their policy goals. Following in the tradition of political scientists like E. E. Schattschneider, I assume that political institutions are not neutral but in fact provide unequal access and leverage to distinct actors and social groups.[14] Individuals and groups who have secured favorable policy outcomes in national struggles over immigration typically have enjoyed special structural advantages over their opponents under given institutional arrangements of the national state and party system. As much as other policy domains, decisive triumphs and nonincremental immigration reforms have been hard to achieve due to the abundance of "veto-points" in American government, thus often biasing the process in favor of existing policy patterns. At the same time, a fragmented American constitutional structure and ever-changing political institutions have meant that dominant political actors and structures may be displaced over time. To understand the possibilities of major policy innovation requires knowledge of how immigration activists have exploited new institutional openings in American governing institutions. Equally striking is the extent to which the guardians of existing immigration policies have consciously built and actively maintained institutional supports for their policy regimes.

Second, I suggest that the dynamics of U.S. immigration policy have long been influenced by the making and *remaking* of distinctive political coalitions on this issue that cut across familiar partisan and ideological lines. At least since the late-nineteenth century, this policy domain has divided pro-immigration free marketeers and restrictionist cultural exclusionists on the American Right, and pro-immigration cosmopolitans and restrictionist economic protectionists on the American Left. As a result, it would be hard to think of an area of U.S. public policy that has engendered more incongruous political alliances in American history.[15] And it is precisely the creation of these unstable yet powerful liberal-conservative coalitions over the years that I argue has proven crucial to achieving major immigration reform in the United States. Significantly, the relative power of the pro-immigration and restrictionist coalitions have shifted over time as new interest groups and political actors have emerged and as older ones have redefined their policy goals. For example, the organization of new nationality groups in Washington (an important by-product of past immigration policies) and decisive shifts in organized labor's immigration agenda have significantly affected the coalitional balance of power. Policy changes have been closely tied to the possibilities of rebuilding Left-Right coalitions to support new policies. But such coalitional breakthroughs have been anything but routine. To avoid the profoundly disorienting and acrimonious politics invited by immigration reform efforts, national political leaders often have attempted to frustrate major action on this issue. Likewise, the tremendous difficulties of building new liberal-conservative coalitions frequently have vexed policy reformers. Although these challenges to coalition building have tended to reinforce the policy patterns of a given period, the episodic rise of new groups and alliances in immigration politics have created opportunities for policy transformation.

A third process that I shall examine is the significant role played by professional expertise in immigration policy making at least since the Progressive Era. At key junctures in each period of political struggle over immigration control, the national state has privileged certain kinds of immigration expertise or social knowledge in the investigations of congressional committees, federal bureaucracies, and special commissions. Privileged expertise has long influenced the very framing of immigration as a national political issue, breathing life into a dominant immigration narrative that resolves competing "causal stories" and helps shape concrete policy responses.[16] Tellingly, competing actors and social groups have understood the importance of causal stories and expert ideas in national immigration politics, recognizing that "the definition of alternatives is the supreme instrument of power."[17] Social science expertise on immigration, as we shall see, has tended to intertwine empirical and normative elements, reflecting historically embedded interests, values, and cultural predispositions. Nonincremental policy change has relied on the privileging of fresh expertise by the national state and on the construction of a newly dominant immigration narrative to rationalize major policy departures. In turn, because prevailing immigration narratives and policy experts have been hard to dislodge, their persistence has fortified existing policy patterns.

Finally, new international crises or threats episodically have served as important catalysts for major immigration reform, altering the incentives and capacities of political actors to break policy stalemates. This is hardly surprising given the fact that immigration control represents a realm of government action that intersects domestic and foreign policy. International strains sometimes have fueled a traditional American impulse toward isolationism and a more modern and inward-looking nationalism that views a homogeneous population as the foundation of a strong state. Heightened animus toward foreign elements in these periods of isolationist fervor have extended naturally to immigrants and other aliens, especially those deemed most threatening to national uniformity. And immigration restrictionists at times have skillfully channeled these xenophobic energies into decisive shifts favoring a particular immigration narrative and attendant policy innovations. Yet other global pressures, such as Cold War competition with the Soviet Union or competitive world trade, have triggered transitions from isolationist to internationalist conceptions of the nation's global role, with the effect of expanding political openings for pro-immigration initiatives. Indeed, initiatives perceived as responsive to international pressures on the United States frequently have drawn cross-party support in government and steeled officials to advance initiatives opposed by key organized interests and mass publics. Whether producing isolationist and internationalist reactions, new global threats or imperatives have proven to be a significant impetus for major immigration reform. Interestingly, specific policy responses often have been formulated by immigration activists before a crisis emerges, with adroit immigration reformers exploiting global strains to achieve long-desired policy outcomes.

As chapter 2 elucidates, the four processes just described do not operate in isolation of each other. Social scientists often have a penchant for separating causal forces from one another, seeking to disaggregate variables for the laudable purpose of determining which are most influential. However, such efforts typically have proven insufficient, if not quixotic, when applied to the daunting puzzles of immigration policymaking in America; noble designs for parsimonious explanation too often have culminated in an unsatisfying reductionism. Disaggregation routinely obscures crucial interlocking processes that lie at the heart of government actions. Indeed, I argue that the dynamic interplay of historically changing political institutions, policy alliances, privileged expertise, and international pressures has profoundly shaped American immigration policies over time. Together these four processes illuminate the enormous challenges and complexities of achieving major policy innovation in a fragmented political system replete with veto-points. Yet they also capture the possibilities of innovation in a U.S. polity whose governing institutions, social interests, and dominant political ideals are often changing.

Chapters 3 through 9 are chronological and developmental, intended both to explain the broad patterns and transformations of American immigration policy in distinctive periods and to reveal how past political events may build on one another. Chapters 3 and 4 analyze the early nationalization of American immigration policy during the nineteenth century's Gilded Age, a period that culminated in limited if not lax regulation of European immigration and sweeping exclusion of Chinese immigration. How do we explain these policy outcomes? Moreover, why were significant new capacities carved out for the U.S. national state to regulate immigration at a time when centralized government was in retreat? The answers, I suggest in chapters 3 and 4, lie within the operations of the nineteenth century U.S. "state of courts and parties." Whereas "party procedures lent operational coherence to the disjointed institutions of the governmental apparatus," Stephen Skowronek notes of this time, "court proceedings determined the meaning and the effect of the law itself."[18]

These institutional arrangements were pivotal to the politics of European immigration control from the nation's founding to the end of the nineteenth century, playing a prominent role in frustrating nativist assaults on Irish, German, and other European admissions. Chapter 3 offers a "path dependence" argument to account for the steady expansion of European inflows of this century even after several momentous judicial rulings hastened the nationalization of U.S. immigration policy. At a time of low immigration, plentiful land, and labor scarcity, the nation's early political leaders established easy naturalization for European immigrants while eschewing federal controls over their admission. The rise of mass-based parties and universal white male suffrage in the Jacksonian era reinforced broad opportunities for European immigration. The Democratic party almost from its inception courted immigrant voters by opposing nativist policy goals. Although the Republican party was sometimes prone to anti-immigrant nationalism, it also was attentive to pro-immigration constituents and eager to prod national economic development through immigrant labor. Judicial activism of the 1870s ultimately led to limited federal regulation of European admissions, but the vibrant partisan and electoral politics was routinely inhospitable to nativist policy designs throughout the nineteenth century. As a result, national restrictions on European inflows were quite modest for more than a century.

The politics of Chinese exclusion presented in chapter 4 offers a very different picture of the immigration policies produced by the early American "state of courts of parties." During the Gilded Age, anti-Chinese activists of the Pacific Coast discovered that they could galvanize robust cross-party, Left-Right support for their proposals in Washington at a time of intense partisan competition for Western votes. Unlike their European counterparts, Chinese newcomers were essentially powerless to resist new exclusionary laws, given their lack of political access or leverage in U.S. courts or partisan elections of the nineteenth century. A broad alliance of politicians and social groups converged behind an immigration narrative that portrayed Chinese sojourners as servile, racially inferior, and fundamentally unassimilable—an exception to virtuous mainstream immigration from traditional European sources. Finally, early presidential resistance to Chinese exclusion due to treaty obligations carried little weight in this isolationist era, and was easily subordinated to the pressing electoral calculations of party managers.

The policy patterns that emerged in the 1880s and 1890s—sweeping Chinese exclusion and very mild regulation of European admissions— became the subject of renewed political conflict in the early-twentieth century. In chapter 5, I examine the monumental struggle between immigration defenders and restrictionists in the first three decades of this century, and address why the latter ultimately triumphed so decisively despite many formidable impediments. During the Progressive Era, opponents of immigration noted with dread that the national origins of most newcomers to the United States were shifting steadily from northern and western to southern and eastern European sources. New activists called for policy innovations that targeted this "new" European immigration for sharp restriction. But these reformers encountered stiff resistance from an unlikely coalition of xenophiles, including various nationality groups, liberal social reformers devoted to cultural pluralism, and business organizations like the National Association of Manufacturers, which hoped to maintain cheap immigrant labor. Opposing camps also formed in the legislative and executive branches, with congressional party leaders and presidents often derailing restrictionist designs. Moreover, champions of existing policies offered compelling pro-immigration narratives that challenged nativist accounts.

Yet restrictionists made the most of institutional changes within the national state that increasingly insulated immigration policymaking from political parties and mass publics, including immigrant voters. They came to dominate congressional immigration committees, a fact that assumed great importance as the strength of party leadership receded in the legislative branch after 1910–11. Like other reformers of the time, restrictionists took advantage of new structural openings for direct advocacy by organized interests in Washington. And nativists enjoyed special influence over the expert findings of two federal immigration commissions, bestowing scientific legitimacy on an essentially eugenicist narrative that portrayed southern and eastern Europeans as *racially* inferior to earlier immigrants and linked these newcomers to a host of new strains on an uneasy American society. This narrative had powerful resonance for a vital new Left-Right coalition comprised of organized labor, patriotic societies, the Brahmin Immigration Restriction League, Southern conservatives, and reform-minded scholars. When the First World War and the Red Scare stoked nationalist anxieties to a new crescendo, pro-immigration nationality groups retreated, business interests reevaluated their policy goals, and an internationalist president lost the power to derail nativist reforms. Against this backdrop, restrictionists were well positioned to channel national security jitters into specific policy innovations that fused immigration control with racial hierarchy. The national origins quota system was born.

Compared to the ambitious immigration lawmaking of earlier years, the 1930s and 1940s are striking for their relative legislative quietude on immigration questions. As chapter 6 discusses, daunting political and structural barriers stood in the way of immigration reform. Eager to avoid issues that might polarize a fragile New Deal coalition, Franklin D. Roosevelt and his lieutenants worked to keep immigration and refugee initiatives off the public agenda. On those rare occasions when immigration reform proposals did receive legislative consideration, they were derailed by hostile congressional immigration committees, which zealously guarded the national origins quota system.

Beyond the legislative arena, however, a two-tiered regulatory regime emerged in these years with fateful consequences for two migrant groups: Jewish refugees and Mexican farmworkers. Frustrated by uneven enforcement at stateside immigration stations like Ellis Island, restrictionists empowered new State Department agencies to control immigrant inspections overseas. Using broad discretion, State Department officials took steps during the Second World War to deny admission to Jewish refugees. A very different regulatory tier dealt with Mexican guestworkers. During this period, an "iron triangle" of Southwestern employers (especially agricultural growers), Western and Southern chairs of congressional immigration committees, and federal immigration bureaucrats supported the legal and illicit importation of Mexican labor. Under pressure from growers to secure cheap Mexican labor, Southern and Western congressmen reasoned that unlike Asians and new European immigrants, Mexican farmworkers were easily "returnable" and thus posed no threat of becoming permanent members of the political community. A formal guestworker program and lax enforcement along the United States–Mexican border ensured that Southwestern employers had a steady supply of cheap labor. This chapter makes clear that the details of administration can have profound policy implications.

Chapter 7 examines the intense battles over alien admissions that reemerged in American national politics from the waning stages of the Second World War to the dismantlement of national origins quotas in 1965. Once again, we find that the dynamism of national government institutions, policy alliances, expertise, and international affairs are pivotal in remaking American immigration policy. Postwar presidents and congressional "committee barons" clashed over Cold War imperatives and their significance for refugee admissions and the national origins quota system; each used independent bases of institutional power to advance competing policy goals in the late 1940s and the 1950s. But pro-immigration reformers enjoyed dramatically new institutional openings in the 1960s, as conservative committee leaders were challenged in both houses of Congress by a growing number of younger and more activist members and as Kenr. Jy and Johnson employed the ample resources of the modern presidency to pursue ambitious policy agendas. Shifting policy alliances among politically active social groups were also significant, most notably organized labor's decision to repudiate national origins quotas it had endorsed for decades. In contrast to the Progressive Era, a new commission and other forms of institutionalized expertise assailed ethnic and racial distinctions in national immigration and refugee law. In 1965, a broad Left-Right coalition of politicians and organized interests embraced a fresh immigration narrative linking expansive policy initiatives to Cold War competition and civil rights reform. These foreign policy and civil rights concerns would make popular majoritarian views increasingly peripheral in an immigration policymaking process already dominated by centralized state actors, organized social groups, and policy experts.

Chapters 8 and 9 focus on the patterns and reforms of American immigration policy during the past three decades, a period in which the general public and a new restrictionist movement grew increasingly uneasy about unprecedented Third World immigration, large-scale illegal immigration, and crises of mass asylum. Opinion polls conducted throughout the period indicated that ordinary citizens favored reductions in nearly all forms of immigrant admissions. Chapter 8 discusses the politics of immigration control during the 1970s, a period that saw significant changes in the volume and regional origin of newcomers settling in the United States. This chapter examines the rise of a modern restrictionist movement and the response of national policymakers, which included the establishment of a respected bipartisan commission that advanced pro-immigration expertise. As we shall see, this period served as an important prelude to significant policy changes in the decade that followed.

The politics of immigration reform during the past two decades is the focus of chapter 9. Between 1980 and 1990, several major immigration reforms established more generous terms of refugee relief, increased opportunities for legal immigration, and extended unparalleled amnesty programs for undocumented aliens. Significantly, policymakers expected these innovations to primarily benefit nonwhite newcomers from Asia and Latin America. But this is only half of the contemporary immigration control story. Many observers perceived a sharp turn against immigration in the United States after the election of 1994, which yielded a controversial anti-immigrant initiative in California and a new Republican leadership in Congress open to restrictionist proposals. Within a few years, however, efforts to reduce alien admissions had lost all momentum. The restrictionist assault on alien welfare and due process rights proved far more successful, but many of these rights were restored by the turn of the millennium. The resilience of expansive immigration policies during the past decade is just as striking as their creation in the decade before. This chapter suggests that two contrasting kinds of politics have promoted expansive immigration policies in this period: one rooted in immigrant enfranchisement and competitive democratic elections and the other in the insulation of elite decisionmakers from ordinary citizens.

I hope the pages that follow offer a fresh view of both immigration control and American political development. Neither can be fully understood without taking stock of the other. This is especially true of the broad patterns and transformations of U.S. immigration policy over time, which have been shaped considerably by processes of national political development. It is a story of the rich variety of institutional and ideological orderings that have emerged in American political history, and their surprising capacity to give form and substance to new policy regimes.

CHAPTER TWO

The Politics of Immigration Control

UNDERSTANDING THE RISE AND
FALL OF POLICY REGIMES

THE LONG-TERM development of American immigration policy raises important issues that merit careful investigation. One is how to explain the distinctive patterns of immigration control that have prevailed for extended periods of U.S. history. What forces have sustained certain immigration policies over time? Another issue is how to account for occasional bursts of major policy change in spite of intense political conflicts that might be expected to produce routine stalemate. What propels significant innovation in this policy area? A final issue is how to make sense of the content or direction of immigration policy over time. Why do pro-immigration policies triumph in some periods and restrictionist policies in others? What explains precisely *how* state actors have chosen to restrict or expand immigration opportunities? This chapter explores these questions, offering an analytical framework for understanding the creation, maintenance, and demise of immigration policy regimes across American political development.

The formation of restrictive and expansive policy regimes is especially intriguing for distinct reasons. Sweeping immigration restrictions require important new forms of intervention by the national state in an American political culture usually uneasy about government power. Particularly remarkable in this regard is the fact that new restrictionist policy regimes have expanded the authority and capacities of the national state during periods when political hostility toward federal governmental activism has been at its zenith, such as the 1870s and 1880s (with its reaction against Reconstruction nationalism) and the 1920s (with its "return to normalcy"). Moreover, the creation of immigration barriers has required the defeat of a formidable coalition of pro-immigration advocacy groups in the United States, including highly organized business and ethnic groups with strong interests in preserving robust immigration opportunities. As one scholar put it, "immigration tends to produce concentrated benefits and diffuse costs, giving those who benefit from immigration greater incentives to organize than persons who bear its costs."[1] If the fragmented structure of the American political process is biased toward concentrated and organized interests, as E. E. Schattschneider argues, then we must explain why powerful pro-immigration groups sometimes have lost decisively in struggles over immigration control.[2]

Liberalizing immigration reforms are equally striking because mass publics in the United States typically oppose new immigrant admissions. Both new immigrant groups and pro-immigration policies have long inspired popular animus. As Rita Simon and Susan Alexander conclude in a study of American public attitudes toward immigration since the late-nineteenth century, "the most consistent theme that emerges . . . is the essentially negative attitudes held by a majority of the U.S. public toward persons wishing to come to the United States."[3] This does not mean that native-born Americans are unromantic about their own immigrant history. Alejandro Portes and Ruben Rumbaut describe a process "dating back to the origins of the republic" in which new immigration is "reviled when it is actually taking place" until "the first generation has passed from the scene and its descendants—now American citizens—are able to revindicate its achievements."[4] Most Americans have embraced the nation's sojourner past while scorning its immigrant present and future. Although the national origins quota system constricted immigrant admissions to a mere trickle from 1928 to 1965, most Americans stiffly resisted expanded admissions during the heyday of this restrictive policy regime— objecting even to extending temporary emergency asylum for refugees fleeing Nazi repression as captured in table 2.1. And well after the Immigration Act of 1965 dismantled the quota system, most of those polled favored decreases in immigrant admissions while scant few supported increases (see table 2.2). Explaining the formation of policies that expanded immigration opportunities during the past four decades requires us to account for the insulation of the policy process from mass publics long opposed to new immigration. In short, why has public opinion often failed to shape policy outcomes? Concomitantly, what are the processes by which populist modes of immigration politics assume a greater or lesser role in influencing government actions?

Research on American immigration policy and history is considerable. Some of the best work in this area can help us understand particular expansive and restrictive policy regimes. For example, John Higham's magisterial *Strangers in the Land* offers powerful insights about the "volatile passions of nativism" that consumed the nation in the late-nineteenth and early-twentieth centuries.[5] Likewise, Gary Freeman's elegant model of immigrant "client politics" in Western democratic receiving states highlights the decoupling of governing elites from mass publics regarding contemporary liberal policies.[6] However, the extended time frame of this study raises a special challenge to account for *both* expansive and restrictive policies. In the pages that follow, I offer a historical-

TABLE 2.1
Opposition to Expanded Immigrant Admissions under Restrictive Regime,
1938–1965

		Percentage Opposing
1938	Opposition to emergency increases in immigration quotas to help "German, Austrian, and other political refugees"	86
1939	Opposition to "a bill to open the doors . . . to a larger number of European refugees than are now admitted under our immigration quota"	83
1946	Opposition to permitting "more persons from Europe to come to this country each year than we did before the war"	83
1947	Opposition to "a bill in Congress to let 100,000 selected European refugees come to this country in each of the next four years"	72
1955	Disagreement with the statement that "the United States is not letting enough immigrants come into this country"	76
1965	Disagreement with the statement that immigration should be "increased"	72

Sources: 1938: *Fortune*, May 1938, in Rita Simon, *Public Opinion and the Immigrant* (Lexington, MA: D. C. Heath, 1985), p. 33; 1939: American Institute of Public Opinion (AIPO), January 1939; 1946: AIPO, January 1946; 1947: *Fortune*, November 1947; 1955: National Opinion Reserach Center, April 1955; and 1965: AIPO, July/August 1965.

institutionalist analysis—one that places special emphasis on the interplay of dynamic governing institutions, policy alliances, expertise, and international crises—to illuminate broad patterns and transformations of American immigration policy over time. More generally, this analysis highlights several political processes that may broaden our theoretical understanding of immigration politics in modern industrial democracies. Before turning to this analytical framework, however, let us first consider several existing theoretical perspectives on the rise and fall of immigration policy regimes.

THE ECONOMY, SOCIAL INTERESTS, NATIONAL VALUES, AND ELECTIONS

Both immigration studies and more general theories of American politics have advanced one of several distinct explanations for policy patterns and

TABLE 2.2
Support for Decreases/Increases in Immigrant Admissions, 1977–1996

	Decrease (%)	Increase (%)
1977	42	7
1981	65	5
1982	66	4
1986	52	11
1988	53	6
1990	48	9
1992	49	8
1994	59	6
1996	58	5

Sources: 1977–82: Rita Simon and Susan Alexander, The Ambivalent Welcome (London: Praeger, 1993); 1986: CBS News/New York Times Monthly Poll, June 1986; 1988–90: Simon and Alexander, Ambivalent Welcome; 1992: American National Election Studies; 1994: CBS News/New York Times Monthly Poll, September 1994; 1996: American National Election Studies, 1996.

innovations. These analyses stress the causal importance of either economic conditions, social interests, national values, or electoral realignments. Each of these rubrics has at least some merit as an explanatory variable, but each is ultimately inadequate for solving our central puzzles. To illustrate their respective limitations, it is useful to examine each explanation in turn.

Economic Conditions

There are at least two ways in which economic conditions generally are assumed to shape the outcomes of national policymaking. One hypothesis is that a stable, high-growth economy acts as a crucial motor for nonincremental policy change. For example, some analysts contend that the burst of nonincremental reforms associated with Lyndon Johnson's Great Society required economic prosperity as a foundation. Similar analysis might be extended to explain programmatic innovations of the Progressive Era. Yet as David Mayhew argues, "the New Deal is a devastating disconfirmation of any theory that associates economic prosperity with lawmaking."[7] That is, the unprecedented policy breakthroughs of the New Deal era occurred against the backdrop of severe economic depression rather than stable growth.

A second model of economic causation, less static than the first, in fact emphasizes sharp economic decline as the chief impetus for policy innovation. From this perspective, the programmatic achievements of the

New Deal are simply explained by the political impacts of the Great Depression that began in 1929. What is difficult for this model to accommodate are examples of dramatic economic slumps that either have derailed bursts of policy innovation or have had virtually no effect. Three examples capture the potential dampening influence of economic downturns on policy creation: the depression of 1873 to 1879 helped end national activism of the Reconstruction era; the "Roosevelt recession" of 1937–38 slowed New Deal innovation; and the "stagflation" of the 1970s imposed new spending and programmatic limits on policymakers. Moreover, some economic slumps, such as the depression of 1893, appear to have little or no impact on nonincremental policy change.[8]

Economic forces are unquestionably significant for immigration policymaking in the United States and other receiving countries. From the earliest days of the American republic, political leaders saw cheap immigrant labor as a valuable means of fueling the nation's economic development. Indeed, state actors, businesses, labor unions, and other policy activists have never stopped viewing immigration as an important vehicle of labor recruitment in an international labor market. Likewise, numerous labor economists persuasively highlight the "cost-benefit" calculations and economic motivations underlying much individual migration (although often in a manner that understates powerful social linkages between sending and receiving countries and between communities and families across national borders).[9] There also is ample evidence that during periods of economic decline and high unemployment in receiving countries like the United States, immigrants can become political scapegoats for a host of societal woes.[10] During such times of economic distress, immigration often is both more salient and repellent to mass publics in receiving countries. The potential importance of economic conditions in the development of American immigration policy is undeniable. However, precisely how economic conditions influence immigration politics and whether they dictate policy choices is quite another matter.

Models of economic causation dominate popular and scholarly accounts of immigration politics and policy in the United States and other Western liberal democracies. That may explain why so few political scientists have studied these subjects. For many analysts, the causes underlying variation in the immigration policies of receiving countries fundamentally reside in the state of their respective economies. In this view, immigration and admissions policies of the United States are driven by business cycles. When the American economy is stable and prosperous, this model predicts that national immigration policy will be liberal and expansive. In turn, precipitous economic downturns are expected to animate anti-immigrant politics and new policies designed to severely constrict immigration.[11]

At first glance, this model is quite appealing. Some of the first efforts by the American national state to regulate immigration in the late-nineteenth century were enacted during economic downturns. The well-springs of Chinese exclusion laws of the same period can be traced to exceptional labor market stresses in California (along with a spatial concentration of newcomers in this region). A temporary restrictive quota system was enacted in 1921 amidst economic depression, and the Great Depression encouraged administrative officers to be harsh in their enforcement of the immigration code. In addition, lawmakers replaced national origins quotas in 1965, a time of impressive national economic prosperity. More recently, California voters overwhelmingly supported the 1994 passage of Proposition 187, a measure denying public benefits to certain aliens, against the backdrop of statewide economic stagnation and high unemployment. These illustrations seem to vindicate the model's central claims: restrictive turns in national policy are produced by sharp economic downturns, while expansive turns are based upon underlying prosperity.

Despite the irresistable elegance of this model's logic, the fact is that its core theoretical assumptions have been disconfirmed time and again in the development of American immigration policy. Consider, for example, the Immigration Act of 1917, a crucial breakthrough for nativists that ushered in a series of severely restrictive laws; its passage was a decisive turning point in the early-twentieth-century struggle over national immigration policy. Our model suggests that this outcome comports with economic decline; yet the American economy was fairly healthy in 1916–17, with sharp increases in real GNP and low unemployment.[12] As noted, enactment of restrictive legislation in 1921 does correspond with an economic recession and high unemployment rates. But the legal foundation for a permanent system of national origins quotas was passed in 1924, well after a return of prosperity that included steady increases in wages, production, and business profits. Moreover, Congress reaffirmed this restrictive plan in early 1929 after several years of economic prosperity and low unemployment, and well before the stock market crash signaled the onset of the Great Depression.[13] That economic confidence was quite high in the days before Congress again registered support for sweeping immigration restriction is captured in the farewell address of President Calvin Coolidge, who blissfully proclaimed: "The requirements of existence have passed beyond the standard of necessity into the region of luxury."[14] Such economic optimism during what one scholar describes as the "prosperity decade" hardly resembles the downturns assumed to drive restrictive reforms.[15]

We can identify further examples of restrictive reforms being produced during times of economic quietude or prosperity. For instance, two important restrictive laws were enacted by Congress over the protests of immigration defenders in 1950 and 1952: the Internal Security Act and the McCarran-Walter Act. Again, we can point to no dramatic economic downturn in these years. Indeed, the nation was experiencing a healthy postwar economic recovery in the early 1950s that featured increased purchasing power for Americans and low unemployment levels.

Along with disconfirming evidence of major restrictive innovations being secured in the United States during economic good times, there are telling cases of expansive reforms being codified during economic downturns. Three recent examples are illustrative. Despite the crisis of economic "stagflation" in the 1970s, especially from 1973 to 1975, special legislation was enacted in these years to assist Indochinese refugees. During the economic recession of 1979–80, a downturn serious enough to derail President Jimmy Carter's reelection bid, legislation enacted in 1980 raised total annual immigration roughly 10 percent and dramatically expanded refugee admissions. Finally, immigration opportunities were significantly expanded by the Immigration Act of 1990, even though an economic recession was already underway.

Upon close inspection, then, a theoretical emphasis on economic conditions is as flawed in accounting for the choices of state actors concerning immigration policy as it is for explaining general surges in national policy innovation. The fact that major restrictive reforms can be codified during times of prosperity and expansive ones during economic downturns should raise serious doubts about how well theories of simple economic causation can address our central puzzles. However, this is not to say economic conditions are inconsequential. Indeed, one of the telling flaws of economic reductionism is that it obscures the strategic efforts of political actors to limit the effects of economic conditions when they might frustrate their goals and to exploit these conditions when propitious. The restrictionist camp depicted immigrants as economic competitors during the Great Depression, but cast newcomers as national security rather than economic threats in the prosperous early 1950s. In turn, key pro-immigration interests responded to economic decline and calls for new restrictions during the late 1970s by creating a special commission that they expected to delay action at least until the economy improved.[16] This camp subsequently linked the competitiveness of U.S. firms in international trade to a robust supply of both skilled and unskilled immigrant workers.

Another important flaw in our economic model is its inability to explain the content of policy change. *How* immigration is restricted or expanded often is just as important, if not more, than *how much* it is. As I will argue, even when economic conditions have been most influential, they have served as preconditions to the *political creation and adjustment* of national immigration policy. Sharp economic declines, for example, have the potential to make the perceived costs and dangers of immigration more salient to mass publics and particular social groups, encouraging stronger anti-immigration sentiments in popular opinion and sometimes the formation of new immigration restriction movements. But as we shall see, such developments can be transformed by political institutions and the policymaking process. For explaining immigration policies over time, standard economic models ultimately leave us well short of the mark.

The Power of Social Interests

A second theoretical approach is found in society-centered theories that view government actions as largely determined by the relative power of social interests. Interest theorists of the pluralist perspective assume that policy outcomes reflect a balanced compromise or "equilibrium" among groups possessing varied power resources, with governing institutions serving as neutral "referees." For example, the political scientist Michael Lemay believes that the classic pluralist theories of Earl Latham, among others, best explain immigration policy outcomes. In this vein, he notes that "the disparities in power among competing groups seeking to influence [a final] balance or consensus is key to our understanding immigration policy."[17] Keith Fitzgerald recently asserted that pluralist interest group theories best account for legal immigration policies. Pluralist theory treats government actions as essentially a prism of the short-term interests of business, labor, and other social groups. An important assumption of pluralism is that the American polity exhibits an extraordinary openness, produced by a wide dispersion of power among groups, which insures that newly organized interests and older ones with new resources may renegotiate policy regimes created in the past.[18]

Interest theorists of the class-conflict school, such as Michael Burroway and Manuel Castells, highlight the disproportionate influence of business interests in shaping immigration policy. From this perspective, immigration policy is designed to serve business interests by exporting the costs of labor reproduction to sending countries and by securing a ready supply of cheap, exploitable immigrant workers. The relative power of business and labor figures prominently in some neo-Marxist accounts, but capitalist interests are presumed to dominate.[19] One of the specific limitations of pluralist explanations is that they assume policy outcomes are equilibriums based on the relative power of each engaged social interest, when American immigration reform often highlights the extent to which some powerful groups lose while others win. Indeed, one of this study's primary concerns is why some advocacy groups and social movements have achieved favorable policy outcomes during certain periods of immigration reform while others have not. Moreover, because national struggles over policy have featured powerful organized interests residing in both pro-immigration and restrictionist camps, decisive official choices to expand or restrict immigrant admissions have made the incremental balancing of interests virtually impossible. Many immigration controls have been enacted even when more powerful organized interests are mobilized in opposition.

A second specific weakness of pluralist explanations is that they treat the state as a neutral broker among competing interests, when in fact the outcomes of immigration politics suggest that governing institutions often distribute power unevenly across social groups. Pluralism's emphasis on the openness of the U.S. political process drastically understates the structural barriers and systematic exclusion of disadvantaged groups, especially nonwhite newcomers. "Whenever a group of people believe they are adversely affected by national policies or are about to be, they generally have extensive opportunities for presenting their case," Robert Dahl once noted optimistically.[20] This assumption reinforces a flawed traditional argument that Chinese exclusion of the 1880s, for example, resulted at least in part because Chinese immigrants refused to mobilize in opposition. In truth, Chinese American groups challenged exclusions through the political recourse available to them, namely, legal challenges in the courts and civil disobedience, but were routinely disadvantaged by structural barriers.[21]

Class-conflict explanations recognize clear winners and losers among social interests, but they cannot account for why business and upper-class interests have suffered major defeats in many policy battles. Chinese exclusion, for instance, was imposed in the 1880s despite opposition from powerful vested interests that valued cheap Asian labor. Business groups were unable to derail efforts to restrict southern and eastern European immigration in the early-twentieth century. Although agricultural growers and other employers of low-skill workers mounted stiff resistance, the so-called Bracero program that long provided supplicant guestworkers primarily to Southwestern growers was terminated in 1963. Business groups failed to forestall employer sanctions for knowingly hiring undocumented aliens in the 1980s, succeeding only in limiting their penalties. And since 1965, family reunification preferences have trumped employer's labor-market preferences in the allocation of annual immigrant visas. Business or capitalist interests certainly have exercised influence on immigration policymaking, but they have rarely, if ever, found themselves in a position to dictate policy choices. Neo-Marxist perspectives also assume struggles over immigration control are grounded in conflicting economic interests, despite the fact that various ethnic, racial, cultural, and foreign policy interests frequently have overshadowed material concerns in immigration politics.[22]

Another key weakness of interest explanations, in both their pluralist and neo-Marxist guises, is that they assume that groups will define their interests in similar ways at different times. LeMay, for one, argues that immigration politics recurrently pits anti-immigrant labor groups against pro-immigrant business groups. Class-conflict theorists similarly assume that powerful business interests routinely advance their interests in cheap immigrant labor.[23] This static view of group interests, however, is undermined by empirical evidence demonstrating that groups in fact alter their policy preferences over time. Business groups like the National Association of Manufacturers, for instance, opposed any form of immigration restriction until the early 1920s, when formidable political pressures and technological changes convinced them to briefly support new limits. But after World War II, business interests again embraced robust immigration to the United States. Organized labor also has redefined its immigration preferences over the course of U.S. political history. Whereas American organized labor fervently supported immigration restriction until midcentury, it became an important champion of expanding immigration opportunities and refugee relief in the 1960s. Since then, the AFL-CIO and other labor groups have embraced legal immigration and refugee admissions while resisting illegal immigration.[24] More recently, organized labor has even reexamined its positions on illegal immigration, demonstrating a stronger concern for recruiting new members from the growing ranks of foreign-born workers.

Another problem with interest explanations of immigration policy is that they often fail to consider why *different kinds of group power* are significant in given political contexts. It is telling that certain group capacities and strategies have proven highly successful in one period of U.S. immigration policymaking while quite ineffective in others. During the late-nineteenth century, for example, a populist anti-Chinese movement in California was able to achieve sweeping exclusions of Chinese immigrants by throwing itself into local party politics. In the early-twentieth century, by contrast, immigration restrictionists helped win national origins quotas by pursuing professional research and "scientific government," direct congressional lobbying, and bureaucratic influence. Why have such distinctive group orientations, resources, and tactics proven politically effective over time? Theories focused on the preferences and power of key social interests provide us with few clues.

Interest explanations tend to ignore how governing institutions can affect the political character and policy fortunes of social groups. As Theda Skocpol observes, "socially deterministic theories overlook the ways in which the identities, goals, and capacities of all politically active groups are influenced by political structures and processes."[25] Jack Walker reminds us that the relationship between governing institutions and social interests is an interactive and mutually redefining one.[26] Policy preferences of social interests are not preordained, and they can be profoundly influenced by the political institutions with which they interact and through which pursue their goals. The evolution of governing institutions presents a changing set of structural opportunities and barriers that may advantage particular social groups and forms of group power at one time but not another. New government policies themselves have the capacity to encourage the political organization of social groups, to shape their relative power, and to alter group alliances; in fact, immigration policies can introduce wholly new groups into national politics or expand the constituencies of existing ones. An explanatory focus on the power of social interests, however, tells us precious little about these important processes.

National Values

Some scholars explain policy choices in terms of powerful values strongly rooted in the American political culture. Inspired by Tocqueville, Hartz, and other theorists who stress a U.S. political culture defined by liberal consensus, these analysts argue that widely shared values set public policy along paths that conform with the hegemonic national ideology.[27] Such an approach might help us explain why the United States has welcomed large-scale immigration for so long. For example, American immigration policies might be linked to a political culture that embraces relatively unfettered markets, including the recruitment of immigrant workers in an international labor market. Likewise, we might contend that U.S. immigration policy reflects a shared devotion to establish a Promised Land or "city on a hill" where the world's oppressed might find refuge, political freedom, and equal opportunity. Scholars such as Lawrence Fuchs argue that the United States has a prevailing "civic culture" that ultimately celebrates ethnic and racial diversity, and that is destined in time to welcome newcomers of every race, ethnicity, and religion.[28]

However, even if we were to accept that a consistent set of national values pervades the American political culture (which I do not), significant variations in the content of particular immigration policies obviously cannot be explained by the unwavering dominance of liberal democratic values (a fact that Fuchs and other scholars clearly recognize). Equally problematic is the fact that it is hard to demonstrate how broad, ambiguous, and sometimes contradictory values of the American "liberal tradition" are translated into specific policy outcomes. Scholars and political leaders disagree sharply on the demands of liberal democracy as it is applied to immigration. Operationalizing values as public opinion that can shape policy outcomes has its own pitfalls, including pro-immigration policies that defy even the most general popular preferences on immigration. A final shortcoming of the values explanation is that it presumes that a preeminent ideological tradition routinely dominates policy discourse and outcomes, when periodic struggles over national immigration control clearly capture an intense competition of rival traditions.[29] Indeed, political discourse and policy outcomes concerning immigration since the late-nineteenth century underscore the degree to which inegalitarian, undemocratic values have long had as much hold on the U.S. political culture as liberal and republican ideals.

Electoral Realignments and Policy Change

"Electoral realignment" theory provides one of the most prominent explanations for policy change among broad theories of American politics. In this account, new policy regimes spring from cyclical, seismic shifts in the partisan alignments of voters. "Critical elections" serve as "constituent acts," as Walter Dean Burnham puts it, that allow for responsible party government in which an energized party majority enjoys unified, purposeful control of government.[30] In the canonical listing of electoral realignments, critical elections are said to have occurred with "remarkably uniform periodicity" in 1800, 1828, 1860, 1896, and 1932.[31] Spurred by elements of stress in the American economy, society, and polity, realignments are credited with creating bursts of highly partisan and ideological policy responses to conflicts and problems that politics-as-usual cannot resolve. After these short surges of intense government activism, politics and policy are assumed to return to a state of prolonged quietude and relative dispassion associated with "normal politics." Critical moments of voter realignment thereby retrofit the American polity for another long winter or blissful summer (depending on how one views the new status quo) of consensual calm.

Two immediate problems present themselves in explaining immigration policy change in terms of electoral realignments. First, it is frequently noted that an electoral realignment as classically defined has not occurred since the 1930s. As such, we are hard-pressed to apply realignment theory to immigration policy variations since the 1940s. Second, crucial turning points in American immigration policy do not correspond with periods of electoral realignment. Major immigration reforms of the Gilded Age were codified well before the 1896 realignment, and policy breakthroughs of the 1910s and 1920s were formed well after. More generally, Richard McCormick argues that "the scholarly findings on policy change after the 1896 realignment have been inconclusive in the extreme."[32] He finds that the 1896 realignment produced "policy inertia" and had small influence on later Progressive Era reforms. There is little doubt that the realignment of the 1930s produced massive policy innovation associated with the New Deal. But significantly, because immigration reform was a polarizing issue for the New Deal coalition, action in this area was deferred in much the same way and for many of the same reasons that civil rights initiatives were avoided. Eager to hold together Southern and Northern coalition members, who were divided on ethnic and racial issues raised by immigration, New Dealers simply deferred action in this policy realm.

The reticence with which New Deal reformers greeted both immigration and civil rights reform proposals in the 1930s points to another crucial limitation of realignment theory, namely, that ethnic and racial struggles are often poorly incorporated within its framework. Martin Sklar aptly notes that analysis of "sex, race, nationality, religious discrimination, or ethnicity" has not been meaningfully provided by dominant understandings of political periodization, including realignment theory.[33] Rogers Smith aims to redress this shortcoming in the literature by arguing that American citizenship laws and basic civic patterns "conform broadly to the periodization suggested by scholars of realignments in the nation's party system."[34] However, as his own historical narrative shows, ascriptive hierarchies do not conform neatly with standard realigning periods. For instance, his account demonstrates that the exclusionary ethnic, racial, and civic agendas of Gilded Age Republicans from the 1870s to 1890s contrast sharply with the egalitarian reforms achieved by Reconstruction Republicans of the 1860s and 1870s. Reconciling these distinct ethnocultural agendas and legislative records as consistent outgrowths of the Republican realignment of 1860 presents an elusive chore. Since major policy reforms addressing ethnic and racial tensions often threaten the cohesiveness of governing coalitions born of electoral realignments, we should not expect immigration, civil rights, or related initiatives to be included typically among the burst of policy changes following a critical election. It is perhaps not surprising, then, that sweeping immigration reform usually occurs during periods of divided government and during the later phases of a partisan "regime" or "realigning period" when party leaders are less capable of quieting rifts in their governing coalitions. Despite its attentiveness to processes of order and change in U.S. political history, realignment theory's periodization scheme does not present a strong "fit" with the tempos of American immigration policy regimes.

A HISTORICAL-INSTITUTIONALIST ANALYSIS OF AMERICAN IMMIGRATION POLITICS

To help better explain the outcomes of national struggles over immigration policy across American political development, I argue that greater emphasis needs to be placed on the ways in which changing institutions

of the national state and party system shape policy choices. Several immigration scholars have recognized the need for careful analysis of the interactions of governing institutions, social forces, and immigration.[35] As
Aristide Zolberg observes, "the role of states in shaping international migration has been largely ignored by immigration theorists. This is acting
like the proverbial ostrich; but ignoring the challenge by burying one's
head in the sand will not make it go away."[36] This study places state
actors and state structures at the center of analysis. However, my goal is not
to supplant the economic, social, or cultural determinism of existing theories of immigration politics with a model of institutional determinism. As
Sven Steinmo puts it, "Institutions are not everything in politics."[37]

In contrast to a "state-centered" perspective,[38] the historical-institutionalist approach presented here highlights four interlocking processes
that help explain the patterns and transformations of national immigration control in American political development. First, the dynamism of
national governing institutions has long shaped the relative structural opportunities for politicians and social groups to pursue policy initiatives or
guard existing policy regimes. Second, policy outcomes have reflected
changing coalitions of organized interests, with political institutions and
past policies influencing the formation and power of these alliances.
Third, professional expertise since the Progressive Era has played a prominent role in privileging certain immigration narratives and policy pack-
ages. Finally, international pressures influence domestic political opportunities for immigration reform or policy stasis. While these processes are
intimately connected, it is analytically useful to examine each in turn.

Immigration Policy Regimes and Changing Structures of Government

The changing shape of American governing institutions—both internally
and in relation to one another—can profoundly affect the relative structural leverage of interest groups, social movements, and other activists in
public policymaking. Schattschneider observed that political institutions
are not neutral, but in fact bias government actions in favor of particular
interests, ideas, and policy alternatives.[39] It is an insight embraced by
many new institutionalists studying public policy. As Theda Skocpol
notes, "degrees of success in achieving political goals . . . depend on the
relative opportunities that existing political institutions offer to the group
or movement in question (and simultaneously deny to its opponents and
competitors)."[40] In short, the organizational biases of governing institutions can favor the capacities and policy designs of specific political actors, while disadvantaging others.

One might reasonably assume that the most prominent bias in the
organization of American political institutions is against major policy in-

novation. After all, the architects of the U.S. Constitution hoped to limit state activism by fragmenting government. The separation of powers, checks and balances, federalism, and bicameralism unquestionably produced a U.S. political system exceptionally replete with veto-points. Yet structural fragmentation also ensured ongoing intragovernmental rivalries in which particular institutional norms, purposes, and power balances were not likely to prevail on a permanent basis. If the framers' penchant for "counteracting ambition with ambition" thus promoted structural barriers to dramatic policy change, it also encouraged a changing set of institutional "opportunity points" to emerge over time. By deliberately fostering intra- and interbranch struggles from the start, the constitutional system became a crucial source of institutional dynamism across American history.

Of course, there are other sources of institutional dynamism in the U.S. polity. Institutional change can also spring from important shifts in the social, economic, and political contexts within which political structures are embedded, departures described alternately as "punctuated change," "critical junctures," "realignments," or "branching points."[41] A less obvious source of institutional change stems from what Karen Orren and Stephen Skowronek characterize as the frictions between political structures endowed with incongruous and intersecting logics due to their "nonsimultaneous origins."[42] It is hardly surprising that stasis and order pervade our dominant conceptions of U.S. political institutions. After all, institutions are by definition associated with regularities in human behavior. But governing institutions have been anything but static variables in the development of American immigration policy.

Understanding the rise and fall of immigration policy regimes over time requires knowledge of how institutional dynamism affects the maintenance of existing policy patterns and the possibilities of major innovation. Ongoing changes in American governing institutions suggest that the structural veto-points that sustain a particular policy regime will often look very different from one historical period to the next (see table 2.3). Indeed, political guardians of certain policy regimes have themselves built new structures to insulate existing policies from new reform efforts. For example, immigration restrictionists worked to ensure the efficacy of their legislative victories in the 1920s by creating new administrative machinery in the State Department. Defenders of a given policy regime may have to actively reproduce earlier choices and outcomes due to the changing contexts within which institutions operate. In short, the structural frustration of policy innovation may evolve markedly over time; the maintenance of policy regimes requires the continual invention of new methods to produce familiar results.

Changing institutional arrangements of the national state and party system over time also helps to explain major policy innovations. First consider the policy effects of dynamism *within* national governing institutions. The policy effects of shifting norms and structures of power within Congress are illustrative. For years, the centralization of legislative power in the hands of pro-immigration congressional party leaders like House Speaker Joseph Cannon served as an important structural bulwark against restrictionist policy initiatives. But the fortunes of Progressive Era nativists shifted markedly after a bipartisan revolt against "Cannonism" in 1911 removed this crucial veto-point and concomitantly strengthened standing immigration committees supportive of their agenda. The rise of the seniority system and powerful committee barons in Congress itself presented a formidable roadblock to pro-immigration reform in later decades. Yet new membership and procedural reforms of the 1960s led to what Roger Davidson calls a liberal activist era of Congress that provided new openings for pro-immigration groups to expand immigration opportunities.[43] Changes associated with the modern postreform and partisan conservative Congresses of recent years have proven equally consequential.

The influence of institutional change on policy regimes is hardly limited to Congress, despite a preoccupation with the legislative branch in the immigration politics literature.[44] The dynamism of the federal courts, the presidency, and executive agencies also have left an indelible mark on American immigration policies over the years. The internal development of legislative, executive, and judicial structures each has presented immigration activists with distinctive institutional opportunities and constraints as they pursue their goals. Crucially, then, processes of change *within* national political institutions have the potential to shift power from opponents to champions of particular immigration reform proposals, and vice versa. Just as important, intrainstitutional changes that hasten policy reform at one time—such as the strengthening of committee leadership in the early-twentieth century—can insulate policy regimes in later eras.

Shifts in power balances and relations *between* governing institutions are equally significant in shaping policy. Again, the interbranch conflict sewn into our constitutional system heightens this source of institutional dynamism in the American political system. To highlight the potential policy significance of shifting institutional relationships, let us consider fluctuations in presidential-congressional relations. Early-twentieth-century presidents used their powers to successfully frustrate major restrictionist reforms favored by congressional majorities. But when Woodrow Wilson's clout declined after the First World War, congressional restrictionists seized the opportunity to press their agenda. While congressional restrictionists dominated immigration policymaking during the

TABLE 2.3
Structural Veto and Opportunity Points in American Immigration Policymaking

Immigration Policy Proposal	Institutional Veto-Points	Institutional Opportunity Points
Chinese Exclusion Bills of 1880s	Fleeting presidential resistance	Receptive national parties Supportive House and Senate leadership Supportive Supreme Court
Literacy Test Bills of the 1890s (intended to restrict Southern and Eastern European immigration)	Strong presidential resistance Democratic party resistance	New congressional Immigration Committees Supportive House Leadership
Literacy Test Bill of 1906	Resistant House leadership (especially Speaker Cannon) Congressional Northern Democrats	Supportive White House Supportive House and Senate Immigration Committees Responsive Senate leadership
Restrictive Bills of the 1910s and early 1920s	Presidential resistance Congressional Northern Democrats	Overthrow of "Cannonism" Stronger Immigration Committees Restrictionist Immigration Commission Supportive new executive agencies
Refugee Relief Bill of 1939	Immigration Committee barons Congressional "Conservative Coalition" State Department agencies	Congressional liberals Executive Branch liberals
McCarran-Walter Bill of 1952 (reaffirming national origins quota system)	Presidential resistance Congressional liberals	Immigration Committee Barons Congressional "Conservative Coalition"

Bill		
Antirestrictionist Bills of the 1960s	Immigration Committee barons Congressional "Conservative Coalition"	Strong presidential support Congressional procedural reform (Democratic Study Group) Receptive congressional leadership
Employer Sanctions Bills of 1970s (to discourage illegal immigration)	Resistant Senate Judiciary Committee chairman	Receptive House Judiciary Committee Presidential support
Illegal Immigration Control Bills of the early 1980s	Resistant House Judiciary Committee chairman Resistant House Speaker Resistant White House officials	Supportive House Immigration Subcommittee Supportive Senate Judiciary Committee Supportive Senate leadership Supportive White House officials
Legal Immigration Reform Bill of 1990 (expanding annual visas)	Fleeting presidential resistance	Supportive House and Senate Judiciary Committees/Immigration Subcommittees Supportive congressional leadership
Legal Immigration Reform Bill of 1996 (reducing annual visas)	Senate Republican leadership Senate rank and file Late presidential resistance	House and Senate Immigration Subcommittees House Republican leadership Fleeting presidential support

1920s and 1930s, a resurgent modern presidency challenged national origins quotas in the postwar years. President Harry Truman first secured special legislation to provide refugee relief for persons displaced by the Second World War. Yet powerful committee chairs in the House and Senate, backed by conservative members, rebuffed broad pro-immigration reform efforts by enacting legislation over presidential veto that reaffirmed national origins quotas and imposed new ideological exclusion categories. As numerous pro-immigration reform proposals languished in committee during the 1950s, President Dwight Eisenhower claimed special powers to unilaterally grant asylum to refugees. The capacity of contending branches to independently shape immigration controls ultimately produced conflicting policy outcomes. It was not until the Johnson White House secured broad support from legislative majorities in 1965, championing immigration reform as part of its Great Society juggernaut, that pro-immigration activists were able to transcend long-standing congressional veto-points. As these examples of changing executive-legislative relations suggest, the possibilities of innovation can reflect the interactions of governing institutions advancing independent goals and power resources. Likewise, institutions that play a marginal role in immigration politics in one period may become salient in another, offering new opportunities for reformers frustrated by the barriers of once-dominant structures.

Finally, the creation of new political institutions also has the capacity to shape the fortunes of competing policy activists. New congressional immigration committees formed in the 1890s provided restrictionists with an important institutional beachhead within the legislative branch during the Progressive Era and the 1920s. The establishment of special commissions to evaluate national immigration policy in 1901, 1907, 1952, 1979, and 1991 played an instrumental role in privileging certain kinds of professional expertise and policy proposals. Policy activists able to influence the deliberations of these commissions often enjoyed distinct political advantages. And the creation of immigration bureaucracies in various executive departments has presented policy activists with distinctive structural openings to shape national immigration control in terms of both policy formation and implementation.

Institutional dynamism has long abounded in U.S. politics, as older political structures evolve, fresh ones are constructed, and the relationships between governing institutions assume new forms. The multiple institutional orderings that have emerged in the American political development present immigration activists with a changing set of structural veto and opportunity points (see table 2.3). As we shall see, institutional processes also play a key role in forging policy coalitions, elevating certain kinds of immigration expertise, and responding to international pressures.

Aggregating Immigration Activists: Liberal-Conservative Coalitions

The political alliances of interest groups, politicians, and other activists engendered by American immigration politics also has deeply affected policy choices and outcomes. Indeed, the creation and maintenance of particular policy regimes has been contingent upon support from strong coalitions that cut across familiar liberal and conservative lines. When these coalitions have broken down, so too have immigration policy regimes.

The significance of Left-Right coalitions in this area of public policy reflects the fact that few issues have produced more incongruous political bedfellows than immigration. As one lawmaker has observed, "Immigration makes arch-enemies into uneasy partners, and old friends into awkward rivals."[45] It is an issue that has alternately linked organized labor to Southern conservatives and New England Brahmin, liberal nationality and human rights groups to large corporate giants, and liberal environmentalists to cultural protectionists.

We can better conceptualize the unlikely coalitions elicited by immigration politics by concentrating on how alien admissions and rights unite and divide political actors. Policy specialists routinely differentiate *immigration* policies from *immigrant* policies. In reality, however, alien admissions and rights are not easily separated. For instance, the entry of significant numbers of unfamiliar immigrant groups can lead to a variety of restrictions on alien rights, from special registration requirements to new limits on eligibility for public benefits, employment, and naturalization. In turn, immigrant policies may be designed to encourage or discourage immigration. Easy acquisition of citizenship and other membership rights were offered by many American states during the nineteenth century to spur European arrivals. More recently, supporters of California's Proposition 187—a measure designed to scale back immigrants' access to public benefits—argued that sharp limits on the rights of undocumented aliens and their children would curb illegal immigration.

We can gain a stronger portrait of the odd coalitions that have emerged over time by mapping rival goals toward alien admissions and rights along two dimensions. One dimension focuses on political interests and values toward alien admissions, with a horizontal continuum that stretches from maximum support for expansive immigration opportunities on the left to maximum support for restricting alien admissions on the right. The second dimension focuses on political interests and values regarding the rights of newcomers, with a vertical continuum that stretches from maximum support for restricting alien rights at the bottom to maximum support for expansive alien membership at the top. As table 2.4 captures, we can identify from this model four distinctive sets (ideal-

TABLE 2.4
The Politics of Alien Admissions and Rights (A Two-Dimensional Model)

Alien Rights Should Be	Alien Admissions Should Be	
	Expanded or Maintained	Restricted
Expansive	**Cosmopolitans** William James Jane Addams Edward Kennedy Xavier Becerra Immigration Protective League, American Jewish Committee, MALDEF, National Immigration Forum	**Nationalist Egalitarians** Frederick Douglass Samuel Gompers Barbara Jordan Richard Lamm AFL (1900–1956), population control and environmental groups
Restrictive	**Free-Market Expansionists** Andrew Carnegie William Howard Taft Ronald Reagan Spencer Abraham American Farm Bureau Federation, National Association of Manufacturers, CATO Institute	**Classic Exclusionists** Henry Cabot Lodge Madison Grant Patrick Buchanan Peter Brimelow Immigration Restriction League, Federation for American Immigration Reform

types) of political interests and ideological commitments in immigration policymaking: cosmopolitans, nationalist egalitarians, free-market expansionists, and cultural exclusionists.

Cosmopolitans endorse expansive alien admissions and the full inclusion of newcomers in the national political community. They believe that large-scale immigration is socially and economically beneficial to the United States, and that the country's assimilative capacities are vast. From Ralph Waldo Emerson and Jane Addams to Edward Kennedy and Xavier Becerra, cosmopolitans have defended cultural pluralism and heterogeneous immigration. Like William James, they believe social justice is nurtured by diversity and harmony rather than by homogeneity.[46] They have supported generous admissions policies for family reunification, refugee relief, and other concerns. Likewise, these immigration activists have favored a broad set of legal protections and entitlements for aliens. In particular, they have been devotees of relatively easy access to citizenship, sharing Michael Walzer's conviction that permanent gradations of membership undermine liberal democracy.[47] For this reason, liberal cosmopolitans have opposed foreign guestworker programs and illegal immigration, which encourage the formation of disenfranchised subclasses in American society. At the same time, their concern for equal membership has led these activists to support policies that enable illegal aliens and asylees to gain legal resident status, such as the unprecedented amnesty programs of the 1980s. To these activists, expansive immigration and alien rights are basic ingredients of universalist democracy.

Nationalist egalitarians support immigration restrictions on the grounds that porous borders undermine equality for native-born citizens, especially in terms of economic opportunity and results. More than a century ago Frederick Douglass endorsed immigration limits, lamenting that "every hour sees the black man elbowed out of employment by some newly arrived immigrant."[48] A later generation of labor leaders like Terence Powderly and Samuel Gompers championed immigration restriction because they believed immigrants undercut the wages, working conditions, and job security of American workers.[49] In both cases, immigration was viewed as a potent threat to advancing social, economic, and political justice among citizens. From this perspective, the American "social contract" requires that certain obligations to disadvantaged members of the national political community must be met before newcomers are granted admission and precious membership goods. For liberal environmentalists like Richard Lamm, immigration restriction has represented a crucial means of preserving American natural resources for existing citizens.[50] Nevertheless, nationalist egalitarians have tended to share with cosmopolitans an uneasiness about aliens residing in the country without the same legal rights as citizens. As a result, they have supported the full social, economic, and political integration of living in the United States. Nationalist egalitarians like Representative Barbara Jordan (D-TX) have favored immigration reductions to enhance economic opportunity for the nation's poorest citizens, but they also have zealously defended cultural diversity and alien rights.[51]

Free-market expansionists welcome expansive alien admissions to meet labor market demands and to promote national prosperity. In his *Report on Manufactures*, Alexander Hamilton noted that it was in the national interest "to open every possible avenue to emigration from abroad." Consistent with his vision of a commercial empire, he perceived newcomers as "an important resource, not only for extending the population, and with it the useful and productive labor of the country, but likewise for the prosecution of manufactures."[52] Almost a century later Andrew Carnegie praised open immigration as "a golden stream which flows into the country each year." He added crassly, "These adults are surely worth $1500 each—for in former days an efficient slave sold for that sum."[53]

Economic prosperity, they believed, was tied to unfettered immigration. More recently, guestworker programs have appealed to many market-oriented conservatives because they provide American employers access to an international labor supply without obligations of extending costly entitlements to foreign laborers. Some have even embraced the labor market dividends of illegal immigration. But whereas cosmopolitans and nationalist egalitarians have been deeply concerned with extending broad membership rights to aliens living and working in the United States, free-market expansionists generally have not. As celebrants of entrepreneurial and self-sufficient newcomers, market-oriented immigration defenders have supported measures denying welfare and other public benefits for noncitizens.

Classic exclusionists favor sweeping restrictions of both immigrant admissions and alien rights, typically on cultural or racial grounds. Since the nation's founding, significant shifts in the ethnic, racial, or religious composition of immigration have been especially threatening to classic exclusionists. They have viewed these shifts as perilous to the country's well-being. In contrast to older immigrant groups, newer ones are associated by these activists with welfare dependency, criminality, disease, and political radicalism. Harvard president A. Lawrence Lowell once argued that ethnic and racial homogeneity stands "as a basis for popular government and the popular opinion on which it rests, that justifies democracies in resisting the influx in great numbers of a widely different race."[54] This restrictionist tradition reached its apex under the national origins quota system, but has been given recent expression by conservatives like Peter Brimelow and Patrick Buchanan.[55] Tamer classic exclusionists have opposed alien admissions and rights due to the fiscal and social burdens they impose on the nation.

It is significant that the configuration of organized interests, social movements, politicians, and other activists within each of our four immigration orientations has shifted over time, as has their aggregation into powerful cross-party coalitions supporting certain policies. Their variation has had enormous influence on the creation, maintenance, and demise of immigration policy regimes in American political history. After the turn of the century, for example, New England nativists relied on support from new groups to secure broad restrictions on southern and eastern European immigration. After flirting with the notion that European newcomers would help build a "New South" only to be defied by settlement patterns, Southern lawmakers joined in championing xenophobic policies. Eugenicists and other intellectuals enamored with racial theories saw exclusionary policies as crucial to preserving "Nordic supremacy" in the United States.[56] Progressives like John Commons and Edward Ross associated immigration restriction with social reform. And under new leadership, organized labor came to embrace any policy regime that reduced European inflows, including one based on ethnic, racial, and religious hierarchies. When important elements of big business wavered in their defense of immigration amid the zealous nationalism of the early 1920s, this formidable Left-Right coalition successfully pressed its case for national origins quotas. This coalitional dynamism has emerged in each period of major policy change.

Revealingly, the national state and party system can profoundly affect policy alliances by actively fostering the formation of new group participants in immigration policymaking, demobilizing others, and shaping how groups define their policy goals over time. Those who assume that political institutions merely transmit the preferences of social groups largely ignore the extent to which the formation of new interest groups and social movements may rely upon government sponsorship. Walker persuasively argued that powerful elderly interest groups like the American Association of Retired Persons were formed to guard and expand government services provided by Social Security, Medicare, and the Older Americans Act of 1965. He concluded that since the initiative for these programmatic breakthroughs came from state institutions, subsequent interest group mobilization reflected "government encouragement and leadership."[57] Similarly, Anne Costain recently found that the presidency and Congress actively "invited" the emergence of a women's movement in the 1960s and 1970s.[58]

The policy legacies of U.S. immigration reform provide a distinctive portrait of how governments may foster the formation of politically active social groups. Government decisions to permit the admission and relatively easy naturalization of new immigrants have had the effect of introducing new groups with a decided interest to mobilize on behalf of admission policies enabling their families and fellow ethnics to enter the country. The mobilization of ethnic and nationality groups against proposals to restrict immigration in the early-twentieth century, for example, included organized interests whose size and identity were profoundly shaped by immigration, such as the American Jewish Committee, the German-American Alliance, the Ancient Order of Hibernians, and the Immigration Protective League. Several generations later, new immigrants fortified the National Council of La Raza, the League of United Latin American Citizens, the Organization of Chinese Americans, the National Immigration Forum, and other pro-immigration groups. The U.S. government has further encouraged group mobilization by funding the creation of advocacy groups with strong ties to newcomers, as was the case in the formation of the Mexican American Legal Defense and

Education Fund.[59] When governments grant entry and naturalization to new immigrant groups, they in effect sponsor eventual alterations in the polity's interest group system.

As much as governing institutions can sponsor and empower certain groups, they also can politically disempower and demobilize others. An important example is provided by the marginalization of Chinese newcomers in immigration politics of the Gilded Age. Some scholars have mistakenly assumed that Chinese immigrants were politically diffident in this period. In fact, Chinese American leaders worked strenuously to resist exclusionary efforts, but faced formidable structural barriers in the "state of courts and parties."[60] Chinese immigrants were denied access to the ballot box and thus had little hope of swaying party leaders. Their efforts to secure judicial relief from exclusionary measures were also routinely frustrated.[61] The structural arrangements of the national state and party system can foster the political *demobilization* of certain groups, with potentially major implications for outcomes of the policy process.

Political institutions also have the capacity to shape how social groups form their interests or policy preferences in the first place. The policy preferences of organized labor in American immigration politics after the 1950s provide an apt illustration. Organized labor is often assumed to have been a staunch champion of immigration restriction across U.S. political history.[62] Yet one of the most intriguing and consequential features of immigration policymaking in American political development was organized labor's late-1950s defection from the restrictionist coalition to join with pro-immigrant groups advancing sweeping innovation. Organized labor lobbied for the 1965 reforms and since then has generally endorsed expansive refugee and legal immigrant admissions.

This redefinition of labor's policy preferences on immigration was affected by the national state and party system in two ways. First, the emergence of the Congress of Industrial Organizations (CIO) owed much to the New Deal regime of the 1930s. As J. David Greenstone notes in his classic *Labor in American Politics*, "From the beginning, CIO unions were so much a product of the New Deal period that their own organizational security became associated in the minds of many of their leaders with the larger struggle for welfare legislation."[63] Government support for the CIO proved crucial for American immigration politics because, unlike the AFL, it opposed ethnic and racial quotas in national immigration law. Although the AFL and CIO offered contrasting voices on immigration for much of the 1950s, they presented a unified voice in favor of dismantling national origins quotas after their merger. This shift contributed to the ultimate passage of the Immigration Reform Act of 1965.

Second, the AFL-CIO has tended to support expansions in legal immigration and refugee admissions since the 1960s, including increases in family-based visas, even though the interests of union members might call for very different policy preferences. Again Greenstone's findings are illuminating. He suggests that the American party system so closely aligned organized labor with the Democratic party that it embraced the interests of other liberal groups and committed itself to broad policy objectives such as civil rights and Medicare rather than pursuing narrower special interests.[64] The role of the New Deal in the rise of the CIO and the labor-Democratic alliance helped reshape how labor defined its policy preferences on immigration control, thus vividly capturing the potential influence of the state and parties on interest formation.

In recent years, the growing complexity of immigration policymaking has contributed to a more fluid and volatile environment in which shifting policy alliances abound. Yet powerful Left-Right coalitions have continued to dominate this policy realm. In 1990, legal immigration reform was propelled by an ideological convergence of free-market conservatives (who hoped to expand immigration to assist American businesses and encourage the free movement of goods, capital, and *persons* across borders) and cosmopolitan liberals (who hoped to reaffirm family reunification preferences and record levels of nonwhite, Third World immigration). The ascendance of free-market philosophies on the American Right and racial liberalism on the Left during the past quarter-century produced a formidable coalition favoring robust immigration in recent decades. By 1996, however, free-market expansionists and conservative restrictionists aligned to impose limitations on welfare benefits and the legal rights of noncitizens. In the same year, however, liberal nationality, civil rights, and humanitarian groups joined conservative business and libertarian lobbies in derailing efforts to restrict either the volume or composition of legal immigration. In short, incongruous cross-party alliances have played a prominent role in the rise and fall of immigration policy regimes.

Privileged Expertise: Institutions and the Production of Immigration Narratives

Inspired by the likes of Max Weber and John Maynard Keynes, a number of political scientists have placed fresh emphasis on the capacity of innovative ideas to create "new world images" that profoundly alter the struggle of social interests.[65] The catalytic role of ideas is especially prominent in several important works on domestic policy, from studies of economic and social policy by Peter Hall and Margaret Weir to investigations of deregulatory politics by Martha Derthick and Paul Quirk.[66] The causal power of ideas is no less important in foreign policy research. For example, Judith Goldstein and Robert Keohane make the case that ideas can be "invisible switchmen" in foreign policymaking, potentially affecting the direction of new policy initiatives driven by external forces.[67] However, immigration policymaking raises difficult questions about the impact of ideas on government decisions.

How do we explain why some ideas have demonstrated greater magnetic power than others in the policy process of distinctive historical periods? For all of its important nuances and distinctive variants, the immigration debate in American political development has tended for some time to juxtapose a familiar set of rival ideas about the economic, sociocultural, and foreign policy effects of immigration controls. So how do we account for why particular immigration narratives have carried the day in the policymaking process? Solving this puzzle requires us to move away from the assumption that institutions are merely the product or passive embodiment of ideas. Instead, we can gain considerable insight by looking more closely at how government structures can privilege certain narratives or "policy paradigms."[68]

Desmond King persuasively observes that liberal democracies such as the United States, deeply rooted in Enlightenment traditions of thought, are systems in which ideas thrive and in which government actors need rational and knowledge-based justifications for new policy initiatives.[69] During the Progressive Era, however, the rationality and scientific legitimacy of policy choices assumed more importance for American policymakers than ever before. In this period began a greater demand for systematic information, gathered and interpreted by professional experts. For Progressives, elevating "scientific government" meant new means for nonpartisan experts to apply social knowledge to vexing public problems and controversies.[70]

Various scholars have noted the influence of states and their programs on the development of the modern social sciences, encouraging a symbiosis between professional experts and public policymaking.[71] But government officials and institutions can assume a more direct role in generating social knowledge or expertise. This is particularly true of the special commissions, congressional committees, and executive agencies charged with gathering systematic information on the impacts of immigration on American society since the turn of the century. In the early-twentieth century, for instance, the so-called Dillingham Commission was established with a generous budget and a large staff of social scientists to study recent immigration and to issue authoritative findings. Deeply informed by racial theories, its expert findings offered a portrait of southern and eastern European newcomers that legitimized the xenophobic narrative and policy agenda of Progressive Era restrictionists. Congressional committees of this period invited academics and specialists to bestow intellectual legitimacy on nativist designs; the House immigration committee even hired an "expert eugenics agent" to conduct studies on its behalf.

Finally, specialists within the immigration bureaucracy also provided expertise that favored ethnic and racial hierarchies for alien admissions.

Whereas professional expertise became a fixture in immigration policymaking after the Progressive Era, its specific content changed over time. Unlike the Dillingham Commission, for example, a new commission created by Truman in 1952 was guided by a new generation of professional experts who disavowed earlier racial theories and embraced a decidedly pro-immigration narrative. Significantly, the migration of influential European scholars to the United States as wartime refugees played a prominent role in recasting American social science and immigration expertise in this period.[72] Likewise, the Select Commission on Immigration and Refugee Policy offered an influential narrative in 1981 that legitimated expansive legal immigration, refugee admissions, and alien rights, while assailing illegal immigration for its deleterious effects on public health, social equality, and the rule of law. Its findings cast long shadows on immigration politics during the 1980s. As we shall see, immigration policies have often conformed with the expert findings and policy paradigms advanced by special commissions, congressional committees, and federal agencies.[73] Tellingly, advocacy groups engaged in American immigration politics have been keenly aware of the importance of shaping immigration expertise and compelling public narratives to secure favorable policy outcomes.[74]

International Crises and Domestic Political Opportunities for Immigration Reform

Immigration control represents an area of government action that intersects domestic and foreign policy. It is little wonder, then, that international crises and concerns have long had the potential to influence immigration controls. The interpenetration of international and domestic politics and its effects on public policy has been the subject of important earlier work. In a study of World War II's influence on U.S. state-building, Bartholomew Sparrow observes that "states are penetrated in many policy domains by the actions or even mere presence of other states." International crises, he goes on to argue, are especially salient in conditioning "a state's own constitution and intranational structure."[75] In similar fashion, Doug McAdam finds that new international pressures can dramatically alter the political possibilities of major policy innovation. Domestic political opportunities, he concludes, often have international origins.[76]

Shifts in international relations have the capacity to substantially alter how U.S. state actors, interest groups, and mass publics define the nation's relationship to the rest of the world, with potentially crucial implications for immigration policy. International crises sometimes have fueled a traditional American impulse toward isolationism. The First World War and Red Scare, for example, helped make Americans and their elected officials see the nation as "vulnerable to European influences of every kind" and in need of insulation from international entanglements.[77] One logically might expect that animus toward foreign engagement during periods of isolationist fervor would extend naturally to immigrants, especially those foreigners perceived as most dissimilar from native-born citizens. We also might anticipate that the leading institutional champions of internationalism in these historical moments will lose some degree of structural power; strikingly, steady efforts by Wilson's internationalist administration to block sweeping immigration restriction lost force at the close of World War I. In turn, congressional restrictionists drew considerable political momentum from resurgent isolationism to enact draconian national origins quotas and to build administrative structures more capable of imposing sweeping restrictions. When international crises produce isolationist responses in domestic politics, then, we should expect that the political and structural capacities of political actors advancing immigration restriction will be enhanced.

At other times, international crises may encourage a transition from an isolationist to an internationalist conception of the nation's global role that can transform the institutional powers and incentives of state actors. In particular, new foreign policy challenges and commitments may confront national political leaders with international imperatives that enhance the domestic political opportunities for pro-immigration initiatives. And as much as international crises that produce isolationist surges may weaken governing institutions advancing internationalist goals, crises that produce new global commitments for the national state may *strengthen* institutions advancing internationalist goals.

The onset of the Cold War, for instance, exposed national political leaders to an ideological struggle with the Soviet Union and emboldened modern presidents to unilaterally extend asylum to refugees displaced by the Second World War and, later, those fleeing communist regimes. Postwar presidents also spearheaded efforts to dismantle national origins quotas, which they argued "make a hollow mockery of confident world leadership"—a campaign that eventually succeeded in 1965.[78] And whereas isolationist surges may help make national policymakers more responsive to popular preferences for immigration restriction, periods of international engagement may encourage state actors to advance pro-immigration policies that conflict with popular opinion. Significantly, World War II and the Cold War effectively ended the traditional isolationist foreign policy that shaped American relations with the world for so long. This secular development helps explain why national political leaders have been generally unwilling to prevent large-scale immigration opposed by mass publics. The end of the Cold War raises the possibility of renewed isolationism, and it is notable that neo-isolationist politicians urged reductions of legal immigration in 1996. Nevertheless, processes of rapid globalization and ongoing American leadership abroad make such restrictionist designs a tall order.

CONCLUSION

Immigration scholars across disciplines have struggled to explain patterns and transformations of American immigration policy over time. If the outcomes of periodic national battles over immigration control were of marginal importance, then our theoretical shortcomings in this area would be of little consequence. But immigration policy choices involve not only the peopling of a nation, but also the framing of a citizenry with shared understandings of what liberal democracy and nationhood demand. The role of economic conditions, social interests, national values, and electoral realignments all have their merits as explanatory variables, I have argued, but ultimately have proven inadequate for the task at hand.

To understand the development of immigration policy in the United States, I have proposed that we need an analytical approach that treats policy regimes as jointly shaped by the dynamism of governing institutions, group alliances, expert narratives, and global pressures. In particular, four processes have been described that together significantly influence immigration policymaking. First, institutional changes in the national state and party system can provide structural advantages for particular groups and activists to pursue their policy initiatives. Second, policy outcomes are influenced by the incongruous yet formidable Left-Right coalitions that emerge in immigration politics over time, with government institutions and policies shaping the organization and preferences of advocacy groups. Third, the solidification of expertise in the policy process since the Progressive Era has politically privileged certain kinds of immigration causal stories that elevate particular policy responses.[79] Finally, international crises affect domestic political opportunities for immigration reform by reshaping the interests and relative power of state actors. We shall proceed chronologically in the pages that follow, exploring these interlocking processes in the creation, maintenance, and demise of immigration policy regimes from the nation's founding to present.

CHAPTER THREE

Immigrant Voters in a Partisan Polity

European Settlers, Nativism, and American Immigration Policy, 1776–1896

FROM THE NATION's founding through the Gilded Age, nativist movements such as the Order of United Americans, the Know-Nothings, and the American Protective Association pressed for their anti-immigrant agendas in electoral contests and partisan structures that then dominated American political life. There was little question for these activists that parties were, as James Bryce put it, "the great moving forces" of American politics in the nineteenth century.[1] When xenophobes were not organizing third party movements like the American Republican party of the 1840s or the fleetingly successful American party of the 1850s, they pressured the mainstream Whig and Republican parties to champion their cause. But nativist political mobilization ultimately bore few policy fruits; efforts to enlist the federal government's support in excluding Irish, German, and other immigrant groups were routinely frustrated. Before the 1880s, John Higham concludes, "nativists had never succeeded in permanently undoing the nation's tolerant, laissez-faire policy toward European immigrants."[2] The only notable exception came from the Federalists' fleeting Alien Acts of 1798. It is important to recognize that immigration was never entirely "open" in this period: state and local governments could regulate the admission and legal status of foreigners. Nor was policy exactly laissez-faire, since both federal and subnational governments recruited new settlers across the Atlantic.

New openings emerged for pursuing national restrictions in 1876 when the Supreme Court declared that state and local immigration laws infringed on the exclusive power of Congress to regulate foreign commerce. Judicial nullification of states' practices placed European immigration control squarely on the national political agenda. And there it sat untouched until New York officials engaged in "brinkmanship" by threatening to close down Castle Garden, the largest immigration depot in the country, unless national lawmakers took steps to manage European inflows. During the next decade, the national state assumed new regulatory responsibilities and bureaucratic capacities for governing European immi-

TABLE 3.1
European Immigration to the United States, 1821–1900

	European Immigrant Admissions	Leading Source Countries
1821–30	98,817	Ireland United Kingdom France Germany
1831–40	495,688	Ireland Germany United Kingdom France
1841–50	1,597,501	Ireland Germany United Kingdom France
1851–60	2,452,660	Germany Ireland United Kingdom France
1861–70	2,065,270	Germany United Kingdom Ireland Norway
1871–80	2,272,262	Germany United Kingdom Ireland Sweden
1881–90	4,737,046	Germany United Kingdom Ireland Sweden
1891–1900	3,558,978	Italy Austria-Hungary Germany Russia

Source: Based on statistics of the Immigration and Naturalization Service.

gration. But such efforts were very modest. Anti-Catholic and other nativists foundered in their efforts to stem the growing volume and ethnic
diversity of European immigration that flowed relatively unfettered
through the close of the Gilded Age (see table 3.1).

How do we explain the recurrent failures of nineteenth-century nativists in their efforts to restrict new European immigration and assimilation? Path dependence theory offers important clues. The central notion
of "path dependence" is that early conditions and choices send public
policy along a distinctive developmental pathway from which it is difficult, though not impossible, to depart in the future. Initial decisions are
reinforced over time by engaged agents, interests and institutions that
have either invested in or adapted to the track along which policy has
traveled.[3] The path dependence argument offered in this chapter rests
upon two basic propositions. One is that the nation's first political
leaders, at a time of low immigration, plentiful land, and labor scarcity,
encouraged European immigration with easy admission and swift acquisition of membership rights. Although the early Alien Acts briefly endan-
gered this policy, the election of 1800 reinforced initial choices by returning full control over alien admissions to the states and by restoring
generous terms of naturalization.

The second is that once massive European inflows began in later years,
many national political leaders (not to mention social interests) became
invested in maintaining robust immigration opportunities. Large numbers of European settlers easily gained both entrance and the suffrage in
the nineteenth century, which created important voting blocs with whom
powerful party politicians, especially Democrats, curried favor by defending immigration and the foreign-born. Because the Democratic party
aligned itself with immigrant and kindred ethnic voters (such as the Irish)
at its inception, it is perhaps not surprising that the Whig and Republican
parties sometimes served as significant vehicles for restrictionist views. On
occasion, these parties made openly xenophobic appeals during national
elections in hopes of attracting native-born voters alarmed by new waves
of immigrants. Yet even these parties sometimes maneuvered to avoid
electoral reprisals from foreign-born and Catholic voters by embracing
the nation's pro-immigration traditions. Scholars like John Gerring have
found that the Whig and Republican parties were ideologically prone to
an anti-immigrant nationalism.[4] Often overlooked, however, is the fact
that Republican leaders also actively nurtured European immigration
during certain periods because of their commitments to "neomercantil-
ism." As Gerring himself notes, "National Republicans pursued specific
industrial policies to stimulate economic growth."[5] Significantly, it was
not uncommon for nineteenth-century Republican politicians to view
large-scale European immigration as consistent with broader ambitions
for national economic development. Republican policymakers actively re-

cruited European settlers in the 1860s. Overall, the vibrant partisan and electoral politics of nineteenth-century America—sufficiently democratized to extend broad political rights to white male newcomers—proved inhospitable to nativist policy designs.

Of course, path dependence does not assume that policy directions are preordained or inevitable; new openings or "critical junctures" may appear over time that present special opportunities for public policy to branch off onto new pathways.[6] Modest openings for new national policies toward European immigration certainly emerged in the nineteenth century. On the eve of the Civil War, the nativist Know-Nothings capitalized on a party system strained and fractured by sectional discord to achieve surprising electoral victories. Nevertheless, their anti-Catholic and anti-immigrant agenda was soon overshadowed by precisely those issues that led to their meteoric rise: slavery and secession. When the federal judiciary stripped states of the authority to screen immigrants in the 1870s, nativists hoped for broad new restrictions on European immigration. Instead, national policymakers codified a limited set of regulations excluding criminals, carriers of contagious diseases, the mentally and physically disabled, and those deemed likely to become public charges, but had no intention of slowing the massive waves of European immigrants settling in the country.

Perhaps the best chance for achieving a major restrictionist policy breakthrough came at the century's end, when Brahmin nativists led by Senator Henry Cabot Lodge (R-MA) and the Immigration Restriction League pressed a literacy test bill through Congress. Tellingly, their success with national lawmakers owed much to the Progressive cast of their political campaign, one that circumvented partisan politics by relying on expertise and new policymaking structures, such as standing immigration committees. Yet nativists struggled to develop crucial coalitional support across familiar partisan and ideological divides. In addition, U.S. imperial successes in the 1890s hurt the restrictionist cause by restoring faith in "America's powers of assimilation" at home.[7] Anti-immigrant reform legislation ultimately died at the hands of a president following a long line of Democratic politicians opposed to assaults on European immigration. The inability of restrictionists to overcome key institutional veto-points or to build a strong Left-Right coalition meant that national policy toward European immigrants would not stray from its original track until the early twentieth century, when Progressive Era reformers deliberately eroded party power in the policy process.

IMMIGRATION, NATURALIZATION, AND AMERICAN NATION-BUILDING

Americans have been ambivalent about immigration since the earliest days of their republic. The founding generation grew up in British North

TABLE 3.2
The Founders and Immigration (Shaping Ideological Traditions)

Immigrant Rights Should Be	Immigrant Admissions Should Be	
	Encouraged	Restricted
Expansive	**Cosmopolitans** e.g., Thomas Paine, *Common Sense*	**Egalitarian Nationalists** e.g., Thomas Jefferson, *Notes on the State of Virginia*
Restrictive	**Free-Market Expansionists** e.g., A. Hamilton, *Report on Manufactures*	**Classic Exclusionists** e.g., Agrippa, Letters in the *Massachusetts Gazette*

American colonies that had contrasting traditions of governing European immigration. Some colonies were routinely hostile to outsiders; some granted entry and equal membership to immigrants who shared their ecclesiastical goals; some recruited immigrant labor but limited the rights newcomers enjoyed; and still others extended generous terms of immigration and membership to all white male settlers (see table 3.2 for competing orientations toward European immigration in the early American republic).[8] By the late-eighteenth century, however, most colonies welcomed European immigrants for economic reasons. British newcomers increasingly arrived from Scotland, Wales, and Ireland, while thousands of Germans, Scandinavians, French, Swiss, and Belgians came as indentured servants. By 1763, only half of British North America was English proper.[9]

Many prominent eighteenth-century English Americans assailed the growing religious and ethnic diversity of European immigration. After Germans voted en masse against his political allies in colonial Pennsylvania, Benjamin Franklin issued a famously blistering attack against "Aliens," who he noted were becoming "so numerous as to Germanize us instead of our Anglifying them."[10] Apprehension about European immigration persisted after the Revolution. In his celebrated "Notes on the State of Virginia," Thomas Jefferson criticized new states for their "present desire . . . to produce rapid population by as great importations of foreigners as possible."[11] In contrast to Franklin's focused diatribe against Pennsylvania Germans, Jefferson worried more generally in 1781 about the capacity of newcomers to cherish republican principles, individual liberty, and self-government. Immigrants, he predicted, would prove either incapable of shedding their loyalties to the "absolute monarchy" of the

Old World or prone to anarchical temptations of the new one.[12] While supporting broad rights for European immigrants residing in the new nation, Jefferson suggested that the quality and durability of republican government required restraints on future admissions.

While Jefferson offered a foreboding portrait of new immigration to the United States, others embraced it on cosmopolitan and capitalist terms. Thomas Paine urged the new nation to adopt the cosmopolitan individualism of Pennsylvania, where the equal membership of English, Dutch, Germans, and Swedes showed that "we surmount the force of local prejudices as we enlarge our acquaintance with the world."[13] New Englanders had long idealized their Puritan forebears as fugitives with a universal mission; theirs was "an errand in the wilderness" meant to "proclaime to all Nations the neere approach of the most wonderful workes that ever the Sonnes of men saw."[14] The Revolution lent national significance to the asylum ideal, finding expression not only in the wistful verses of Paine's *Common Sense*, but also in George Washington's exuberant 1783 pledge that "America is open to receive not only the Opulent and respectable Stranger, but the oppressed and persecuted of all Nations and Religions."[15] Others were more pragmatic in encouraging new settlers. Far removed from the provincial politics of his native state, a more august Benjamin Franklin issued a general letter in 1782 enticing prospective European immigrants with the promise that "all the Rights of the Citizen" were easily acquired. At the same time, he candidly noted that his country's welcome was motivated by a need for immigrant workers to spur U.S. economic and territorial growth. "America is the Land of Labour," he declared, best suited for "hearty young Labouring men."[16] George Washington hoped in 1785 that the "fertile plains of the Ohio" would be populated by stout European immigrants.[17]

The Constitution is all but silent about immigration. Yet the constitutional architects had much to say about the relative merits of immigrant admissions and rights during their deliberations at Philadelphia in 1787. The question of who should be eligible for federal elective office served as the impetus for a broad-ranging immigration debate that revealed considerable disagreement among delegates. Some came to the conclusion that immigrants could never throw off what Elbridge Gerry called "foreign attachments," making them an inherently subversive presence in the new nation. Others, like Governeur Morris and Pierce Butler, called for long periods of citizenship (fourteen years or more) before the foreign-born were eligible for congressional office. Ultimately, they shared Gerry's deep suspicions of immigrants. "What is the language of Reason on this subject?" asked Morris. "Admit a Frenchman into your Senate and he will study the commerce of France; an Englishman, he will feel an equal bias in favor of England."[18] Tellingly, those who favored excluding the foreign-born from public office included pro-immigration delegates such as George Mason, who welcomed the economic benefits of alien laborers but resisted extending broad political rights to "foreigners and adventurers."[19]

Many delegates assailed this position. James Wilson, a Scottish-born delegate, spoke of "the discouragement and mortification" felt by immigrants due to "degrading discrimination" in social and political membership.[20] Well before scholars like Seymour Martin Lipset and John Kingdon concluded that immigrants "were systematically different from those who stayed behind,"[21] Franklin observed that those who came to American shores were predisposed to embrace its social and political ideals. James Madison worried that denying immigrants public office would "give a tincture of illiberality to the Constitution." He also noted that states which endorsed robust immigrant admissions and rights were the most advanced in wealth, territory, and the arts.[22] Delegates eventually compromised by making the foreign-born ineligible only for the presidency and establishing modest residency requirements for congressional office. The Philadelphia convention also adopted a proposal empowering Congress to establish a uniform rule of naturalization. In contrast to British tradition, these constitutional decisions signaled a rejection of fixed gradations of membership among foreign- and native-born white men in the American political community.[23]

Commentary on immigration during the ratification process mirrored that of the Philadelphia convention. Most state newspapers and convention speakers highlighted the need "to draw numbers from the other side of the Atlantic," and praised the framers for facilitating broad immigration opportunities.[24] Others expressed hostility toward immigration. Several Anti-Federalists argued that European inflows enervated the civic virtue and martial spirit fostered by cultural homogeneity.[25] As New England's Agrippa warned fellow nativists, a newly empowered Congress was sure to establish a generous rule of naturalization that would undermine the right of some states to exclude foreigners and "to keep their blood pure."[26] With the ratification of the Constitution, the young nation called on the federal government to assume new responsibilities, including a "common defence" against foreign threats.[27] Significantly, the framers never viewed immigration as an external threat. Instead, they embraced a laissez-faire national policy toward European newcomers that allowed states to regulate and recruit new settlers as they saw fit. The fact that subnational governments had their own immigration policies could not have escaped the framers, who would have faced enormous practical and political hurdles in establishing a uniform admissions policy for the country.

Labor scarcity, abundant territory, and strong yearnings for rapid economic development were all factors that informed the framers' initial immigration decisions—or *nondecisions*, to be precise. Early on, nation-building was closely associated in the American mind with European immigration. "The United States was conceived as a great adventure in the conquest and taming of a vast land," notes Donald Horowitz. "It was a country in the making, and immigration was essential to settling it."[28] Yet it is perhaps equally important that few framers could have anticipated either the massive scale or increasing diversity of European immigration in the next century. The Constitution's silence on immigration and its implicit recognition of states' existing policies came at a time when newcomers were few (roughly 3,000 to 6,000 per year in the late-eighteenth century) due to the dampening effects of revolutionary warfare and restrictions European governments imposed on emigration.[29] Finally, early U.S. nationalism featured a natural-rights philosophy and lingering revolutionary spirit that led the country's most prominent leaders to embrace tolerance, nonsectarianism, and European immigrants.[30]

It did not take long for Congress to realize Agrippa's fears that it would establish generous terms of naturalization. The first Congress in 1790 enacted a uniform rule of naturalization that made citizenship very easy to acquire for European men. It provided that "free white persons" who resided in the United States for as little as two years could be naturalized by "any common law court of record in any of the States."[31] One-half century later, nativists pointed to this legislation as beginning an ill-conceived tradition of swiftly granting citizenship and voting rights to "men, many of whom, but a few short years previously, scarcely knew of our existence." But initially, naturalization law was a source of friction between the nation's first political parties, namely, the Federalists led by Alexander Hamilton and the eventual Democratic-Republicans led by Thomas Jefferson.

During the 1790s, support for immigration was eroded by Anglo-French conflict and partisan polarization at home. For the Federalists, new French and Irish immigrants were untrustworthy because of their celebration of French Revolutionary ideals and their participation in democratic clubs associated with new forms of dreaded factionalism. But perhaps most disquieting to Federalists about European newcomers was their support for Democratic-Republicans. In cities like New York and Philadelphia, naturalized Irish and other immigrants usually voted for Democratic-Republican candidates. "If some means are not adopted to prevent the indiscriminate admission of wild Irishmen and others to the right of suffrage," the Federalist Harrison Gray Otis warned, "there will be an end to liberty and property."[32]

Federalist congressional majorities ultimately imposed stringent new limits on the rights of European immigrants, including their access to citizenship and enfranchisement. A new naturalization law was passed in 1795 that increased the residency requirement for citizenship from two to five years. Three years later, embattled Federalist lawmakers enacted the Alien and Sedition Acts, which included new policies governing immigration and naturalization. Foreigners were now eligible for citizenship only after *fourteen* years of residency. All aliens were required to register with federal officials. In addition, the Alien Act empowered the president to deport any alien "whom he shall judge dangerous to the peace and safety of the United States." Finally, the Alien Enemies Act allowed the federal government to apprehend and confine male enemy aliens age fourteen years or older during times of war.[33]

   The Alien and Sedition Acts proved to be short-lived, an effort by the Federalist party to forestall its imminent loss of political power. These restrictive measures only strengthened ties between enfranchised immigrants and the Democratic-Republican party, as foreign-born voters, especially the Irish and French, cast their ballots in 1800 for Jeffersonian candidates. Once assuming power in 1801, Democratic-Republicans acted quickly to rescind Federalist restrictions on European immigrants and to restore generous terms of naturalization. Registration requirements for aliens were repealed, while presidential powers to deport foreigners deemed dangerous to the public safety were simply allowed to expire after their two-year limit. The Jeffersonians also passed legislation in 1802 making naturalization contingent once again upon only five years of U.S. residency. Party leaders such as Jefferson and Madison also took pains to endorse easy admissions and naturalization policies for European men that prevailed during the eras of the American Revolution and constitutional formation. The United States was destined, Jefferson declared, "to consecrate a sanctuary for those whom the misrule of Europe may compel to seek happiness in other climes." He added that European settlers should view the United States as a New Canaan, where they would "be received as brothers."[34] From its inception, the Democratic-Republican party (later the Democratic party) closely allied itself with white male immigrants.

   At the opening of the nineteenth century, then, federal policy toward European immigration already appeared hard to change. The Jeffersonian "Revolution of 1800" reaffirmed the constitutional architects' initial decision not to impose federal controls on alien admissions, anticipating that most states would recruit European settlers as a means of promoting economic development at a time when untamed territory abounded and labor was scarce. The restoration of generous terms of naturalization for European men after 1800 also meant that they would be a potent force at the ballot box once immigration swelled. Jeffersonians began a long Democratic tradition of guarding robust European immigration and alien rights, for which they received electoral support from most newcomers. Well before massive immigration of later decades, national policy toward transatlantic immigration had become essentially insulated from anti-foreign sentiment and organized restrictionist groups. Departing from this path would be a pipe dream for nativist movements for years to come.

Mass Immigration, Democratization, and Party Politics, 1801–1850

From the start, the political consequences of the Democratic party's alliance with enfranchised immigrant groups, especially the Irish, were not lost on its rivals. As Democratic-Republicans rescinded anti-alien legislation of 1798, Federalists lamented the electoral implications of easy naturalization. Federalist newspapers like the *Columbia Sentinel* featured naturalization policy in an extended series exploring how Jeffersonians translated pro-immigrant policies into foreign-born votes. There was little question, the *Sentinel* claimed, that Jefferson urged congressional loyalists to ease naturalization requirements in 1802 with the purpose of "gratifying the wishes" of licentious immigrant voters in order to secure "his own greatness . . . by another election."[35] With nativist indignation, Federalists accused Jeffersonians of sacrificing national purity and stability for electoral gain.[36]

But like the Whigs and Republicans to follow, Federalist leaders disagreed on how they should respond to European immigration and its beneficent impact for Democratic office-seekers. Whereas some endorsed nativist policy solutions, Hamilton and others argued that the party's future depended on its coming to terms with immigrant voters. As Washington's Treasury secretary, Hamilton had vigorously advocated open immigration policies as crucial to national economic development.[37] After the devastating election of 1800, he urged Federalists to actively court immigrant voters. His arguments resonated with Federalist politicians of urban centers where immigrant voting blocs were the most formidable. Philadelphia Federalists created a "committee to aid in the naturalization of foreigners," while their New York brethren used new campaign slogans and anthems to openly appeal to newcomers ("Come Dutch and Yankees, Irish, Scot, with intermixed relation; From whence we come it matters not; We all make, now, one nation").[38] Hamilton himself proposed a Washington Constitutional Society dedicated to providing assistance to immigrants who might later repay Federalist generosities on election day. This pro-immigration strategy ultimately died with its chief author. At the Federalists' Hartford Convention a few years later, nativist partisans railed against Democratic-Republicans for their naked appeals

TABLE 3.3
Immigration and Population Growth of the United States, 1821–1860

	Immigration	Population	Immigration as % of Population Increase
1821–30	143,439	12,866,020	4.4
1831–40	599,125	17,069,453	14.3
1841–50	1,713,251	23,191,876	28.0
1851–60	2,598,214	31,443,321	31.5

Source: Table created from data in *The Statistical Yearbook of the Immigration and Naturalization Service* (Washington, DC: Government Printing Office, 1994). The U.S. government did not collect statistics on immigration before 1820.

to foreign and Irish support. Hartford delegates summoned memories of 1798 by calling for new restrictions on the political rights of naturalized citizens.[39] But theirs were the yearnings of defeated politicians whose party would soon disappear.

The decades before the Civil War were marked by an unprecedented increase in immigration to the United States, with most immigrants beginning their journeys from countries such as Germany, Ireland, England, Scotland, France, Sweden, and Norway. During the 1820s, immigration accounted for only 4 percent of the steady increase in American population; by the 1850s, immigration accounted for nearly one-third of U.S. population growth (see table 3.3). Three million arrived in one decade alone, during an extraordinary antebellum surge from 1845 to 1854; this flood of new settlers constituted about 15 percent of the total U.S. population—the highest proportion of immigrants at any time in the young nation's history. Overall, the American population more than tripled from roughly 9.6 million in 1820 to 31.5 million in 1860, with immigration accounting for a sizable portion of this increase. Mass immigration had become a defining feature of American national development.

Surges of xenophobia accompanied robust immigration, with Catholic newcomers the most frequent targets of nativist hostility. The U.S. Catholic population grew sharply in the decades before the Civil War, thanks to Irish and German inflows. From the burning of the Ursuline Convent in 1834 to the Kensington riots of the 1840s, anti-Catholic venom sometimes exploded into mob violence.[40] Catholic immigrants also were assailed in new books and newspaper articles. One popular work written by New York newspaper editor and telegraph inventor Samuel Morse, *Foreign Conspiracy* (1841), alleged that the Vatican was flooding the United States with Catholic immigrants in order to supplant republican government with Catholic theocracy. "We are dupes of our hospitality," warned Morse. "The evil of immigration brings to these shores illiterate Roman

Catholics, . . . the obedient instruments of their more knowing priestly leaders."[41] Xenophobia and anti-Catholicism mixed easily in new nativist movements, which favored limits on Catholic political rights and restrictions on immigrant admissions.

Many of these movements, such as the anti-Masons, organized new parties dedicated to guarding the polity from Freemasons, Catholics, and immigrants. The Anti-Masonic party was a notable political force in New York, Pennsylvania, and New England states when the "Age of Jackson" began, and served as political opposition to Jacksonian Democrats until the rise of Henry Clay's Whig Party in the mid-1830s.[42] After the demise of the anti-Masonic movement, militant nativists in port cities receiving the bulk of immigration traffic formed new parties committed to restricting the admission of Catholic, criminal, and pauper aliens from Europe. In the 1840s, the American Republican party (later the Native American party) gained a strong following in New Orleans, New York, Philadelphia, Boston, Newark, St. Louis, and Charleston. Casting themselves as the reform alternative to the two major parties, American Republicans pledged "to introduce honesty and purity in politics" by using "every means in our power to diminish foreign influences."[43] Yet nativist third parties never garnered more than a handful of victories in local elections, and none effected any change in the expansive terms of American immigration and naturalization policies.

Professional politicians of the mainstream Whig party proved no more successful in dislodging established immigration policy patterns. For both ideological and strategic reasons, Whig politicians were more prone to xenophobia and anti-Catholic nativism than were their Democratic counterparts. Most immigrants in turn associated the Whig party with aristocracy, temperance, and nativist prejudice, resulting in a virtual Democratic monopoly on foreign-born votes.[44] It is little wonder, then, that Whig leaders were known to appeal to nativist voters before the Civil War by embracing anti-immigrant and anti-Catholic positions. During the depression of 1837, for instance, Whig congressional leaders presented petitions from nativist groups across the country before urging federal legislation to restrict immigration and to toughen naturalization requirements. But the bill died without a floor vote; David Bennett finds that most lawmakers were "not anxious to alienate the growing immigrant vote," and thus preferred to wait for the economic crisis to pass.[45]

During the presidential campaign of 1844, Whigs actively solicited endorsements from nativist groups for its national ticket of Henry Clay and Theodore Frelinghuysen. Frelinghuysen had impeccable nativist credentials, and was known for his leadership of several organizations openly hostile to Catholicism and new immigration.[46] But the Whigs lost the presidential contest to the Democrat James K. Polk by a narrow margin (fewer than 40,000 votes separated the tickets after about 2.8 million ballots were cast).[47] Revered Whig leaders such as Daniel Webster, Millard Fillmore, and Clay himself came to the conclusion that the heavy support Democrats enjoyed among immigrant and Catholic voters—especially in crucial states such as New York—cost them the White House.[48] Whether or not their electoral analysis was accurate, it clearly informed the Whig decision to quickly sever ties with nativist groups like the American Republicans in 1845. As a result, nativist legislative plans languished.

By 1850, U.S. immigration policy remained unchanged by the ebb and flow of nativist sentiment or the political activism of new anti-immigrant groups. Morse and other anti-Catholic nativists saw their cause as fundamentally "a national question, not only separate from, but *superior* to all others" (original emphasis).[49] But in the first half of the nineteenth century, the national government remained all but silent on European immigration even as its volume reached unprecedented levels. In fact, the only immigration controls enacted in this period required that new arrivals be counted after 1819 to maintain uniform statistics, and mandated minimum living standards for vessels carrying immigrant passengers to the United States.[50] The task of regulating immigration continued to devolve to state and local governments, an arrangement begun by the nation's founders but reinforced by the political philosophies of Jeffersonians and Jacksonians, who dismantled many national institutions and programs.[51]

In practice, the modest regulatory structure governing immigrant traffic in antebellum America was the creation and ongoing responsibility of a few states with large ports, such as New York (where most immigrants landed), Pennsylvania, Massachusetts, Maryland, and South Carolina. State immigration laws authorized exclusion of newcomers with criminal records, contagious illnesses, or a perceived likelihood that they would become wards of the state.[52] Troubled by the financial burdens of regulating alien inflows and offering poor relief to destitute immigrants, coastal states charged ship masters small head taxes on each passenger and required bonds to be posted for those considered likely to become public charges. The authority of state governments to regulate immigration in this fashion was affirmed by the Supreme Court in the 1837 case of *Mayor of New York v Milne*. As the Taney Court ruled, "precautionary measures against the moral pestilence of [foreign] paupers, vagabonds, and possibly convicts" were consistent with the right of states to exercise police power within their borders.[53] The 1848 *Passenger Cases* reversed this holding, suggesting that state head taxes violated federal prerogatives, but states made minor policy adjustments and assumed continued primacy in this area.[54]

Even in coastal states with laws excluding European criminals and paupers, the mechanisms for enforcing these measures did not favor major restrictions. The immigration boards states created to regulate alien inflows were comprised almost entirely of "social reformers and humanitarians who served without pay." As enforcement structures, the all-volunteer state immigration boards operated more as "protective charity foundations" concerned with immigrant welfare than as watchdog agencies consumed with excluding unwanted outsiders.[55] The devolution of immigration control posed significant hurdles for nativist groups pursuing sweeping immigration restriction.

The nativist agenda faced other daunting obstacles. In the same decades that the United States was being reshaped by massive waves of new European arrivals, several national developments made future immigration highly desirable. The dramatic expansion of U.S. territory with the Louisiana Purchase and the Mexican-American War created a strong demand for new immigrants to settle a large, open frontier. Territorial governments actively recruited European newcomers, employing immigration agents to launch ambitious advertising campaigns overseas or to court new arrivals as they landed in New York. Another crucial sea change was the emergence of a growing industrial economy that required an expanded labor force that European immigration helped realize. "The open-door policy," Kitty Calivita observes, complemented "the advent of industrialization and the need for an industrial work force."[56] Political leaders of varied partisan stripes embraced immigrant labor recruitment.

Perhaps the most profound source of policy frustration for antebellum nativists, however, rested in a crucial political transformation of the Jacksonian era: the extraordinary shift in American government from what Martin Shefter calls a "regime of notables" to the world's first mass-based democracy in which universal white male suffrage, party organizations, and competitive elections predominated.[57] Democratizing reforms of the 1830s and 1840s, when combined with broad immigration opportunities and easy acquisition of citizenship, made white male immigrant groups an electoral force that Democratic leaders and other politicians had a compelling interest in winning over. As we have seen, the Democratic party pledged support for generous terms of European immigrant admission and naturalization from its inception. Local Democratic organizations worked hard to enfranchise white male newcomers as swiftly as possible; local judges naturalized large numbers of immigrants on the eve of presidential elections, and many states and territories even established voting rights for white male *aliens*.[58] An 1845 congressional investigation found that urban Democratic political machines were well practiced at naturalizing thousands of immigrants just before elections.[59]

For nativists and Democratic opponents, the rise of potent immigrant voting blocs was a grim development. Clay castigated "this constant manufacture of American citizens out of foreign emigrants" as a great "evil."[60] Morse bitterly criticized the nation's founders for establishing easy naturalization and broad political rights for white male newcomers on a nonsectarian basis. "How is it possible," he demanded, "that so vital a point as the ballot box was not constitutionally surrounded with double, ay, with treble guards?"[61] Early restrictionists understood clearly that the enfranchisement of immigrants made them a political force, facilitating alliances with established party politicians who supported mass European immigration and the federal government's laissez-faire response to it. Even the Democrats' fiercest competitors wavered between conciliating nativist or immigrant voters. Like Hamiltonian Federalists before them, many Whigs came to the conclusion that it was not in their interest to antagonize significant voting blocs by embracing anti-immigrant causes. Mindful of the economic benefits and electoral clout of new European settlers, Whig president John Tyler publicly declared that his administration extended "to the peoples of other countries an invitation to come and settle among us as members of our rapidly growing family."[62] The fact that the Whigs lost presidential elections in which they openly courted anti-immigrant votes, as was the case with Clay's 1844 defeat, was not lost on national party leaders who increasingly rebuffed nativist goals. In short, immigrant enfranchisement and mass-based party competition fortified national policies that encouraged European immigration.

SECTIONAL CRISIS AS POLICY OPENING: THE RISE AND FALL OF THE AMERICAN PARTY

At midcentury, nativists concluded that the existing two-party system was fundamentally inhospitable to their anti-Catholic and anti-immigrant agenda. While Democrats remained firmly allied with new European immigrant groups, the once friendly Whig party could no longer be trusted to protect "Native Americans" from impure foreigners. "Both whigs and democrats," nativist leaders noted, "regarded the matter as ephemeral and insignificant, and went on as usual, wheedling and coaxing the naturalized citizens, and sycophantically bargaining for their suffrage."[63] By 1850, these leaders looked for independent vehicles for their policy goals, joining secretive fraternal societies such as the Order of United Americans (OUA) and the Order of the Star Spangled Banner (OSSB). These societies eschewed the two major parties, and the OSSB in particular began independent political organizing in local wards and electoral districts throughout states like New York.[64] Mocking the OSSB for its secrecy, Horace Greeley noted in the *New York Tribune* that its members should be called "know-nothings"—a label the movement itself cheerfully embraced.[65] Like nativists before them, fraternal orders of the

Know-Nothing movement formed a new American party to serve as their primary instrument for reshaping national public policy.

There was little reason when the 1850s began to expect the Know-Nothings and their American party to be any more successful than earlier nativist campaigns. However, the 1852 presidential election would mark the Whig party's last national campaign and signal the impending demise of the "second party system" dominated by Jacksonian Democrats. The enactment of the Kansas-Nebraska Act in 1854 served to intensify sectional conflict over slavery in the territories, while new parties emerged from the ashes of the Whig party to challenge an increasingly balkanized Democratic party. They included the Temperance, Fusion, Free Soil, Anti-Nebraska, People's, Republican, and American parties. Establishment politicians like Stephen A. Douglas believed third party movements were incapable of commanding cross-sectional support but contributed to the animosity that characterized national political life. U.S. politics, he lamented, had become "a crucible into which is poured Abolitionism, Maine liquor law-ism, . . . Protestant feeling against the Catholic, and the native feeling against the foreigner."[66]

The 1854 and 1855 elections, however, demonstrated the broad appeal of the American party both north and south of the Mason-Dixon line. Know-Nothing candidates won statewide victories in New Hampshire, Massachusetts, Rhode Island, Connecticut, New York, and Kentucky. They also secured offices in Texas, Maryland, and Delaware, and garnered substantial electoral support in Virginia, Georgia, Alabama, Mississippi, Louisiana, and Texas.[67] In addition to electing seven Know-Nothing governors, the American party gained a presence in Congress (see table 3.4). The 34th Congress, which opened in 1855, included forty-eight new representatives of the American party, while fifty-nine others closely aligned themselves with the the American party platform.[68] The movement's overnight success transcended the ballot box. As David Bennett notes, "nativism became a new American rage: Know-Nothing candy, Know-Nothing tea, and Know-Nothing toothpicks were marketed, buses and stage coaches received the charmed name, the clipper ship *Know Nothing* was launched in New York."[69]

By crippling the Whig and Democratic parties, the slavery extension crisis clearly provided key openings for the Know-Nothings.[70] But the American party's meteoric rise in 1854–55 more specifically reflected a nativist agenda that promised to unify native-born citizens polarized by slavery and sectional discord. Prevailing hostilities between fellow citizens could be redirected by political nativists against Catholics, immigrants, and other groups whose presumed foreign connections corrupted the nation. On the eve of civil war, many Americans preferred to associate national political turmoil with external rather than indigenous forces.

TABLE 3.4

House and Senate Seats Won by the American Party, 33d–38th Congress

| Congress | Years | American Party | |
		Senators	House Members
33d	1853–55	0	0
34th	1855–57	5	43
35th	1857–59	5	14
36th	1859–61	2	23
37th	1861–63	7	28
38th	1863–65	0	0

Source: Table based on data in E. P. Hutchinson, *Legislative History of American Immigration Policy* (Philadelphia: University of Pennsylvania Press, 1981), pp. 621–43.

Know-Nothingism "was in a sense an ideal solution to be able to berate, to let off steam and resentment on, non-Americans rather than fellow citizens."[71] The American party offered a xenophobic basis for renewed national solidarity. "Our country, our whole country, and nothing but our country," it proclaimed.[72]

The surge in political nativism also sprang from a more direct source: stunning increases in the volume and ethnic diversity of immigration to the United States in the 1850s. The 3 million European immigrants who poured into the country in the decade before 1855 shattered previous levels, and constituted nearly 15 percent of the total U.S. population. The fact that Irish Catholics represented more than 40 percent of new residents was especially galling to nativists.[73] American party politicians linked new immigrants to alleged increases in crime, poverty, and public expenditures on poor relief and law enforcement.[74] Accordingly, the American party called for bold national reforms that repealed lax naturalization laws, limited elective office to native-born citizens, established "more stringent and effective" immigration laws, deported foreign paupers, and waged "war to the hilt on Romanism."[75]

American party members of Congress sought in 1855 to press their anti-immigrant legislative program. They initiated several bills in both houses mandating stringent naturalization requirements, but none was enacted.[76] When attempting to secure federal immigration restrictions on foreign paupers, criminals, and those deemed mentally and physically disabled, they again failed to secure majority support.[77] By the second session, immigration virtually disappeared from the congressional agenda. The frustrations of American party representatives owed much to lawmakers' preoccupation with the slavery issue and armed conflict in Kansas. But when national lawmakers *did* turn their attention to immigration and naturalization, nativist proposals were soundly rejected by pro-immigration majorities.

Despite deep fissures within Democratic ranks, its congressional standard bearers remained strong defenders of both an expansive immigration policy and generous naturalization rules. Democratic leaders continued to affirm the principle that the United States was an "asylum of the oppressed of every nation," and pledged to fight "every attempt to abridge the privilege of becoming citizens and the owners of soil among us."[78] Democratic dominance of the Senate ensured the defeat of nativist bills.

The relationship between the Know-Nothing movement and House Republicans, who held a slim majority, was more ambiguous. Many Republicans were attracted by the Know-Nothing cause due to perceptions of Irish immigrants as supportive of slavocracy, as wage-earning workers who threatened free labor, and as sources of new urban social problems.[79] Joel Silbey notes that "Republicans and Northern Know-Nothings hated the slave power, but they also hated the Irish immigrant—both for the last named's excessive use of political power and foreign intrusion into what was seen as the right way for America to develop."[80] Several dozen of the 108 newly elected Republicans were once members of Know-Nothing lodges. Indeed, one Republican formerly associated with the Know-Nothings was Nathaniel Banks of Massachusetts, whom fellow partisans elected Speaker of the House.[81] However, other House Republicans battled with Know-Nothings for anti-Democratic votes in their districts and chose to tread lightly on the immigration issue. Still others embraced European immigration as essential to Northern economic expansion and the dominance of free labor in Western territories. More important, many Republicans came to view temperance and nativism as dangerous distractions from the cause of abolition; some radicals suggested Know-Nothingism was inspired by Southerners to protect slavery. "Neither the Pope nor the foreigners ever can govern the country or endanger its liberties," Charles Dana wrote in the *New York Tribune* in 1856, "but the slave-breeders and slave traders *do* govern it."[82]

Republican politicians were particularly supportive of European immigration in the Midwest, where German and Swedish immigrants represented important voting blocs. In Midwestern states, party activists courted foreign-born voters and welcomed leadership from German abolitionists like Carl Schurz and Gustav Koerner. Northeastern Republicans also came to challenge the Know-Nothing movement. At an 1855 Republican rally in Massachusetts, Senator Charles Sumner boldly confronted the legions of Know-Nothing supporters in his state party. "Are you for Freedom, or are you for Slavery?" he demanded of a hushed, overflow crowd in Boston's Faneuil Hall. Although Northern Know-

Nothings opposed slavery, Sumner warned that their true goal was "to attaint men for religion, and also for birth." Not only did this agenda "disturb the energies" of the antislavery crusade, he argued, but its assault on "Civil Freedom" and religious toleration "should not be associated with our cause."[83] He called on his party to fight "any check upon the welcome" to European immigrants:

> There are our broad lands, stretching towards the setting sun; let them come and take them. Ourselves children of the Pilgrims of a former generation, let us not turn from the Pilgrims of the present. . . . The history of our country, in its humblest and as well as most exalted spheres, testifies to the merit of foreigners.[84]

In the face of solid Democratic and notable Republican opposition, Know-Nothing lawmakers stood no chance of securing their anti-immigrant agenda.

The demise of the American party was as swift and dramatic as its ascent. The key to the Know-Nothings' fleeting electoral success was the cross-sectional appeal of its assault upon all things foreign, which fundamentally relied upon state American party organizations of the North and South setting aside differences over slavery in the interest of shared nativist goals. Whereas Southern Know-Nothings took care to steer clear of "the dangerous rock of slavery," their Northern counterparts drew electoral support by fusing nativist and abolitionist positions.[85] While this formula worked magic at the ballot box in 1854, it collapsed when Northern and Southern delegates battled over slavery extension at the American party national convention of 1855. Delegates from Northern states like Ohio demanded that the national party call for the reinstitution of the Missouri Compromise, while Southern counterparts favored an endorsement of the Kansas-Nebraska Act. Southern delegates ultimately controlled the convention, winning explicit national party support for the Kansas-Nebraska Act. But Northern delegations responded by bolting the convention and issuing independent antislavery planks.[86]

In 1856 sectional discord over slavery extension again sundered the American party's national convention with similar results: dominant Southern delegations defeated Northern planks endorsing the Missouri Compromise and Northerners spurned the convention.[87] The party's selection of Millard Fillmore as its 1856 presidential candidate further offended Northerners, who loathed him for signing the Fugitive Slave Law of 1850. By 1860, former Northern supporters of the American party threw their support behind the Republican party. Ironically, the same slavery extension controversy that helped elevate political nativism in antebellum America proved to be the driving force behind its swift demise.

REPUBLICAN GOVERNMENT AND IMMIGRANT LABOR:
RECRUITING NEWCOMERS

The path established for national immigration policy in the late-eighteenth century was well guarded by the Democratic party until the onset of the Civil War. Yet this once dominant old party was decimated by the crises of slavery extension and Southern secession, leaving immigrant admissions and rights in the hands of an essentially one-party Republican government after the 1860 election. If the Whigs and Republicans were more sympathetic to xenophobic sentiment than were the Democrats, then this period of one-party rule might seem opportune for Republican nativists to win passage of restrictionist legislation. But no such initiatives were enacted. One might presume that the extraordinary demands of preserving the Union consumed Republican leaders and foreclosed consideration of peripheral issues like immigration. However, Republican officials were remarkably attentive to immigration matters during and immediately after the Civil War, initiating several significant federal efforts to *encourage* immigration. Higham, Gerring, and others correctly observe that the Republican party was prone to embrace anti-immigrant views and to serve as a vehicle for nativist political goals. Yet this same party also had a penchant for government policies designed to directly facilitate national economic growth, including immigration inducements expected to fuel industrialization and Western territorial development. These neomercantilist concerns, rather than nativist ones, shaped Republican views of immigration during the Civil War and Reconstruction years. Cosmopolitans in the party also fortified the federal government's pro-immigration orientation, celebrating the universality of America's asylum ideal.[88]

During the 1860 campaign, prominent Republicans worked to purge Know-Nothing elements from their party and to win a national platform that explicitly disavowed nativist reform proposals. In addition to economic and cosmopolitan motivations, the GOP leadership had good reason to endorse immigration for pragmatic electoral purposes. Sizable immigrant groups such as the Germans, Swedes, and Dutch were important potential voting constituencies of the young party (the Irish remained loyal to the Democratic party).[89] These voting blocs were largely hostile toward nativist movements, and had demonstrated as much to the Whig party when it embraced xenophobic causes in the past. The 1860 Republican platform stated its firm opposition to any revision of existing naturalization law or any effort to constrict immigrant rights.[90] Party politicians also promised a new Homestead Law offering free lands, an initiative that party strategists knew immigrant voters would find attractive. Before becoming the Republican presidential candidate, Abraham

Lincoln allegedly courted Know-Nothing votes in Illinois while privately expressing disdain for the movement.[91] By 1860, however, Lincoln took pains to publicly express opposition to immigration restriction because "the value of life is to improve one's condition." If newcomers "can better their condition by leaving their old homes," he assured a German audience, "there is nothing in my heart to forbid them coming; and I bid them all God speed."[92]

Under Republican control during the 1860s, the national government favored expansive immigration opportunities. Warfare took a heavy toll on the American labor force, reinforcing the ideological predilections of many national Republicans to spur large-scale immigration in these years. To encourage settlement of the West "so that every poor man may have a home," the Homestead Act of 1862 offered 160 acres of land free to citizens *and aliens* who worked it for at least five years.[93] The stated purpose of the legislation was not to encourage European immigration, but Secretary of Treasury Salmon Chase and Secretary of State William Seward saw it as a means of doing just that. With Lincoln's blessing, Seward instructed U.S. consular officials in Europe to mass-distribute government-published pamphlets advertising the opportunities provided to newcomers by the Homestead Act.[94] In one 1863 circular, Seward promised "industrious" European men "abundant means of support, and comfortable homesteads for themselves and their families."[95] Some U.S. consuls hired full-time agents to attract prospective settlers with free land. The federal government was far from alone in this venture. While Western states and territories continued to use immigration agents and publicity campaigns to induce immigration from Europe, railroad companies sent agents to Germany to recruit farmers to develop vast railroad lands.[96]

The Republican party again endorsed immigration in its national platform during the 1864 election, proclaiming that "foreign immigration . . . should be fostered and encouraged by a liberal and just policy."[97] That same year Lincoln urged Congress to establish a system for inducing immigration to redress "a great deficiency of laborers" produced by the Civil War. Within a few months, lawmakers obliged with An Act to Encourage Immigration, which created a full-time commissioner of Immigration and a Bureau of Immigration to disseminate information in Europe that might attract newcomers (twenty thousand dollars per annum was allocated for recruitment literature). The law also authorized immigrant labor contracts enabling prospective European immigrants to contract their labor for one year in exchange for free transportation to the United States. The law specifically prohibited contracts exceeding one year as well as conditions of slavery or involuntary servitude.[98] As a Republican congressional committee concluded in 1864, "the advantages which have accrued heretofore from immigration can scarcely be computed."[99]

A few months before his assassination, Lincoln hailed open immigration "as one of the principal replenishing streams, which are appointed by Providence to repair the ravages of internal war, and its wastes of national strength and health."[100] Under pressure from labor groups in 1868, congressional Republicans repealed their earlier authorization of contract labor. But the original law spawned private immigrant recruitment agencies such as the Foreign Emigrant Aid Society and the American Emigrant Company that fostered European inflows for years to come.[101] At the same time as European immigration rose to roughly 200,000 per year (mostly from German inflows), the Burlingame Treaty of 1868 hastened Chinese immigration to the country (see chap. 4). In ensuing years, the federal government returned to a laissez-faire policy in hopes that its benign neglect would allow European immigration to flourish. The Republican party again endorsed robust immigrant admissions in its 1868 and 1872 platforms, but their pro-immigration planks were matched in these years by a resurgent Democratic party eager to reclaim its close ties with immigrant voters.[102] In growing cities like New York, the Democratic party enjoyed new strength thanks largely to immigrant voting blocs and new Irish-dominated party machines such as the Tweed Ring of Tammany Hall. As two-party competition reemerged after Reconstruction, immigration policy continued along the path begun at the founding, remarkably undisturbed by political convulsions that shook American politics in the 1850s and 1860s.

RELUCTANT REGULATORS: THE SLOW NATIONALIZATION OF
EUROPEAN IMMIGRATION CONTROL

In the early 1870s, official efforts to regulate European immigration remained largely the province of state governments with major ports of entry. The vast majority of newcomers—originating from Germany, Ireland, and the United Kingdom—arrived in New York, where they were channeled through a central immigrant depot, Manhattan's Castle Garden. The few modest immigration controls established by state legislation both authorized the potential exclusion of individual immigrants deemed "undesirable" (such as criminals, the diseased, unmarried pregnant women, and disabled persons considered likely to become public charges), and created a system of bonding and head taxes to support immigrant poor relief and other services.[103] Enforcement of these measures continued to be the task of philanthropists and volunteers of state immigration boards. Their chief concerns were to maintain an efficient reception process and to assist immigrants in need of temporary support.[104]

The death knell for state-level regulation of immigrant admissions was sounded by the Supreme Court in its 1875 *Henderson v Mayor of New York* ruling. The decision specifically nullified state requirements that shipmasters pay bonds and head taxes for passengers. But its sweeping prohibition on state immigration controls was of monumental significance. Whereas the Court's *Milne* decision said state governments possessed police powers within their territories that authorized them to control immigration, the *Henderson* majority held that state regulations were an unconstitutional usurpation of exclusive congressional power to regulate foreign commerce.[105] Moreover, the Court urged national uniformity in alien admissions. "The laws which govern the right to land passengers in the United States from other countries ought to be the same in New York, Boston, New Orleans, and San Francisco."[106]

Judicial intervention denied officials in coastal states the power to exercise even modest control over the vast immigrant traffic that flowed through their urban ports. In the absence of congressional action, however, state immigration boards of the Northeast continued to assist European newcomers arriving on their shores. Officials in New York, Massachusetts, Maryland, and other "front-line" states found this arrangement intolerable. Deprived of head tax revenues from steamship companies by the *Henderson* ruling, they now faced the prospect of raising taxes or realigning their budgets to offset the financial burdens of receiving and providing public benefits to record numbers of immigrants. The legislatures and immigration boards of New York and other Northeastern states lobbied Congress with petitions and reports urging federal relief from the costs of administration and immigrant care. They also advocated federal legislation to exclude convicts and "confirmed paupers" altogether.[107]

Neither Republican nor Democratic leaders rushed to establish federal regulations on European inflows. Steamship companies and industrial employers of immigrant laborers resisted any national restrictions that might slow European immigration.[108] Moreover, Northeastern states received little sympathy from their Western and Southern counterparts. Representatives of Western states still yearned for new European settlers, while Southern politicians noted that steady European immigration would guarantee white electoral supremacy.[109] Finally, leaders of both major parties were reluctant to adopt any new federal policies that might offend immigrant voters. Although he smeared Democrats for falling under the spell of Catholic influence in his campaign for governor of Ohio in 1875, Republican Rutherford B. Hayes was careful to distance himself from nativist impulses during his presidential bid the following year. "You can denounce all charges of hostility to foreigners . . . as utterly unfounded," Hayes publicly assured Carl Schurz in the heat of the 1876 race. "I was not a Know-Nothing when my political associates generally

ran off after that ephemeral party."[110] For their part, Democratic platforms affirmed "the liberal principles embodied by Jefferson . . . which
makes ours the land of liberty and the asylum of the oppressed of every
nation" as "cardinal principles in the Democratic faith."[111] For six years
after the *Henderson* ruling, Congress turned a deaf ear to Northeastern
officials clamoring for a national response to the economic and social
burdens of European immigration.

Despite congressional reluctance to restrict European immigration in
any fashion, there was no escaping the fact that judicial actions had made
immigration a national issue. Frustrated by federal delays, New York's
Board of Emigration Commissioners threatened in 1881 to shut down
Castle Garden and to cease all regulatory activities unless federal action
was forthcoming. Congress quickly responded by adopting legislation
that essentially nationalized state policies governing European immigration that had been struck down by the Court. The Immigration Act of
1882 borrowed language from state statutes to restrict admission of "any
convict, lunatic, idiot, or any person unable to take care of himself or
herself without becoming a public charge."[112] It also established a system
of funding immigrant inspections and providing for the welfare of newcomers by assessing head taxes on each entrant. However, the federal
government lacked the administrative capacities to enforce these new
regulatory policies. Congress resolved this dilemma by authorizing state
immigration boards and commissioners to enforce federal legislation with
direction from U.S. Treasury officials.[113] Policy patterns long associated
with state governments were now maintained by the federal government;
the 1882 law placed the national imprimatur on well-established state
regulations and restored the power of state and local officials to implement these policies under Treasury Department guidance.

Amid immigration swells and economic depression a few years later,
labor unions clamored for federal legislation to prohibit industrial employers from importing immigrant workers to break strikes and hold
down wages. Democrats, who controlled the House, responded to these
pressures with great care. While the Democratic party cast itself as the
traditional defender of European immigrants, it also nurtured close ties
with labor unions, including the first mass movement of American workers, the Knights of Labor. To avoid offending either of these key constituencies, House Democrats assailed only that European immigration
which resulted from "greedy capitalists" importing foreign laborers under
contract.[114] Party leaders proposed an Anti-Contract Labor Bill in 1884
that prohibited solely prepaid passage and contractual arrangements for
the recruitment of unskilled alien workers. Lest foreign-born voters view
the bill as restrictive, Democrats emphasized that it "in no way seeks to
restrict or prohibit voluntary or free immigration."[115] During floor debate

over the bill, House sponsors assured Irish and German immigrants that the measure would discourage only so-called new immigrants: Italians, Poles, Hungarians, Slavs, and other southern and eastern Europeans arriving in small number in this period.[116] During the 1884 campaign, the Republican party also endorsed a ban on contract labor. Democrats countered that contract labor owed its origin "to an act passed by a Republican Congress in 1864."[117] Within a year, a federal contract labor ban was enacted.

The Knights of Labor welcomed distinctions between old and new European arrivals. With a large foreign-born and pro-immigration membership, the Knights in fact had no desire to secure sweeping restrictions on European immigration. The international orientation of the Knights, which spread throughout the industrial world, made the movement more concerned with attaining the solidarity of all workers, regardless of nationality. Indeed, Knights leaders such as Terence Powderly praised "voluntary immigration" from Europe, and assailed contract labor as a monopolist perversion of the nation's traditional commitment to unrestricted immigration. One Knights' publication decried "the stupendous folly of an industrial system which makes so naturally beneficent a thing as an increase in population a menace to the welfare of the wealth producers."[118] In its early form, then, American labor struck an ambivalent (if not tolerant) posture toward large-scale European immigration.

Before the century's end, Congress enacted only one other piece of legislation concerning European immigration: the Immigration Act of 1891. Sailing through both chambers, the law created a new federal bureaucracy within the Treasury Department to assume the tasks of screening immigrants. The new Immigration Bureau relieved state agencies and private associations from screening newcomers, replacing them with a corps of U.S. immigration inspectors stationed at the nation's major ports of entry. In addition, persons suffering from contagious diseases and polygamists were now deemed excludable, and aliens who became public charges were made subject to deportation.[119] Within the year, Castle Garden was replaced by a new federal immigration station in New York City harbor, Ellis Island. Employing 119 of the 180 total staff who comprised the young Immigration Bureau, Ellis Island was to be the largest and busiest immigration station for decades to come.[120]

It is significant that the 1882, 1885, and 1891 laws were neither intended to nor had the effect of disturbing the nation's long-standing celebration of robust European immigration. Early choices of decisionmakers—especially generous terms of naturalization—continued to reinforce established policy patterns of encouraging new waves of European immigrants. In the decade these three laws were enacted, European immigration to the United States reached 5 million and represented close to 40 percent of the country's total population growth.

THE AMERICAN PROTECTIVE ASSOCIATION AND PARTY POLITICS

Political nativism was resurgent in the final decade of the nineteenth century. Amidst labor agitation and immigration swells of the late 1880s, xenophobic sentiment gained new currency but remained politically diffuse and unorganized. The 1886 bombing of Haymarket Square in Chicago occurred during a national strike initiated by the Knights of Labor, but its hasty attribution to seven anarchists of whom six were immigrants persuaded many Americans that terrorism, labor upheaval, and political radicalism originated abroad. "There is no such thing as an American anarchist," the journal *Public Opinion* insisted at the time. "The American character has in it no element which can under any circumstances be won to uses so mistaken." The Haymarket tragedy, it contended, was the work of "reckless foreign wretches."[121] For secretive fraternal associations like the Junior Order of United American Mechanics and the Patriotic Order Sons of America, labor unrest and class antagonisms were unquestionably the products of foreign, rather than homegrown, influences.

Anxieties about foreign radicalism reawakened anti-Catholic nativism. The missionary Josiah Strong's best-seller, *Our Country*, warned the nation's Protestant majority of a "Romanist Peril" that would overwhelm American government, schools, and culture.[122] Robust European immigration, he warned, was "mother and nurse" to socialism, labor unrest, "continental ideas" of faith and liquor, party machines, and "rabble-ruled cities."[123] This revival of pietistic moralism was centered principally in the rural Midwest, where anxieties about urbanization ran deep. Rural Protestants viewed the country's burgeoning industrial cities as home to corrupt party bosses and political subversives, paupers, criminals, saloon keepers, corporate barons, and financiers. Moreover, they believed that the corruption and immorality of urban America was directly attributable to the vast numbers of Catholics and immigrants who populated them. Prohibition and Sabbatarian movements soon identified immigrants with the urban and industrial forces they found so distressing. Protestant moralists like the Reverend T. W. Cuyler, president of the National Temperance Society, saw immigration restriction as a fundamental element of their reform program. "Temperance reform and the Christian Sabbath and intelligent freedom will not survive," he warned, "if our land shall keep open doors for all the godlessness and all the crime and all the reckless pauperism of the whole wide world."[124]

In terms of grass-roots organization, the most formidable nativist movement that emerged in the 1890s was the American Protective Association (APA). Comprised of an odd alliance of Protestant businessmen and workers disaffected with the Knights of Labor, the APA maintained local councils throughout the Midwest and Northeast and boasted a membership of more than 2 million faithful.[125] The APA political agenda called for tax exemptions on Catholic property to be waived, the promotion of "non-sectarian free public schools," immigration restriction, new language and citizenship tests for voting, and tougher naturalization requirements.[126] Reminiscent of the Know-Nothings, the APA's leadership urged its local councils to focus their energies on gaining leverage in local and state party politics. "The American Protective Association was, in practice, as decentralized as the political circumstances in which it dabbled," the historian Donald Kinzer notes.[127]

There was little question that the APA's localistic political activities were specifically designed for, as one contemporary put it, "capturing the machinery of one of the existing parties."[128] Yet only one of the major parties afforded opportunities for APA influence. Democratic organizations were openly hostile to the movement. Irish Catholics remained one of the party's most dependable and important voting blocs (especially in New York, a state that every president-elect won between 1880 and 1912), and they dominated many Northern urban "machines." Even the reform-minded Democrat Grover Cleveland, who made a career of challenging machines like Tammany Hall, actively courted Catholic and immigrant voters in his presidential campaigns.[129] Little wonder that local APA councils focused on gaining leverage within *Republican* organizations. "The plan of capturing Republican primaries and conventions [is] . . . the predominant activity of the APA," the *Century Magazine* noted.[130]

By 1894, the *New York Times* reported that a large number of local and state GOP organizations had fallen into the "grasp of the APA." APA leaders estimated that their local councils exercised strong influence on the Republican "political machinery" in fourteen states, and controlled several million votes.[131] To Democratic party managers struggling to hold together a restless electoral coalition amidst profound economic dislocations, the identification of the APA with the Republican party was fortuitous. Back in 1884, the Republican party was punished by immigrant and native-born Irish voters when its leaders remained silent after a prominent Protestant minister famously called the Democrats a party of "rum, Romanism, and rebellion." In the early 1890s Democratic politicians hoped the GOP's association with nativism and cultural conservatism would again cost it precious votes. The association of the APA with the Republican party, concluded Wisconsin Democratic chair Edward Wall, would "keep before the people . . . plainly the fact that personal liberty is only surely safe with the Democratic party in power."[132] Democrat John Peter Altgeld of Illinois became a model for other party candidates when he successfully exploited the GOP's association with anti-Catholic nativism in his 1892 gubernatorial bid. The APA was loudly denounced at Democratic conventions in dozens of states during the 1894 election, a strategy intended to duplicate victories of 1890 and 1892.[133]

In truth, APA influence within the Republican party was greatly exaggerated by the APA's leadership, the press, and Democratic politicians. When asked of the strength of the APA in his home state of Indiana, former GOP president Benjamin Harrison quipped, "I have not heard of any in our state, except as our Democratic friends talk of it."[134] Most Republican leaders in fact temporized on the APA movement and its reform agenda for most of the 1890s, wary of alienating either pietistic moralists or potentially supportive Catholic voters. The executive committee of the Republican National Committee (RNC), for example, turned down a motion by two of its Catholic members that the APA be publicly condemned by the national party. But the RNC did adopt a resolution in supporting religious freedom: "The Republican party, as it always has been, is in sympathy with the largest liberty of religious opinion."[135]

Over time, Republican leaders looked to electoral defeats in 1890 and 1892 and concluded that the moral crusading of ideologues in its ranks had become a serious liability. In these elections, the GOP lost ground not only among the traditional victims of nativism—Irish and German Catholics—but also among German Lutherans and newer immigrant groups. In order to forge a successful and enduring national majority coalition, many party professionals began to look for candidates and issues capable of liberating the GOP of the divisive cultural agenda of pietistic nativists.[136]

Among the scores of Republicans who lost office in 1890 was William McKinley, a congressman from Ohio who chaired the House Ways and Means Committee and served as one of the party's leading champions of protective tariffs. The year following his defeat, McKinley entered Ohio's gubernatorial race determined to win votes across ethnic and religious lines by focusing on the tariff issue and the goal of national economic growth. The issues which defined the campaign were not "local questions," he insisted, but the "general and National" concerns of "financial honor" and "industrial welfare."[137] Spurning the divisive rhetoric of moralistic reformers, McKinley tried to persuade voters that the Republican party stood for "the doctrine of hope, and cheer."[138] Rather than duck cultural and ethnic issues, McKinley placed them within his vision of national economic development. If the protective tariff and a secure national currency were promoted, he contended, renewed prosperity would ease the economic tensions that underlay cultural animosity between ethnic, religious, and occupational groups. In stump speeches across the state, McKinley sounded unifying themes of cultural harmony; true patriotism, he insisted, "believes in America for Americans, native *and naturalized*" (emphasis added).[139] He also expressed optimism that a flourishing economy would allow American shores to remain open to "those who are well disposed to our institutions, seeking new and happier homes, ready to share the burdens as well as the blessings of our society."[140] As prophet of the protective tariff, undepreciated currency, and cultural harmony, McKinley defeated his Democratic rival by a convincing margin. The coattails of his campaign also helped supplant Ohio's Democratic legislature with a two-thirds Republican majority.

The depression of 1893 served to focus even greater public attention on economic, rather than nativist, issues. As Grover Cleveland struggled to resist an agrarian and silverite challenge within Democratic ranks, the GOP engineered landslide victories across the country in 1894. Republicans gained 121 seats and a new majority in the House.[141] Such stunning GOP gains in congressional and state-level offices, attributed to Democratic inaction in the face of economic depression, persuaded many Republican leaders that they could win support from foreign-born voters and that pietistic nativism posed an obstacle to their dominating national political life. McKinley easily won reelection as governor in 1893, despite upsetting the Ohio APA by refusing to discharge two Catholic employees. He also established a stronger national reputation in the 1894 campaign, delivering close to four hundred speeches in three hundred cities on behalf of GOP candidates.[142] Two years later, APA leaders watched with dismay as McKinley and his managers orchestrated a successful bid for the presidential nomination. Mark Hanna, McKinley's leading adviser, wrote of the "prime importance" of rallying "to the support of Republican ticket many thousands of Roman Catholics."[143] The electoral strategy of McKinley's presidential campaign closely resembled that of his earlier gubernatorial bid, focusing on the prosperity and cultural harmony that would result from the protective tariff and an unmodified national currency.

Many APA leaders organized in opposition to McKinley's candidacy. Prior to the GOP national convention of 1896, the National Advisory Board of the APA's Supreme Council served notice that it found all Republican candidates *except* McKinley acceptable. In newspaper articles as well as circulars distributed across the country, APA activists denounced McKinley's candidacy on the grounds that he "discriminated in his appointments in favor of Romanists and against American Protestants."[144] They also threatened to punish other party candidates who were not pledged to their political agenda. Tellingly, many McKinley managers welcomed APA hostility as an opportunity to recast the party's nativist image and to court Catholic and foreign-born voters.[145] McKinley himself privately assailed the APA for its hubris: "Think for a moment: the leaders of a secret order seeking through its organization to dictate a presidential nomination." He concluded that APA agitation posed little danger to his electoral ambitions, telling a friend that "it may hurt locally here and there but in the broad sense it cannot hurt."[146] Before the GOP national convention in St. Louis, APA leaders boasted that they would dominate both the drafting of the party platform and the presidential nomination process. Yet almost every detail of the convention was carefully orchestrated by the McKinley-Hanna organization. To emphasize cultural harmony, a rabbi was selected to deliver the opening prayer. While planks proposed by the APA were soundly defeated, the convention adopted two planks, one favoring Irish home rule and another decrying the persecution of Jews in Russia, that were intended to bring immigrant voters into the Republican fold.[147]

In the general campaign, GOP speeches and literature depicted robust immigration as a natural and welcome product of national prosperity. As the *Republican Campaign Textbook* put it, "Immigration follows high wages—high wages follow the tariff."[148] Those voters who flocked to McKinley's front porch in Canton, Ohio, during the 1896 campaign were told that the Republican party embraced cultural tolerance and unity. "We have always practiced the Golden Rule," McKinley proclaimed. "The best policy is to 'live and let live.'"[149] To attract immigrant votes, Hanna organized the distribution of 120,000 campaign pamphlets, printed in foreign languages, that made direct appeals to immigrant voters.[150] With increased voter support from all ethnic groups except Irish Catholics, McKinley defeated his Democratic rival, William Jennings Bryan, by a comfortable margin, at least by late-nineteenth-century standards. His 4.3 percent edge over Bryan in popular returns was greater than the aggregate margins of victory—a total of 3.2 percent—polled by the previous *four* presidential victors.[151] In later years, presidential candidates of varied partisan stripes would vie with one another for the votes of immigrant industrial workers.

The American Protective Association shared more than anti-Catholicism and xenophobia with earlier nativist movements; like its forerunners, the APA pursued a grass-roots, party-based strategy that was derailed by the dominant parties it sought to influence. The Republican party's quest for electoral mastery in 1896 led its leaders to purge the APA from its ranks. The perceived electoral significance of immigrant voters—the legacy of early official choices offering generous terms of European immigration and naturalization—meant that competitive party politicians had little interest in embracing nativist policy goals. Cut loose from its partisan moorings, the APA quickly faded from the political landscape.

ANTI-IMMIGRANT PROGRESSIVISM: THE IRL AND THE LITERACY TEST BATTLE

It is perhaps not surprising, given the leverage of immigrant voters and kindred ethnic groups with one and sometimes both of the nation's major parties, that the nineteenth-century nativist group that came closest to securing broad restrictions on European immigration spurned parties. The Immigration Restriction League (IRL) set out to transcend traditional party politics in favor of Progressive notions of "direct democracy" and "scientific government."[152] The IRL was an unusually intellectual and professional organization, formed by Harvard alumni disquieted by how immigration diminished their political and economic clout. The IRL drew funds and members from the ranks of upper-class academics, businessmen, politicians, and various professionals who saw themselves as the last line of defense for Anglo-Saxon traditions. Whether self-defined as conservative or Progressive, IRL members agreed that sweeping restrictions on European immigration were critical to achieving greater social control in America.[153] The IRL's new brand of political nativism nearly produced a major shift in U.S. immigration policy in 1896, thanks to important institutional and intellectual developments.

Regarding institutional arrangements, IRL activists had little interest in pursuing policy innovation through partisan or electoral means in the 1890s. Instead, they chose to pursue new extraparty openings to directly lobby national policymakers on behalf of immigration restriction.[154] "Our organization is a non-partisan one," the IRL proudly declared, "and we would not support or oppose a candidate for office on party grounds."[155] Instead, the group adopted a "dignified," "factual," and antiparty strategy, embracing social science research, mass publicity, and direct Washington advocacy to advance its policy aims. From the start, the IRL Executive Committee drafted an agenda of "Legislative Work" and established a Washington office headed by James Patten, a Harvard-trained lawyer who worked closely with restrictionist members of Congress and monitored bureaucratic developments. "An office in Washington," IRL leaders concluded, "is practically indispensable for successful prosecution of the League's work."[156] Of course, the IRL's efficacy was contingent upon whether key officials and institutions of the national state were receptive to their extraparty efforts.

The standing immigration committees established by Congress in 1890 became a crucial institutional beachhead for IRL nativists in this period. Their creation was illustrative of the expanding scale and complexity of congressional work in the late-nineteenth century.[157] Astute observers of the day, such as Woodrow Wilson, described standing congressional committees as "little legislatures" that stood as "the most essential machinery of our governmental system."[158] The House and Senate immigration committees were no exception. Dominated by New England patricians like Senators William Chandler (R-NH) and Henry Cabot Lodge (R-MA) and Representative Samuel McCall (R-MA), the committees welcomed independent expertise, favored policy activism, and specifically backed new restrictions on European immigration. In the process, these structures institutionalized formal input from immigration experts and activists and regularized the drafting and proposal of reform legislation. A national immigration policy network soon grew around them.

At a time when independent expertise was gaining new currency in the policymaking process, IRL nativists also benefited from the restrictionist tenor of most social-scientific research on immigration. In an outpouring of scholarly articles published during the 1890s, several of the country's most respected intellectuals fundamentally recast the American immigration debate. As *Lippincott's Monthly Magazine* informed readers, it was not "professional alarmists who are taking up the vital question of immigration and call for a halt; it is students of social science and the conditions of stable social equilibrium who toll a warning bell."[159] Claiming the mantle of scientific authority, academics differentiated between old and new immigration in economic, political, and racial terms.

Harvard economist Richard Mayo-Smith was among the most respected commentators on the economic impact of new immigration of this period. In his writings, Smith challenged the traditional assumption that American economic development depended on robust European immigration, noting that the "progress of civilization" had lessened the need for unskilled immigrant labor. "The steam drill, the dredge, the derrick, do the work which was formerly done by men."[160] Smith also observed that new immigrants rarely settled in the undeveloped frontier lands, where their "muscular labor" might be of some use. "The truth about these unskilled laborers is . . . that they are generally stranded in the large cities where they form an ignorant, often depraved mass, living from hand to mouth, a burden to the poor rate and social incubus on the community."[161] In his *Emigration and Immigration: A Study in Social Science* (1890), Smith condemned nineteenth-century principles of liberal individualism, limited state authority, and open immigration: "we must disabuse ourselves of the notion that freedom of migration rests upon the right of the individual. It is simply a privilege granted by the state."[162]

The intellectual assault on new European immigration also took aim at the political behavior of foreign-born voters. Numerous scholars and civic reformers perceived immigrants as the lifeblood of corrupt urban party machines that sacrificed good government on the alter of patronage, personal power, and narrow partisanship. As George Gunder of the Institute of Social Economics warned in a lecture bulletin to colleagues and students, recent immigrants represented "the material for the worst forms of political corruption and viciousness," more apt than citizens to fall under the spell of unprincipled "Tammanyists."[163] Settlement worker Robert Woods suggested that in Boston's immigrant sections, voters spurned the important Progressive causes of civil service reform and new mechanisms for "direct" elections in favor of "ward politics" based on "racial, religious, and industrial affiliations."[164]

Perhaps most outspoken regarding the deleterious political influence of immigrants was Wisconsin sociologist Edward A. Ross. A Progressive who favored electoral reform, Ross argued that a primitive and corrupt relationship existed between party "bosses" and immigrants, one that was akin to that between "a feudal lord and his vassals."[165] In every U.S. city with a large immigrant or African American vote, he observed, "appeared the boss, the machine, and the Tammany way." Most vexing to Ross was the ability of party machines to use the "simple-minded foreigner or negro" as a means of "neutralizing the anti-machine ballots of an equal number of indignant intelligent American voters."[166]

Many social scientists incorporated these economic and political critiques of immigration into a broader *racial* analysis of new immigrant groups. Total immigration in fact declined from 5.2 million in the 1880s to 3.7 million in the 1890s. But various analysts noted that the composition of alien inflows had shifted from traditional source countries of northern and western Europe to newer ones of the southern and eastern regions of the Old World (see table 3.5). Record numbers of Italians, Slavs, Hungarians, Greeks, and Jews fleeing persecution in Poland, Russia, and Romania entered the country.

Francis Walker, president of the Massachusetts Institute of Technology and former chief of the national census, was among the first prominent intellectuals to apply Darwinian and Spencerian theories of racial hierarchy to new European immigration. In 1891, Walker theorized that earlier in the century only the most resourceful and fittest Europeans immigrated to the United States, being required, first, to accumulate the financial means for travel and, second, to survive the harrowing transatlantic passage. By contrast, the development of the European railway and ocean steamship service reduced "almost to a minimum the energy, courage, intelligence, and pecuniary means required for immigration."[167] Far more troubling, according to Walker, was the fact that immigration was "increasingly drawn from the nations of southern and eastern Europe—peoples which have got no great good for themselves out of the race wars of centuries, and out of the unceasing struggle with the hard conditions of nature; peoples that have the least possible adaptation to our political institutions and social life; and that have thus far remained hopelessly upon the lowest plane of . . . life."[168] A few years later, the revered MIT president embraced Teutonic theory to justify excluding newer European immigrants. "They have none of the *inherited instincts and tendencies* which made it comparatively easy to deal with the immigration of olden time," he concluded. "They are beaten men from *beaten races*, representing the worst failures in the struggle for existence" (em-

TABLE 3.5
European Immigration to the United States, by Region, 1871–1910

	Northern and Western European Immigration	Southern and Eastern European Immigration	Top Three Countries of Last Residence
1871–80			Germany
			United Kingdom
	2,070,373	200,551	Ireland
1881–90			Germany
			United Kingdom
	3,778,633	956,169	Ireland
1891–1900			Italy
			Russia
	1,643,492	1,893,437	Germany
1901–10			Italy
			Russia
	1,910,035	6,106,060	Hungary

Source: Table created from data in the Statistical Yearbook of the Immigration and Naturalization Service (Washington, DC: Government Printing Office, 1994).

phasis added).[169] At the century's close, Walker marveled at the extent to which intellectual opinion concerning European immigration had changed since the 1870s. "Probably not a member of the American Social Science Association at that time entertained a doubt of the desirability of promoting the movement of population to this country," he declared.[170] Two decades later, he observed, most social scientists saw the value of excluding southern and eastern Europeans.

In an age preoccupied with racial typologies and ascriptive hierarchies, it is little wonder that southern and eastern Europeans were distinguished in biological, evolutionary terms from older-stock Americans. Social Darwinism and the eugenics movement caught hold in colleges and universities across the United States during the 1890s, gaining currency among social scientists, biologists, and other scholars.[171] These intellectuals made much of the fact that Charles Darwin himself described the "wonderful progress of the United States" as an outcome of "natural selection" and "the great stream of Anglo-Saxon immigration to the West."[172] They were also well versed in the writings of Darwin's cousin, Francis Galton, who founded eugenics as a new science of human heredity. As he put it, eugenics was dedicated to "the study of agencies under social control that may improve or impair the racial qualities of future generations either physically or mentally." Such ideas were easily grafted onto existing racial themes in American science, mass opinion, and public discourse.[173] Indeed, they bestowed intellectual legitimacy on popular racism in American political culture, and offered a comprehensive explanation for the host of new social and economic problems that vexed the nation.

Significantly, Senator Lodge was himself among the first to publish scholarly articles favoring immigration restriction in the 1890s. Having received Harvard's first doctorate in political science by writing a thesis on Anglo-Saxon law and heritage, Lodge considered himself an able practitioner of social science research and analysis. In 1891, he conducted a study of the "distribution of ability" in the American population, purporting to show "the enormous predominance" of Americans of English descent in the development of American economic and political institutions.[174] Using 1890 census data, Lodge argued elsewhere that "the conditions have changed utterly from the days when the supply of vacant land was indefinite, the demand for labor almost unbounded, and the supply of people very limited." Like Walker, he noted with alarm that European immigration was "making its greatest relative increase from races most alien to the body of the American people and from the lowest and most illiterate classes of those races."[175] But adherence to impartial scientific methods of studying the immigration question, Lodge wrote, "will enable us to deal with it intelligently and efficiently." He was thoroughly convinced that independent expertise could and should dictate clear policy choices; as he put it, "facts and figures speak for themselves only too plainly."[176]

The growth of social science research supporting immigration restriction acquired policy relevance largely because new governmental institutions, first standing congressional committees and later special commissions, provided an official channel through which these experts could shape policy outcomes. Reform-minded lawmakers serving on congressional immigration committees in turn looked to this new expert social knowledge as a means of shaping and rationalizing major policy innovation. Far from a passive beneficiary of these institutional and intellectual developments, the Immigration Restriction League actively nurtured stronger connections between restrictionist academic experts and the immigration committees. Academic, social, and professional luminaries were the driving force behind the IRL, and their chief purpose was to give political effect to the Teutonic findings of Walker and others that targeted southern and eastern Europeans for exclusion.[177] The league's first annual report explained that charter members intended the new movement to arouse public sentiment and congressional action concerning the threats posed by these immigrants to the "national character."[178] The IRL's Washington office furnished statistical information, special studies, and expert witnesses for the House and Senate immigration committees.[179]

In addition to enjoying new institutional and intellectual openings for their agenda, IRL nativists and their congressional allies had the advantage of pressing for immigration restriction legislation at a time when pro-immigration groups were not well organized in Washington. Under Republican control in 1892, the Senate immigration committee chaired by Chandler conducted ambitious investigations of immigration and issued lengthy reports of expert testimony and statistical analysis pointing to the dangers of southern and eastern European immigration. An outbreak of cholera aboard several passenger vessels bound in 1892 provided Chandler with what he thought was the perfect "opportunity" to exclude "degraded immigrants" from these regions.[180] Yet congressional leaders of both major parties tabled Chandler's proposal for a one-year universal suspension of immigration.

When Republicans took control of Congress after the 1894 midterm election, the nativist leadership of the House and Senate immigration committees became enamored with a proposal that was authored by economist Edward Bemis and advanced by the IRL. Bemis suggested that all immigrants be required to pass a literacy test, reasoning that the new regulatory mechanism would filter out those immigrants who were naturally inferior. The educational test, he argued, would be especially onerous on southern and eastern Europeans, while favoring immigrants from traditional source countries.[181] Working closely with the IRL, the immigration committees held hearings and drafted legislation in 1896 calling for a new literacy test.[182] The IRL's lobbyists reported to their Executive Committee that they were "on the most intimate terms" with key lawmakers, "especially those on the Immigration Committees," having "drafted amendments and sat up nights with them devising plans of campaign."[183] Early in 1896, the House and Senate immigration committees reported out comparable bills stipulating that "all persons over 14 years of age who can not read and write the language of their native country" were inadmissible.[184] This legislation was accompanied by lengthy committee reports, for which IRL members were asked to furnish expertise and "numerous tables of statistics."[185]

On the Senate floor, Lodge led the battle for the committee's literacy-test bill. Invoking extensive research assembled by the committee, Lodge claimed that nonpartisan experts agreed that a literacy test would burden only immigrants comprising the "slum population" of "congested cities," criminals, and those who "come most quickly upon private or public charity for support." These qualities were usually found, he averred, in the inferior stock of southern and eastern European arrivals. Failure to enact the literacy test raised the specter of diluting an Anglo-American race descended of Germanic tribes from Norway to the Alps:

[O]ther races of totally different race origin, with whom the English-speaking people have never hitherto been assimilated or brought in contact, have suddenly begun to immigrate to the United States in large numbers—Russians, Hungarians, Poles, Bohemians, Italians, Greeks, and, even Asiatics. . . . It involves nothing less than the possibility of a great and perilous change in the fabric of our race.[186]

The genius of the literacy test, Lodge underscored, was its capacity to screen out these racial undesirables. He assured colleagues that the literacy test "will bear most heavily" upon southern and eastern Europeans, "and very lightly, or not at all, upon English-speaking emigrants or Germans, Scandinavians, and French."[187]

On the heels of economic depression and well-publicized surges in Italian immigration, Chandler told newspaper reporters that there was every reason to expect both houses to enact literacy-test legislation.[188] Despite opposition from German American and Irish American colleagues, McCall ultimately won House support for the immigration committee bill by emphasizing expert findings that the literacy test would not slow traditional northern and western European immigration. In the Senate, Republican party managers balked at taking action on the controversial proposal during an election year. Their reluctance was heightened by Democratic speeches suggesting that the "real purpose" of the bill was "hostility to the Catholic Church" and appeasement of the APA.[189] Senate GOP leaders eventually compromised with Lodge, promising to reconsider his bill after the election.[190]

When the Senate opened its new session, Lodge's literacy test bill won passage with solid Republican support. Its success owed much to the endorsement of the immigration committee, prominent support from social scientists, and the relative absence of interest group opposition. But as House and Senate conferees met, pro-immigration business and ethnic groups mobilized to defeat the measure. German American groups sent protests to every congressional member, demanding them to explain "what right have we to assume that the character of those to come under a continued liberal policy of immigration will be one particle lower than of those who came before?"[191] In foreign-language newspapers nationwide, the literacy test was vigorously condemned. Joseph Senner, the U.S. commissioner of immigration, challenged Lodge's claim that Italians and other new immigrants were any different from earlier groups. Even in the first generation, he argued, new immigrants were transformed by the nation's "irresistible influence of freedom and prosperity."[192] Business groups complained that the literacy test would deny them access to essential immigrant labor.[193] The conference report passed the Senate by only two votes, a reflection of growing organized opposition.

Significantly, the IRL and other nativists were unable to secure solid support from organized labor for either immigration restriction generally or the literacy test in particular. The nation's most important labor group of the late 1890s, the American Federation of Labor (AFL), remained deeply divided on the issue. As key ethnic constituencies of the Democratic party lobbied outgoing president Grover Cleveland to reject the bill, organized labor's most powerful voices remained silent.[194] Following a long line of Democratic leaders committed to robust European immigration, Cleveland vetoed the literacy test bill. "It is said that the quality of recent immigration is undesirable," his blistering veto message noted. "The time is quite within recent memory when the same thing was said of immigrants who, with their descendants, are now numbered among our best citizens."[195]

The bill's sponsors remained optimistic that the large Republican majorities in Congress would override Cleveland's lame-duck veto. But Senate party managers, taking stock of mounting opposition from business groups, German associations, and other organizations, elected not to attempt an override. Their decision also reflected a keen awareness among Republican leaders that immigrant voters contributed markedly to their 1896 electoral triumphs. After the election, the chief of the federal Bureau of Statistics found that the twelve states with the country's largest foreign-born populations gave McKinley a staggering 202-to-1 edge in electoral votes. Such a stunning outcome, he noted in a popular journal, showed that Italians, Russians, Poles, and other new immigrants were not "as dangerous an element in politics as has been frequently asserted," and "not beyond our power of . . . healthful assimilation."[196] In subsequent campaigns, both major parties printed tens of thousands of campaign documents in foreign languages in an explicit appeal for immigrant votes.[197] The historian Paul Kleppner concludes that the 1896 election encouraged Republican party managers to waver on immigration restriction for years to come.[198]

The near success of the literacy test in 1896 stunned defenders of the nation's immigrant tradition and mobilized pro-immigration organization in Washington. When Lodge prepared a literacy test bill in 1898, a formidable group of pro-immigration intellectuals, business leaders, and social workers formed the Immigration Protective League in 1898, designed to mirror the advocacy work of the IRL.[199] Business groups like the National Association of Manufacturers, steamship companies, and various industrialists lobbied hard to maintain robust European immigration. Southern leaders, hopeful that European arrivals would replace African American workers migrating to northern cities (if not encourage further black exodus), resisted xenophobic designs in these years. Only three Southern Senators voted for the literacy test in 1898.[200]

Huge rallies were organized nationwide by ethnic and business groups in 1898 to denounce Lodge's reform bill. In New York City, for example, Jewish, German, Italian, and Catholic leaders collaborated with the Chamber of Commerce and various captains of industry on a mass meeting against immigration restriction.[201] On a platform adorned with a colorful array of national flags, speakers charged that the literacy test "separates families," invoking a concern for family unity that was a prominent theme in future policy debates.[202] Others warned Republican politicians that "the votes of foreign-born men elected William McKinley President" and won them control of Congress. "The Republicans in assailing the intelligence and honesty of the foriegn vote," rally organizers threatened, "assail their own source of strength."[203]

Republican congressional leaders also felt heat from elder statesmen of their party. Carl Schurz, the respected German-born Republican who was instrumental in purging Know-Nothings from the party in 1860, scolded Lodge and other nativists in an open letter to the public. How could they fear "the immigration of some thousands of people of the Caucasian race," he asked, in "a country still, on the whole, so thinly settled, and blessed with an abundance of undeveloped resources."[204] Party managers well understood these arguments, as well as the importance of conciliating foreign-born voters. On the eve of the 1898 election, the Republican Congressional Committee openly embraced newcomers: "[O]ur country has received great bodies of honest, industrious citizens, who have added to the wealth, progress, and power of the country."[205] The aging abolitionist William Lloyd Garrison took comfort that "however impervious" congressional Republicans were "to the appeals of rights and justice" on the immigration issue, "they are acutely sensitive to signs affecting re-election."[206]

Even the nation's imperial adventures abroad reinforced existing immigration policies, unleashing renewed confidence in the country's assimilative capacities. Conquest abroad and new colonial experiments persuaded exuberant American empire-builders that the United States could easily, as John Higham put it, "incorporate and dominate inferior races." In 1898, Americans could relish victory over Spain in a "splendid little war" as well as the acquisition of new dependencies in the Philippines and the Caribbean. The implications were not favorable to restrictionists. "If destiny called the Anglo-Saxon to regenerate men overseas," Higham notes, "how could he fail to educate and discipline immigrant races at home?"[207] Lodge's fears about Europeans newcomers now seemed overwrought.

Amid growing resistance from many quarters, Representative McCall informed the IRL and its allies in 1898 that the prospects of securing literacy-test legislation were dim. "German newspapers have frightened a good many of the members having a large German vote in their districts," he lamented, adding that House Speaker Thomas Reed "will be influenced by the wishes of these members."[208] As opposition mounted, pro-immigration representatives provided congressional leaders with a temporary solution: the creation of a "nonpartisan" immigration commission empowered to collect information and to recommend legislation addressing the impact of new immigrants on "the problems of labor, agriculture, and capital."[209] The resulting Industrial Commission on Immigration offered party managers a reprieve from immigration debate, one that would postpone decisive action for several years.

CONCLUSION

Nonincremental policy change is routinely a tall order in an American constitutional system replete with structural veto-points. The nation's time-honored celebration of European immigration, along with easy naturalization and voting laws that transformed newcomers into a recognized electoral presence, made major restrictions like the literacy test especially elusive. In contrast to most nineteenth-century nativists, restrictionists associated with the IRL made no effort to influence immigration policy through partisan or electoral means. Instead, they sought to capitalize on the openings provided by new committee structures and growing reverence for "scientific government" to advance their policy goals. And whereas nativist movements from the anti-Masons to the APA were fervent anti-Catholics, the IRL and its allies targeted southern and eastern Europeans for exclusion. Their novel political campaign for the literacy test very nearly succeeded and set the tone for policy struggles of the early-twentieth century.

The failure of Lodge and the IRL to recast national policy toward European admissions underscores the enormous challenges of securing major immigration reform. The prominence in the policymaking process of new expertise and new congressional immigration committees supporting broad restrictions on southern and eastern European immigration was not enough. Restrictionists were unable to build the kind of broad Left-Right coalition necessary to overturn more than a century of robust European immigration. Lacking solid support on the Left from organized labor, IRL patricians faced formidable opposition from powerful business groups, ethnic associations, and various liberal cosmopolitans (see table 4.6). American imperial adventures overseas produced a confidence about the nation's standing in global affairs that did nothing to help the restrictionist cause.

Most importantly, Lodge and the IRL ultimately could not overcome the powerful partisan and electoral forces that they initially hoped to circumvent. Their literacy test bill was vetoed by a president affiliated with a

Democratic party that from its inception defended expansive admissions and rights for European immigrants. Their efforts to revive the legislation was derailed by congressional leaders of a Republican party that long endorsed the economic benefits of importing immigrant labor and often competed for new immigrant votes, especially beyond the ranks of the solidly Democratic Irish bloc. The coup de grace was mounting evidence in the late 1890s that young immigration stations like Ellis Island were firmly under the spell of party machines that encouraged patronage hires and lax enforcement.[210] The linkage between the nation's dominant political parties and the federal government's tolerant and expansive policies toward European arrivals were forged in the early American republic, when early political leaders embraced European immigration and established easy naturalization and voting rights for white male newcomers. Their initial choices set national policy toward European immigration on a particular course that nativists would not fundamentally disturb until after the First World War. However, the nineteenth-century "state of courts and parties" produced decidedly different policies toward Chinese immigrants.

Chinese Exclusion and Precocious State-Building in the Nineteenth-Century American Polity

IT IS A common and not altogether surprising presumption that the United States was essentially "stateless" during the nineteenth century, especially given the American polity's penchant for localism and limited government in these years. In terms of developing centralized governmental functions and powers, so the argument goes, the American republic trailed far behind its western European counterparts at least until the Progressive Era and New Deal (if not later). Of course, several scholars have highlighted the shortcomings of this received wisdom.[1] Despite a relatively weak "sense of the state" in nineteenth-century America, Stephen Skowronek observes, coercive power and institutional behavior patterns were molded by an unmistakable "state of courts and parties."[2]

Drawing on these theoretical insights, Theda Skocpol has offered evidence that the United States developed an expansive and advanced social spending state well before the twentieth century. Indeed, she describes the American federal government's early involvement in social welfare provision as part and parcel of a "precocious" state, one that belies notions of the United States as a social policy laggard.[3] Consistent with Skowronek's emphasis on the prominence of political parties during the country's early political development, Skocpol finds that generous national social spending on Civil War pensions in this period was precisely the kind of government activism one would expect from a patronage-oriented system dominated by party politicians.[4] These social policies exemplify the defining features of what Theodore Lowi has described as "distributive" policies, seemingly "positive-sum" benefits for particular individuals and groups that raise few visible costs or conflicts. As such, Civil War pensions fit neatly with Lowi's generalization that federal governmental activities of the nineteenth century were routinely distributive, with regulatory and redistributive policies blossoming after the turn of the century.[5]

The triumph of Chinese exclusion policies during the post-Reconstruction era offers a contrasting portrait of the "precocious" American state that emerged during the nineteenth century. Rather than distributing generous public benefits directly to a special subset of the nation's population, Chinese exclusion called for the federal government to assume unprecedented regulatory authority over immigrant admissions and rights for the explicit purpose of guarding the racial purity of American society. Indeed, most advocates of Chinese exclusion shared a strong "sense of the state"—one that linked national state-building to the preservation of existing orders of ethnic, racial, and religious hierarchy. "The strong nations of the earth are now, as they always have been, the most thoroughly homogeneous nations, that is to say, the most nearly of one race, language, and manners," proclaimed one prominent anti-Chinese group. "All political history shows homogeneity to be a vast power in a State, and that heterogeneity is a corresponding source of weakness."[6] Despite a U.S. tradition of devolving most regulatory authority over immigration to the states, anti-Chinese activists secured precisely the kind of ambitious official national interventions they envisioned. Federal laws and judicial rulings of the Gilded Age granted the federal government broad powers to restrict both Chinese immigration and the rights of Chinese aliens already living in U.S. territory.

This chapter analyzes the late-nineteenth-century partisan, legislative, and judicial processes that helped produce sweeping anti-Chinese policy breakthroughs at a time when most Americans were intensely hostile toward new forms of centralized governmental activism.[7] It also points to a formidable political alliance of classic exclusionists favoring racial cleansing and egalitarian nationalists of a nascent labor movement seeking protection from Chinese contract labor. The political reification of social science expertise did not blossom until the Progressive Era, but we still find national policymakers of this period concerned with rationalizing their Chinese immigration decisions on the basis of careful bipartisan investigation. Most notably, a Joint Special Committee to Investigate Chinese Immigration issued sweeping recommendations in 1876 that legitimated exclusionary reforms on the basis of the facts it gathered. Foreign pressures slowed adoption of Chinese exclusion due to the opposition of presidents concerned that the United States not abrogate its Burlingame Treaty with China by prohibiting immigration. Yet party politics ultimately overwhelmed these executive concerns, with fealty to international treaties dwarfed by national electoral competition.

The rise of a "precocious" *exclusionary* state in this period, one dedicated to what a prominent restrictionist later described as the need to preserve "the quality of our race and citizenship,"[8] casts early American state-building in a light very different from the dominant views of nineteenth-century "statelessness" or even of a distributive social spending state. It also foreshadows the construction of a far more elaborate set of government policies and structures after the turn of the century that made the promotion of cultural uniformity and "Nordic supremacy" an even firmer purpose of the national state.[9] Most significantly, the triumph of Chinese exclusion highlights the remarkable capacity of American political institutions to adapt in service to inegalitarian traditions of racial hegemony, and challenges various scholars who closely associate the growth of national state capacity with the achievement of social equality. The enhancement and centralization of government capacities have certainly contributed to egalitarian reform in American political development, but they also have produced profoundly retrograde policies as well. For these reasons, the politics and policies of Chinese exclusion merit fresh investigation, especially in terms of the interactions between anti-Chinese social movements and the dominant political institutions of the nineteenth century.

SETTING THE STAGE: CHINESE IMMIGRATION, LABOR ORGANIZATION, AND CALIFORNIA POLITICS

Following the California gold rush of 1848, Chinese immigrants, recruited to fill labor needs of Western mining and railroad construction, first came to the United States in large numbers. Roughly 250,000 Chinese were admitted to the country from 1850 until sharp restrictions were imposed on Chinese immigration in 1882 (see table 4.1).[10] The vast majority settled in California, where its governor initially welcomed them as "one of our most worthy classes of newly adopted citizens."[11] Before long, however, the state's white settlers viewed the Chinese, as Chief Justice Hugh G. Murray of the California Supreme Court put it, "as a race of people whom nature has marked as inferior . . . differing in language, opinions, color, and physical conformation."[12] Chinese newcomers frequently were depicted by white leaders as perilous to the "moral and physical" well-being of Western communities, promoting the spread of paganism, opium addiction, prostitution, polygamy, leprosy and other diseases, criminality, and other impurities.[13]

To many white Americans of the 1840s and 1850s, the territories of New Mexico and California presented a foreboding racial frontier where Anglo-Saxonism and republican government would be sorely tried by a perilously diverse population. As one observer fretted, the Far West was "inhabited by a mixed population, of habits, opinions, and characters incapable of sympathy or assimilation; a race whom the experience of an entire generation has proved to be unfitted for self-government, and unprepared to appreciate, sustain, or enjoy free institutions."[14] Delegates at the California constitutional convention of 1849 strongly endorsed reserving the suffrage to "white" men, while excluding "the inferior races of mankind." Although California entered the Union as a "free" state in 1850, it adapted many Southern slave codes governing black rights for its constitution, discriminated against Mexicans (although the Treaty of

TABLE 4.1
Chinese Immigration to the United States, 1821–1880

	Total Immigration	Chinese Immigration	Percentage of Total Immigration
1821–30	143,439	2	0.0014%
1831–40	599,125	8	0.0013%
1841–50	1,713,251	35	0.002%
1851–60	2,598,215	41,397	1.6%
1861–70	2,314,824	64,301	2.8%
1871–80	2,812,191	123,201	4.4%

Source: Author's compilation based on the *1998 Statistical Yearbook of the Immigration and Naturalization Service* (Washington, DC: Government Printing Office, 1999).

Guadalupe Hidalgo of 1848 guaranteed them citizenship rights), and waged, as Governor Peter Burnett declared, "a war of extermination . . . until the Indian race becomes extinct."[15] In this exclusionist racial order, the arrival of Chinese newcomers was not likely to go unnoticed by white settlers of California and the Pacific Northwest.

Most of California's earliest political leaders embraced the anti-Chinese cause. During the 1850s, the California Assembly passed laws excluding Chinese immigration, imposing special mining and police taxes on minority groups, and barring Chinese and other racial minorities from public schools. While laws prohibiting Chinese immigration were routinely nullified by the federal courts, the California Supreme Court clarified in an 1854 case that Chinese were ineligible for equal protection under the Constitution. In the case, the Court overturned the murder conviction of a white man because it rested heavily on the testimony of a Chinese witness. Applying a state law stipulating that "[n]o Black, or Mulatto person, or Indian shall be allowed to give evidence in favor of, or against a white man," the Court prohibited Chinese from testifying in California courtrooms. Chief Justice Hugh G. Murray, a member of the Know-Nothings, argued that "the same rule that would admit them to testify, would admit them to all the equal rights of citizenship and we might soon see them at the polls, in the jury box, upon the bench and in our legislative halls."[16] The effect of the ruling was to make Chinese vulnerable to countless acts of violence and lesser crimes perpetrated by white settlers.[17] Reflecting on random violence and political attacks targeting Chinese immigrants in this period, a black Californian writing for *Frederick Douglass' Paper* speculated in 1855 whether "the Chinese have taken the places of the colored people, as victims of oppression."[18]

Organized labor stood at the center of the anti-Chinese movement in California politics.[19] Labor antagonism toward the Chinese found expression during the 1850s at mass meetings of white miners, who protested that "Capitalists" hoped to make profits through an "asiatic inundation."[20] As a developing industrial and urban center with powerful manufacturing and shipping interests, San Francisco became the locus of California union organization and politicization in the 1860s. Between 1860 and 1870, the city's population soared from 57,000 to nearly 150,000. In the late 1860s, the closing of unproductive mines, the completion of the transcontinental railroad, and the steady migration to the state of new settlers led displaced workers to San Francisco in search of scarce jobs. Employers responded to this labor oversupply by reducing wages and extending the working day.[21]

Union leaders blamed these labor market developments on Chinese workers (comprising 13 percent of the city's labor force), who were said to displace white laborers by accepting "servile" wages and working conditions. "[The Chinese] do not constitute as European immigrants do, an addition to the industrial element," one California newspaper declared. "On the contrary, they are substitutes and supplanters, every one of them who obtains employment is taking the place of a white man, and depriving him of work."[22] While many Chinese traveled to the United States as voluntary immigrants, labor groups and newspapers presumed all arrived as bonded or "coolie" laborers, thereby representing a new slave trade that degraded free white labor.[23]

Labor resentment of Chinese workers also stemmed from their employment as strikebreakers. When Irish railroad workers went on strike for higher wages in 1863, for instance, financiers of the Pacific Railroad recruited thousands of Chinese laborers to work for meager wages and under poor conditions. White laborers first organized secretive anti-coolie clubs in this period, but wartime prosperity and railroad construction quieted Sinophobic tempers. But as unemployment and labor unrest grew after the war, these clubs reappeared and spread to every ward of the city. Calling itself the Central Pacific Anti-Coolie Association, the organization's ward club structure facilitated individual and group membership.[24]

Some within labor's ranks, like H. C. Bennett, argued fervently that anti-Chinese efforts diverted the labor movement from fundamental working-class issues. "The poor Chinese are set up as a decoy," he declared, "to draw attention from the real evil." Bennett reminded Irish workingmen that they "were for centuries held as an inferior race by their Saxon rulers," and warned that "the very same men who are now leading the Irishmen against the Chinese, were the leaders of the know-nothing party."[25] But his views were rare among San Francisco labor leaders. As labor historian Lucille Eaves has observed, union organizers recognized that anti-Chinese agitation "contributed more than any other one factor to the strength of the California labor movement."[26] During the 1860s, labor organizations and anti-coolie clubs focused on state party politics and elections to press their exclusionary agenda.

In antebellum California, the Democratic party dominated state politics and government, electing six of the state's first seven governors, seven of its first eight U.S. senators, and controlling all but one session of the state legislature between 1849 and 1862. When the Republican party first appeared in the state during the tumultuous election of 1856, Democrats were effective in discrediting GOP candidates as "radical" champions of racial equality. In response, state Republican leaders carefully explained to voters that they supported slavery in Southern states but opposed the spread of slavery westward. Republican speeches and newspaper editorials rivaled state Democrats in the ferocity of their racial epithets.[27] Although the 1856 campaign proved disastrous for California Republicans, Abraham Lincoln carried the state by a slim margin in 1860, due largely to a hopelessly divided state Democratic party.[28]

In the early 1860s, California Republicans embraced the anti-Chinese cause. Leland Stanford, the state's first GOP governor, used the occasion of his 1862 inaugural address to cast himself as a champion of Chinese exclusion, pledging that he would do all he could to secure "the repression of the immigration of the Asiatic races."[29] Stanford's rhetoric was largely disingenuous, given that his own railroad and agricultural enterprises employed hundreds of Chinese laborers. Nevertheless, Stanford eagerly endorsed a variety of anti-Chinese enactments passed by the state legislature, including a so-called Chinese Police Tax of $2.50 per month levied on all Chinese laborers residing in the state.[30]

"OPENING OF OUR GATES TO ALL OF MANKIND": REPUBLICANS AND THE BURLINGAME TREATY

During the Civil War and its immediate aftermath, California Republicans quietly retreated from a staunch anti-Chinese stance, as they reaped the electoral benefits of a moribund opposition, wartime patriotism, and the promise of a transcontinental railroad. Indeed, the state party increasingly followed national Republican leaders on immigration, foreign trade, and economic development.[31] National Republican leaders, such as Carl Schurz, Charles Sumner, Salmon P. Chase, and William Seward, successfully purged Know-Nothings from the party during the 1860 election.[32] As chapter 3 suggests, the Republican leadership's decision to spurn nativists in 1860 was motivated not simply by the electoral expediency of courting Midwestern German voters, which was a key concern. More fundamentally, immigration restriction conflicted with two critical goals of Republicanism: Northern economic growth and the dominance of free labor in Western territories.[33]

After the Civil War, national Republican leaders looked to immigration as essential for resuscitating a labor force thinned by war casualties. The Republican party's promotion of immigration during and after the Civil War had important implications for the Chinese question in Western states. Although most congressional Republicans supported an 1867 resolution prohibiting "coolie trade" from China, they generally were receptive to voluntary Chinese immigration. By contrast, Western Democrats expressed hostility toward all forms of Chinese admission. Indeed, they unsuccessfully attempted to insert language into the Fourteenth and Fifteenth Amendments excluding Asians from constitutional protection. By contrast, national Republicans hoped to foster economic development in the Far West by reaching out to Asian nations. In 1868, Congress ratified the Burlingame Treaty with China, which established stronger commercial ties as well as "the inherent and inalienable rights of man to change his home and allegiance" from one country to the other.[34] It also assured that Chinese visiting or residing in the United States "shall enjoy the same privileges, immunities, and exemptions" as American citizens.[35]

The Burlingame Treaty inspired many to celebrate the new protections they anticipated for Chinese arrivals. Mark Twain noted optimistically that the Burlingame Treaty meant "the days of persecuting Chinamen are over, in California."[36] Former abolitionist Wendell Phillips expressed hope that the nation would "welcome every man of every race to our soil and to the protection of our laws."[37] At the Republican National Convention of 1868, one speaker exulted that the party's commitment to unrestricted immigration, railroad construction, and Asian trade would produce unprecedented national wealth and power. "China, Japan, India, and the South Sea Islands will be made tributary to California and Oregon," he declared. "The flood-gates of emigration are still open . . . pouring out over our land millions of willing hands and stout hearts, adding millions to our prosperity."[38]

As the Burlingame Treaty and the transcontinental railroad raised the promise of profitable trade with China and Japan, various California leaders voiced new enthusiasm for Chinese immigrant admissions and rights. This was particularly true of business leaders and their Republican allies in the state. The decidedly Republican *Sacramento Union* abandoned a long-standing commitment to Chinese exclusion in the late 1860s, telling readers that the "interchange of populations" was an acceptable outcome of healthy trade relations. Its editorials also gave expression to the egalitarian moralism of Radical Republicans, arguing that restrictions on Chinese immigration and liberties conflicted with "the natural rights of man as defined by the Declaration of Independence."[39] The *San Francisco Daily Alta* was even more profuse in its new devotion to Chinese rights, embracing a future time when Chinese newcomers could vote and occupy seats in Congress.[40] Years later, the state's Republican senator Aaron Sargent, an eventual champion of Chinese exclusion, explained that he and other California Republicans were swept up in the idealism of the period when the Burlingame Treaty was affirmed. "The 'enthusiasm of humanity' was a great moving power in the nation . . . when [it] was ratified," he observed. "The national exaltation growing out of the emancipation of a race and the sorrowful events of the civil war, had its climax in the opening of our gates to all of mankind."[41]

POLITICAL BACKLASH: ANTI-CHINESE ACTIVISM AND WESTERN PARTY COMPETITION

In the late 1860s, California Republicans began to pay an enormous political price for national Republican commitments to civil rights reform and robust Chinese immigration. During state elections of 1867, a network of labor groups and anti-Chinese clubs presented each of the state's parties with a list of exclusionary demands that included the prohibition of Asian immigration. State Republicans tried to finesse the issue by endorsing all forms of "voluntary immigration." By doing so, they hoped to satisfy anti-Chinese activists, who cast Asian inflows as "servile" and involuntary, without repudiating their national party's economic and racial policies.[42] During the heat of the campaign, the GOP gubernatorial candidate, George C. Gorham, urged the Central Pacific Anti-Coolie Association to draw an important distinction between the evils of an exploitive "coolie system" and its victims, Chinese immigrants. "The same God created both Europeans and Asiatics," he noted. "No man of whatever race has any better right to labor . . . than has any other man."[43] State Republicans were willing to limit all forms of foreign contract labor, but they refused to exclude Chinese immigrants or any other groups on ethnic, religious, or racial grounds.

Significantly, the anti-Chinese cause unified rival factions of the California Democratic party and helped it reemerge as a formidable presence in state politics. In the 1867 election, Democrats seized upon the Reconstruction Congress's record on race as a means of courting support from growing trade unions, anti-coolie clubs, and white working-class voters. At the party's state convention, delegates passed resolutions condemning Chinese immigration and Republican efforts to extend new rights to racial minorities.[44] One leading Democratic newspaper told voters that racial policies comprised the most important distinction between the parties:

[T]he self-styled Union or Mongrel party have [*sic*] but one principle . . . and that is the doctrine of universal equality for all races, in all things. The Democracy are, and ever have been the party . . . for a white man's government, constitutionally administered, against a great Mongrel military despotism, upheld by a union of the purse and the sword, and sought to be perpetuated through negro and Chinese votes.[45]

Not surprisingly, labor organizations and anti-Chinese clubs mobilized on behalf of Democratic candidates. When the dust settled in 1867, Republicans found themselves swept out of Sacramento. In his victory speech, Democratic governor-elect Henry Haight pledged that his party would fight "against populating this fair State with a race of Asiatics," "against sharing with inferior races the Government of this country," and "against the military despotism which now exists in the South."[46] Reeling from their electoral debacle, state Republicans warned the national party organization that Democratic inroads on Chinese exclusion could imperil the 1868 Republican presidential campaigns.[47] "Our young state may determine the whole contest,"one California Republican cautioned the National Republican Committee. "The wicked and malignant rebellion which has been stamped out upon the battlefield . . . yet exhibits vitality upon the ballot box."[48] When the votes were tallied, electoral competition in Western states proved fiercer than in any other region of the country (see table 4.2). Ulysses S. Grant ultimately carried California in 1868 by the narrowest margin in the country, outpolling Horatio Seymour by a mere five hundred votes.

In 1869, California Republicans again lost electoral ground by defending commercial relations with China and the rights of Chinese immigrants.[49] Before the next campaign, state Republican politicians retreated from the pro-Chinese leanings of the national party, declaring themselves "inflexibly opposed" to Chinese naturalization and immigration. An imported Chinese workforce, they now asserted, denigrated a cherished party ideal: "the dignity of labor."[50] In California party politics, the bidding war for anti-Chinese votes had begun.

Similar pressures were being exerted on Western Republicans serving in Congress. As Democrats proposed resolutions declaring that Congress never intended the Fifteenth Amendment to extend suffrage to Chinese, Western Republicans scrambled to distance themselves from the racial policies of Radical Republicans.[51] Indeed, the growing ideological divide between Radical and Western Republicans boiled to the surface during a rancorous Senate debate over naturalization requirements and the future status of Chinese living in the United States. In 1870, Senator Charles Sumner (R-MA) offered an amendment to naturalization laws to replace references to "free white men" with simply "free men."

Senator William Morris Stewart, a fellow Republican from Nevada,

TABLE 4.2
Party Competition in the 1868 Presidential Election, by Region

Region	Grant (R) (%)	Seymour (D) (%)	Margin of Victory (%)
Northeast	53.7%	46.3%	7.4%
Midwest	55.6%	44.4%	11.2%
Southern	46.2%	53.8%	7.6%
Border	40.9%	59.1%	18.2%
Western	50.6%	49.4%	1.2%

Sources: Created by author from data in R. Diamond, ed., *Guide to U.S. Elections* (Washington, DC: Congressional Quarterly Press, 1976). Regional classifications from D. Brady, *Congressional Voting in a Partisan Era* (Lawrence, Kansas: University of Kansas Press, 1973), p. 239.

rose in opposition to the amendment. He was a surprising foe, since only a year before he had championed Chinese civil rights in the well of the Senate against "wicked" local laws and "mob violence," even advocating federal intervention if necessary to protect those rights:

> The Chinese can mine, they can manufacture, they can farm, they can build, they can construct railroads or do any other thing to develop a country and produce wealth. There is no question about their right to be here. . . . All the Chinese ask is the right to labor and to live. [The 1866 Civil Rights Act] must be extended by Congress to all persons residing in the United States. . . . I am not here to threaten, but to advise the people of the [Pacific] coast to consider the consequences of injustice and outrage toward the Chinese. It is better to do right voluntarily than to be forced to obey the laws and respect the rights of others.[52]

In response to Sumner's amendment a year later, however, Stewart warned that Chinese political empowerment would "hand over our republican institutions" to "pagans in religion, and monarchists in theory and practice." Enfranchising emancipated blacks was justified, he argued, because former slaves were both American-born and Christian. He considered the easy naturalization of European immigrants equally defensible. "They are of our own race, and assimilate rapidly, and aid in the development and progress of our country," he explained. "Let them come." But extending equal rights to Chinese, Stewart insisted, undermined individual liberty, free democratic institutions, and free labor.[53]

Sumner was incredulous at this change of heart, admonishing Stewart for "thrice" betraying the Chinese and the "mighty words" of the Declaration of Independence. "The greatest peril to this Republic is from disloyalty to its great ideas," he proclaimed. "How mean, how dark, how muddy is that road which has found counselors to-day!" Dramatically opening the Bible of the Senate secretary, Sumner recited the Gospel story of Peter weeping after betraying Jesus three times. Over the protests of Western colleagues, Sumner declared: "Thrice has a Senator on this floor denied the great principles of the Declaration of Independence. The time may come when he will weep bitterly."[54]

Despite Sumner's impassioned appeal, his amendment lost 26 to 12. When Illinois Senator Lyman Trumbell (R) later tried to add "Chinese" to the naturalization laws, he was defeated 31 to 9. In the aftermath of this acrimonious legislative battle, the Republican *San Francisco Daily Alta* chastised Sumner for failing to realize that his bill "would occasion popular repudiation against the Republican party, which would destroy it before the Chinese could gain citizenship."[55] Republicans, it concluded, would be swept out of office long before Chinese immigrants gained access to the ballot box. By contrast, Frederick Douglass congratulated Sumner for his moral courage. "I rejoice . . . to see you on the right place upon the Chinese question," he noted. "As usual, you are in the van, and the country is in the rear."[56] But Douglass was anything but sanguine about the future, anticipating the decline of Radical Republicanism and civil rights. "A bitter contest, I fear, is before us," he warned, with most political leaders "entangled in the meshes of temporary expediency and hesitation."[57]

JUDICIAL ACTIVISM AND THE NATIONALIZATION OF ANTI-CHINESE POLITICS

As unemployment in California reached new highs in the 1870s, the anti-Chinese issue consumed state politics. Although insulated from the immediate economic impact of the Eastern Panic of 1873, Western states soon found themselves flooded with overland migrants. Between 1873 and 1875, 153,000 overland migrants came to California, with most settling in San Francisco. Chinese immigration reached record levels in the same years: 20,000 arrived in 1873; 14,000 in 1874; 16,000 in 1875; and 23,000 in 1876. Resentment of Chinese immigrants intensified when railroad and industrial employers turned to unskilled Chinese laborers instead of unionized white workers. The Central Pacific Railroad employed more than 15,000 Chinese workers in this decade, while other Chinese newcomers found jobs in the clothing, furniture, and cigar industries. The People's Protective Alliance was formed in the 1870s to direct the activities of anti-coolie associations across the state.[58] Responding to these pressures, state and local governments imposed new anti-Chinese regulations.

One of these state laws prohibited Chinese from landing without a bond unless they could prove their "good character" to the state commissioner of Immigration. This assertion of state control over immigration had followed a pattern of devolution in this policy area since the nation's founding. In 1874, however, state efforts to restrict Chinese inflows were challenged before California's federal circuit court, in a case involving twenty-two Chinese who were denied entry by state officials pending receipt of $500 bonds for each of them. In his decision, Justice Stephen Field expressed sympathy with the "general feeling" of Californians that "the dissimilarity in physical characteristics, in language, in manners, religion and habits, will always prevent any possible assimilation of them with our people." He nevertheless invalidated state efforts to curb Chinese entry, advising that "recourse must be had to the Federal government, where the whole power over this subject lies."[59] The final blow to state-level immigration control came two years later, when three Supreme Court rulings nullified state immigration laws because they encroached upon exclusive congressional authority to regulate foreign commerce.[60]

Judicial activism in immigration law dramatically altered the strategy of the anti-Chinese movement. In the immediate postwar years, anti-Chinese activists directed most of their energies to shaping state and local policies. They tended to vigorously oppose enhanced responsibilities for the national state, which they associated with Radical Republican designs of extending civil rights protections and circumscribing state and local racial practices. But judicial limitations on state police powers created new imperatives; Chinese exclusion could be achieved only if new federal regulatory controls were established. "Our only hope," California senator Aaron Sargent declared after Field's decision was announced, "is in the National Government."[61]

The Anti-Chinese Movement and National Party Competition

In the fiercely competitive party system of the late-nineteenth century—one characterized by rock-hard, sectional partisanship both north and south of the Mason-Dixon line—many national party leaders saw the steadily growing and protean voting blocs of Far Western states as crucial to future electoral mastery. Shortly after Field struck down state restrictions on immigration, Western members of Congress from both parties called for national limits on Chinese immigration. Amid divided government in 1875, the White House and congressional leaders endorsed legislation addressing two perceived evils associated with Chinese immigration without abrogating treaty agreements with China: Chinese prostitution and "coolie" labor. At the same time, Northeastern lawmakers voiced concern that European countries were pardoning criminals who agreed to emigrate to the United States. The Immigration Act of 1875 made it illegal to transport Asian immigrants without their voluntary consent (a response to "coolie labor"), and designated prostitutes and those convicted of felonious crimes as excludable classes.[62] Anti-Chinese groups of Western states praised the legislation, but demanded more decisive national action. Paralleling the anti-Chinese bidding war that consumed California politics six years earlier, leaders of both major parties courted Western voters in the pivotal 1876 election with pledges to restrict Chinese immigration.

However, efforts to court anti-Chinese votes generated contrasting reactions within each party. At the National Democratic Convention of 1876, considerable attention was devoted to a Chinese exclusion plank. The party platform highlighted the "omissions of a Republican Congress and the errors of our treaties" that "exposed our brethren of the Pacific coast to the incursions of a race not sprung from the same parent stock."[63] According to the *Official Proceedings* of the Democratic Convention, the plank was met with "Cries of 'Good!' 'Bully!' and cheers."[64] The Democratic party's traditional welcome to European immigrants was matched by an intense hostility expressed toward racial minorities—immigrant or otherwise. Thus, Democratic support for Chinese exclusion posed little conflict with the party's vigilance against anti-Catholic nativist movements.

For Republicans, by contrast, the Chinese issue was a source of bitter conflict. At its state convention in 1876, California Republicans abandoned nuanced positions of the past and declared unwavering support for Chinese exclusion. The presence of Chinese in the United States, state delegates resolved, was inimical to national advancement.[65] Western members of the Republican National Platform Committee also drafted and won committee support for a plank calling on Congress to investigate the effects of Chinese immigration. But the proposal instantly drew fire from racial progressives in the party. In contrast to the acclamation with which Democrats greeted the anti-Chinese plank in their national platform, a milder Republican plank provoked acrimony. When the official platform was read at the Republican national convention, Northeastern delegates rose in opposition to the Chinese plank as anathema to the party's egalitarian heritage. "The Republican party is twenty years old . . . and this is the first time in all that long period that any attempt has ever been made to put in its platform a discrimination of race," one delegate protested. "I denounce, therefore, that resolution as a departure from the life and memory of Abraham Lincoln."[66] A former abolitionist asked delegates if they understood that the platform was a "declaration of faith." Chinese exclusion belied party doctrine, he declared: "If you mean to draw a cordon along the coasts of this country—if you mean to say that any man of any race shall be excluded—then you have revoked the original principle of your party."[67]

Proponents of the plank responded that "servile" Chinese immigrants violated the most sacred principle of the Republican party: free labor. A New Mexico delegate claimed that it was consistent for a party "that has always been opposed to the slave trade" to reconsider Chinese contract labor. Another stressed that "our own American-born freemen as well as European freemen" who immigrate to the United States "have rights which we should guarantee and protect."[68] Others described Chinese newcomers in subhuman terms. As one Nevada delegate averred, "the people on the Pacific coast have suffered an invasion there worse than the grasshopper plague, worse than the plague of locusts."[69] When a motion to strike the plank was put to a vote, it was defeated 532 to 215.[70]

During the summer of 1876, leaders of the Democratic House and Republican Senate raced to create a Joint Special Committee to Investigate Chinese Immigration. Few rank-and-file members opposed its formation.[71] One disgusted House Republican observed "an alliance forming between those opposed on general principles to the negro, the Chinese, and the Indian, to make common cause for the purpose of razing these tribes from the face of the earth."[72] Confronted with a resurgent Democratic party, however, GOP leaders catered to an anti-Chinese movement that had already demonstrated its capacity to punish Republicans on election day. A year before Republicans agreed to withdraw federal troops from the South, the national leadership's shift on Chinese immigration signaled the decline of Radical Republican goals of racial progress and equal citizenship. Close presidential balloting in Western states in 1876 further underscored the political importance of the anti-Chinese movement (see tables 4.3 and 4.4).

Foreshadowing the significance of professional expertise in later periods, lawmakers thought it important to build some semblance of a rational, factually based justification for anti-Chinese reform in the 1870s. The Joint Special Committee to Investigate Chinese Immigration, created in the heat of the presidential election, was officially charged to gather information on "the character, extent, effect of Chinese immigration to this country." A transparent product of party competition for Sinophobic votes, the Special Committee nevertheless launched an extended fact-finding mission on the Pacific Coast. It relied on statistics and the testimony of 128 witnesses, nearly all of whom supported Chinese exclusion.[73]

Clergy, diplomatic officials, and business leaders defended Chinese immigration to the committee. Railroad entrepreneur Charles Crocker, for example, asserted that Chinese labor "goes very far toward the material

TABLE 4.3
Voting Results of Presidential Elections in California, 1868–1896

	Republican Candidate		Democratic Candidate		Other Candidates		Margin of Victory	
	Votes	%	Votes	%	Votes	%	Votes	%
1868	Grant 54,588	50.2	Seymour 54,068	48.9	6	<1.0	520	0.4*
1872	Grant 54,007	56.4	Greeley 45,685	42.5	1,061	1.1	13,290	14
1876	Hayes 79,258	50.9	Tilden 76,460	49.1	63	<1.0	2,798	1.8
1880	Garfield 80,282	48.9	Hancock 80,426	49.0	3,510	2.2	144	0.1*
1884	Blaine 102,369	52.0	Cleveland 89,288	45.3	5,331	2.7	13,081	6.7
1888	Harrison 124,816	49.7	Cleveland 117,729	46.8	8,794	3.5	7,087	2.9
1890	Harrison 118,027	43.8	Cleveland 118,151	43.8	31,407	12.4	124	.05*
1896	McKinley 146,756	49.2	Bryan 144,877	48.5	7,065	2.4	1,879	0.7
Total	706,096	48.9	680,999	47.2	56,176	3.9	25,097	1.7

*smallest plurality in the country

Source: Compiled by the author from data in Robert Diamond, ed., Guide to U.S. Elections, (Washington, DC: Congressional Quarterly Press, 1976).

TABLE 4.4
Party Competition in the 1876 Presidential Election, by Region

Region	Hayes (R) (%)	Tilden (D) (%)	Margin of Victory (%)
Northeast	51.1	48.9	2.2
Midwest	52.2	47.8	4.4
Southern	40.1	59.6	19.5
Border	42.1	57.9	14.8
Western	51.2	48.8	2.4

Sources: Created by author from data in R. Diamond, ed., *Guide to U.S. Elections*, (Washington: CQ Press, 1976). Regional classifications from D. Brady, *Congressional Voting in a Partisan Era* (Lawrence: Kansas: 1973), p. 239.

interest of the country."[74] Large-scale ranchers and farmers also testified that Chinese newcomers filled low-paying rural jobs that were spurned by white settlers. But these witnesses were countered by a phalanx of local politicians, police, health officials, labor leaders, officers of anti-coolie clubs, and other activists favoring Chinese exclusion. Henry George warned committee members that unrestrained Chinese inflows create an inferior subclass in the West comparable to that of African Americans in the South. "Like the negroes," he observed, "they [Chinese] learn very fast, but beyond that point . . . they are incapable of attaining the state of civilization the Caucasian is capable of."[75]

The Special Committee's majority report was prepared in 1877 by California's own Senator Sargent, now an honorary vice president of the Anti-Coolie Union of San Francisco. It predictably concluded that Chinese were economically harmful to working-class citizens and incapable of sharing social and political institutions established by the "Aryan or European race." Sargent took pains to insist that the committee's findings were based on impartial facts. "The deduction from the testimony," the report noted, "would seem to be that there is not sufficient brain capacity in the Chinese race . . . for self-government." To add urgency to the report, Sargent warned that Chinese were "tending eastward" to the "banks of the Mississippi, and perhaps on the Ohio and the Hudson."[76] The committee majority urged the White House to renegotiate the Burlingame Treaty, and legislative colleagues to enact new prohibitions on Chinese immigration.

The Democratic House responded to the report with two resolutions calling for new treaty negotiations with China. But while Republican senators delayed action, both major parties faced a third-party challenge in California. In 1878, the charismatic Denis Kearney drew white laborers into a new Workingmen's party with demagogic speeches linking working-class insecurity to an evil marriage of corporate privilege and servile Chinese labor. The new party spread rapidly across the state, establishing major branches in forty of the state's fifty-two counties.[77] In statewide election, Workingmen's party candidates won key legislative seats, mayoral races, and 50 of 153 delegate slots for a special convention to revise the California constitution. California ultimately adopted a new constitution that contained sweeping anti-Chinese provisions. Firms were prohibited from hiring Chinese workers; employers who imported Chinese contract laborers were made subject to criminal or civil punishment; Chinese residents were officially denied suffrage and public employment; and cities and towns were instructed to confine Chinese to "prescribed portions."[78]

By the late 1870s, a formidable Left-Right coalition had clearly emerged in favor of Chinese exclusion (see table 4.5). Within the labor movement, classic exclusionists like Kearney railed against the racial dangers of Chinese immigration while egalitarian nationalists like Frank Roney worried about how Asian labor affected the economic opportunities of native-born workers.[79] Labor organizations across the country presented Congress with numerous petitions protesting "the systematic importation and immigration of Chinese laborers into the United States, to be employed at rates of wages ruinous to the free labor of our citizens."[80] The strong grass-roots movement of anti-Chinese clubs and organizations also established a firm presence in Western states, drawing an array of Sinophobic social elites and working-class activists into their ranks. The movement's electoral clout ultimately led Western politicians to become active members of anti-coolie clubs and Asian exclusion leagues.[81]

Pro-Chinese forces included a small yet diverse set of social groups. Cosmopolitan and market-oriented defenders of Chinese immigration included merchants concerned with expanding trade with the Far East, industrial and agricultural employers reliant on cheap Chinese labor, and Protestant clergy interested in promoting missionary work in China. The latter would form an Evangelical alliance that organized and bankrolled the creation of a Chinese Equal Rights League in the 1890s that challenged exclusionary policies for many years.[82] Chinese American leaders also actively opposed the exclusionist agenda in various political settings,[83] but the denial of voting rights for Chinese newcomers was devastating. In an era of competitive national elections and decentralized party politics, the anti-Chinese movement enjoyed strong mass-based support with which to pressure party politicians.

The political resources of Chinese immigration defenders were no match for those of the exclusionist coalition. In 1878, an unusual bipartisan caucus of Western congressmen formed to map out a strategy for

TABLE 4.5
Political Groupings on Chinese Exclusion

The Rights of Chinese Immigrants Should Be	Chinese Immigration Should Be	
	Encouraged	Prohibited
Equal to Those of Native-Born Whites	Protestant missionaries Former abolitionists Chinese Equal Rights League *"Our nation's invitation to the world cannot and ought not be limited by race or color."* Sen. George Frisbie Hoar William Lloyd Garrison Rev. Josiah Strong	Trade union leaders Republican pragmatists *"I never warmed to [anti-Chinese xenophobia], but agreed to sail under the flag so emblazoned to address real subjects of worker protection."* Frank Roney Rutherford B. Hayes
Fewer Than Those of Native-Born Whites	Merchants, ranchers, farmers, and manufacturers Six Chinese companies *"The presence of Chinese as laborers among us goes very far toward the material interst of the country."* Leland Stanford Charles Crocker Col. F. A. Bee	Anti-coolie clubs Workingmen's party Chinese Exclusion League Southern Democrats *"Like the negroes, . . . they are incapable of attaining the state of civilization the Caucasian is capable of."* Sen. Aaron Sargent Denis Kearney Henry George

securing Chinese exclusion.[84] For their part, Southern congressional Democrats promoted a "political alliance of the South and the West" dedicated to white supremacy and defeat of Northeastern "radicalism."[85] Yet the pro-Chinese stance of New England Republicans like Senator George Frisbie Hoar (MA) represented quixotic stands in a party unwilling to sacrifice Western electoral support. The position of the party's establishment was more aptly captured by the prominent support Chinese exclusion received from GOP senator and presidential favorite James G. Blaine. In 1879, former abolitionist William Lloyd Garrison publicly criticized the "demagogical, partisan rivalry between Republican and Democrat . . . as to who should the most strongly cater to the brutal, persecuting spirit which for the time being is so rampant in California."[86] Tellingly, Blaine responded that Garrison "libels almost the entire white race" by equating Chinese newcomers to European immigrants. "Mr. Garrison would not feel obliged to receive into his family a person that would physically contaminate or morally corrupt his children," he added. "As with a family so with a nation."[87]

During California's 1879 election, the Workingmen's party won key offices on a sweeping anti-Chinese platform that castigated "the managers of both parties" for appeasing "monopolists" by delaying action on Chinese exclusion.[88] A state referendum calling for Chinese exclusion won by a lopsided 150,000 to 900 vote.[89] The same year Congress passed the Fifteen Passenger Bill, barring vessels from transporting more than fifteen Chinese passengers. Despite broad cross-party support in Congress, the legislation faced executive resistance due to its foreign policy implications. President Rutherford B. Hayes vetoed the bill on the grounds that only the executive could abrogate the Burlingame Treaty. The maelstrom of criticism that followed the decision shook the president, who expressed dismay that his veto was "bitterly denounced in the west" and had led to his being burned in effigy.[90] Under intense pressure, Hayes sent delegations to China to renegotiate immigration sections of the Burlingame Treaty.[91]

As much as the 1876 campaign, the 1880 presidential election elicited promises from both parties to restrict Chinese immigration. James Garfield, the Republican presidential candidate, thought it politically important to express strong support for Chinese exclusion in his formal acceptance letter. Democrats countered by circulating documents in which Garfield allegedly declared his support for unrestricted Chinese labor. Moreover, no fewer than six pages of the Democratic campaign handbook of 1880 concentrated on Garfield's legislative transgressions on the Chinese issue, thereby illustrating "his contempt for the working man of his own race."[92] Fierce party competition in presidential elections of the post-Reconstruction era had transformed the anti-Chinese crusade into a political juggernaut. As the *New York Times* noted, "Which great political party is foolish enough to risk losing the votes of the Pacific States by undertaking to do justice to the Chinese?"[93] Once votes were counted, party politicians must have noticed that Western states again yielded the narrowest electoral margins in the country—states where Chinese exclusion was most salient as an issue (see table 4.6).

In 1881, a new treaty agreement with China was announced in which Peking recognized the right of the United States to "regulate, limit, or suspend" Chinese immigration but not "absolutely prohibit it."[94] In exchange, voluntary immigration from China was reaffirmed, and Chinese residing in the United States were assured new protections including the

TABLE 4.6
Party Competition in the 1880 Presidential Election, by Region

Region	Garfield (R) (%)	Hancock (D) (%)	Margin of Victory (%)
Northeast	51.9	46.5	5.4
Midwest	52.7	42.1	10.6
Southern	36.1	61.6	25.5
Border	42.4	54.2	11.8
Western	50.1	49.2	0.9

Sources: Created by author from data in R. Diamond ed., *Guide to U.S. Elections*, (Washington, DC: Congressional Quarterly Press, 1976). Regional classifications from D. Brady, *Congressional Voting in a Partisan Era* (Lawrence, Kansas: University of Kansas Press, 1973), p. 239.

right "to go and come of their own free will."[95] GOP leaders were jubilant, declaring it "a cause for congratulation that this question . . . has at length been settled." California Republicans boasted to voters that the new treaty was "framed by Republican commissioners and ratified and approved by a Republican administration."[96] Western Democrats and the anti-Chinese movement countered that the new treaty did not go far enough to prohibit Chinese immigration.[97]

THE TRIUMPH OF CHINESE EXCLUSION

In 1882, Chinese exclusion bills were proposed in both the House and Senate. During Senate debate, Hoar was virtually alone among Republicans in defending the rights of Chinese immigrants. In the West, anti-Chinese groups held rallies in which Hoar, like President Hayes before him, was denounced and burned in effigy. "The Senator from Massachusetts attempts to revive the 'Fatherhood of God and Brotherhood of Man' doctrine, which met its quietus in California many years ago," noted one California newspaper. "The great chair of Webster is held, but not filled, by a dwarf."[98] By large margins in both houses, Congress passed legislation that suspended the admission of all Chinese laborers for twenty years. President Chester Arthur, Garfield's successor, vetoed the bill due to "treaty obligations," but told lawmakers that he would welcome a modified version that satisfied "the expectations of the people."[99]

California Democrats were described by newspapers as "hugging themselves with joy over the President's veto." As one party leader celebrated, "We can get on the stump now and show the laboring men of the country that we have stood as a bulwark against the influx of a horde of Asiatics."[100] The California Democratic party issued a resolution instructing national policymakers that "it is the duty of the general government to . . . extend its strong arm for their protection."[101] Against this backdrop, a new Chinese exclusion bill was introduced in Congress. To mollify White House concerns, it shortened the suspension period on Chinese labor immigration to ten years. Significantly, it also contained new provisions providing for the deportation of Chinese, barred any state government or court from naturalizing Chinese immigrants, and required current Chinese residents to obtain special certificates for reentry if they left the United States.[102] After sailing through Congress, Arthur signed the Chinese Exclusion Act of 1882 into law.

National policy initiatives aimed at excluding Chinese grew more draconian over the next decade. In 1884, Congress closed loopholes created in the 1882 law when federal courts determined that Chinese immigration from U.S. territories, such as Hawaii and the Philippines, was not prohibited. But the grass-roots anti-Chinese movement of the Pacific Coast demanded still stronger national action. During the 1880s, violent attacks against the Chinese and Chinese American population residing in the United States spread from California to many Pacific Northwest and Mountain states. Anti-Chinese riots erupted in Denver in 1880; Rock Springs, Wyoming, in 1885; as well as Seattle, Tacoma, and Portland in 1886. As many as thirty-one California cities witnessed riots, Chinatown burnings, and physical expulsions of Chinese.[103] Special anti-Chinese conventions were organized to find ways to "rid the state of the Chinese now here."[104] In short, the Sinophobic movement now sought to complement immigration barriers with vigorous efforts to thin the country's Chinese population.

In 1888, amid sustained anti-Chinese agitation in the West, Democratic president Grover Cleveland reopened treaty negotiations with China. A new treaty barred Chinese labor immigration for another twenty years, with a clause for twenty more years (until 1928) if approved by both governments. But during ratification, the Senate attempted to add provisions denying reentry to Chinese residents who had left the country—including those with the special certificates for readmission mandated by the 1882 law. China informed U.S. negotiators that it would withdraw its approval of the treaty if the Senate clause prevailed, and the new treaty was never ratified.[105] Significantly, Cleveland's campaign manager, Representative William Scott (D-PA), quickly introduced legislation to strengthen Chinese exclusion. As the *New York World* observed, electoral calculations were unmistakable in the action: "The motive for this extraordinary haste is so transparent as to appear like a bit of comedy. . . . The Republicans were as anxious as the Democrats to make votes on the Pacific coast."[106]

The Scott Act passed with large bipartisan majorities in both houses.

The 1888 law made it unlawful for Chinese persons to enter the United States unless they were government officials, teachers, students, or travelers. Despite objections from Peking, reentry certificates issued to Chinese residents who temporarily left U.S. territory were declared legally null and void. To be readmitted, Chinese who left the country were required to show that they had a wife, child, *and* U.S. property valued over a thousand dollars. In his signing statement, Cleveland sounded the death knell for the Burlingame Treaty and Radical Republican ambitions for welcoming immigrants of all races and ethnicities. The "experiment of blending the social habits and mutual race idiosyncracies of the Chinese laboring classes with those of the great body of the people of the United States," he averred, "proved by the experience of twenty years . . . in every sense unwise, impolitic, and injurious to both nations."[107]

In the 1888 presidential campaign, both parties reaffirmed their steadfast commitment to Chinese exclusion. Both major party platforms claimed exclusive credit for securing federal action on Chinese exclusion.[108] During the next presidential election year, Congress passed the Geary Act of 1892, which shifted attention from Chinese immigration to the Chinese population residing in the United States. Under the new law, Chinese aliens were required to prove that their residence was legal by producing a white witness to testify that they resided in the country prior to 1882. In addition, the Geary Act denied bail to Chinese defendants in habeas corpus proceedings, and required all Chinese to carry a certificate of residence. The law also renewed the immigration ban of the Chinese Exclusion Act.[109]

In New York City, Chinese American merchants formed the Chinese Equal Rights League to protest these new policies, appealing for "an equal chance in the race of life in this our adopted home."[110] On the Pacific Coast, Chinese Americans challenged exclusionary measures in the courts and many refused to register for certificates of residence.[111] During the first period within which registration of all Chinese residents was to be completed, only about one of every ten Chinese actually registered. In response, "the federal government expanded the facilities for registration and sent officers directly to encampments of Chinese to expedite the process."[112] Congress later renewed the Chinese Exclusion Act in 1902, and subsequently made exclusion permanent.

CHINESE EXCLUSION IN THE COURTS

Traditional scholarship argues that Chinese immigrants and their native-born children were politically diffident in the late-nineteenth century, suffering "with helpless stoicism whatever indignities were thrust upon [them]."[113] But Chinese American leaders in fact pursued with great acumen one of the few political recourses available for blocking new federal exclusions: legal challenges in the courts.[114] From 1880 to the turn of the century, twenty cases involving Chinese rights were heard before the Supreme Court; numerous other legal challenges were mounted in lower courts. These legal appeals resulted in many modifications and invalidations of discriminatory state laws, and are significant for their contribution to American civil rights law.[115] Yet, the Supreme Court routinely affirmed congressional assaults on Chinese rights. In the same period that the Court stripped away civil rights protections enacted during the Civil War and Reconstruction, emphasizing the "powerlessness" of legislation to revise racial mores, it also articulated a doctrine of congressional "plenary power" that included the authority to weed out unassimilable races.[116]

The first constitutional challenge to Congress's power to exclude immigrants on the basis of race or national origin came before the Court in 1889 with the *Chinese Exclusion Case.*[117] Chae Chan Ping, a Chinese laborer, came to California in 1875 when the Burlingame Treaty protected unrestricted immigration from China. But the 1884 supplement to the Chinese Exclusion Act required Chinese resident aliens to obtain authorization certificates if they wished to leave the United States and then reenter. In 1887, Chae Chan Ping obtained such a certificate before returning to China to visit his family. While overseas, Congress passed another law barring admission to all Chinese laborers, including those with reentry certificates. Confined for months to a ship in the San Francisco Bay, Chae Chan Ping challenged the 1888 statute on two grounds in a petition for habeas corpus. First, his attorney argued that the new law violated the renegotiated Sino-American treaty that granted Chinese resident aliens the right to reenter the United States after short exits. Second, his petition held that 1880s legislation was "beyond the competency of Congress to pass it," challenging the constitutionality of laws that targeted a particular ethnic group and abridged the vested rights (including property rights) of resident aliens to reenter the country.[118]

Justice Stephen Field, writing for the majority, acknowledged that the 1888 statute and 1880 treaty conflicted, but reasoned that they were on equal footing, thereby giving preference to the most recent legal development. More important, Field's response to the second argument gave expression to the fundamental doctrine of classic immigration law, namely the "plenary power doctrine." His opinion declared that the federal government not only has the power to regulate immigration, but that the political branches could exercise this power without being subject to judicial scrutiny. Congressional authority to regulate immigration was based on the imperatives of national security, territorial sovereignty, and self-preservation. "[If Congress] considers the presence of foreigners of a different race in this country, who will not assimilate with us, to be dangerous to its peace and security . . . its determination is conclusive upon the judiciary." Moreover, Field stressed that reentry of Chinese resident aliens was not a legally protected right but a privilege or license, revocable at any time by the federal government.[119]

In 1892, the Court's *Nishimura Eiku v United States* decision expanded the doctrine of plenary power.[120] The petitioner, a Japanese immigrant deemed excludable by an officer of the Treasury Department because she was considered likely to become a public charge, argued that due process protections required a judicial proceeding. The majority ruled that the plenary power doctrine trumped any challenges by aliens to individual constitutional rights: "It is an accepted maxim of international law, that every nation has the power . . . to forbid the entrance of foreigners within its dominions, and to admit them upon such conditions as it may see fit to prescribe."[121] Plenary power also extended to "executive officers," the Court determined, who were entrusted by Congress to act as "sole and exclusive judge" of policy enforcement.[122]

A year later, in *Fong Yue Ting v United States*, the plenary power of Congress was applied by the Court to the deportation of aliens residing in the United States.[123] The 1892 extension of the Chinese Exclusion Act required Chinese resident aliens to prove residency prior to 1892 via a white witness or face deportation. Fong claimed he resided in the country prior to 1892 but could not produce a white witness to verify his claim; the white witness requirement, his attorney argued, denied Fong of procedural due process. The Court responded that the power to exclude and the power to deport were indistinguishable: the process of deportation did not mandate constitutional protections associated with "punishment."[124] Rather, the Court again stressed the contractual relationship between the sovereign nation-state and aliens:

> The order of deportation is not a punishment for crime. . . . It is but a method of enforcing the return to his own country of an alien who has not complied with the conditions upon the performance of which the government of the nation, acting within its constitutional authority . . . has determined that his continuing to reside here shall depend.[125]

In just five years, a solid legal groundwork was laid for the exclusion, restriction, and expulsion of immigrants. Subsequent judicial rulings reaffirmed the broad, unencumbered power of Congress and its administrative agents to regulate immigration. Inspectors of the Chinese Bureau, a subdivision of the U.S. Customs Office, were pressured by Sinophobic groups and lawmakers to enforce federal laws more severely than required by statute or Treasury Department rules.[126] By the turn of the century, the dramatic policy innovations achieved by the anti-Chinese

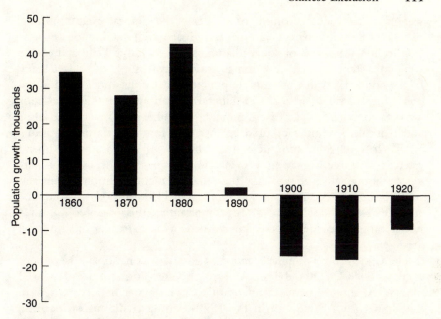

Fig. 4.1.   Late-Nineteenth-Century Chinese Population Growth and Decline in the United States (Source: Census Bureau, *Statistical Abstract* [Washington, DC: Government Printing Office, 1924])

movement effectively shut down Chinese immigration and significantly thinned the nation's Chinese American population (see fig. 4.1).

Conclusion

The politics of Chinese exclusion casts some doubt on whether liberalism, republicanism, and ascriptive hierarchies represent separate and rival traditions in American political development,[127] or whether in practice these traditions have been blended and contorted by political actors (in albeit intellectually inconsistent ways) to serve their policy goals. This chapter reinforces Rogers Smith's contention that liberal and racist ideas (including new evolutionary notions of racial difference) play a significant role in shaping policy choices and outcomes.[128] It also affirms Smith's argument that in the American polity, "[c]hanges toward greater inequality and exclusion, as well as toward greater equality and inclusiveness, . . . can and do occur." This claim is well illustrated by the decisive shifts from Reconstruction policies welcoming Chinese immigration to Gilded Age policies slamming the gates shut. Yet a careful examination of the political discourse of this period suggests that rival ideological traditions were not clearly aligned on opposite sides of the Chinese exclusion question. To be sure, Senators Sumner and Hoar gave unambiguous expression to liberal notions of equal treatment, just as Judge Field and others were consistent in their devotion to Anglo-Saxon superiority. But many of the combatants in this struggle pursued their policy goals with a disconcerting blend of liberal and illiberal aspirations. Anti-Chinese labor activists combined ugly racist arguments with liberal claims for free labor and workplace democracy (and against new forms of slavery). Various employer groups in turn defended Chinese immigration with liberal references to free human movement, limited government, and the market economy, while at the same time making racist assertions about the need for inferior Asian workers to meet menial labor needs that were unsuitable for white men. More importantly, this chapter captures how Sinophobic ideas were intertwined with particular institutional arrangements.

The Gilded Age's popular reaction against activist national government as envisioned by Republicans during the Reconstruction era is well known. As intense party competition resumed and federal troops were withdrawn from the South in the 1870s, strong traditions of localism, laissez-faire liberalism, and limited government gained renewed force in American politics. In turn, the ideological reaction against the active Civil War state also resurrected older institutional arrangements that typified the nineteenth-century polity. The historian Morton Keller observes that the federal government's "purposeful activism" of the Reconstruction years was in sharp decline by the 1870s, with "the fostering of public policy" overshadowed by the renewed imperatives of "party organization." As a result, "Congress and the executive became less significant instruments of governance than state legislatures, the courts, and major political parties."[129] In similar fashion, Skowronek describes the Gilded Age as recapturing a "normal mode of operations" for American politics: a "state of courts and parties" preoccupied with distributing particularistic benefits to localities.[130] The "precocious" social spending state given special emphasis by Skocpol fits neatly within this political order, a natural product of what she aptly calls "patronage democracy."[131]

The return of competitive party politics and judicial influence in the wake of Reconstruction had familiarly pernicious implications for recently emancipated African Americans. The withdrawal of federal troops from the South in 1877 presaged the federal government's full-scale retreat in terms of protecting the civil rights of racial minorities, as the leaders of both major parties embraced state and local solutions to the "race problem." At the same time, the federal courts systematically dismantled most of the constitutional rights gained by African Americans during Reconstruction, affirming local white practices that rendered them a "separate" and unequal subclass in the American polity.[132] In short, white supremacy and hostility toward an active national state went hand in hand with dismantling legal protections for African Americans and nurturing Jim Crowism during and after the Gilded Age. Little wonder that William Riker once lamented that "the main effect of federalism since the Civil War has been to perpetuate racism."[133]

The triumph of Chinese exclusion, however, offers a different portrait of how dominant institutional arrangements of the post-Reconstruction American polity promoted racial hegemony. Whereas the assault on African American rights was achieved through national acquiescence to state and local racial practices fostered by resurgent parties and courts, the exclusion of Chinese newcomers in the same era required an ambitious new sphere of national regulatory control to be created. That reform-minded state legislatures, intense electoral competition between both major parties, and new forms of judicial activism propelled unprecedented restrictions on Chinese immigrant admissions and rights strongly confirms "the state of courts and parties" that Keller and Skowronek place at the center of Gilded Age political life. What is perhaps most striking, however, is not the power of American political institutions to routinely derail "purposeful" national government in this period, but their capacity to adapt in service to traditions of racial hierarchy.[134]

The ripple effects of American Chinese exclusion politics transcended national borders, as political actors in Canada, New Zealand, and Australia drew inspiration from the Sinophobic movement of the American West. "Australasian colonies were much influenced by events in California," Charles Price notes, with various activists working to "transfer holus bolus the arguments used there . . . or else to hold up the 'terrible conditions' of California as an example of what at all costs they must themselves avoid."[135] For the United States, Chinese exclusion was intended to be an isolated development with no connection to its long-standing policy of openness toward European immigrants. Yet new exclusionary laws and enforcement structures embodied logics that conflicted with traditional immigration policies. In particular, Chinese exclusion initiated and legitimated state capacities for restricting immigration on ethnic and racial bases that challenged the nineteenth-century trajectory of U.S. policy toward European inflows.[136] Chinese exclusion proved several decades later to be anything but an isolated development, as national policymakers constructed an increasingly elaborate immigration control system of racist design.

CHAPTER FIVE

Progressivism, War, and Scientific Policymaking

THE RISE OF THE NATIONAL ORIGINS QUOTA SYSTEM, 1900–1928

IMMIGRATION RESTRICTIONISTS OF the early-twentieth century, like most other Progressive Era reformers, believed that bold new forms of national governance were necessary to restore economic, social, and political order to a country enduring wrenching change. Many viewed the late-nineteenth century as a time of disquieting turbulence. The closing of the frontier and the expansion of an urban industrial economy fostered greater economic interdependence that threatened cherished local autonomy. The period saw the rise of new forms of poverty that strained local relief efforts, as well as labor upheaval and socialist movements—sedate versions of class conflict and radicalism that Americans thought would never surface on this side of the Atlantic.[1] As one scholar wrote at the time, "the fate of our country has been in what Edmund Burke describes as 'a perilous and and dancing balance.' Every day is a day of crisis."[2] The decentralized, self-regulating society that prevailed for much of American history was, in the view of Progressive Era restrictionists, a luxury of the past. To the civic reformer and IRL vice president Joseph Lee, immigration was the sort of dangerous force that the federal government most desperately needed to tame through rational legislation and administration. "In political life, liberty meant until recently the minimum of control necessary to secure equal opportunity," he noted. "We have begun to realize the control of man over nature, and to see that the highest results come from the collective effort consciously directed to an end. These considerations have a direct bearing upon the question of immigration regulation."[3]

Early-twentieth-century nativists saw immigration restriction as the preeminent Progressive cause. Numerous scholars have challenged efforts to define "Progressivism" or to identify core principles and organizational forms of the "Progressive movement."[4] The Progressive Era, Daniel Rodgers suggests, breathed life into a new fragmented and issue-oriented politics in which often-contradictory reform movements sought to capitalize on the declining influence of traditional political parties on government.[5] Significantly, immigration restrictionists understood well that the Progressive political landscape was crowded with competing issues and movements. Undaunted, they explicitly linked their cause to a host of other prominent reform impulses of the day. Restrictionists reminded prohibitionists and good-government reformers that new immigrants undermined temperance and fueled corrupt urban party machines. As much as pure-food legislation guarded the physical health of American citizens, Progressive nativists promised immigration restriction would "benefit not alone our bodies but . . . insure the welfare of our homes, our States and our nation." Moreover, they cast restrictionism as "but a part of the great conservation movement," dedicated to conserving the quality of American citizenship. However attentive to other reform campaigns, nativists insisted that their cause was the most urgent. "There is less of real critical moment in any other national question than there is in this immigration question," IRL leaders declared. "It is *the Great American problem*."[6]

Drawing inspiration from new scientific research, Progressive Era restrictionists aimed to build a national regulatory system that excluded immigrants of national and ethnic groups they deemed inferior. Certain that crucial *racial* distinctions existed between Europeans, they yearned for new immigration barriers to guard the nation from the contamination of southern and eastern Europeans. By 1900, Chinese were the only nationality group openly excluded in immigration law. Large cross-party majorities in Congress renewed the ban on Chinese admissions in 1902 and made their exclusion permanent in 1904; the Chinese population in the United States declined in these years from 107,000 to 71,000. By contrast, a record 8 million European newcomers streamed into the United States between 1901 and 1910; more than 6 million of these arrivals claimed southern and eastern European origins in nations such as Italy, Russia, Hungary, and Greece.

The IRL and its allies worked vigorously in the first decade of the twentieth century to secure major policy innovations designed to stem this unprecedented immigrant tide. To broaden the resrictionist coalition, they forged key alliances with organized labor, Southern conservatives, and various "social control" Progressives. They continued to maintain strong ties with the House and Senate immigration committees, helping members and staffers draft and defend restrictionist legislation. And they successfully nurtured support for their cause from an activist president with Progressive inclinations, Theodore Roosevelt. By 1910, however, Progressive nativists had little to show for their efforts. To be sure, laws enacted between 1882 and 1903 excluded a modest number of immigrants who failed to pass certain tests of mental, physical, financial, and moral fitness. Yet these filters did nothing to dampen southern and eastern European inflows. The nation's traditional receptivity to European immigrants and the ease with which they obtained citizenship rights seemed impervious to change.

The early frustrations of Progressive Era restrictionists owed much to the fact that they could not easily escape the partisan structures that had bedeviled nativists throughout the nineteenth century. For example, one institutional legacy of the "party period" in U.S. political history posed special obstacles to modern nativists: the "partisan speakership."[7] Major revision of House rules in 1890 (the so-called Reed Rules) consolidated control of the body in the hands of the majority party leadership, producing a dominant Speaker's office that was until 1910 "an artifact and architect of party government in the United States."[8] One of the most fervent defenders of expansive policies toward European immigration was House Speaker Joseph Gurney Cannon (R-IL), who used his extraordinary Speakership powers to derail restrictionist policy proposals from 1903 to 1910. Presidential candidates of major parties also continued to court the votes of new immigrants at least through the 1912 campaign.[9]

Despite early roadblocks, the immigration restriction movement blossomed in the Progressive Era. The fortunes of anti-immigrant reformers improved markedly with the passage of Progressive political reforms that gradually eroded the power of political parties. The decline of both traditional American party government and partisan electoral competition in the early-twentieth century meant that extraparty groups like the IRL increasingly enjoyed greater structural openings to *directly* influence immigration policymaking. In turn, insurgent national politicians became less hamstrung by party leaders and more responsive to reform-minded interest groups and associations. Moreover, activists capable of marshaling social-scientific expertise on behalf of their proposals commanded an authority unparalleled in earlier political contexts; the rise of scientific government also created new distance between elite policymaking and mass-based politics that gave special leverage to immigrant voters.

The transformed political and institutional arrangements of the Progressive Era polity were decidedly more hospitable to nativist immigration reformers than had been the nineteenth-century "state of courts and parties."[10] But as partisan bulwarks against immigration restriction broke down, a diverse coalition of pro-immigration associations and interest groups mobilized to preserve existing policies. They proved to be formidable rivals, adapting effectively to fresh demands of the Progressive Era polity. For most of the early-twentieth century, immigration defenders and restrictionists were locked in a monumental battle over restrictionist initiatives such as the literacy test and national origins quotas. The outcome of this struggle would be settled decisively by newly empowered governmental institutions, officially sanctioned expertise, coalitional dynamism, and an isolationist reaction to jolting international pressures.

IMMIGRATION COALITIONS OF THE PROGRESSIVE ERA

The Immigration Restriction League and its nativist allies faced daunting political opposition in the early-twentieth century. Organized associations of older ethnic groups, such as the German-American Alliance and the Ancient Order of Hibernians, joined forces in the 1900s to resist restrictionist proposals.[11] Although many new immigrants supported McKinley and the Republican party in the national elections of 1896 and 1900, they maintained an electoral affinity for Democrats at the local level.[12] Consequently, Irish politicians of urban Democratic political machines often defended the interests of new southern and eastern Europeans.[13] Political professionals of the Republican party continued to court new immigrant voters after McKinley's death, especially in national elections. They fed patronage to groups like New York's Hungarian Republican Club in 1900, while prominent "organization" Republicans like Speaker Cannon frustrated restrictionist efforts in Congress. Jewish organizations such as the American Jewish Committee, the Liberal Immigration League, and the Hebrew Immigrant Aid Society counterpoised the IRL in both their lobbying and research activities.[14] Business groups including the National Association of Manufacturers, railroad and steamship companies, and industrial employers defended their unfettered access to the immigrant labor market.

A handful of scholars like Franz Boas and Harvard president Charles Eliot challenged restrictionist academic findings concerning the economic and racial influence of new immigration. In a similar vein, Lincoln Steffens's celebrated *Shame of the Cities* (1902) pointed to the natural-born majority that sustained the corrupt Philadelphia party machine and argued that political graft was an indigenous problem. "The 'foreign element' excuse is one of the hypocritical lies that save us from clear sight of ourselves," he concluded.[15] At gatherings of social reformers and charity organizations, settlement workers like Jane Addams and Frances Kellor spoke against restrictionist plans and praised the contributions of new immigrant groups to American life. For Addams, who helped organize groups from the National Association for the Advancement of Colored People to the National American Woman's Suffrage Association, economic security and equal membership represented integral elements of a unified reform movement—a movement to transform government into an agent of social justice.[16] Only by accepting with "magnanimity" the "right" of outsiders to "join in our progress," she asserted in 1905, could the nation develop "the larger sense of justice which is becoming world-wide."[17]

While business groups, ethnic associations, and liberal cosmopolitans organized in defense of European immigration after the 1896 literacy-test battle, restrictionists also expanded their bases of support. In the

1890s, IRL activists worked vigorously to draw labor unions into the restrictionist column.[18] While organized labor passionately advocated Chinese exclusion and prohibitions on contract labor immigration, it was deeply ambivalent about whether voluntary European immigration should be constrained. Terence Powderly, leader of the Knights of Labor, claimed that his organization was internationalist and thus resistant to sweeping restrictions lest it "be construed as opposing any portion of humanity."[19] When the Knights faded in the 1890s, the IRL courted the American Federation of Labor (AFL) as the nation's preeminent labor organization (AFL membership rolls increased from 250,000 to 1.5 million from 1898 to 1903).[20] At early AFL national conventions, European immigration restriction so deeply divided union rank and file that their leaders chose to delay action on the issue. AFL president Samuel Gompers observed that "the labor movement approached the problem of immigration restriction reluctantly," largely because foreign-born members like himself had "mixed feelings" about denying entry to those they had left behind.[21] Yet Gompers ultimately embraced the literacy test because he believed large-scale immigration was fundamentally corrosive to the economic security of American workers; a foreign labor force was easily manipulated by large corporate employers to crush workers' rights. Rejecting Powderly's vision of labor internationalism, he argued that "freedom" for workers across the globe required "those devoted to the cause to remain within their own countries and help in national struggles." National labor movements were the only means of protecting domestic workers from "low wages and bad working conditions." His restrictionist stance also was deeply influenced by what he perceived as a troubling "drift" in U.S. immigration to "unskilled" laborers who "were largely undisciplined in trade union policies."[22] While AFL unionism celebrated traditional craft principles, most southern and eastern European immigrants occupied new semiskilled industrial jobs that were unorganized by AFL member unions.[23] For Gompers and his loyalists, new immigrant workers enabled industrial monopolists to undermine the independence of American laborers, "to substitute machine work in the place of previously indispensable craft skill."[24]

Gompers's views on European immigration were initially resisted by AFL member unions representing large numbers of foreign-born workers. His efforts to win support for the IRL's literacy test proposal failed at early AFL national conventions. Yet Gompers eventually persuaded AFL delegates to empower his Executive Council to study the impacts of new European immigration on American laborers and to recommend an official position on the issue. Not surprisingly, Gompers's Executive Council ultimately endorsed stringent limits on southern and eastern European immigration. After heated debate and a "sharply divided" vote among the AFL's rank and file, the country's most prominent labor organization lent its official support to immigration restriction at the start of a new century.[25] Significantly, AFL leaders instructed its young Washington Department of Legislation to work closely with the IRL and other nativist groups to secure restrictionist immigration reforms. AFL lobbyists soon established themselves as key members of an immigration policy network associated with the congressional immigration committees and new investigatory commissions.[26] Throughout the Progressive Era, the AFL's Washington office made "Literacy Test/Immigration Restriction" a centerpiece of its legislative agenda.[27] As a result, immigration restriction produced unlikely political alliances between organized labor and xenophobic patricians of the IRL and various fraternal societies.

Northeastern nativists also actively nurtured cross-sectional support for their reform agenda in the early-twentieth century. IRL activists developed new ties with Asian exclusionists in 1905, and successfully persuaded Japanese and Korean Exclusion Leagues of the Pacific Coast to endorse sweeping restrictions of southern and eastern European immigration.[28] Immigration restriction initially elicited little support below the Mason-Dixon line. During the late-nineteenth century, more than a few Southern leaders hoped to recruit European immigrant laborers to help build a "New South" defined by unprecedented agricultural and industrial development, even as native blacks migrated to Northern cities in record numbers.[29] At gatherings like the Southern Interstate Immigration Committee, leaders from across the region planned ways to attract more European settlers.[30] Just as Western states and territories once enticed immigrants with assurances of land and broad rights, Southern agents promised newcomers that life in the South would be "comfortable and prosperous and happy."[31] Despite spirited appeals to by Southern business interests and officials, fewer than 500,000 newcomers settled in the region by 1910 (more than 13 million immigrants resided in other parts of the country).[32]

As Southern recruitment efforts floundered, the IRL launched an anti-immigrant publicity campaign throughout the region. The IRL's James Patten wrote articles for Southern journals on the racial inferiority of new European immigrants and their capacity to bring fearsome urban problems to the pastoral South. "The North would be glad to have its city slums emptied upon the sunny lands of the South," one article warned.[33] While IRL representatives attended conferences and met with opinion leaders throughout the region, its Washington lobbyists wooed Southern congressmen.[34]

During the 1890s, Southern members of Congress routinely opposed new restrictions on European immigration. But sectional animosity toward new European immigrants grew sharply in the new century, as

Grangers, Farmers' Alliances, and conservative Democratic politicians joined the restrictionist cause. One IRL survey of Southern political officials conducted in 1905 found that 84 percent favored the exclusion of southern and eastern Europeans, and 92 percent favored a literacy test.[35] The same year, Representative Oscar Underwood (D-AL) invoked the ethnic and racial distinctions made by Francis Walker and other scholars. God "created the great Celtic and Teutonic races to carry forward the banners of our present civilization and the principles of Christianity," he proclaimed on the House floor, "and when we contaminate our blood with an inferior race we will not be carrying out the object of our creation."[36] Senator F. M. Simmons (D-NC) contended that unless immigration was limited to "persons of Celtic, Scandinavian, or Anglo-Saxon origin," the nation would be subjected to "further race and class problems" that would keep it from becoming "a homogenous whole."[37] In the same period, Southern state legislatures adopted resolutions calling for the exclusion of southern and eastern Europeans, especially Italians and Russian Jews.[38]

Northern nativists also came to view the dangers of immigration as emblematic of a larger national "race problem." Whereas Northern Know-Nothings were almost as hostile to the extension of slavery as they were to Catholic immigrants, Northern restrictionists of the Progressive Era often expressed sympathy with Southern efforts to disenfranchise blacks and with Western demands for Asian exclusion. Harvard president A. Lawrence Lowell argued that the health of republican democracy in the America required Anglo-Saxon dominance:

> We know now that in carrying on popular government in the South the negroes have been disfranchised, that is, they made democracy there homogenous by thrusting out one race from the body politic. So far as the Chinese are concerned, we have kept this country homogenous by excluding them. I used to think when I was young that that was all wrong, but I have come to the conclusion that, on the ground . . . of the need for homogeneity in democracy, [it] was absolutely right.[39]

In similar fashion, the New England–based IRL frequently asserted that "Indians, Negroes, Chinese, Jews, and *Americans* cannot all be free in the same society."[40]

During the early-twentieth century, the restrictionist crusade in Congress would be led not only by Northern patricians like Lodge, but also by Western and Southern immigration committee chairs, such as John Burnett, an Alabama Democrat, and Albert Johnson, a Washington Republican. Among interest groups, the IRL formed alliances with the AFL and other labor groups, patriotic societies like the Junior Order of

TABLE 5.1
Immigration Coalitions of the Progressive Era

Alien Rights Should Be	*Alien Admissions Should Be*	
	Expanded or Maintained	*Restricted*
Expansive	**Cosmopolitans**	**Nationalist Egalitarians**
	Horace Kallen	Samuel Gompers
	Jane Addams	Terence Powderly
	Louis Marshall	John R. Commons
	Immigration Protective League, American Jewish Committee, German American Alliance, "social justice" progressives	American Federation of Labor, Knights of Labor, Wisconsin progressive economists
Restrictive	**Free-Market Expansionists**	**Classic Exclusionists**
	William Howard Taft	Henry Cabot Lodge
	Stephen Mason	Madison Grant
	Joseph Cannon	Albert Johnson
	National Association of Manufacturers, steamship companies, U.S. Chamber of Commerce	Immigration Restriction League, patriotic societies, the Grange, eugenicists, Asian Exclusion Leagues

United American Mechanics and the Daughters of the American Revolution, agrarian groups like the Grange and the Farmers' Alliance, and anti-Asian movements of the West. An equally diverse coalition of ethnic associations, social justice reformers, cosmopolitan intellectuals, steamship companies, and large industrial employers mobilized in opposition to restrictionist initiatives (see table 5.1).

THE PARTISAN SPEAKERSHIP AND THE DEMISE OF IMMIGRATION REFORM, 1903–1907

When Republican House and Senate majorities became polarized over the literacy test in 1898, they responded in typical Progressive fashion by creating a special commission to study the issue. As the Industrial Commission on Immigration engaged in fact gathering, restrictionists were heartened by Theodore Roosevelt's ascent to the White House following McKinley's assassination. An energetic president, Roosevelt devoted more attention to immigration than his predecessors had. Although he later courted new immigrant voters by appointing the country's first Jewish cabinet secretary, Oscar Straus, many nativists believed he was sympathetic to their reform agenda. A close friend of Lodge, TR assured the IRL executive committee in 1896 that "I *do* heartily sympathise with the [literacy] bill" since it was "introduced by Senator Lodge."[41] In a letter to Lodge a year later, Roosevelt shared that he was "horrified" that the "[*New York*] *Sun* put me down as opposed to the restriction of immigration," and insisted that the editors print a correction.[42] In his first annual message to Congress, Roosevelt called for the exclusion of anarchists, "a certain standard of economic fitness," and the literacy test.[43]

A few days after Roosevelt's address, the Industrial Commission submitted to Congress nineteen volumes of testimony and research on immigration. Most of the commission's reports were in fact prepared by academic experts, most social scientists, who were delegated specific subjects to study. One of the most widely read reports was written by the economist John R. Commons and focused on "immigration and its economic effects." His statistical analysis of the occupational distribution of immigrants purported to show that "the races having the largest proportion of unskilled workers" were Asians and southern and eastern Europeans (even though his own data showed that Irish newcomers tended to have fewer job skills than groups defined as "Hebrew," Italian, or Japanese).[44] Concerned about guarding the wages of American workers, Commons also found that southern and eastern Europeans were accustomed to significantly lower wages than were workers in other European regions.[45]

Commons's report easily blended notions of gender hierarchy with the ethnic and racial assumptions that informed his investigation. Women, he reasoned, should be barred from industrial jobs because they lowered wages, displaced male breadwinners, and generally were "not suitable in factories on account of carelessness, ill temper, and unreliability." But whereas "the daughters of native Americans and of the earlier immigrants" had the good sense to "find employment as clerks, schoolteachers, and similar occupations," southern and eastern European women eagerly took industrial jobs, he grimly noted.[46] Related to the proposed literacy test, another report provided statistical information indicating illiteracy rates were high among southern and eastern Europeans and relatively low among other Europeans.[47] This research seemed to confirm Lodge's claims during the 1896 floor debate.

In addition to its social scientific findings, the Industrial Commission made several of practical legislative recommendations to Congress. Although the experts who conducted research for the commission urged major restrictions, most commissioners were cautious political actors.

While majorities endorsed a ban on anarchists, increased head taxes, and stronger prohibitions on contract labor, only two of fourteen commissioners supported a literacy test. Citing commission recommendations, Congress passed legislation in 1903 that increased the head tax from one to two dollars, and established exclusions for epileptics, anarchists, the "insane," and "professional beggars."[48]

Efforts to restrict immigration were tabled during the 1904 election year, as the dominant Republicans distanced themselves from nativist positions that might undercut support from foreign-born voters. Party strategists crafted campaign documents designed to appeal to particular ethnic and religious voting blocs; Republican canvassers were especially attentive to Jewish immigrant voters.[49] The party's sponsorship of organizations like the Roosevelt Committee for Jewish Voters and the National Roosevelt League for German Americans reminded nativists that new European immigrants continued to exercise clout at the ballot box.

Immigration restriction resurfaced soon after the election due to anti-Japanese agitation on the Pacific Coast. In 1905, the *San Francisco Chronicle* published a series of articles alerting readers of increased Japanese immigration (see table 5.2) and warning that "the Japanese is no more assimilable than the Chinese."[50] Grass-roots organizations that propelled Chinese exclusion now targeted Japanese newcomers. In California, politicians of both parties promised voters they would pursue Japanese exclusion; the state legislature swiftly passed resolutions calling on Congress to bar Japanese admissions. The San Francisco School Board also required Japanese children to attend segregated schools, sparking diplomatic tensions when an outraged Japanese government protested that segregation violated its "most favored nation" status. A reluctant Roosevelt administration was thus pulled into the fray.[51] Proponents of the literacy test were encouraged by these developments. "There is a rise in feeling against immigration," Lodge wrote Roosevelt in the summer of 1905. "The intense feeling on the Pacific Slope may help us get some

TABLE 5.2
Japanese Immigration to the United States, 1871–1930

1871–80	149
1881–90	2,270
1891–1900	25,942
1901–10	129,797
1911–20	83,837
1921–30	33,462

Source: Based on data from the *Statistical Yearbook of the INS* (Washington, DC: Government Printing Office, 1994).

good general legislation." With "the anti-Japanese-Chinese agitation" and the support of organized labor, he predicted, "we might win."[52] Lodge and IRL lobbyists privately told Western lawmakers that their support for the literacy test was necessary "if they expect us to back their Asiatic proposition."[53] In contrast to the Chinese Exclusion Leagues, new Asiatic Exclusion Leagues called for a suspension of all nontraditional immigration, Asian *and European*.

With the active support of organized labor, new Southern animus toward southern and eastern Europeans, and anti-Japanese agitation on the Pacific coast, the IRL was optimistic about the chances of securing literacy test legislation in 1906. After having "met and talked with many Senators and Congressmen," the IRL's Washington lobbyist James Patten told the Executive Committee that "the outlook for legislation is very bright indeed."[54] He added that the IRL and AFL strategy of flooding members with letters was having an effect: "Never has there been a time when Congressmen and Senators have been so overwhelmed with personal correspondence urging legislation."[55] Gompers personally made dozens of trips to Capitol Hill to shore up support for the literacy test.[56] As in the 1890s, the IRL worked closely with congressional immigration committees in drafting restrictive legislation. In the Senate, Lodge secured broad support for a literacy-test amendment to a 1906 immigration bill sponsored by Senator William P. Dillingham (R-VT), chair of the Senate immigration committee. It stipulated that immigrants over sixteen years of age (excluding wives, children, parents, and grandparents of citizens or admitted immigrants) were required to pass a reading test.[57]

The House battle over literacy test legislation was in many ways a clash between old and new political norms and institutions of an American polity in transition. The House Committee on Immigration and Naturalization was dominated by Progressives who identified the literacy test with social reform and racial purification. Committee members took pains to link their restrictionist bill to expert research. The bill's chief sponsor, Augustus P. Gardner (R-MA), defended the legislation by speaking reverently of commission findings that could be interpreted as supporting a literacy test. But restrictionists faced withering opposition from Speaker "Uncle Joe" Cannon whose dedication to standpat principles contrasted with the Progressive reform spirit that was then catching hold in national politics. There were special reasons why Cannon and "organization" Republicans opposed the immigration bill. Lobbied intensely by ethnic associations and the Liberal Immigration League, House party managers worried that the measure would provoke electoral reprisals from foreign-born voters; Cannon's own district contained a large and active constituency of naturalized voters.[58] They also supported business groups who claimed that sweeping immigration restrictions would deprive manufacturers and other employers of a vital labor supply. Unlike nativist Progressives who restlessly clamored for legal mechanisms to deter southern and eastern European inflows, Cannon and his loyalists saw the country as "a hell of a success" requiring little change.[59] Despite cross-party House support for the literacy test, Cannon was ready to use his ample powers to block immigration reform.

The powers of the partisan speakership were a significant institutional legacy of the heyday of political parties in the second half of the nineteenth century. Even before the Reed Rules were adopted in 1890, Woodrow Wilson observed in his classic work *Congressional Government* that "the Speaker of the House of Representatives is the most powerful functionary of that system. So sovereign is he within the wide sphere of his influence that one could wish for accurate knowledge to the actual extent of his power."[60] Thomas Reed established a highly centralized and partisan power structure in the House not long after assuming the Speakership in 1889, which was used aggressively to enforce party discipline among rank-and-file members. He determined all committee assignments and committee chairmanships. The self-appointed chair of the Rules Committee, Reed also dictated which bills were to be considered for a vote and what limitations on debate were imposed. As one of Reed's key lieutenants in 1890, Cannon took charge of the controversial "disappearing quorum" rules change that permitted the counting of members who were present but not responding to a roll call vote. His subsequent rise to the Speaker's chair reflected his long service as an ardent soldier of the Republican party.[61]

When the House immigration committee reported out its literacy-test bill, Gardner and the IRL were confident that Republicans and Democrats would join to enact the measure. But Cannon could not abide this ambitious reform legislation; the fact that he opposed new limits on immigration and that the bill was supported by Republican insurgents and various Democrats made his opposition firm. For several months of 1906, he flatly refused to permit the initiative to reach the House floor. It is often argued that Cannon and his "court" of dedicated Republicans were oblivious to the growing reform spirit of fellow partisans in Congress,[62] but it is telling that he and his lieutenants agreed to take action on the bill once Gardner and his allies threatened an appeal to the entire House Republican Caucus. It was a major achievement for restrictionists to get their proposal on the House floor agenda. However, Cannon's subservient Rules Committee set floor rules that were designed to block passage of the literacy test. To provide Cannon loyalists cover from AFL and IRL retaliation, it prohibited a recorded vote on either amendments or the bill as a whole. It also reported a special rule stipulating that no yea and nay vote could be taken on the literacy-test provision, limited debate to three hours, and permitted only one amendment for each section of the bill.

During the truncated debate over Gardner's bill in June, immigration committee sponsors underscored the extent to which independent expertise highlighted the need for a literacy test. They urged colleagues to consult the impartial findings of the Industrial Commission and reminded members that theirs was a bipartisan measure consistent with other Progressive causes of the day. In the final minutes of floor debate, the purposes of the Rules Committee became apparent when Charles Grosvenor (R-OH), a key member of Cannon's leadership team, stunned restrictionists by proposing an amendment substituting a new investigatory commission for the literacy test. An incredulous Gardner countered with a point of order that Grosvenor's proposal was not germane to the literacy test section. "Why, here is the report of the Senate, and here is the report of the House, and here is the report of the Industrial Commission," Gardner exclaimed. "Yet you are talking this nonsense about another commission."[63] The presiding chair, a Cannon lieutenant, overruled his objection. When a simple division (entailing those for and against a measure to stand until counted by the chair) was held on Grosvenor's substitution amendment, it was defeated by a vote of 136 to 123.

In a dramatic show of power, Cannon ordered a recount of the vote, claiming the simple division was not sufficient. Members now were required to register their votes by passing between official tellers stationed in the well of the House. Early in the debate, Cannon vacated the Speaker's chair to take personal command of Republicans on the floor.[64] As rank-and-file members milled down to the tellers, they were confronted personally by Cannon and his lieutenants (several newspapers reported that Cannon shook members by their coat lapels during the vote). "Speaker Cannon not only used the vast power and influence of his office to defeat [the literacy test]," an AFL lobbyist bitterly complained, "but he left the exalted position of the Speaker, went upon the floor of the House, and made enough members either go to the cloak rooms or go between official tellers of the House" in order to strike the literacy-test provision.[65] In the recount, Grosvenor's amendment supplanted the literacy test by a 128 to 116 vote. Twenty Republican supporters of the literacy test had been pressured into either switching their votes or abstaining altogether. The *Philadelphia Record*'s morning headline read: "Speaker Scurries about Aisles, Threatening, Cajoling and Importuning Members to Support of Machine." The *New York Times* reported that Cannon "overrode the Committee on Immigration" in "one of the most extraordinary spectacles ever seen on the floor of the House."[66]

The revised immigration bill, stripped of literacy test requirements, won easy passage in the House. To no one's surprise, Gardner, the member most closely associated with the immigration bill, was not named by Cannon to represent the House in conference committee. All three House conferees appointed by the party leadership were Cannon loyalists and fervent opponents of the literacy test. They squared off against Senate conferees led by Lodge and Dillingham who pressed for the Senate bill's literacy test provisions. Amidst conference committee meetings, pro-immigration groups placed renewed pressure on Cannon and House conferees to hold the line. "We are moving heaven and earth to prevent the bill as it passed the Senate from becoming a law," Louis Marshall, head of the American Jewish Committee, assured pro-immigration allies.[67] For eight months, the conference committee remained deadlocked. "[W]e have been unable to get the House conferees, who of course represent the Speaker, to come to any kind of agreement," wrote Dillingham in February 1907. "They will not even agree to disagree and so report to their body."[68]

Because of the intensifying diplomatic conflict over Japanese school segregation in San Francisco, Roosevelt eventually urged conferees to reach compromise. He confided to some White House visitors that the Japanese immigration issue needed to be addressed in an "entirely different manner from the method used in regard to the Chinese." Because of Japan's military prowess, he feared that resentment over Japanese exclusion might lead to warfare and the potential loss of the Philippines and Hawaiian Islands.[69] Attempting to calm Japanese authorities and appease Californians, Roosevelt persuaded the San Francisco mayor to exempt Japanese students from Asian segregation in exchange for prohibitions on Japanese entering the continental United States from Hawaii. In addition, as part of this so-called Gentlemen's Agreement, the Japanese government pledged to discourage labor immigration from its country. To prevent Japanese from moving to the West Coast after a stay in Hawaii, Secretary of State Elihu Root suggested amending the immigration bill to authorize the president to exclude all aliens whose entry would be "to the detriment of labor conditions" in the country. The amendment was devised to ban Japanese laborers without making explicit reference to Japan.[70]

With a solution to the Japanese conflict at hand, Roosevelt sent Secretary Root to Capitol Hill to negotiate with the immigration conferees. Cannon ultimately set the terms of compromise, making his support for Root's amendment contingent upon the conference committee's acceptance of the House bill. In deference to Roosevelt, Lodge ended the conference stalemate by conceding his literacy test provision in favor of the House bill establishing yet another immigration commission—one that House Republican leaders hoped would sidetrack European immigration restriction. The conference deal became the Immigration Act of

1907, which established an immigrant head tax of four dollars and created a new investigatory commission. The frustrations of restrictionists in the House led many to join a growing insurgency campaign to overthrow the partisan speakership and restructure the distribution of congressional power. But the more immediate concern of Progressive Era nativists was the new commission that Cannon embraced for dilatory purposes. The IRL and other anti-immigrant reformers hoped its findings would prove as useful to their cause as those of the Industrial Commission.[71]

THE DILLINGHAM COMMISSION: RACE AND SCIENTIFIC GOVERNMENT

The new investigatory commission was led by Senate restrictionists who comprised one-third of its membership. Among them were Lodge and Dillingham, the commission chair. While two of the three commissioners from the House shared Cannon's disdain for restrictive immigration reform, the third, John Burnett (D-AL), welcomed the literacy test. The three presidential appointees were expected to provide special immigration expertise. Mindful of Lodge's sacrifice on behalf of the Gentlemen's Agreement, Roosevelt reassured his Senate ally that a credible scientific study by the commission would "put before the Congress a plan which would amount to a definite solution of this immigration business."[72] Most political actors soon recognized that the Dillingham Commission would be much more than an institutional way station for immigration reform.

Interest groups of opposing camps also saw the commission's enormous potential influence at a time when expertise or social knowledge was emerging as an institutionalized feature of the American policymaking process, enjoying a privileged role in the design and implementation of public policies.[73] As James Morone observes, "There was, in the Progressive vision, no Democratic or Republican way. . . . Rather, there was a *best* way—precise, expert, scientific."[74] This development had much to do with the rise of a "new knowledge-bearing elite" evidenced in the changing universe of professional associations and academic research.[75] New forms of social-scientific expertise lent intellectual authority to general policy "paradigms" and specific initiatives.[76] Government structures such as executive bureaucracies, congressional committees, and investigatory commissions in turn gave political force and expression to particular expert ideas about the causes of and solutions to social problems. For immigration activists of the early-twentieth century, the Dillingham Commission had the power to either privilege or discredit restrictionist claims that new immigration from southern and eastern Europe hurt American society. Max Kohler, chief lobbyist of the AJC and the Union of American Hebrew Societies, cautioned pro-immigration allies that the commission's "report is likely to shape our immigration policy for a number of years . . . and its publications will be the chief collection for the study of the immigration question for a long time to come."[77] The IRL Executive Committee drew similar conclusions: "If their report is negative, it will hurt us for many years," the committee observed, "whereas a positive report, favoring especially the illiteracy test," would "carry great weight with Congress."[78] IRL leaders notified their Washington office that there was "no more valuable work" than to monitor its investigation and, when necessary, "to hammer the commissioners."[79]

The work of the Dillingham Commission was unprecedented, even by the standards of Progressive era fact gathering and social engineering. The commission conducted investigations for more than three years, spent more than a million dollars, employed a staff that reached three hundred, and ultimately published a hefty forty-two-volume report. One of the most influential commissioners was Jeremiah Jenks, a presidential appointee who served as the chief theoretician and staff coordinator for the Dillingham Commission's studies. Jenks was a respected Cornell economist whose Progressive credentials were beyond reproach, having served on government investigations of corporate trusts and long championed social engineering as a means of solving national problems. He also was enamored with the earlier ethnic and racial theories of Walker and Mayo-Smith. In a 1909 address to academics and social reformers entitled the "Racial Problem of Immigration," Jenks called for immigration policy to shift from "an individualistic basis" to one based on "racial characteristics." "Most of us are proud of being Anglo Saxons," he intoned in the same speech, adding that British offspring were "particularly good."[80]

The Dillingham Commission held no public hearings. Instead, its staff compiled an extensive body of empirical research that purported to demonstrate the perils that new European immigrants posed to the nation. The recurrent theme of its forty-two reports was the vast contrast between immigrants from traditional European source countries and those from southern and eastern Europe. Whereas old immigration brought skilled and industrious settlers who were well acquainted with republican institutions, newer arrivals represented an invasion of "unskilled laboring men" from "less progressive countries of Europe."[81] Individual reports underscored a close association of new immigrants with a host of vexing social problems.

In the commission's report on "immigrants in mining and manufacturing," researchers found that newcomers "almost completely monopolized unskilled labor activities in many of the more important industries . . . and as a result a class of employees was gradually displaced."[82] Its study of "immigrants in cities" suggested that southern and eastern European dwellings exhibited "considerably greater congestion per room" and a higher "proportion of unclean rooms" than older European groups (researchers determined that African American dwellings were the most overcrowded and unsanitary).[83] Commission staffers also studied "the children of immigrants in schools," comparing the "rate of progress" and intelligence of students across what were described as distinct racial categories. The performance and capacities of students were ranked by the commission report in the following descending order: "white native-born" immigrants from "English-speaking races"; Swedish, Dutch, and German immigrants; and at a much lower ranking, "Hebrew" immigrants, Italians, "Magyars and Slovaks," Poles, and Asians; and finally, "native-born negroes."[84] Tellingly, these studies failed to control for duration of residence in the United States. The social scientists serving on the commission's staff drew conclusions about innate group characteristics by comparing immigrant nationality groups that had resided in the United States for a few years with those that had lived in the country five times as long.[85]

One commission study did yield results that challenged the findings of the forty-two reports. Franz Boas, an anthropologist and Jewish immigrant from Germany, conducted a study for the commission on changes in bodily form of descendants of immigrants. In contrast to American eugenicists, Boas found that the mental and physical qualities of second-generation immigrants differed markedly from the parent stock. Indeed, he argued that his measurements showed that second-generation immigrants regardless of national origin or racial classification tended to converge into a uniform "American type." Immigrant assimilation, he concluded, was determined by the physical and social environment and not by inherited hereditary traits.[86]

Jenks and his key staff assistant, anthropologist Daniel Folkmar, expressed some concern about Boas's findings but ultimately determined that it failed to disconfirm the overwhelming evidence that southern and eastern Europeans were decisively less assimilable than older stock immigrants. While Boas's study was submerged, Jenks and Folkmar collaborated on an extensive *Dictionary of Races* that became an important feature of the Dillingham Commission's report to Congress. Both were influenced by Walker, Mayo-Smith, and Harvard's William Z. Ripley. Ripley's influential *The Races of Europe* (1898) argued that "the plain truth of the matter" is that "there is no single European or white race of man." He determined that there existed three European races: a Nordic race, a Teutonic race, and a Mediterranean race. Southern and eastern Europeans were categorized as Mediterranean, the "darkest" and most primitive of these races.[87] In their *Dictionary of Races*, Jenks and Folkmar stated that their principal task was to discover "whether there may not be certain races that are inferior to other races . . . to show whether some may be better fitted for American citizenship than others." Integrating eugenicist methods and findings, the volume placed emphasis on what it described as definitive physical qualities of races, especially of different European races. To this end, Jenks and Folkmar presented information on the "shortness and height of . . . heads," the relative darkness of eye, hair, and skin, as well as "facial characteristics" such as "the 'Jewish nose.'" Based on such data, they came to the predictable conclusion that "all these peoples from eastern and southern Europe . . . are different in temperament and civilization than ourselves."[88] The *Dictionary*, along with other commission reports, was cited frequently by restrictionists in subsequent immigration debates.

Steeled by the forty-two volumes of empirical research, restrictionist commissioners focused their energies in 1910 on a summary of recommendations that was to serve as a blueprint for legislative action. Nativist groups enjoyed close working relationships with a number of commissioners. As policy recommendations were being drafted, IRL lobbyists met with Burnett "to go over the illiteracy test carefully and thoroughly with him, before he goes before the Commission."[89] Lodge pledged in a "heart to heart talk" with restrictionists that he would "do all in his power to have the Commission recommend and the Senate enact the literacy test."[90]

Restrictionists celebrated the Dillingham Commission's expert reports and policy recommendations, which were affirmed unanimously by the commissioners (two commissioners assumed to be immigration defenders were swayed by the commission's empirical research). Its policy prescriptions included the literacy test, an increased head tax, as well as a proposal, given little notice at the time, to restrict immigration on the basis of national origins quotas. IRL lobbyist James Patten determined it was such a "strong document" that he ordered ten thousand copies of the full report and twenty thousand copies of the summary of findings, more than ten times the number printed by the government.[91] At a special dinner, the IRL honored Lodge for "statesmanship" that "will make more difference than all of the tariffs and everything else that Congress will do for the next ten years."[92] Gompers called off an electoral assault on Lodge that was planned by Massachusetts trade unions frustrated by his reactionary stance on most labor issues.[93] His decision captured the importance the AFL attached to immigration restriction.

Well before the Dillingham Commission finished its work, pro-immigration groups anticipated that the dominant trends in American natural and social sciences were likely to help restrictionists. On questions of race and immigration, the AJC's Cyrus Adler noted, "the sound sense and humanity of the average politician are much more to be trusted than that of the average scientific man."[94] The AJC sponsored a study by economist Isaac A. Hourwich demonstrating that new immigration produced economic growth and national prosperity.[95] Yet most empirical research on immigration favored restrictionism. When the Dillingham Commission findings were released, immigration defenders had little expertise with which to respond. At an annual gathering of social workers and reformers, Cyrus Sulzberger assailed commission findings as "unwarranted."[96] Jane Addams spoke of the many illiterate immigrants she had worked with in Chicago who were far more successful than highly educated ones. But few lawmakers gave much credence to these criticisms of the commissions findings. Immigration restrictions could claim the intellectual high ground in national policy debates for years to come.

VETO-POINTS, OLD AND NEW: FROM CANNONISM TO EXECUTIVE RESISTANCE

As the Dillingham Commission completed its work in 1910, a coalition of House Democrats and Republican insurgents stripped the partisan Speakership of its most formidable powers. The House revolt against Cannonism involved significant rules changes that aimed to loosen the stranglehold of centralized party government in the House. In the memorable phrase of Republican insurgent George Norris on party discipline, "I would rather be right than regular."[97] House nativists like Gardner eagerly supported the "unhorsing" of Cannon and the decline of the partisan Speakership. Indeed, Cannon's assault on the literacy test in 1907 was a vivid illustration for many Progressive Era restrictionists of the unholy alliance of party bosses, monopolists, and subservient immigrant voters that corrupted American constitutional democracy. Many anti-immigrant groups championed "direct democracy" reforms. Despite its close ties with the Democratic party, the AFL had long called for political reforms that would "wipe out plutocratic dictation" of party machines so as to "let the people rule."[98] Likewise, IRL patricians consistently supported political reforms intended to enervate political parties. But restrictionists considered Cannon's obstruction of the the literacy test especially offensive. For Gompers, "that action was one of the final straws that broke the camel's back and hastened the revolt against 'Cannonism.'"[99] While overstating linkages between the 1907 literacy-test battle and the House revolt, restrictionists appreciated that the diminution of the partisan Speakership and traditional party government dissolved important structural barriers to immigration reform.

The demise of the Reed Rules led to a devolution of power in the House, breathing life into an institutionalized seniority system and the rise of autonomous standing committees. In the wake of the 1910 revolt, the chair of the House immigration committee assured IRL lobbyists that neither party leaders nor the Rules Committee could easily block future committee bills. "Rules Reform and immigration," he observed. "It does not seem possible for them to avoid either."[100] Although other issues would dominate the public agenda for some time, immigration restrictionists enjoyed new political and institutional opportunities to press their reform agenda in the 1910s. Indeed, their cause was strengthened by two powerful yet seemingly contradictory aspirations of Progressivism: "direct democracy" and "scientific government." The former was a driving force in the demise of the partisan Speakership and traditional party government, both of which impeded immigration reform, while the latter deeply informed the creation of the Dillingham Commission and the political influence of its findings. The fact that southern and eastern European immigration soared from 1.9 million in the 1890s to 6.1 million in the 1900s lent a sense of urgency to nativist demands for a literacy test. In popular Jack London novels, southern and eastern Europeans were depicted as "the dark-pigmented things, the half-castes, the mongrel-bloods" who threatened native-born protagonists named Saxon.[101]

If restrictionists gained fresh political momentum from the commission report and the decline of centralized party power in Congress, the presidential office remained an important veto-point. In key respects, presidential resistance was part of an old story: European men continued to easily obtain admission and political membership. Their assumed importance in national elections persuaded presidents and party managers to welcome newcomers and distance themselves from restrictionists. In the Progressive Era, new European immigration was defended in Washington by dozens of well-organized interest groups. Strikingly, older ethnic groups which no longer dominated immigration totals, such as the Ancient Order of Hibernians and the German-American Alliance, ardently defended immigration opportunities for southern and eastern Europeans. New interest-group pressures and the perceived importance of foreign-born voters convinced even chief executives like Roosevelt, who supported the restrictionist cause, that it was necessary to conciliate immigrant groups.

The implementation of immigration laws during the Roosevelt administration is telling in this regard. When Roosevelt began his presidency, sensational press accounts described the Immigration Bureau and the Ellis Island inspection station as riddled by patronage appointments and rampant corruption. The new president confided to a friend that he was "more anxious to get this office straight than almost any other." Troubled by lax enforcement, Roosevelt named new immigration administrators who possessed strong professional credentials and favored restriction.

Emblematic of this personnel shift was the selection of William Williams, a Wall Street executive, to run Ellis Island. Williams was known for his unflagging devotion to civil service reform and administrative science; his first memo to Ellis Island inspectors compared government agencies to corporations that must be run with efficiency and frugality.[102] Williams made little effort to hide his zeal for restricting immigration,[103] and he drew fire from various pro-immigration groups for issuing independent orders that required immigrants to land with between ten and fifty dollars in their possession (with the amount scaled according to physical condition).[104] He also offended New York Republicans by ending a long-standing practice of awarding profitable contracts for money exchange, food, and baggage concessions at Ellis Island to loyal partisans.[105] Williams was supported by the Immigration Bureau's commissioner general, Frank Sargent, who believed that only "sturdy Scotchman, Irishmen and Germans" should become citizens.[106]

Yet relations between Williams and the White House grew strained when White House strategists urged less-stringent enforcement during the 1904 election. Williams ultimately resigned when Roosevelt could not resist filling the Ellis Island chief assistant's position with a patronage appointment, New York Republican Joseph Murray. Partisan considerations also informed Roosevelt's decision to name Oscar Straus, a prominent Jew and immigration defender, to the post of secretary of Labor and Commerce, the executive department that supervised the Immigration Bureau. In the months leading up to the 1906 election, Republican strategists grew alarmed by the Democratic candidacy of William Randolph Hearst for New York governor. Hearst had carefully used his chain of newspapers to cast himself as champion of new immigrant groups and to criticize Williams and literacy-test proposals. Many foreign-language newspapers and ethnic leaders embraced Hearst's candidacy. Amid reports that he was likely to win large majorities in New York City's Lower East Side (a section dominated by Jewish voters), party managers worried that naturalized voters would abandon Republican candidates. It is against this backdrop that Straus was named to the cabinet. Tellingly, one of his first official duties was to campaign in New York on behalf of Charles Evans Hughes, the GOP gubernatorial candidate.

As Labor and Commerce secretary, Straus recast the restrictive administrative tone set by Sargent and Williams. His speeches praised immigrants for fostering economic growth. In private, he lamented that Asian exclusion cost the United States lucrative trade opportunities in Asia. Straus also openly appealed to labor leaders to remember their own immigrant past:

> Look back . . . upon your own escutcheons. If it is not you, your fathers came over here. I cannot get away from the old American idea

that was voiced by Roger Williams. . . . He said: "When you have crossed over the black brook of some soul bondage yourself, leave a plank for distressed souls who come after you."[107]

As one might expect, organized labor was more alarmed than moved by such statements. The AFL and IRL resolved to "keep watch of Straus," and to alert allies on the congressional immigration committees "of any steps which Straus is taking to break down the law."[108]

At Ellis Island, another immigration defender, Robert Watchorn, was named by the White House to replace Williams as its chief administrator. Watchorn rescinded Williams's monetary test as "drastic" because it excluded "a very large number of able-bodied men and women, who could not show $10 . . . though they were in every other way eligible to land." A cultural pluralist, he also refused to permit Christian missionaries to proselytize Jewish arrivals. Straus praised Watchorn as "a man possessing extraordinary qualifications of head and heart for tempering justice with mercy;"[109] Straus later gave his trusted Ellis Island commissioner funds sub rosa to assist needy aliens who passed through the inspection station.[110] The executive branch and electoral politics continued to pose important hurdles for nativist immigration reformers.

Immigration reform politics in 1912 aptly captures the barriers that remained for restrictionists. Early in the year, new literacy-test legislation drafted by the Senate immigration committee was passed with broad support from the Republican majority and Southern Democrats. In the House, Burnett was now chair of the immigration committee, and he championed a similar literacy-test bill. But as the session drew to a close in June, Burnett agreed to take up the bill after the election in deference to his party's presidential candidate. While cross-party majorities in Congress favored restrictions on southern and eastern European immigration, all of the major presidential hopefuls were actively courting immigrant and ethnic voters opposed to reform.

The beleaguered incumbent, William Howard Taft, praised new immigrants in campaign speeches and authorized the Republican National Committee to issue statements promising that he would veto any literacy-test legislation if reelected. Party strategists also recruited Louis Hammerling, a Polish editor and leader of the American Association of Foreign Language Newspapers, to coordinate pro-Taft publicity in newspapers that catered to the foriegn-born.[111]

Theodore Roosevelt and the Progressive party were even more aggressive in currying favor with immigrant voters. Despite his past endorsement of Lodge's literacy test, Roosevelt distanced himself from restrictionists in his political reincarnation as third-party standard bearer. Pro-immigration liberals like Jane Addams and Frances Kellor served in high councils of the Progressive party and were influential in shaping a platform that presented newcomers as victims of malevolent domestic forces.[112] One platform plank decried that "our enormous immigration population" had "become the prey of chance and cupidity." Progressives pledged to establish "industrial standards" that would smooth tensions between immigrant and native workers, and promised to promote "assimilation, education, and advancement" in their pursuit of "social justice."[113] The party's publicity campaign deliberately put rivals on the defensive with foreign-born voters. The *Progressive Bulletin* charged Taft, who reappointed William Williams in 1909, with presiding over a "reign of terror on Ellis Island" that reflected his "purist nativism." Woodrow Wilson, the Democratic candidate, was attacked for scholarly writings he published in 1902 that praised Chinese inflows while endorsing the social-scientific view of new European immigrants as inferior.[114] In Progressive campaign literature distributed widely among new immigrant communities, Wilson was quoted as saying that "the immigrants from Southern Italy, Hungary and Poland are the very lowest class of human beings possessing neither intelligence nor initiative."[115] The Progressive appeal to naturalized voters won support. In three of four New York City districts that returned pluralities for Roosevelt, most voters were naturalized citizens of Slavic and Russian Jewish descent. After the election, Kellor would be instrumental in creating an Immigration Bureau within the Progressive National Service, a structure dedicated to linking the insurgent party to the electoral power of new European immigrant voters.[116]

Wilson struggled throughout the campaign to disavow his earlier writings on Chinese and new European immigration. His praise for Chinese immigrants drew hostility from Californians, where he lost the Democratic primary, while his offensive statements about southern and eastern Europeans alienated new immigrant voters. To hold union labor and Western support, Wilson pledged fealty to Chinese and Japanese exclusion, suggesting that the country was already overburdened by the "Negro question." "We cannot make a homogeneous population out of a people who do not blend with the Caucasian race," he stated. "Oriental coolieism will give us another race problem to solve and surely we have had our lesson." But Wilson assumed a pro-immigration stance toward southern and eastern Europeans. In a public letter to an Italian American, Wilson promised that the country would never close its gates to Europeans "who loved liberty and sought opportunity" during his presidency.[117]

When Congress reconvened after the 1912 campaign, the House quickly passed Burnett's literacy-test bill. In contrast to 1907, a conference report containing the literacy test was approved by both houses shortly thereafter. In their final push for the literacy test, however, restrictionists encountered stiff White House resistance. Subjected to intense lobbying by German American and Jewish organizations, Taft confided to A. Lawrence Lowell in 1913 that "until recently I have been in favor of a literacy test, but I am not quite clear in my mind now."[118] Perhaps the most important lobbyist was Taft's own secretary of Commerce and Labor, Charles Nagel, who argued that American industry would be crippled by immigration restrictions. With the labor needs of industrial employers in mind, Taft vetoed a literacy bill in his administration's last days, as Cleveland had done in 1896. Ironically, the Republican Senate voted to override the veto, 72 to 18, but the Democratic House failed to do so by the margin of 213 to 114.

Although he polled a minority of the popular vote, Woodrow Wilson entered the White House with Democratic majorities in both houses. He was an energetic leader, determined to control Congress by obtaining unprecedented cooperation from its Democratic caucuses for his reform program.[119] To the frustration of nativists, however, the Progressive economic and social policies championed by Wilson in 1913 pushed immigration reform off the public agenda. One year later, the congressional immigration committees pressed for literacy-test legislation. Both committees were chaired by Southern Democrats: Elison "Cotton Ed" Smith (SC) in the Senate and Burnett in the House. According to Republicans such as Gardner, bipartisan cooperation prevailed on the committees among restrictionists. "In 1906 and 1910, I was in control of the illiteracy test bill," Gardner noted. "In both instances, my right hand man . . . was Mr. Burnett of Alabama. Nowadays, Mr. Burnett is in control of the bill and I am his right hand man."[120] One immigration defender serving on the House committee warned the AJC that Burnett and Gardner were determined to enact literacy-test legislation, regularly holding the committee in session for "sixteen continuous hours beginning at 10 AM adjourning at 2 AM the following morning, only to meet again the same morning at 10 O'clock."[121] Literacy-test legislation once again passed the House in 1914 by a vote of 253 to 126, and the Senate in early 1915 by 50 to 7 (39 abstaining).

Because of Wilson's discrepancies between his scholarly writings and his campaign appeals to new European immigrants, immigration restrictionists were uncertain how Wilson would respond to literacy-test legislation. Wilson met with ethnic leaders, as well as with a delegation of prominent women social reformers led by Addams who challenged the moral soundness of the literacy test.[122] The New York branch of the Immigration Restriction League tried with limited effect to influence the new president through its associations with adviser Colonel Edward House.[123] But more compelling was a resolution passed by most Democrats and Republicans in the New York Assembly urging Wilson to veto the measure.[124] When Southern Democrats privately quizzed Wilson on the bill, he candidly explained that his hands were tied by 1912 campaign promises to foreign-born voters. "I find myself in a very embarrassing situation about that bill," he confessed. "I myself made the most explicit statements at the time of the Presidential election about this subject to our fellow-citizens of foreign extraction. . . . In view of what I said to them I do not see how it will be possible for me to give assent to this bill."[125] However ambivalent he may have been, Wilson's 1915 veto message was infused with characteristic moralism. He blasted Congress for creating a test of outsiders that was based on economic privilege rather than character; the literacy test, he wrote, conflicted with "the humane ardors of our politics" and the country's devotion to "the natural and inalienable rights of men."[126] Wilson was anything but an egalitarian on matters of race, permitting dozens of federal offices and facilities to be segregated after 1913.[127] Yet he was unwilling to renege on a campaign promise to new immigrants. After bargaining with key Democratic members, Wilson fended off a veto override by only four votes. The nation's traditional openness to European immigration regardless of national origin narrowly survived.

WORLD WAR, ANTI-HYPHENISM, AND THE LITERACY TEST

The onset of the First World War for a time reduced immigration from 1.4 million in 1914 to 300,000 in 1916. Restrictionists welcomed the decline, but they also feared the flow would resume at record levels once the war came to a close. Anti-immigrant reformers had effectively nurtured a broad Left-Right coalition for the literacy test since the turn of the century. They had made the most of new institutional opportunities in Congress to press their cause, perhaps most notably the emergent power of standing immigration committees that were receptive to their agenda. Finally, Progressive Era nativists both facilitated and benefited from the elevation of social-scientific expertise in the immigration policymaking process, as the Industrial and Dillingham Commissions bestowed intellectual legitimacy on their xenophobic ideas and initiatives. Nevertheless, pro-immigration activists comprised an equally formidable coalition that enjoyed its own structural advantages in the governing process. And even during the reformist heyday of the Progressive Era, the American constitutional order and its institutional legacies continued to frustrate major policy innovation with veto-points. The fact that the policy of granting easy entry to European immigrants was as old as the American republic added to the elusiveness of nativist policy designs. Yet the outbreak of global warfare, with its attendant stimulus to xenophobia and yearnings for national uniformity, allowed immigration restriction to truly flourish. Organized groups like the IRL and AFL had laid an institutional and ideological groundwork for restriction over many years; as fears of foreign radicalism reached a fevered pitch after the war, restrictionists were well positioned to provide specific policy solutions to new isolationist demands.

One of the initial effects of the war was to discredit political activism on the part of nationality groups that identified strongly with their countries of origin. Throughout the Progressive Era, ethnic groups openly mobilized against immigration restriction through direct and grass-roots lobbying efforts. But rallies held by the German-American Alliance in support of peace with Germany dismayed the American public in 1915–16, accentuating native fears about the loyalties of the country's large foreign-born population.[128] While urgent questions arose about the nation's assimilative capacities and the impact of ethnocultural diversity on American security, politicians and opinion leaders increasingly called for government policies promoting national conformity. As Theodore Roosevelt proclaimed, a strong defense against outside aggression required vigilance "not merely in military matters, but in our social life," infusing in the American people "a high and fine preparedness of soul and spirit."[129]

Doubts about the adequate assimilation of immigrant groups troubled immigration defenders and restrictionists alike; key leaders from both sides called for an intensive program of "Americanization" that would introduce greater "order" and "efficiency" to the assimilation process.[130] The call for Americanization attracted a broad array of social groups and activists. Many groups—including settlement houses, the North American Civil League for Immigrants, the Young Men's and Young Women's Christian Associations, the National Council of Jewish Women, and various women's clubs—viewed their participation as philanthropic toward aliens. Their concerns were to protect newcomers from exploitation, to secure for them an "American standard of living," and to help them become citizens.[131] Business groups including the U.S. Chamber of Commerce and the National Association of Manufacturers (NAM) formed the National Americanization Committee, which offered English and civics lessons for immigrants in factories. The committee also told newcomers that labor agitation was inconsistent with American political ideals and harmful to "commercial and industrial development."[132]

Drawing on earlier immigration work for New York State and the Progressive party, Frances Kellor emerged as an important pro-immigration leader in the Americanization movement, speaking for both social workers and business groups. In the interest of preserving robust immigration without sacrificing social control, it was Kellor, not restrictionist groups, who later proposed blueprints for national alien registration and distribution.[133] Nativist patriotic associations like the American Legion and the Daughters and Sons of the American Revolution also crusaded for Americanization. They urged employers not to promote unnaturalized workers, and shared Kellor's zeal for alien registration. Thirty states ultimately created Americanization programs, some limited employment opportunities only to aliens intending to become citizens, and

Iowa even adopted legislation making it illegal to speak a foreign language. Federal agencies, with little congressional or White House direction, also devoted considerable energy to the assimilation crusade. The Bureau of Education in the Interior Department, the Bureau of Naturalization in the Labor Department, and the Department of Justice each established their own distinctive Americanization policies.[134]

The challenge of transforming "hyphenated Americanism" into "citizenship absolutely undivided" was irresistible to many Progressives.[135] Kellor believed that the Americanization movement would "forge the American people in this country into an American race that will stand together in times of peace and war." Roosevelt remained until his death the most celebrated spokesman for the "Swat-the-Hyphen" effort, reminding rapt audiences that the true test of the American melting pot "is the completeness of the fusion."[136] And as German Americans openly opposed his reelection bid, Wilson denigrated the political activism of ethnic organizations he had courted only four years earlier: "You can not become thorough Americans if you think of yourselves in groups."[137]

Only a few public voices, out of touch with the existing political culture, defended immigrant group identities against the Americanizers' quest for conformity. The author Willa Cather expressed nothing but disdain toward acculturation and Progressive reformers who treated immigrants as mere "laboratory specimens." As she lamented, "this passion for Americanizing everything and everybody is a deadly disease with us. . . . Speed, uniformity, nothing else matters."[138] Horace Kallen extolled the value of cultural pluralism in these years, observing that "democracy involves, not the elimination of differences, but the perfection and conservation of differences. It aims, through union, not at uniformity, but at variety."[139] Yet such views commanded a small audience during the war.

Patriotic associations, labor unions, and other restrictionist groups welcomed the new forms of social control that accompanied Americanization programs. Significantly, IRL members expressed contempt for such programs. By perpetuating faith in "the melting pot," these nativists observed, even draconian assimilation programs were an "inversion of Darwin's real teaching." According to IRL leaders, the war's most profound lesson was that the goal of assimilating southern and eastern Europeans was chimerical: "The superficial changes constituting 'Americanization' were entirely inadequate to affect the hereditary tendencies of generations." For enthusiasts of social Darwinism and eugenics, then, national conformity was best secured through a system racial selection and exclusion.[140]

With publicity and lobbying support from the IRL, the AFL, patriotic groups, and agrarian associations, Burnett and the House immigration committee reintroduced a literacy-test bill in 1916. Its language stipulated that close family members of admitted immigrants were exempted from the test, reflecting a reverence for family unity that would later come into its own. But the bill also included further restrictive measures: an increase in the head tax from four to eight dollars and the exclusion of those judged by immigration officials to be vagrants, stowaways, persons suffering from tuberculosis or possessing a "constitutional psychopathic inferiority," and advocates of property destruction. The term "constitutional psychopathic inferiority" was a term developed by eugenicists, and was defined by the bill as "a congenital defect in the emotional or volitional fields of mental activity which results in inability to make proper adjustment to the environment."[141] In contrast to the 1906 battle, all amendments proposed by immigration defenders on the House floor were soundly defeated unless approved by Burnett and the committee; an amendment that exempted political refugees from the literacy test was among those that failed. The bill passed the House easily.

Literacy-test legislation also was broadly supported in the Senate. Dillingham initially proposed a bill limiting immigration by fixed percentages for certain nationality groups based on the ethnic breakdown of the U.S. population in the most recent census. During debate, however, he endorsed the literacy test as a more workable method for restricting immigration. The only major departure from the House bill was the addition of an "Asiatic barred zone" that extended legal exclusion to "Hindus" while leaving the Gentlemen's Agreement with Japan intact.

Beyond the Senate chambers, the AJC's Louis Marshall urged Congress not "to build a Chinese wall around our country, to make us an isolated and parochial people, in the narrowest sense of the word."[142] The Hebrew Immigrant Aid Society (HIAS) circulated material across the country denouncing the literacy test. Jewish leaders also pointed to the irony that one of the measure's leading proponents, Democratic senator "Cotton Ed" Smith of South Carolina, hailed from a state that attracted few immigrants but had one of the highest illiteracy rates in the country. Addams scolded restrictionist labor organizers and social reformers for failing to recognize that conservative nativists cared little about the improvement of industrial and social conditions. "To the national dishonor of the 'assisted' immigration of the slave trade days," she noted sadly, "we are adding another chapter."[143]

The Senate passed the Burnett bill by an overwhelming margin, with only seven dissenting votes. "The League is now all powerful in Washington," IRL leaders boasted. "No bill as to immigration can be passed if we object, while any bill we favor has a good chance of passage."[144] Wilson again vetoed the literacy-test legislation in 1917, but this time the *Democratic-controlled* Congress overrode him.

Closely monitoring the inspection of immigrants at Ellis Island, IRL activists were among the first to notice that the literacy test failed to filter out a large portion of southern and eastern Europeans. Because "the spread of elementary education in the backward countries" undermined the literacy test, nativist leaders concluded, a new mechanism for "discriminating in favor of immigrants from northern and western Europe" was required. Accordingly, the league and the activist immigration committees labored for a new system "to restrict a possible large immigration of inferior quality after the war" with "some numerical scheme of restriction" based on nationality quotas.[145] In the war's aftermath, the Red Scare heightened public concern that the nation's large immigrant population made it vulnerable to Bolshevik revolution, anarchy, and other forms of political radicalism. Americanization programs assumed a harder edge, and Attorney General A. Mitchell Palmer launched a campaign to combat espionage and sabotage by rounding up communists and other suspect persons. Hundreds of alleged alien radicals captured in the Palmer raids of 1920 were expelled from the country in what Assistant Secretary of Labor Louis Post called a "deportations delirium."[146]

When Republicans took control of Congress in 1919, the House Immigration Committee, with Albert Johnson (R-WA) now at the helm, focused on easing standards for deportation. Legislation passed in 1920 sanctioned the expulsion of aliens who advised, advocated, taught, or published any views promoting the overthrow of government, or who were somehow affiliated with organizations which did so. As European immigration soared to 800,000 the same year, a sharp leap from the trickle of the war years, Johnson and his committee persuaded House colleagues to approve "emergency" legislation suspending immigration for one year. Many House members were galvanized by a State Department report, circulated by the immigration committee, warning that the country was receiving a large wave of "filthy" and "unassimilable" Jews displaced by persecution in eastern and central Europe.

By the time the Johnson bill reached the Senate, agricultural growers, the National Federation of Construction Industries, NAM, and other immigrant employers were aggressively lobbying against a suspension that would entirely cut off immigrant labor. As NAM president Stephen Mason protested, "such action will hamper the future expansion of industry and agricultural development in many sections."[147] But at a time when organized nationality groups were losing the political leverage they had enjoyed before the war, the Red Scare encouraged the brief yet crucial defection of key business groups from the pro-immigration camp. As William Bernard notes, "for the first time important sections of Big Business, as a result of the fear that immigrants might propagate the ideas of the Russian Revolution, took a stand for the restriction of immigration."[148]

American Industries, the leading journal of the NAM and other large industrial employers, surprised many by acknowledging the urgent need for new federal regulations on European immigration.[149] While opposed to suspending immigration, many business interests accepted a compromise offered by Dillingham: a one-year quota that limited immigration to 3 percent of each European nationality living in the United States at the time of the 1910 census.

A pocket veto by the enfeebled Wilson administration ultimately derailed the legislation, but Warren G. Harding's sweeping 1920 election on an isolationist "America First" platform signaled an end to executive resistance. "Nationalism was the vital force that turned the dearly wrought freedom of the republic to a living impelling power," Harding averred. "Nationalism inspired, assured, upbuilded."[150] At the 1920 Republican convention, a now august Senator Lodge put the matter more eloquently: "We must be now and forever for Americanism and Nationalism, and against Internationalism."[151] Harding's acceptance speech reflected profound anxieties about the radical threat "the great Red conflagration" posed to American nationhood, and he explicitly endorsed the cause of immigration restriction during the campaign.[152] Against this backdrop, the House and Senate immigration committees wasted no time in resurrecting Dillingham's quota plan in 1921. The new immigration bill retained its earlier form, but contained additional provisos limiting the number admitted in any one month to 20 percent of the annual quota; requiring legal aliens who temporarily visited abroad to be charged to the appropriate quota upon their return; and granting a preference for the wives, parents, children, brothers, sisters, and the betrothed of citizens, resident aliens who had applied for citizenship, and aliens who had served in the armed forces during the First World War. Finally, the legislation limited the total number of immigrants to 355,000 per year. With broad support in both houses, as well as the approval of the White House, the measure became the Quota Act of 1921. Congress renewed this "emergency" legislation twice, extending its coverage to 1924.

Albert Johnson, once a member of the Asiatic Exclusion League and the Dillingham Commission, believed a more permanent and restrictive quota system was desperately required. He identified closely with IRL calls for "the proper eugenic selection of the incoming alien millions." The country might improve its racial stock, the IRL advised, "not by killing off the less fit, but by preventing them from coming into the State, either by being born into it or by migration."[153] In 1923, Johnson was elected president of the Eugenics Research Association. Eager to develop fresh scientific validation for racial exclusion in immigration policy, Johnson employed an "expert eugenics agent" to study newcomers for the

House Immigration Committee. He eventually hired Harry H. Laughlin, a geneticist who supervised the Eugenics Records Office in Long Island, New York, to serve as the committee's eugenics specialist. Under these auspices, Laughlin conducted an "analysis of America's modern melting pot" that purported to show decisively that a higher percentage of southern and eastern European immigrants possessed socially inadequate qualities than northern and western Europeans. "We in this country have been so imbued with the idea of democracy, or the equality of all men," Laughlin reported in 1923, "that we have left out of consideration the matter of blood or natural inborn hereditary mental and moral differences. No man who breeds pedigreed plants and animals can afford to neglect this thing."[154] Johnson also kept in regular contact with Madison Grant, a leader of the New York IRL and the renowned author of *Passing of the Great Race* (1914), an apocalyptic account of Anglo-Saxon decline due to race mixing.

As Laughlin's work suggests, the scholarship of restrictionist intellectuals assumed more candidly racist overtones in the 1920s. Prescott Hall, for example, wrote in the *Journal of Heredity* of the urgent need to apply Darwinian principles on a global scale. As he explained,

> Eugenics among individuals is encouraging propagation of the fit, and limiting or preventing multiplication of the unfit. World eugenics is doing precisely the same thing as to races considered as wholes. Immigration restriction is a species of segregation on a large scale, by which inferior stocks can be prevented from both diluting and supplanting good stock. Just as we isolate bacterial invasions, and starve out the bacteria by limiting the area and amount of their food supply, where its over multiplication in a limited area will, as with all organisms, eventually limit its numbers.[155]

Edward Ross boasted in *Century* magazine that his "practised eye" had recognized the biological inferiority of southern and eastern Europeans as soon as they arrived on American soil. "In every face there was something wrong—lips thick, mouth coarse, upper lip too long, cheekbones too high, chin poorly formed, the bridge of the nose hollowed, or else the whole face prognathous," he wrote.[156] As American scholars attended eugenics conferences in Europe, the IRL devoted itself to "the development of public opinion" and expert research favoring new restrictions.[157]

Working closely with restrictionist groups, Johnson and the immigration committee crafted legislation in 1924 that revised the 1921 quota system.[158] The new formula assigned a quota to each nationality based on 2 percent of the number of foreign-born from that country who lived in the United States at the time of the 1890 census. The new limits promised to lower quota slots from 387,803 under the 1921 system to

186,437. In the Senate, David Reed (R-PA) championed a different quota scheme, one that calculated quotas not on the composition of the foreign-born population at a given census but on the "national origins" of the American population as a whole. Lodge, now at the twilight of his career, lent his prestige to Reed's national origins quota plan. Proponents of both bills took pains to remind lawmakers that the legislation was inspired by commission and committee immigration research.

Reed and Johnson ultimately agreed upon a compromise between their respective quota plans. Madison Grant assured Johnson that the new plan would reserve 84 percent of the immigration slots for northern and western Europeans and 12 percent for southern and eastern Europeans (see table 5.3). The harmonized measure was passed by overwhelming majorities in both houses, and was signed by Calvin Coolidge, who supported immigration restriction. The Immigration Act of 1924 stipulated that Johnson's 1890 census formula was to operate until July 1927, after which Reed's national origins quotas were to take effect. In addition to maintaining an "Asiatic barred zone," the Reed-Johnson Act called for Japanese exclusion to be phased in during 1925. Immigrants

TABLE 5.3

A Comparison of the Immigration Quota Laws of 1921 and 1924

	Immigration Act of 1921	Reed-Johnson Act of 1924
Quota scheme	Immigration limited to 3% per year of each European nationality already residing in the U.S., using figures from the 1910 census	Immigration limited to 2% per year of each nationality already residing in the U.S., using figures from the 1890 census
Annual ceiling	387,803	186,437
Projected distribution	northern and western Europe: 55% southern and eastern Europe: 45%	northern and western Europe: 84% southern and eastern Europe: 16%
Additional restrictions	No more than 20% of quota alloted in any one month Return of resident aliens visiting abroad to be charged against quota	Asiatic Barred Zone created Gradual Japanese exclusion Preference for "near relatives"

who were exempted from the quota system included citizens' wives and children under eighteen years of age, professors, ministers, and Western Hemisphere natives—the latter a concession secured by southern Democrats and Western lawmakers who relied on cheap Mexican labor. Within the quotas, preferences were to be given to older children and parents of citizens, immediate family of certain alien residents, and immigrants with agricultural skills. At the urging of ethnic associations, congressional members from Northern urban districts defended exemptions and preferences for "near relatives."[159] The new system of national origins quotas helped secure what the literacy test had not: a dramatic reduction of southern and eastern European immigration. "The United States is our land," a jubilant Albert Johnson proclaimed. "The day of unalloyed welcome to all peoples, the day of indiscriminate acceptance of all races, has definitely ended."[160] The national origins quota system would be deferred twice by Congress in 1927 and 1928, but then enjoyed a tenure beginning in 1929 that endured well into the 1960s.

CONCLUSION

For some reformers, the national origins quota system was a necessary government response to the insecurities of modern industrial economic life. Many within the ranks of organized labor premised their support for sweeping restrictions in this period on the real or imagined costs of immigrant labor to working-class citizens. This perspective was shared by those social reformers who believed that "the effectual restriction of immigration is absolutely necessary if we are to raise the American standard of living and reduce the mass of poverty that still exists."[161]

The construction of a restrictionist regime also promised potent new forms of social control at a time when American self-defense against foreigners seemed more crucial than ever. The breakdown of nineteenth-century society breathed life into "a new national self-awareness," as Barry Karl has put it, and "a sense that the complexities of modern life required a kind of observation and control of the lives of others that threatened older ideas of freedom."[162] Prohibition and Americanization imposed a regimented morality designed to melt away differences thought to endanger democracy and national unity. Similarly, sweeping immigration restrictions promised to insulate the country from disquieting international forces, especially political radicalism . As the *New Republic* concluded, unfettered European immigration was the luxury of an era when the demands on the state for social justice and control were few:

> Freedom of migration from one country to another appears to be one of the elements of nineteenth century liberalism that is fated to disappear. The responsibility of the state for the welfare of its individual

members is progressively increasing. The democracy of today cannot permit . . . social ills to be aggravated by excessive immigration.[163]

But if economic and national security were important concerns of early-twentieth-century immigration reformers, the primary intent and effect of their national origins quota system were manifestly racist. In the face of increasing ethnic pluralism, restrictionists saw the literacy test and national origins quotas as means of "rationally" controlling the nation's ethnic and racial composition. American nativists perceived clear physical and racial differences among Europeans (for example, as Matthew Frye Jacobson documents, it was widely believed at the time that one could see Jewishness and other forms of racial difference among white Europeans).[164] Eugenics provided scientific confirmation of these racist conclusions, offering seemingly powerful evidence that immigrants from southern and eastern Europe lacked the advanced hereditary makeup of earlier immigrant groups. Smith reminds us that strong inegalitarian ideologies long have flourished alongside liberal and democratic values, finding persistent expression in the development of the country's political thought, institutions, and policies.[165] More than a fleeting exception, ethnic and racial hierarchies were firmly embedded as the defining feature of American immigration policy for nearly half a century.

However, it is important to remember that proponents of national origins quotas, like Chinese exclusionists before them, fused liberal and racist ideas in making their case for restriction. Lowell and other nativists celebrated American liberal principles in their calls to close the gates, arguing that Western democratic societies could not accommodate ethnic and racial pluralism and still maintain popular government, individual rights, the rule of law, and a healthy marketplace. The IRL's preoccupation with scientific justifications for immigration restriction reflected, as King astutely discerns, a perspective deeply infused with liberal enlightenment standards of rational justification for policy choices.[166] In short, the entanglement of liberal and racist ideas in early-twentieth-century immigration debates raises important questions about whether liberal and illiberal traditions have in practice warred with one another as philosophical rivals in American political development.

As policy innovations clearly inspired by xenophobic and racist intentions, Chinese exclusion and national origins quotas might understandably tempt one to adopt a simple functional or cultural model of immigration control in which new restrictions are triggered by the hostilities of native-born Americans to outsiders deemed racially suspect. Writing on the "centrality of race" in U.S. immigration policymaking, Ellis Cose suggests that "racial animosity" in immigration politics resembles "a virus that at times lives dormant but can suddenly erupt with a vengeance" when unwanted groups arrive.[167] But Cose also recognizes that immigration controls are the product of complex processes that can filter or defy racial and ethnic tensions between the native-born and immigrants. The problem with simple functional or cultural explanations is, of course, that immigration policies both before this period and later in the century were often at odds with the surges of restrictionist sentiment that greeted each wave of new immigrants. Moreover, the political and institutional processes that propelled Chinese exclusion and national origins quotas contrast significantly. Both of these restrictive breakthroughs departed decisively from the traditional path of federal immigration policy begun at the nation's founding. But they did so for markedly different reasons.

Focusing on the specific mechanisms that reinforced pro-immigration policies toward Europeans in the nineteenth century, we readily see why these processes were not in play for Chinese newcomers.[168] Whereas large-scale European inflows and easy naturalization gave dominant political parties ample electoral (and mercantalist) incentive to reaffirm expansive policies, Chinese came in smaller number, were ineligible for citizenship, and thus served as easy targets for party leaders competing for crucial Western votes. However powerful the self-reinforcing dynamics of expansive European admissions and naturalization policies in the Gilded Age, their reach did not extend to disenfranchised Chinese immigrants. In short, Chinese exclusionists did not so much disrupt as elude the mechanisms that had reproduced pro-immigration policies since the early republic.

The restriction of southern and eastern European immigration, by contrast, required the wholesale breakdown of "reproductive mechanisms" animating expansive admissions policies. Like earlier European groups, southern and eastern Europeans arrived in large number, easily acquired voting rights, were defended by powerful ethnic and business interests, and were courted by major party leaders. Processes of increasing returns or positive feedback thus endured, encouraging policy equilibrium.[169] But the social and political landscape is not permanently frozen, and new developments can dislodge a long-lasting equilibrium.[170] Progressive political reforms fundamentally weakened the power of political parties whose centrality to nineteenth-century American politics was critical to sustaining expansive immigration policies. To broaden popular participation and weaken the hold of party leaders in American politics, Progressives embraced the direct primary, ballot initiatives, suffrage for women, and the direct election of senators. In Congress, Speaker Cannon was overthrown and the seniority system was adopted. The purpose of these measures was to loosen the hold of party leaders over both houses and to insulate independent lawmakers from the wrath of these leaders. Successful Progressive efforts to elevate "scientific government" and such principles as "expertise" in the policymaking process were by definition hostile to the decentralized and partisan system of nineteenth-century politics. If the Progressives' twin devotion to "direct democracy" and decisionmaking by experts seem incompatible, Brian Balogh and John Kingdon remind us that both ideals targeted political parties for attack as the corrupt agents of concentrated wealth and privilege.[171] The effect of these reforms was to erode the strongest nineteenth-century institutional and political supports of pro-immigration policies. When immigration defenders set about to build new mechanisms for reproducing policy equilibrium, they were undermined by the prevailing tenor of social-scientific expertise and intense protectionist impulses that grew out of the First World War and the Red Scare.

For their part, Progressive nativists made the most of the political opportunities afforded by significant changes in both American political institutions and the international order. Explicitly committed to transcending traditional party politics, the Immigration Restriction League and its allies pursued direct influence with national legislators, administration officials, and commissioners across partisan lines. They were unusually attentive to fact gathering and the scientific findings of congressional committees and special investigatory commissions, recognizing the growing prominence of expertise in Progressive Era policymaking and the particular reverence policymakers accorded eugenicist conclusions about immigrant groups.

Although the intellectual convictions of immigration experts would change over time, their prominent role in shaping policy paradigms and outcomes would become a fixture of American immigration politics. Once national origins quotas and Asian exclusion were established in the immigration code by the late 1920s, restrictionists worked to establish fresh mechanisms for maintaining their new policy regime. One of the most important sources of restrictionist policy equilibrium in ensuing decades was the chair of the standing Immigration Committee, in each house of Congress, who was almost invariably a Southern or Western conservative and who worked closely with nativist groups to frustrate pro-immigration reformers seeking to dismantle national origins quotas. Their power was buoyed by the seniority system and a formidable "conservative coalition" of Southern Democrats and Western Republicans. "It is only necessary to defeat movements of repeal," a restrictionist celebrated in 1928. "The burden of proof is on the anti-restrictionists."[172] Legislative opportunity points of the Progressive Era were transformed into formidable veto-points for half a century to follow. As the next chapter elucidates, restrictionist committee barons were also quite attentive to guarding their policy commitments in the administrative realm by taking pains to fashion a distinctively nativist implementation process.

CHAPTER SIX

Two-Tiered Implementation

JEWISH REFUGEES, MEXICAN GUESTWORKERS, AND ADMINISTRATIVE POLITICS

THE LEGISLATIVE ACHIEVEMENTS of immigration restrictionists in the 1920s were staggering. The Quota Acts marked a regulatory shift of unprecedented scale, one that decisively ended the path national immigration policy had followed for more than a century. The 1929 quota plan set an annual ceiling for legal immigrant admissions at 153,714, a sharp decrease from the annual average of roughly 700,000 immigrants since the turn of the century. By design, the vast majority of these cherished immigration slots were reserved for northern and western Europeans; Greek, Hungarian, Italian, Polish, and Russian quotas soon produced ten- to seventy-five-year waiting lists. But even as nativist political actors built a strong legal foundation for their restrictionist regime, they had nagging fears that their policy aims would be compromised in the administrative realm. In particular, the IRL and other advocacy groups worried that lax enforcement by the Immigration Bureau would provide openings for Europeans at immigration stations like Ellis Island and for Latin Americans along the United States–Mexican border.[1] For these reasons, restrictionist groups pressed for innovations in bureaucratic structure and practices that were equal to their legislative breakthroughs. They proved to be only partially successful in their efforts to dominate the implementation process.

What ultimately emerged in the 1930s and 1940s was a two-tiered immigration bureaucracy. One layer of immigration control was administered by new State Department agencies and consular officials who eagerly employed broad exclusionary powers overseas to all but shut down European and Asian immigration. A second layer administered by the Immigration Bureau and Labor Department focused on Western Hemisphere immigration and came to be dominated by a formidable "iron triangle" that promoted legal and illegal entry of Latin and South American guestworkers. Several distinctive factors lay behind each of these administrative processes, but both reflected the policy preferences of Southern and Western conservatives, who wielded enormous power in

Congress generally and on the Immigration Committees (later subcommittees) particularly during this period. As we shall see, the resolve of nativist immigration committee barons and their allies to maintain formidable legal and administrative barriers against Europeans and Asians whom they perceived as racially inferior was unshakable. But many nativist lawmakers—especially influential immigration committee members—represented Southern and Western regions where agricultural growers pressured for cheap foreign farm labor. The two-tiered immigration bureaucracy that emerged was at once draconian toward overseas immigrants and strikingly tolerant toward the importation of temporary workers across the nation's Southern border. This chapter focuses on the legal and administrative experiences of two groups for whom this bifurcated regulatory system had particularly fateful consequences: Jewish refugees and Mexican farmworkers.

Appallingly few Jewish refugees who sought sanctuary in the United States from the rise of the Nazi regime until the end of the Second World War secured authorized entry. The frustrations of European Jewry and their American kin during this period captures how impenetrable the admissions process was for southern and eastern Europeans with even the most compelling moral claims for refuge. Responding to modern critics who charge that the Roosevelt administration could have done more to open America's gates to desperate European Jews, Peter Novick argues effectively that the Great Depression, the restrictionist sentiment of both the general public and Congress, and Roosevelt's foreign policy priorities meant that any alteration of existing quota limits was simply not feasible "as a practical political matter."[2] In his zeal to revise prevailing accounts of U.S. abandonment of European Jewry, however, Novick overstates his case by insisting that the American immigration regime was not particularly resistant to Jewish refugees and did not single them out for special discrimination. To be sure, the existing quota system afforded little or no room in the implementation process to admit Jewish refugees above and beyond annual limits. Yet whether *all* quota slots were to be made available in any given year and *who* was to occupy those slots were decisions over which administrators exercised enormous control. In the pages that follow, I present evidence that the State Department's Visa Bureau and consular officers were especially resistant to Jewish refugees and often did use their discretion to target European Jews for harsh treatment.

In strong contrast to the sweeping scope and stringent character of restrictions imposed on Asian and European immigration in the 1930s and 1940s, no concerted effort was made by the federal government to limit entry of aliens from Western Hemisphere countries. Indeed, bureaucrats and members of Congress not only allowed, but invited, Mexican immigration in this period. Through administrative initiatives and eventually legislation, policymakers aggressively recruited a large supply of Mexican guestsworkers to provide primarily cheap agricultural labor in what became known as the Bracero Program.[3] Moreover, the surreptitious entry and presence of undocumented Mexican aliens in the United States typically was met by uneven and lax enforcement (usually during harvest seasons). Southern and Western lawmakers were quick to point out that nonwhite Mexicans, unlike Asians and southern and eastern Europeans, could be easily expelled across the southern border and thus posed little danger of becoming permanent and full members of American society. Mexican labor inflows would be sustained for decades by an iron triangle of Southwestern growers, Immigration Bureau officials, and powerful congressional committees dominated by Southern and Western conservatives. The administrative structures and practices governing Jewish refugees and Mexican farmworkers in this period provide vivid portraits of the two-tiered regulatory system that executed American immigration policy until after the Second World War.

CLOSING THE FRONT DOOR: VISA AND CONSULAR REVIEW

In a recent cross-national study, John Torpey attributes the origins of passport and visa systems among countries of the North Atlantic to the "general rise of the protectionist state out of the fires of the First World War."[4] As did its European counterparts, the United States developed a visa system and complementary State Department agencies as a form of self-defense against foreigners considered dangerous or inferior. But the U.S. establishment of "remote border control," to borrow Aristide Zolberg's apt phrase, was particularly colored by the restrictionist movement's past frustrations with the Immigration Bureau. For restrictionists, the Immigration Bureau's implementation of national laws at U.S. immigration stations like Ellis Island was at best uneven due to changing management and priorities, inadequate budgetary and personnel resources, and vulnerability to external pressure from pro-immigration politicians and interest groups.

From the start, neither the pro-immigration nor restrictionist coalition trusted the discretion of Immigration Bureau officials. Galvanized by reports of immigration inspectors and medical staff accepting bribes from steamship and railroad companies, nativist groups established a presence at immigration stations around the country in the 1890s for the purpose of "watching inspection and calling attention to inefficiency and violations of law."[5] Ethnic, religious, and immigrant aid associations were equally concerned about the discretion of inspectors and also maintained a presence at immigration stations. "The power conferred on the inspectors [is] of the most arbitrary character," Louis Marshall of the AJC cautioned in 1907. "He will soon regard himself as Czar."[6] The political crosswinds that riddled the Immigration Bureau manifested themselves most dramatically in response to Bureau appointments. Key appointees, such as Labor and Commerce secretaries, the commissioner general of Immigration, and the immigration commissioner of Ellis Island, faced tough scrutiny from policy activists. Whereas pro-immigration groups and politicians hounded appointees like William Williams for their strict enforcement of the law, their restrictionist rivals dogged Robert Watchorn and other officials who they believed were co-opted by business and ethnic-group pressures.[7]

Jewish bureaucratic managers were especially suspect. Joseph Senner, a former Jew of German Austrian birth who served as immigration commissioner for the federal immigration station in New York in the 1890s, was thought by nativist political actors to be quietly sabotaging immigration standards on behalf of Jewish immigrants. On one occasion, the restrictionist Senate Immigration Committee chair William Chandler interrogated Senner about what nativist groups alleged was a Jewish conspiracy at Ellis Island:

Chandler: Of your 13 inspectors, are any Jews?

Senner: I think one is.

Chandler: I have a letter . . . which says that several inspectors are Jews, and they have combined in eluding immigration laws. What is your religion?

Senner: I am a Christian.

Chandler: Have you ever been a Jew?

Senner: I have.

Chandler: When did you change?

Senner: Long ago.

Chandler later told reporters that Senner was unfit to serve as an immigration commissioner, arguing that "a native American should tend the gate."[8] Years later nativist organizations were convinced that the Jewish Labor and Commerce secretary Oscar Straus was working behind the scenes to "break down the law."[9] In general, restrictionists saw the Immigration Bureau as inefficient, corrupt, and unduly influenced by pro-immigration ethnic, religious, and business interests.

As nativist reformers devised numerical schemes for limiting southern and eastern European immigration in the early-twentieth century, they also set about building a bureaucratic structure that was more insulated from the vagaries of electoral politics and pro-immigration pressure groups. The House Immigration Committee and its activist chair, Albert Johnson, took the lead in recasting the administrative process. His committee won passage of the Passport Control Act of 1918, designed to protect the country from enemy agents during the war by adding a second layer to the immigration review process. Before aliens were permitted to arrive at American immigration stations, they were now required to first obtain a visa from American consuls or accredited representatives abroad. Enacted as temporary wartime safeguards, entry visas and consular examinations soon appealed to nativist lawmakers and groups as a promising long-term solution to their administrative woes.

Under the terms of the Passport Control Act, consular inspections and visa requirements were scheduled to expire at the war's end. However, dozens of consular officers later urged State Department superiors and congressional immigration committees to retain the visa system, warning that the country remained vulnerable to national security threats. One journalist detected other motivations, suggesting that "these representatives, having built up a visa machinery and acquired added wealth and importance, were naturally loath to relinquish this power and to scrap their organization."[10] Whatever the motivation, the State Department and congressional majorities agreed that a short-term extension of consular powers would help prevent "agitators and other dangerous persons" from entering the country.

In contrast to restrictionists' uneven relationship with the Immigration Bureau, Albert Johnson and the House immigration committee enjoyed consistent cooperation from State Department officials. When Johnson was in need of material to bolster his 1921 immigration suspension bill, Wilbur J. Carr of the Consular Bureau issued a lengthy official statement warning that a stream of more than 5 million "physically and socially deficient" Jewish aliens were clamoring to enter the United States. Carr paraphrased reports of American consuls in Vienna, Berlin, Warsaw, and other European cities describing Jewish applicants as "a class of economic parasites"—"filthy, un-American, and often dangerous in their habits."[11] The House committee's special "eugenics agent," Harry Laughlin, collected considerable data regarding the racial inferiority of southern and eastern Europeans by "collaborating with the Consular Service."[12] "I have not only secured a mass of new material through American consular offices," Laughlin told Johnson, "but I have also made some first-hand field studies into the case histories and family stocks of would-be immigrants."[13] Congressional restrictionists and consular officers of the State Department shared a close working relationship in the twenties, one that was forged on a shared vision of ethnic and racial hierarchy.

Significantly, officials of the Immigration Bureau and the Labor Department welcomed consular examinations and visa controls following the First World War. Warren Harding's commissioner at Ellis Island, Robert Tod, did not relish the thought of untold numbers of aliens teeming to American shores during his tenure. After completing a tour of

American consulates in Europe, Tod strongly endorsed screening aliens overseas on a permanent basis. Tod approvingly observed that aliens examined overseas were less likely to gain entry into the United States than those inspected at Ellis Island, where they "can appeal to the Courts here and with the powerful assistance of different organizations will succeed in landing."[14] Labor secretary James Davis later sounded similar themes in support of "moving our inspection machinery abroad." Screening aliens on American soil engendered a "clamor by well-meaning individuals, organizations, and newspapers," Davis told the White House, making enforcement "exceedingly difficult." Many inadmissible southern and eastern Europeans gained entry into the United States, he warned, because of "the efforts of friends, relatives, and members of his own racial group, to influence immigration officials to waive the restrictions and admit him." Eager to liberate the Labor Department from headaches associated with immigration control, especially its virulent political cross-pressures, Davis embraced the State Department's new role in controlling immigration. "If we halt these cases before they leave their native countries we will end the troubles at our ports of entry," he noted.[15]

During congressional debates over the future of the visa system and consular review, the State Department assured pro-immigration activists that consular officials would never be able to "regulate the rise and fall of the immigration tide." The 1924 Quota Act mandated on a permanent basis that all European immigrants obtain an entry visa and pass a consular inspection overseas prior to their embarkation to the United States. To implement this new screening process, the Consular Bureau was complemented by a new Visa Bureau, created out of the former visa section of the State Department's Passport Control Division. In addition, technical advisers and medical examiners of the Immigration Bureau were stationed at American consulates to assist in the examination process.

Critics soon charged that the Consular and Visa Bureaus had established arbitrary and labyrinthine rules that demonstrated "unmistakable prejudice against Jewish immigrants."[16] Washington bureau officials instructed consular examiners that all aliens with passports from states that were formerly parts of Russia were "per se suspicious and should be scrutinized with particular care."[17] The Visa Bureau instructed its agents to be equally suspicious of anyone presenting a passport of a country other than that of which she was a subject or citizen. Tellingly, most immigrants from former Russian states were Jews, and most seeking entry into the United States had fled their native countries. "The powers of the chief of the Visa Office are almost unlimited, and appeal against his decision is practically impossible,"wrote journalist Reuben Fink.[18]

Immigration restriction became even more severe during the Great Depression. President Herbert Hoover issued an executive order in 1930 calling for "strict enforcement" of section 3 of the Immigration Act of 1917, barring aliens deemed "likely to become a public charge"—often called the LPC clause. "[T]here is serious unemployment among all wage earners in this country," Washington instructed consular officers. "The result is that any alien wage earner without special means of support coming to the U.S. during the present period of depression is, therefore, likely to become a public charge."[19] Most working-class aliens were deemed inadmissible, even those guaranteed financial sponsorship by organizations like the AJC and HIAS. During the 1932 presidential election, the Hoover campaign appealed to unemployed voters by stressing that tougher enforcement of the LPC clause had resulted in a 94 percent *underissue* of available quota slots. Legal immigration plummeted from 242,00 in 1931 to 36,000 in 1932 (fewer than 3,000 visas went to Jews).

THE NAZI REGIME AND EARLY EFFORTS TO RESCUE EUROPEAN JEWRY

The Nazi party's rise to power in 1933 Germany ushered in a succession of anti-Jewish measures. Jewish stores, products, and services were officially boycotted by Germans. The Law for the Restoration of the Professional Service and subsequent decrees prohibited Jews from occupying positions in public administration, education, journalism, the arts, public health, transportation, banking, and numerous other fields. Horrified by this first phase of official persecution, tens of thousands of German Jews sought refuge in other countries.

Even before the specter of Nazism, American Jewish groups protested Consular and Visa Bureau practices that disadvantaged Russian and Eastern European Jews. But several American Jewish leaders discerned an unprecedented urgency for German Jews . As Morris Waldman, secretary of the AJC, told his Executive Committee:

> The incredible has happened. And the Jews of the world are shaken to their depths. . . . [W]hat has happened to the Jews in Germany (and indirectly to the Jews of the world) is worse even than the expulsion of the Jews from Spain. It not only involves the possible extermination of 600,000 Jews, but threatens to react dangerously upon the political, social, and economic status of the Jews in other countries. . . . We have a tremendous job on our hands, not a passing episode, but one that threatens to be a problem for a long time. . . . Many civilized countries of the world will have to be enlisted—to offer shelter to the refugees.[20]

The AJC resolved to recruit "brains, money, and influence" to rescue German refugees. Other Jewish organizations agreed that "emigration is the only hope."[21] Efforts to influence the State Department and the

Roosevelt White House began in earnest.[22] In March 1933, Rabbi Stephen Wise urged FDR to revoke Hoover's executive order "as a part of the New Deal."[23]

Many prominent Americans lent their support to the cause of Jewish refugees in 1933. ACLU director Roger Baldwin counseled Jewish leaders that "the only way to persuade Mr. Roosevelt to act is to bring the matter forcefully to his attention from non-Jewish sources."[24] Under Baldwin's leadership, luminaries like Jane Addams, Reinhold Niebuhr, Lillian Wald, and Charles Beard publicly challenged New Deal reformers to advance the American "tradition of asylum." They thought it politically wise to stress that "not only German Jews, but other Germans opposed to the present government of Germany" were in danger, and urged an executive order requiring the State Department to grant visas to "bona-fide political or religious refugees."[25] An array of church groups also called for the admission of German refugees, pledging to sponsor needy aliens who might become public charges. The Consular and Visa Bureaus of the State Department were unfazed by these pressures. When a delegation of Jewish leaders attempted to meet with State Department officials in 1933, they were informed that the official with the most discretion over visa issuance, Wilbur Carr, was "on vacation."[26] It was Carr who so unabashedly allied himself with Albert Johnson and other nativists in Congress during the late-1910s and 1920s, and who issued the 1920 report warning of an impending invasion of racially inferior Jewish refugees. Little wonder that Jewish policy activists placed "very little hope" in gaining assistance from the State Department.[27] "This branch of the State Department under your charge has been deliberately discriminating in practice, if not avowedly, against Jews, immigrants or otherwise," a frustrated Max Kohler wrote Carr, "and committed itself to the un-American and ridiculous 'Nordic' theory."[28]

What surprised Jewish advocacy groups most was not the State Department's intransigence, but the silence of the White House. Policy activists wondered why Roosevelt had carefully avoided official conferences with Jewish organizations about the German refugee crisis. "Surely he recognizes that the situation is too serious for the State Department to hide behind legal verbiage" to exclude Jewish refugees, B'nai B'rith's I. M. Rubinow fumed.[29] At press conferences, Roosevelt referred all questions regarding the plight of German Jews to the State Department.[30] FDR's public reticence on the issue undoubtedly reflected what he saw as basic political realities. Confident in Jewish support for the New Deal (the prominence of Jewish advisers in the Roosevelt administration led anti-Semites to call it the "Jew Deal"), the White House was reluctant to antagonize Southern Democrats and key elements of organized labor over the refugee issue. As much as Roosevelt distanced himself from anti-lynching legislation opposed by Southern politicians, he had similar incentives to say little publicly about Jewish refugee relief. More importantly, the Depression was at full tilt, and the only immigration reforms entertained seriously by Congress in this period were popular proposals to cut immigration further.

Labor secretary Frances Perkins did meet with Jewish leaders concerning the plight of European Jewry in 1933 and later years, and she became one of their most supportive advocates within the Roosevelt administration. With the Immigration Bureau under the supervision of her department, Perkins attempted to circumvent the LPC clause by allowing private groups to provide bonds for Jewish refugees who might become public charges.[31] In 1933, Perkins also appointed a special committee of prominent citizens to evaluate "the general amenities in the administration of the immigration."[32] While recognizing the need for immigration control amidst widespread unemployment, the committee recommended that administrators extend "special consideration" to relatives of citizens and resident aliens ("the family constitutes the foundation and strength of our society") and to refugees ("asylum for those who flee from religious, racial and political persecution is one of the oldest and most valued of American traditions").[33] While refusing to revoke Hoover's order regarding strict enforcement of the LPC clause, Roosevelt instructed consular officials in 1934 to accord refugees "the most humane and favorable treatment possible under law."[34]

Such efforts to ease administrative practices on behalf of Jewish refugees encountered strong resistance from the Consular and Visa Bureaus. Refugee advocates demonstrated that Jewish immigration admissions in fact *declined* in the months following FDR's 1934 instructions to consular officers. The Immigration Bureau, which became the Immigration and Naturalization Service (INS) under a 1933 executive order, assumed a similar stance when it informed all of its personnel serving at American consuls overseas that "the economic situation" continued to dictate "a rigid application of the public-charge clause." Consular officials required Jews to present letters from "bankers or other reputable persons" of their native country attesting to their good character, irrespective of whether they were subject to official persecution. In addition, American consuls were urged to share information about excluded aliens so that cases would not be reheard at a different consular office. "There is no appeal from the consul's [initial] decision," Washington officials told inspectors.[35] As the *New York Times* reported, German Jews faced "double barriers" since U.S. consuls required evidence of economic self-sufficiency while Nazi officials prevented émigrés from removing capital from Germany.[36]

The immigration bureaucracy looked quite different at Ellis Island. Early in his term, Roosevelt named an Italian immigrant and social worker, Edward Corsi, as the Ellis Island commissioner. His immigrant service background made him an instant favorite of ethnic associations. But Corsi was largely irrelevant to the implementation of admissions policy; he soon found that "deportation was the big business at Ellis Island."[37] Earlier, the liberal interpretation of immigration statutes by Straus and Watchorn aided thousands of Europeans streaming through Ellis Island and other immigration stations. Three decades later, another pair of immigration defenders, Perkins and Corsi, held virtually the same offices but had little influence on the immigrant screening process. That power now rested largely with new State Department agencies and consular officials.

POLITICAL RESISTANCE TO JEWISH REFUGEES

Nineteenth-century political leaders of varied ideological stripes celebrated the ideal of asylum as a special commitment of the American polity. Yet the restrictionist policy regime that emerged in the early-twentieth century made almost no distinction between refugees and other immigrants. Only the Immigration Act of 1917 waived the literacy test for those escaping political or religious persecution. Refugees essentially confronted the same admissions barriers as immigrants: national origins quotas, various physical, mental, and moral tests, and strict bureaucratic application of the LPC clause.

Several Jewish policy activists privately criticized Roosevelt for failing to take direct action on behalf of German Jews in his first term. Some noted the irony that White House inaction occurred at a time when so many prominent American Jews had been elevated to key political posts. "As yet our great and progressive American government has not shown any particular anxiety to open the doors to Jewish immigrants from Germany," Rubinow wrote Kohler in frustration. "I would rather see a hundred Jews brought in from Germany than any high dignitary of the Jewish faith in Washington."[38] When New York governor Herbert Lehman protested to the White House in 1935 and 1936 that Roosevelt's directive to American consuls regarding "favorable treatment" of Jews was routinely ignored, FDR reissued his instructions.[39] But beyond that, the administration was quiet on the matter.

White House reticence on the refugee issue was a barometer of the formidable political opposition to any relaxation of existing restrictions. Whereas Al Smith pressed Democrats to "vindicate the principles on which this nation was established by making room here for our share of the refugees from Germany," organized labor and Southern Democrats opposed such action.[40] Critical of Nazi persecution of Jews and trade unionists, the AFL joined Jewish groups in boycotting German goods.[41] But at its 1933 convention, AFL members rejected special admissions for

German refugees. "There is not a country in the world where there is not religious or political persecutions," delegates concluded.[42] Southern Democrats also assailed refugee relief. "We must ignore the tears of sobbing sentimentalists and internationalists, and we must permanently close, lock, and bar the gates of our country to new immigration waves and then throw the keys away," Representative Martin Dies (D-TX) declared in 1934.[43] Southern demagogues directly tied unemployment to immigration. "If we had refused admission to the 16,500,000 foreign born who are living in this country today," one House member declared, "we would have no unemployment problem."[44] The Depression unquestionably muted moral claims for refugee relief. Even in New York, rumors swirled of domestic workers being replaced by German refugees.[45]

At the same time, eugenics research continued to offer pseudoscientific validation for basing immigration preferences on prevailing notions of racial hierarchy. With support from the Carnegie Institution and the New York Chamber of Commerce, former House eugenics agent Harry Laughlin studied 246 mental health institutions and prisons. Based on this research, he issued a well-publicized report in 1934 denouncing any "exceptional admission for Jews who are refugees from persecution in Germany." "Scientific investigation" demonstrated the need for "race-standards" to determine national immigration policy. The crucial question policymakers should ask themselves, he added, was whether they would want certain foreigners as "sons-in-laws to marry their own daughters."[46]

Jewish critics pointed out that eugenics research bore a "suspicious resemblance" to Aryan theories espoused by the Nazi regime.[47] The *New York Times* noted that "human beings are not fruit-flies living in a bottle-world under control," and questioned whether there was a "scientific way of determining what races are assimilable."[48] Moreover, the prominence of Niebuhr, Beard, and other leading academics in the campaign to rescue Jewish refugees perhaps signaled a gradual scholarly retreat from scientific racism. Nevertheless, scientific arguments for "race-standards" continued to appeal to immigration decisionmakers, especially those in Congress and the State Department.

VETO POLITICS: REFUGEES AND CONSERVATIVES IN CONGRESS, 1938–1942

Numerous advocacy groups and politicians expressed new alarm about the worsening plight of European Jews in the late 1930s. Germany's annexation of Austria in 1938 helped mobilize the White House. Soon after the Austrian *Anschluss*, Roosevelt called for an international conference to discuss means of assisting German and Austrian refugees. Yet

State Department invitations to twenty-nine European and Latin American countries signaled the conference's limited scope by stipulating that "no country would be expected or asked to receive a greater number of immigrants than is permitted by its existing legislation."[49] At a press conference the same month, Roosevelt bristled at the suggestion that refugee relief efforts focused on German and Austrian Jews. "It means a great many Christians, too, a very large number," he insisted. Roosevelt also served notice that all German and Austrian quota slots would be made available (consular officials had routinely underissued quota slots in past years). But as one reporter observed, the combined annual quotas of Germany and Austria amounted to only 26,000 slots at a time when hundreds of thousands of refugees needed asylum. When pressed whether he favored legislation "to relax our immigration laws," FDR stated that there would be "no change in the law."[50]

Roosevelt still had compelling reasons to tread lightly on the refugee issue. When *Fortune* magazine surveyed ordinary citizens in 1938, 86 percent said they opposed emergency increases in immigration quotas to aid "German, Austrian and other refugees."[51] Worsening economic conditions stiffened the opposition of Congress to any loosening of existing immigration restrictions. Finally, geopolitical priorities discouraged a more heroic administration position. As Novick notes, "Roosevelt had to convince the public at large, and in particular nativists and isolationists, that the greater involvement he sought in the European conflict was in the national interest—a matter of self-defense, not some globalist do-gooding; he was not letting Jewish interests determine American policy."[52]

The White House hoped that revoking Hoover's LPC order would make existing quotas fully available to refugees. In April, Roosevelt issued an executive order merging the meager Austrian quota with that of Germany, permitting Austrian refugees to have access to a larger number of quota slots. During the summer of 1938, representatives of European and Latin American countries met in Evian-les-Bains, France to deliberate on the German-Austrian refugee crisis. The Evian conference ultimately accomplished little, a result preordained by the fact that participating countries were not expected to ease restrictive immigration policies on behalf of political and religious refugees.

Despite modest White House efforts to help German and Austrian refugees within quota limits, bureaucratic resistance endured. INS personnel stationed in consular offices overseas were informed that the likelihood of refugees becoming public charges "must be considered dispassionately, in spite of the tragic circumstances surrounding their plight."[53] The State Department denied visitors' visas to refugees who could not obtain immigrant visas within quota limits. As Frances Perkins discovered,

In the earliest stages of the European situation which began with the annexation of Austria to Germany, there was . . . great pressure on our consular officers abroad to issue visitors' visas for refugees who could not get positions on the regular quota. The State Department promptly sent an officer abroad to instruct all consuls personally that visitors' visas should only be issued to aliens having an unrelinquished domicile in the country of their nationality and a provable intention of returning there.[54]

American consuls also required German and Austrian visa applicants to obtain police certification of good character. Only after the ACLU and Jewish advocacy groups notified the White House of this practice were such requirements waived for political and religious refugees.

Nazi persecution of the Jews intensified after a German diplomat was killed in Paris by a Jewish assassin. Nazi Storm Troopers and angry mobs responded by attacking Jewish stores, hospitals, schools, synagogues, and homes on November 9, 1938. Kristalnacht—the night of broken glass— was accompanied by a demand from the German government that German Jewry pay a fine of nearly $400 million for allegedly conspiring in the diplomat's death. New segregation laws also were imposed against Jews, and more than 60,000 were arrested and forced into concentration camps.[55]

In response, Roosevelt recalled his German ambassador and ordered an extension of visitors' visas for 15,000 refugees already in the United States. The escalation of persecution and violence against European Jews engendered new support for the refugee relief movement. Since 1933, a core of Jewish advocacy groups, Protestant and Catholic organizations, the ACLU, social workers, and liberal academics hoped to rescue European Jewry. After Kristalnacht, they were joined by growing numbers of artists, entertainers, academics, and politicians, as well as the NAACP and a new force in the American labor movement, the Congress of Industrial Organizations (CIO). The AFL also voiced concern about the plight of European Jews, but it remained opposed to special admissions for refugees.

The contrasting AFL and CIO positions reflect the fact the American labor movement was in transition during the 1930s, as surging union membership was accompanied by new schisms. In this period, groups within the labor movement pressured the AFL to organize nonunionized industrial workers of the steel, automobile, rubber, textile, and other industries of mass production. John L. Lewis, president of the United Mine Workers, headed a contingent of industrial labor leaders who demanded AFL assistance in organizing nonunionized industries. Their goal was to join workers under one industrial, or "vertical," union. However, this vision was at odds with the craft union tradition forged by Gompers and still promoted by AFL leadership. That is, the AFL continued to celebrate the "horizontal" organization of workers of similar skills or trades. The AFL's trade union tradition encouraged a nativist political agenda. Whereas new immigrants from southern and eastern Europe tended to work in unorganized industries, AFL trade unions were dominated by older ethnic groups. Thus, the American labor movement's approach toward immigration was shaped largely by the interests of native-born members far removed from their own immigrant past. However, a new labor order was ushered in by Lewis's 1935 formation of the CIO, one in which workers of southern and eastern European background figured prominently. From the start, the CIO was more favorably disposed to immigration than was the AFL and was willing to override quota limits on behalf of refugees.

Although the AFL opposed nonquota status for Jewish refugees, Nazi persecution of European labor leaders and Jewish labor groups led the AFL Executive Committee to denounce anti-Semitism. "Religious persecution is a matter of deep concern for Labor," an AFL convention resolved, "for it is either a forerunner of the persecution of Labor or in some cases it has followed the suppression of Labor."[56] In 1938, the Labor League for Human Rights was created to support the rescue of those persecuted by the Nazi regime. AFL president William Green agreed to serve as an honorary chair and AFL secretary George Meany as an honorary secretary. Green also praised the White House for organizing the Evian Conference, but reiterated AFL opposition to refugee admissions beyond quota limits. Instead of admitting Jewish refugees en masse to the United States, the AFL endorsed a Jewish homeland in Palestine. The contrasting CIO and AFL positions suggested that organized labor no longer spoke with one voice in the refugee debate. Nevertheless, congressional restrictionists remained staunch defenders of closed borders.

As Nazi persecution escalated in 1938, an interfaith coalition of religious and ethnic leaders, civil rights activists, and social workers met quietly to develop a political strategy for rescuing German and Austrian Jews. After discussing bureaucratic barriers, participants agreed that special legislation would have to be secured in order to circumvent quota limits. They understood the odds were long. New York Democratic representatives Emanuel Celler and Samuel Dickstein had proposed legislation providing nonquota status to German refugees for several years, but their bills never made it out of committee. Wary of past failures, the interfaith coalition drafted blueprints for a more modest bill that granted nonquota status to 20,000 German refugee children. To coordinate this legislative agenda, a Non-Sectarian Committee for German Refugee Children was organized.

The Non-Sectarian Committee quickly secured the backing of two respected Northeastern lawmakers, Senator Robert F. Wagner (D-NY) and Representative Edith Nourse Rogers (R-MA), who introduced identical asylum bills in February 1939. An impressive array of public figures—including the nation's leading clergymen, numerous college presidents, Herbert Lehman, William Allen White, Helen Hayes, Henry Fonda, George Rublee, and Rexford Tugwell—were recruited as chairs of the Non-Sectarian Committee. Politicians as diverse as Herbert Hoover, Philip La Follette, and Fiorello La Guardia endorsed the measure. Thousands of American families representing forty-six states volunteered to host German refugee children.

The House and Senate immigration committees held joint hearings in April 1939 on the Wagner-Rogers bill. Both committees were dominated by Southern and Western conservatives who were staunchly restrictionist—indeed, none of the asylum bills proposed by Dickstein or Celler from 1933 to 1938 made it out of committee. The Non-Sectarian Committee hoped to avoid stirring anti-Jewish sentiment by having Catholic and Protestant clergymen testify that the bill would rescue many Christian children from Germany. Southern and Western academics urged committee members of their regions to support the measure. The chief of the Children's Bureau assured the joint subcommittee that refugee children would be properly cared for by private sponsors without burdening the public fisc. Philip La Follette and Helen Hayes also offered impassioned appeals on behalf of the legislation. Frances Perkins and Eleanor Roosevelt strongly favored the Wagner-Rogers bill, but the White House cautiously demanded that both maintain a neutral silence.

Aligned against the legislation were the American Legion, Daughters of the American Revolution, the IRL, and other patriotic and anti-immigrant groups. Restrictionist witnesses skillfully appropriated New Deal rhetoric in opposing the Wagner-Rogers bill, frequently reminding lawmakers that refugees would compete with "one third of a nation ill-housed, ill-clad, ill-nourished."[57] The AFL also opposed the Wagner-Rogers bill, asserting that "the quotas should not be enlarged nor should unused quotas of other countries be used." The AFL's Washington office argued that "whatever immigrants should come here should come as immigrants and not as refugees."[58] Many Americans seemed to agree with restrictionists that "charity begins at home": polls suggested that the vast majority of those interviewed opposed the legislation.[59]

The Wagner-Rogers bill received an icy reception from the full House and Senate Immigration Committees. Representative John Anderson (R-CA) argued that Congress should concern itself first with *American* refugees, the 1.5 million citizens "wandering around our country at the present time without shelter, without necessary food, without proper clothing." Another House committee member demanded, "[H]ow many of those homes that might admit those [refugee] children will not admit the needy children in our own country?" Dickstein, who served on the House committee, warned refugee advocates that their asylum bill was in trouble. "There has been a rumor around the Capitol here, and there was before we started the hearings, that this committee was pretty well controlled to kill this legislation," he said grimly. "In fact, they talked about having 11 votes in their pockets." A confidential State Department polling of committee members confirmed this conclusion, noting that Southern and Western members, who comprised a majority of the committee, strongly opposed the measure. American Legion lobbyists had "full confidence that this committee will not report out a bill at all."[60]

The Senate Immigration Committee was also dominated by Southern Democrats and Western Republicans who adamantly opposed Jewish refugee admissions. Only four of the committee's fourteen members favored the Wagner-Rogers measure. Senator Robert Reynolds (D-NC) threatened to filibuster the bill if it reached the floor. The committee's restrictionist chair, Richard B. Russell (D-GA), tacked on an amendment that struck language regarding the admission of German children above quota limits. The revised asylum bill simply called for children to have first preference under the existing German quota. Wagner immediately announced that the amended bill was "unacceptable," and the legislation died in committee. To anti-immigrant activists, Reynolds boasted that the amendment was designed to paralyze the Wagner-Rogers bill without carrying the stigma of "killing the resolution entirely."[61] By session's end, neither house had acted on the measure.

Tellingly, Congress passed legislation a year later that extended refuge to British children on a nonquota basis. The State Department also assured the public that "all the red tape has been cut and all the nonessential requirements have been eliminated" for evacuating British refugee children imperiled by German bombing.[62] The ethnic and racial hierarchy of American immigration and refugee policy was unmistakable: once the focus of refugee relief shifted to British children, legislative and bureaucratic barriers quickly disappeared. The same year, Congress passed the Alien Registration Act, requiring all aliens in the United States to register at local post offices across the country and those over the age of fourteen to be fingerprinted. Over the objections of the ACLU and the National Council for the Protection of Foreign-Born Workers, 5 million aliens were registered in 1940. Fears of enemy agents entering the country also prompted the FDR administration to present a Reorganization Plan that transferred the INS from the Department of Labor to Justice for, as he put it, "national defense reasons."[63]

Within the State Department, Assistant Secretary of State Breckenridge

Long directed subordinates in 1940 to make every effort to avoid granting visas to European refugees. "We can delay and effectively stop for a temporary period of indefinite length the number of immigrants into the United States," he wrote in a departmental memo. "We could do this by simply advising our consuls to put every obstacle in the way and to require additional evidence and to resort to various administrative devices which would postpone and postpone and postpone the granting of the visas."[64] Overseas, the American Friends Service Committee was informed by consular officials in Vienna that the State Department had determined "that emigration for German Jews coming from Germany was . . . finished."[65]

In later years, the Roosevelt administration entertained the notion of proposing refugee relief legislation that would allow immigration ceilings to be pierced. INS commissioner James Houghteling had the task of exploring potential congressional support for such a reform. After conferring with lawmakers and attending dozens of Immigration Committee sessions, Houghteling concluded that "the chance of any liberalizing legislation" was "negligible" due to the dominance of Southern and Western restrictionists.[66] The only notable immigration reform achieved during the Roosevelt presidency was legislation allocating a token number of visas for Chinese immigrants. Although it marked an important step away from Chinese exclusion, most lawmakers saw it as an exceptional wartime measure intended to strengthen the country's alliance with China. The persistence of racial gradations in American immigration law was underscored by the meager annual quota for Chinese immigrants.

Although key Roosevelt administration officials hoped to provide refugee relief, the State Department continued to frustrate Jewish admissions. In 1941, Breckenridge Long secured cooperation from the Visa Bureau in cutting immigration to 25 percent of available annual quotas. Visa issuance was later cut to 10 percent of available immigration quotas. State Department officials also devised a special rule in 1943 that denied visas to refugees deemed by consular officials to be "in no acute danger." As the historian David Wyman observes, "This arrangement permitted the State Department to close the doors at will. Where Jews *were* in acute danger, in Axis-held territory, there were no American consuls to issue visas. But those who escaped to countries where consuls still operated were 'not in acute danger' and for that reason could be kept out of the United States."[67] Consular officials imposed other hurdles as well. Frances Perkins fought the State Department over its exclusion of rabbis who, it decided, were ineligible for the nonquota status granted to other alien clergy (section 4d of the 1924 act classified clergy as nonquota immigrants). "One should expect every person who is engaged in preaching, teaching, conducting services, funerals, weddings, etc. to be considered as a minister," Perkins insisted.[68] She frequently told Jewish friends that their European relatives would be unlikely to gain admission and urged them to seek refuge in South America.[69]

The administrative barriers to Jewish refugees finally came under fire when Treasury secretary Henry Morgenthau, Jr., was informed by the World Jewish Congress that the State Department purposefully delayed a "wide rescue plan" endorsed by Roosevelt. Treasury officials launched a careful investigation of the matter in 1943 that culminated in a lengthy, confidential memorandum, "Report to the Secretary on the Acquiescence of This Government to the Murder of the Jews." The report found the State Department guilty of "willful attempts to prevent action from being taken to rescue Jews from Hitler."[70] After a dramatic confrontation with Breckenridge Long,[71] Morgenthau briefed FDR at the White House. "There is a growing number of responsible people and organizations today who have ceased to view our failure [to admit Jewish refugees] as the product of simple incompetence on the part of those officials in the State Department," he said. "They see plain Anti-Semitism motivating the actions of these State Department officials and . . . it will require little more in the way of proof for this suspicion to explode into a nasty scandal."[72] After the meeting, Roosevelt issued an executive order creating the interdepartmental War Refugee Board to oversee Jewish rescue efforts.

The White House pursued modest refugee relief through additional administrative actions. The State Department was instructed to issue visitors' visas to roughly 3,000 prominent political refugees, and consuls outside of Germany were ordered to grant visas to German refugees. Likewise, an arrangement was made with Canada to facilitate permanent settlement in the United States of refugees residing in the country on temporary visas. Under existing law, aliens with temporary visas could not be deemed immigrants until they obtained immigrant visas from a consular office outside the United States. "Canadian pre-examination," however, enabled refugees to enter Canada, where they could receive a quota visa from the American consul. Of course, these interventions were mostly too little, too late. Significantly, a very different regulatory regime would operate in these years for Mexican guestworkers.

WELCOMING MEXICAN GUESTWORKERS:
WINKING AT LAX ENFORCEMENT

From the time the federal government began regulating immigration in the late-nineteenth century, policymakers focused almost exclusively on European and Asian inflows. Whereas inspection stations could be found at nearly every major American port of entry by the turn of the century, efforts to control the country's land borders were negligible. This contrast was not lost on the nation's first commissioner general of Immigration. In the Immigration Bureau's 1903 annual report, he warned that the Canadian and Mexican borders were largely unmonitored.[73] Only a handful of inspection stations were scattered along national land borders. By 1906, bureau managers lamented that the seventy-five inspectors patrolling the nineteen-hundred-mile Mexican border on horseback were unable to curtail illegal immigration, which it described as "constantly on the increase."[74] "Lack of funds, men, and facilities" along land borders was a frequent complaint of bureau officials in the early-twentieth century.[75]

Significantly, Congress authorized a modest Border Patrol force largely in response to Immigration Bureau reports that inadmissible Asians and Europeans were being smuggled across the Canadian and Mexican borders. That is, the problem of illegal immigration was initially associated in the American mind not with Latin American migrants, but unwanted Asian and European ones. In fact, the Dillingham Commission wrote approvingly of the easy flow of Mexican laborers across the southern border. Its final report praised Mexicans as an indispensable source of migratory labor for sections of the South and West, crucial to herding and perishable crop production.[76] "The Mexican immigrants are providing a fairly acceptable supply of labor in a limited territory in which it is difficult to secure others," the commission rationalized. "Their incoming does not involve the same detriment to labor conditions as is involved in the immigration of other races who also work at comparatively low wages."[77] But what the Dillingham Commission perhaps found most appealing about Mexican laborers was "their more or less temporary residence." Although commissioners thought Mexicans were as racially inferior as Asian or southern and eastern Europeans, they saw little danger of their becoming permanent U.S. residents. "While the Mexicans are not easily assimilated, this is not of very great importance as long as most of them return to their native land in a short time," noted the Dillingham report.[78]

INTEREST GROUP PRESSURE AND MEXICAN CONTRACT LABOR

The Immigration Act of 1917 imposed the country's first legal constraints on Mexican immigration, making all alien admissions contingent upon passage of a literacy test and payment of an eight-dollar head tax. However, the meager size of the Immigration Bureau's Border Patrol forces meant that these new requirements hastened illegal Mexican immigration. The free movement of Mexican migrant workers was largely undisturbed. What did lead Mexican workers to return home in large numbers was U.S. entry into the First World War; rumors that they would be drafted into the American armed forces spurred the mass exodus. For the first time in years, Southwestern employers found themselves without a ready supply of cheap migrant labor.

In the aftermath of the Mexican exodus, Southwestern growers, ranchers, and other employers implored administration officials to remove potential barriers to the swift return of Mexican farmworkers. Wartime victory, employers desperately reasoned, depended on their capacity to produce food for the country amidst a severe labor shortage that only Mexican guestworkers could alleviate. The Immigration Bureau and the Labor Department bowed to these outside pressures by initiating the importation of thousands of Mexican contract laborers to work in agriculture, mining, railroad maintenance, and building construction. To do so, Labor secretary William B. Wilson invoked a special clause of the Immigration Act of 1917 (the ninth proviso of section 3) that enabled him to "issue rules and prescribe conditions . . . to control and regulate the admission and return of otherwise inadmissible aliens applying for temporary admission."[79] The literacy test, head taxes, and contract labor restrictions were waived for Mexicans. Mexican laborers were assured that they would not be conscripted into the armed forces. To guarantee their return to Mexico, the U.S. government withheld a significant portion of guestworkers' wages until they left the country.

Although many Southern and Western members of Congress joined employers in urging Secretary Wilson to facilitate the swift return of Mexican laborers, House Immigration Committee chair John Burnett (D-AL) reacted with alarm. As he privately wrote Wilson, the Labor Department's interpretation of section 3 of the Immigration Act of 1917 might open the door for Asians or southern and eastern Europeans. Wilson responded that he was under enormous pressure to take action, noting that "numerous statements with regard to the shortage of farm labor and its extent have reached the Department from all sections of the country, and especially . . . from those interested in agricultural enterprises." He added that many Southwestern interests even advocated renewed Asian immigration to meet labor needs: "Many representations have been made to the Department with the view to obtain permission to import large numbers of Oriental laborers, especially Chinese and Filipinos." But the distinct advantage of Mexican contract labor, he assured Burnett in a manner reminiscent of the Dillingham Commission's, was their decidedly impermanent status. In his words, "the admission of [Mexicans] can be made strictly temporary and can be regulated and controlled to a very large degree, and will be so regulated and controlled under the practice [of] the Department."[80] Burnett and other racial exclusionists in Congress were generally satisfied by Wilson's explanation.

Mexican contract labor was justified as an emergency wartime measure. When hostilities ceased in 1918, Secretary Wilson planned to terminate the temporary admissions program. But intense pressure from agricultural interests and congressmembers led Wilson to extend the program until 1920. Tellingly, congressional oversight of the Labor Department's Mexican contract labor program in this period centered on how many workers returned home and whether Mexicans were easily deported. Between 1917 and 1921, almost 75,000 Mexican guestworkers labored in the United States, along with an indeterminate number of undocumented workers.

THE RESTRICTIONIST COALITION AND MEXICAN LABOR IMMIGRATION

The issue of Mexican migratory labor threatened to rent the immigration restriction movement in the 1920s. The diverse nativist coalition that emerged from the Progressive Era was united in its hostility toward Asian and new European immigration, as well as in its devotion to eugenicist principles of racial order and Anglo-Saxon superiority. But Mexican labor immigration was another matter. The AFL, the Immigration Restriction League, patriotic associations, and various nativist lawmakers favored stringent limits on Latin and South American immigration. By contrast, many Southern and Western restrictionists extolled the virtues of a cheap and flexible Mexican labor force. Representative John Nance Garner (D-TX), Roosevelt's future vice president, marveled that "the prices that [Mexicans] charge are much less than the same labor would be from either the negro or the white man."[81] While agreeing with those who opposed the permanent addition of Mexicans to the American population, many Southern and Western nativists contended that Mexican guestworkers were by definition temporary, powerless, and easily expelled.

Under the Quota Act of 1921, Western Hemisphere immigrants enjoyed nonquota status. In later debates over the 1924 and 1928 quota laws, however, nativists clashed over the nonquota status of Latin and Southern Americans while agreeing on Canada's exemption. "With Canada, the case is different," the IRL noted. "Immigrants from Canada are of racial origins similar to our own."[82] In turn, it was crucial to place quotas "on Mexico and on other countries in North and South America whose population is not predominantly of the white race."[83] While still serving as the Immigration Committee's eugenics agent, Laughlin warned that any "intermixture or intermarriage" of Mexicans and Anglo-Saxons imperiled "whatever population it touches."[84] Nativist intellectuals scorned the economic narcissism of Southern and Western restrictionists who backed nonquota status for Mexicans, noting that racial contamination went hand in hand with importing African slaves and Chinese "coolie" labor.[85]

The National Grange and the American Farm Bureau Federation strongly opposed a change in Mexico's nonquota status. The Great Western Sugar Company of Colorado told the House immigration committee that it did

> not want to see the condition arise again when white men who are reared and educated in our schools have got to bend their backs and skin their fingers to pull those little beets. . . . You have got to give us a class of labor that will do this back-breaking work, and we have the brains and ability to supervise and handle the business part of it. There is no danger of that class of labor taking over the supervising work.[86]

From this perspective, Mexican laborers were essential because they performed menial jobs unsuitable for "white men" of "brains and ability." Garner assured House colleagues that Mexicans "do not cause any trouble, unless they stay here a long time and become Americanized."[87] Southern and Western lawmakers, solidly restrictionist toward European and Asian immigration, were deeply divided over Mexican labor. The controversy seemed to place the national origins quota system itself in jeopardy.

Immigration defenders attempted to exploit these fractures within the nativist camp during the legislative debates of 1924. In the House, Fiorello La Guardia (D-NY) and Adolph Sabath (D-IL) offered an amendment that placed quotas on Western Hemisphere countries. Their hope was to kill the 1924 quota legislation entirely by sundering a restrictionist majority on the question of Mexican migrant labor. Faced with imminent stalemate, restrictionists called for a compromise on the divisive issue. As one closed-border advocate declared, "I want the Mexicans kept out, but I do not want this bill killed by men who want these and all others admitted in unrestricted numbers."[88]

The Immigration Act of 1924 ultimately placed stringent barriers on southern and eastern European immigration and reaffirmed Asian exclusion, but was quite permissive on Canadian and Latin American admissions. Aliens with ten years continuous residence in a Western Hemisphere country could enter the United States as nonquota immigrants. "Restrictions of immigration and setting up of un-American racial tests has been enacted through a fusion of northern Republicans from urban districts with southern Democrats, with a bribe tossed to the latter by keeping Mexico open," Kohler observed.[89] As nativist reformers prepared new quota legislation in 1928, they agreed to treat Latin American immigration as a distinctive issue. "These two kinds of restriction are quite separate and independent, and will stand and fall on their own merits," declared New York reformer Demarest Lloyd. "We all agree that unity of restrictionists is desirable."[90] IRL activists made similar observations concerning "the National Origins–Mexican Quota situation," arguing for a decoupling of the issues.[91] The IRL even expressed sympathy for the dilemma faced by the Southwest in 1928. "Although the West has become racially conscious and wants to be a white civilization, it also wants to develop and to develop rapidly," observed one IRL newsletter. "For this it needs unskilled labor of a mobile type, like the Mexicans, for it cannot get white labor to do its unskilled work."[92] Congress eventually codified a bifurcated regulatory structure: one stringently restrictive, the other relatively open and flexible.

Opening and Closing the Door: The Returnable Labor Force

As Congress formalized consular inspection procedures and visa requirements in 1924 to insure stringent enforcement of national origins quotas overseas, the Immigration Bureau struggled for adequate resources to guard the Canadian and Mexican borders. "It must be conceded that the present law was enacted primarily for the purpose of providing for the closer inspection of aliens coming to the seaports of the United States," U.S. Immigration commissioner John Clark stated plainly. "When we come to consider the dangers of unlawful invasion along the land boundaries, however, we find our law conspicuously weak, and almost totally inadequate to protect the interests of our Government."[93] Congress finally established the Border Patrol in 1924, prodded by Labor Department warnings that inadmissable Asians and Europeans were flocking to Canada and Mexico "to gain admission by stealth."[94] From the start, however, the Border Patrol was significantly understaffed.[95] By 1928, the Immigration Bureau warned lawmakers that "we have simply got to have the men or else we cannot enforce the law."[96] IRL leaders complained that the congressional immigration committees intentionally underfunded border enforcement at the behest of "selfish powers and interests."[97]

During the 1920s, Mexican immigration increased substantially. Yet neither legal nor illegal Mexican inflows prompted great concern among national policymakers. However, the onset of the Great Depression changed public perceptions of Mexican labor immigration considerably. AFL president William Green asserted that years of unfettered Mexican immigration displaced American workers. "[T]here are at least 2,000,000 Mexicans in the United States . . . and all wage earners should be warned of this calamitous condition," Green declared.[98] At national conventions, the AFL strongly denounced Mexican migrant labor.[99]

In response to growing public discontent, the Immigration Bureau launched a general crackdown on undocumented Mexican aliens in 1929. Although the bureau seized only a small portion of illegal entrants residing in the country, its well-publicized deportation campaign had the intended effect of encouraging hundreds of thousands of Mexican aliens to return home. "We have passed in practically one year from a wide open Mexican border to a practically closed Mexican border," noted one observer.[100] The Depression's constriction of job opportunities also has-tened Mexican repatriation. As a later presidential commission on migra-tory labor noted, "whereas in the twenties we absorbed a Mexican popu-lation of about a million, in the thirties we disgorged almost half a million people of Mexican origin."[101]

During the First New Deal, AFL leaders campaigned for legislation that would place national origins quotas on Mexico and other Western Hemisphere countries. In 1934, the AFL's Washington office vigorously pursued a bill that established a 1,500 annual quota for Mexican immi-grants, and barred all those ineligible for citizenship, namely, nonwhite Mexicans. But these AFL efforts failed due to the staunch opposition of House and Senate Immigration Committees dominated by unsympathe-tic Southern and Western conservatives.[102] By 1938, the INS reported that illegal immigration from Mexico was again on the rise, hastened by the construction of new highways and "automobile travel."[103]

In a manner reminiscent of the First World War, Southwestern growers and congressmen complained to executive branch officials in the 1940s that war-induced labor shortages necessitated a new contract-labor pro-gram. Other sectors of the American economy also struggled to cope with a reduced labor supply. In the early 1940s, an interagency commit-tee was formed to facilitate the importation of Mexican guestworkers to address these needs. The committee was comprised of officials from the War Manpower Commission as well as from the Agriculture, State, Jus-tice (which now oversaw the INS), and Labor Departments. In 1942, the State Department negotiated a special agreement with Mexico establish-ing the Bracero Program. Despite resistance from liberal Democrats with close ties to organized labor, lawmakers approved the bilateral agreement as Public Law 45 in April 1943. As in the past, policymakers reassured critics that bracero workers were easily returnable; the exodus of hun-dreds of thousands of Mexicans during the Depression seemed to con-firm this assertion.[104]

Because of abuses endured by migrant laborers earlier in the century, the Mexican government was reluctant to cooperate in a new contract labor program during the Second World War. A bilateral agreement was secured only after State Department officials promised safeguards for bra-ceros. The United States pledged that braceros would not perform any military service and that wages, living conditions, workplace safety, and medical services would be comparable to those of domestic workers. The Mexican government was to supervise the recruitment and contracting of braceros, and employers were responsible for all transportation costs. To guarantee that braceros returned home, a major portion of wages were to be deposited in a Mexican bank until their return home. The agreement assured that Mexicans "shall not suffer discriminatory acts of any kind."[105] Congress later approved similar contract labor programs with British Honduras, Jamaica, Barbados, and the British West Indies.[106]

From the start, organized labor fervently opposed the Bracero Program as both exploitive of Mexican braceros and detrimental to the working standards of native laborers. The AFL questioned the motives of employers clamoring for cheap Mexican labor. "The same elements that have always exploited illiterate Mexican labor have used the war emergency as a special plea to waive restrictive immigration laws," it warned.[107] The CIO worried about "the vicious exploitation and discrimination directed against the Mexican workers" and, in contrast to the AFL, welcomed them "into the ranks of organized labor in the United States for the improvement of their conditions."[108]

Once the Bracero Program began, neither employers nor federal administrators saw that the terms of the United States–Mexican agreement were honored. Mexican braceros routinely received lower wages than domestic migrant workers and endured substandard living and working conditions. Contrary to the bilateral agreement, the INS permitted growers to directly recruit braceros at the border. If they did not allow employers to recruit their own guestworkers, one INS official recalled, "a good many members of Congress would be on Immigration's neck."

The INS also felt considerable congressional and interest-group pressure to accommodate illegal Mexican immigration. The INS avoided search and deportation procedures against illegal aliens during crop seasons because it "could likely result in loss of the crops."[109] One Texas farm group explained enforcement arrangements to Senator Thomas Connally (D-TX) in this way:

> "For a number of years citizens of Mexico entered the United States both legally and illegally, engaging in agricultural work. . . . While from time to time they have been picked up by the Border Patrol, there has been a tendency on the part of the Border Patrol to concentrate their efforts on deporting only those who were bad. . . . This arrangement, although it did not have the stamp of legislative approval, has worked out very nicely for our farmers down here."[110]

Strict enforcement was reserved principally for those Mexican guestworkers who attempted to organize fellow laborers in pursuit of better wages, housing, and working conditions. The alliance of agricultural growers, Southern and Western "committee barons," and immigration officials would permit the easy flow of Mexican labor immigration for most of the century.

CONCLUSION

The two-tiered administrative structure that emerged in the early-twentieth century captured the power Southern and Western congressmen had over immigration policy. Barring Jewish refugees while creating a subclass of exploitable foreign laborers reflected comparable notions of racial hierarchy. National origins quotas and other bureaucratic barriers assured that Asian and southern and eastern European immigrants would not "dilute" the American population. Likewise, the belief that Mexicans could be easily repatriated convinced congressional conservatives that guestworkers could perform menial labor unsuited for white workers without becoming, as they put it, another "Negro problem."

While many Roosevelt administration officials scorned the racial order envisioned by Southern and Western restrictionists, they concluded that a direct challenge to the national origins quota system was politically chimerical. It was not until after the war that most liberal Democrats would come to view immigration reform as unambiguously consistent with their civil rights and international agenda. In subsequent decades, the struggle over national origins quotas would pit the resources of the modern presidency against the entrenched power of a bipartisan conservative coalition in Congress.

CHAPTER SEVEN

Strangers in Cold War America

THE MODERN PRESIDENCY, COMMITTEE BARONS, AND POSTWAR IMMIGRATION POLITICS

IN 1940, ONE year after the demise of the Wagner-Rogers refugee bill, an array of liberal activists met in Washington at a conference of the American Council for the Protection of the Foreign Born (ACPFB). Among the 310 participating delegates were representatives of various ethnic groups (including Asian, Latino, and southern and eastern European leaders), civil rights organizations, humanitarian and religious groups, professional associations, academics, and several labor groups led by the CIO. At the meeting, speakers articulated a broad agenda that would animate pro-immigration reformers for the next quarter century. The AC-PFB was principally dedicated to preventing "discrimination against noncitizens or foreign-born citizens because of their nationality, political, economic, or religious belief, or lack of citizenship."[1] Yet the deliberations of delegates cast a wider net, assailing the existing national origins quota system for separating families, denying asylum to desperate refugees, and contradicting "fundamental American concepts of equality, regardless of race, color, nationality, creed, or place of birth . . . the guarantees of democracy."[2]

Whereas the AFL remained supportive of national origins quotas, the more racially progressive CIO denounced the country's immigration policy. James B. Carey, the CIO's national secretary, told conference delegates that American labor must wake up to the fact that restrictionists in Congress were equally hostile to the needs of American workers. "The propagandists who preach today that [immigrants] aggravate our unemployment problem," Carey declared, "are the very persons who never intended and who do not now intend to do anything about our own, American unemployment."[3] Delegates also heard from the leader of the Spanish-Speaking People's Congress of California, who poignantly described Mexican guestworkers as "drifting unattached fragments of humanity"—a subclass denied equal wages, schooling, welfare, use of public places, and access to citizenship. After the conference, various liberal groups mobilized in opposition to national origins quotas, Asian and African exclusion, and the exploitation of Mexican braceros and illegal aliens. Many of these groups successfully lobbied in 1943 for the repeal of Chinese exclusion. But it was a hollow victory, a symbolic gesture by reluctant lawmakers on behalf of a wartime ally; the legislation alloted a token number of annual visas for Chinese immigrants (roughly one hundred in total).

As the Second World War neared conclusion, pro-immigration activists found themselves on the defensive. In 1944, congressional nativists proposed several bills to suspend all immigration to ensure domestic jobs for returning servicemen. In Washington, a Committee on Postwar Immigration Policy was hastily organized. Its membership included the AJC, HIAS, B'nai B'rith, the National Catholic Welfare Conference, the Federal Council of Churches, the American Committee for Christian Refugees, the ACLU, the Common Council for American Unity, and the YWCA. At early committee meetings, group representatives fretted about Congress's decidedly anti-immigrant mood and the impact returning American soldiers might have on immigration policy. "Once the war is over and our men begin competing for jobs, pressure for restriction will be vastly intensified," the committee observed privately. "Unless steps are taken at once to combat such sentiment, educate public opinion and organize liberal forces of the country, there is grave danger Congress will bar all immigration."[4] Given the dominance of restrictionists in Congress, the Committee's membership resolved to initiate "close consultations with the Executive Branch" to block legislative efforts to close American borders.[5] In addition, a subcommittee of leading scholars and experts was appointed to conduct fresh research on the economic, social, and cultural benefits of immigration.[6]

This sort of defensive effort against anti-immigrant reform was largely an act of political futility in the twenties. But it had very different meaning and consequences in the transformed international and domestic political world that was emerging in postwar America—a time when, as Eric Goldman put it, "nothing seemed unchanging except change."[7] Immigration advocates were correct to assume that they faced formidable opposition in Congress. But it was immigration restrictionists who would be gradually placed on the defensive in the postwar decades. Americans may have been eager to look inward after 1945 (just as they had in the isolationist twenties), but this was a luxury of the past. As Allied forces celebrated victory in Europe, the United States found itself locked in what Arthur Schlesinger, Jr., described as a "permanent crisis" with the Soviet Union, one that would "test the moral, political and very possibly the military strength of each side."[8] The Cold War would provide liberal immigration reformers with important new rationales for dismantling offensive national origins quotas as the nation vied with the USSR for the "hearts and minds" of foreign leaders and populations. According to compelling new political narratives, immigration policies designed during the isolationist twenties could not be squared with the modern demands of superpower competition.

Significantly, the executive office occupied by Truman, Eisenhower, Kennedy, and Johnson would serve as a powerful institutional champion of expansive immigration reform in the postwar decades. The Cold War gave the U.S. presidency unprecedented clout over foreign policy *as well as* domestic initiatives framed as efforts to influence global affairs. As John White observes, "The change in the president—from a person of civic virtue in George Washington's day; to Martin Van Buren's partisan leader; to 'boss' and commander in chief during the Cold War—was considerable."[9] Fred Greenstein points out that executive control over the deployment of nuclear weapons, beginning with Truman's decision to release atom bombs over Hiroshima and Nagasaki, imbued the presidency with "quite literally life-and-death importance" that dramatically expanded the office's formal and informal powers.[10] Modern presidents of the postwar era usually were often most influential when standing atop the national security state; the role of Leader of the Free World could place them "above politics."[11]

Postwar immigration defenders turned to the executive branch for support largely by default. The structural roadblocks in Congress were daunting, and the courts continued to cite the plenary power doctrine as reason for its deference to lawmakers on immigration matters. Yet presidential administrations from Truman to Johnson saw special interests of their own in not only opposing new immigration restrictions at war's end, but in dismantling national origins quotas in favor of a more flexible and open system of immigration control. Each of these administrations resented the severe limits that existing policies placed on admitting refugees when doing so served national foreign policy interests. Especially galling to White House internationalists were the barriers that national origins quotas placed on providing haven to those escaping communist regimes behind the Iron Curtain. Postwar presidents responded by calling for major immigration reform and by taking independent executive action to provide relief to refugees outside the dictates of existing legal restrictions.

There was another reason postwar presidents embraced expansive immigration reform. As much as Cold War competition created new imperatives for ending the U.S. government's long silence on black civil rights, it raised equally compelling concerns about the explicit ethnic and racial biases in national immigration policy. Truman officials frequently linked civil rights and immigration reform as "important to . . . moral leadership in the struggle for world peace," warning that failure to pursue racial progress would help "those with competing philosophies . . . prove our democracy an empty fraud and our nation a consistent oppressor of underprivileged people."[12] Executive branch internationalists particularly worried about the message national origins quotas sent to the newly independent states of the Third World. "Since the end of World War II, the United States has been placed in the role of critical leadership in a troubled and constantly changing world," a remade State Department later concluded. "Inasmuch as our immigration laws are regarded as the basis of how we evaluate others around the world their effect on people abroad and consequently on our influence can be readily seen."[13] In earlier national political struggles over immigration, even energetic presidents were generally content to remain on the sidelines as lawmakers shaped policy initiatives. Most confined their involvement to the penultimate moment when they would either sign or veto reform legislation. With the onset of the Cold War, American presidents assumed a far more active role in making immigration policy than they had at any other time.

During the isolationist heyday of the twenties, immigration restriction was all the rage among legislators. Yet the membership of Congress was considerably more divided on the issue after the war, as internationalists in both parties raised new questions about nativist policies that seemed better suited to the isolationism of a bygone era. However, Cold War anticommunism also fueled familiar fears of domestic infiltration by foreign enemies and concomitant passions for imposing draconian limits on alien admissions and rights. Nativist lawmakers of the 1940s and 1950s praised the national origins quota system for keeping immigrant inflows to a minimum and maintaining the nation's "cultural and sociological balance" at a time of grave peril to the American republic. At the height of McCarthyism, restrictionists pressed for new exclusionary categories to better shelter the country from agents of an international communist conspiracy. The most ardent defenders of this perspective in Congress were conservative Republicans and Southern Democrats, who forged a powerful alliance against liberal policy activism during and after the New Deal. This "conservative coalition" would enact immigration legislation in the early 1950s that reaffirmed national origins quotas and established new restrictions against foreign security threats. The competing policy goals of restrictionist legislators and expansionist presidents produced a postwar interbranch struggle over immigration control that closely resembled the "liberal-presidential" and "conservative-congressional" fault lines Hugh Davis Graham observed in civil rights politics.[14]

Despite some initial triumphs amidst McCarthy-era hysteria, the political luster of immigration restriction eroded steadily throughout the 1950s and 1960s. In the early-twentieth century, eugenicists and other specialists supplied expert research to commissions and congressional committees that rationalized severe restrictions on immigration from outside northern and western Europe. Yet the racist fascism of America's wartime foes encouraged an official ideological retreat from notions of ascriptive hierarchy; principles of biological determinism fell into intellectual disrepute in the postwar era.[15] Significantly, the academic retreat from racist pseudosciences owed much to the growing prominence on the faculties of U.S. colleges and universities of European scholars who had fled Nazi repression. The Cold War itself further elevated the role of scientific expertise in affairs of state. As we shall see, the expert findings of a new immigration commission would challenge the scientific basis upon which the national origins quota system was built. In the process, a new narrative would emerge among "knowledge-bearing elites" justifying wholesale immigration reform.

Changing postwar coalitional alignments were also advantageous for proponents of a more open immigration policy. Whereas the brief defection of key business groups from the pro-immigration camp of the 1920s helped restrictionists secure favorable policy outcomes, a comparable but longer lasting shift in the alignment of organized labor profoundly altered the shape of postwar immigration politics. The 1955 merger of the AFL and CIO would prove pivotal in turning labor's strongest organizational voices against immigration restriction. Labor's dramatic shift on immigration would be spurred by several developments: changing union membership, the rise of a postwar alliance with the civil rights movement, the AFL-CIO merger, and hostility toward conservative congressmen who defended national origins quotas while promoting Mexican guestworker programs. At the same time that liberal immigration reformers gained a powerful political ally, a number of influential nativist groups like the Immigration Restriction League disappeared from the political landscape.

Despite these developments, the impediments to expanding immigration opportunities remained formidable for two decades after the war. As one liberal senator conceded as late as 1964, this was "an issue that really isn't politically good" because most Americans opposed any increases in annual immigrant admissions.[16] Moreover, structural arrangements in Congress during the postwar years were often inhospitable to expansive immigration reform. The Legislative Reorganization Act of 1946 was adopted to strengthen legislative capacities for exercising policy leadership and overseeing executive bureaucracies after a period of perceived congressional decline. It streamlined committee arrangements (the former Immigration Committees, for instance, were folded into the Judiciary Committees), expanded committee staff and legislative expertise, and created a new budgetary process. In operation, these institutional reforms did not replace the old order of committee government or the seniority system that defined legislators' standing on their committees. Indeed, the new committees possessed broader jurisdictions and increased staff resources that made them stronger than ever. These structural arrangements were pivotal because nativist lawmakers tended to dominate the Immigration Subcommittees and Judiciary Committees throughout the postwar years. As Congress was reshaped by growing numbers of liberal Democrats and moderate Republicans after the 1958 election, the resilience of Southern Democrats like Senator James Eastland (MS) meant that the minority controlling the committee system could derail expansive immigration reform for some time. Only cross-party congressional majorities favoring immigration reform and strong presidential intervention would bring decisive policy change.

The Crisis of Displaced Persons and Liberal Mobilization

The plight of Europe's displaced persons at the war's end served as an important catalyst for liberal political mobilization on immigration reform. As Allied and Soviet forces converged on Germany in the summer of 1945, the State Department estimated that roughly 13 million Germans had joined the "20 to 30 million of the people of Europe already torn from their moorings by the terrific impact of war."[17] The Allied military command and the newly created United Nations Relief and Rehabilitation Agency (UNRRA) were entrusted with the task of assisting these displaced persons (DPs). The Allied Command and the UNRRA dealt with the vast majority of DPs by safely transporting them back to their countries of origin. It was decided, however, that several groups were especially vulnerable to persecution and could not be repatriated: Ukrainians, Baltic and Polish nationals, and Jewish refugees.

The future of tens of thousands of Jewish survivors living in European DP camps was the preeminent concern of American Jewish groups. Long active in immigration politics, the AJC rallied Jewish organizations, congressmen, and administration officials in 1945 to assist Jewish refugees. After persistent urgings from Rabbi Stephen S. Wise, Representative Emanuel Celler, and Treasury Secretary Robert Morgenthau, the Truman White House sent Earl Harrison, a former commissioner of immigration, to Europe to investigate the conditions of the DP camps, and especially the well-being of homeless Jews. In his report to the president, Harrison grimly noted that many concentration camp survivors were dying due to a shortage of food, shelter, and fuel. Appallingly, he found that a lack of clothing meant that many Jewish DPs were forced to wear concentration camp uniforms or German SS uniforms. In the strongest possible terms, Harrison scolded Allied leadership for not doing more to provide immediate relief to Jewish survivors: "We appear to be treating the Jews as the

Nazis treated them, except we do not exterminate them." To alleviate the crisis, he advised Truman to urge on Britain the opening of Palestine, and to establish special U.S. immigration slots for Jewish refugees.[18]

After Harrison issued his dramatic report, Celler encouraged pro-immigration groups to press the White House for action. Since entering the House in the twenties, Celler had watched dozens of reform bills languish in the hands of restrictionist committee barons. After "close consultations" with Celler, Jewish organizations and their allies agreed that "it would be much wiser to have action taken by the President than to attempt any sort of Congressional action."[19]

While members of Congress debated whether to close American borders, Truman took independent executive action. He issued an executive order in December 1945 that extended special relief to a portion of Europe's displaced persons. It directed the State Department to reopen consular offices near DP camps in order to process immigration claims, and to extend preferential visas from unused annual quotas to Holocaust survivors and other refugees. Anticipating criticism of providing special assistance to Jewish DPs, the White House carefully characterized the beneficiaries of preferential visas as "persons of all faiths, creeds, and nationalities." The presidential directive ultimately enabled 40,000 DPs, most of whom were Jewish refugees, to gain admission to the United States.

Congressional policy activists, such as Senator Richard Russell, chair of the Senate Judiciary Committee, wasted no time in assailing Truman for usurping legislative authority and for placing foreigners before American veterans. A Gallup poll conducted a few weeks after Truman's executive order suggested that most Americans were unsympathetic to Europe's dispossessed: 51 percent of those polled favored a decrease or suspension of immigration, 32 percent supported the policy status quo, and a mere 5 percent approved of increases in immigration. Veterans and members of labor unions were among the most staunchly restrictionist respondents.[20]

Significantly, the Gallup poll also indicated a developing gap between elite and mass opinion on the subject of immigration. While most of those with at least a college education supported increased or existing levels of immigration, those with a high school education or less overwhelmingly favored decreased immigration or closed borders.[21] Whereas Progressive intellectuals and other elites were a driving force behind early-twentieth-century nativism, their ideas were suspect to many scholars and social luminaries of the postwar years. The impetus for this postwar retreat from scientific racism was not only its close association with Nazi fascism, but also the growing prominence of "inferior" groups within the academic community itself. As Elazar Barkan notes, "immigrants, women and Jews, created new spaces and provided necessary data to refute claims of their own 'inferior' qualities."[22] Many of these findings would be embraced and publicized in the 1950s by a new immigration commission.

To the American Jewish community and its political allies, it was readily apparent that Truman's directive would assist only a fraction of the refugees who crowded into Allied-controlled zones of Europe in 1946. Their concern grew more acute when large numbers of Jewish refugees fled Eastern Europe and communist rule in the spring and summer of 1946, including many who survived an outbreak of anti-Semitic violence in Poland. In response, the AJC, HIAS, B'nai B'rith, and other organizations accelerated their campaign for special legislation to aid Jews and other DPs. While American Jewish groups largely coordinated and financed the DP relief effort, they established a Citizens Committee on Displaced Persons (CCDP) comprised of Catholic and Protestant leaders, prominent members of the business community, social workers, public officials, and academics. Earl Harrison was named chair of the CCDP, William S. Bernard its executive director, while its national board boasted respected liberals like Eleanor Roosevelt, James Farley, Lehman, and LaGuardia. At the same time, a National Committee on Immigration Policy, also headed by Harrison and Bernard, was established to press for sweeping changes in U.S. immigration policy. The rationale for separate committees on refugees and immigration reform was strategic: refugee relief would be easier to secure, and might be undermined if too closely associated with a major overhaul of the immigration code.

The decoupling of refugee relief from efforts to dismantle national origins quotas was specifically designed to gain crucial AFL support for displaced-persons legislation. Relations between the AFL and congressional Immigration Committees (and, later, Judiciary Committees) were strained during the 1930s over Mexican braceros and illegal immigrants. Moreover, the AFL came to recognize during the war that "the march of dictatorships in the world" subjected both "free trade unions" and "racial and religious minorities" to vicious suppression. After the war, AFL leaders urged members to "wage an unrelenting struggle against groups . . . spreading the poison of anti-Catholicism, anti-Protestantism, anti-Semitism, anti-Negroism and other forms of racial prejudice."[23] However, the AFL was not yet willing to sacrifice national origins quotas, resolving that "any lowering of the immigration bars be opposed, and . . . all phases of traditional immigration policy be maintained."[24] To gain AFL support, then, the CCDP worked to separate the plight of displaced persons from broader immigration reform efforts. The strategy proved successful, as delegates at the 1946 AFL convention endorsed "the immediate entry of immigrants composed of displaced persons in Europe of whom the Jews are a large number," while opposing broader changes in U.S. immigration law.

THE STRATTON BILL OF 1947

As the CCDP engaged in coalition-building activities, Truman used his "bully pulpit" to pressure Congress to enact special DP legislation. In his 1947 State of the Union address, he announced that the executive branch had done "all that is reasonably possible under the limitation of existing law and established quotas" to assist displaced persons. The task now rested on Congress, he declared, to "fulfill our responsibilities to these thousands of homeless and suffering refugees of all faiths."[25] A few months later, Representative William Stratton of Illinois introduced a displaced-persons bill designed to assist 400,000 DPs over four years. Drafted by the CCDP, the Stratton bill defined "displaced persons" broadly, encompassing both Jewish survivors and those fleeing communist rule. The CCDP described the bill as "emergency" legislation that would do nothing to enervate the national origins quota system. Likewise, the committee reminded policymakers and the general public that 80 percent of DPs were Christian, while "another portion of them, by far the smallest number, only one out of five is of the Jewish faith."[26] Jewish groups and their allies were all too familiar with the ethnic and religious hierarchies that still pervaded the nation's political culture, and worked to alter popular perceptions of DP relief as designed principally to assist Jewish Holocaust survivors.

The CCDP also engineered a sophisticated publicity campaign attentive to a variety of media. As Executive Director Bernard recalled, the effort focused on "some 3,000 opinion makers" representing leading newspapers, magazines, radio stations, and movie producers. The effort paid early dividends, as prominent journalists and entertainers championed the cause of European DPs. The country's leading newspapers and magazines—many of which once alarmed Americans with sensational accounts of unassimilable immigrants teeming to American shores—now urged swift refugee relief. "Surely a nation whose population is mainly composed of immigrants and their descendants cannot logically maintain that the only 'good' immigrants are those who are already here," the *Saturday Evening Post* averred.[27] Likewise, the *Christian Science Monitor* questioned whether the United States could assume global leadership in the Cold War era if it was unwilling to help the DPs: "Let Americans prove their concern for free peoples by giving a few of these hapless and hopeless refugees a chance to be free."[28]

Despite such efforts, restrictionist congressmen and patriotic associations formed a solid phalanx against the Stratton bill. Paul Griffith, national commander of the American Legion, warned followers that many refugees were "Communist atomic spies" and "poor material for assimilation." Each new immigrant, he added, "represents a discrimination against the veteran who needs a job, a home, a car and a suit because he gave them all up to fight for America."[29] In a 1947 radio debate with Harrison and Celler, one VFW representative candidly stated that "we need a more homogenous people."[30] Perhaps the most vicious attack on DP relief was launched by nativist representative Ed Gossett (D-TX), who railed against a Jewish-organized "refugee racket." The "blood" of Jewish DPs, he reasoned, would expose American society to "weakness and pollution." In his view, closed borders and isolationism best served national interests: "Our very survival in a mad world depends on our internal strength and unity."[31]

The Republican-controlled 80th Congress generally was unmoved by White House, CCDP, and media pressure for DP relief. Whereas a Northeastern minority called for action on the Stratton bill, the majority of Southern Democrats and Republican conservatives in Congress were in no hurry to solve Europe's refugee crisis. Yet the Stratton bill received strong support from organized labor, most notably the crucial backing of AFL president William Green. Truman sent Secretary of State George Marshall and Secretary of War Robert Patterson to Capitol Hill to testify for the Stratton bill. "You cannot assert leadership and then not exercise it," Marshall told lawmakers. Despite such efforts, the measure remained bottled up in both houses. Senator Chapman Revercomb (R-WV), chair of the Judiciary Committee's Immigration Subcommittee, was especially hostile to Jewish refugees, who he insisted were ordinary economic immigrants rather than the victims of systematic persecution.[32]

In the House, Celler found Judiciary Committee leaders also advancing "a campaign to stall action" on the Stratton bill.[33] Nevertheless, he pleaded with Judiciary chair Earl Michener to report the bill out of his committee. "It was the desire to escape persecution and establish a better way of living that inspired our forefathers to found our great Republic," Celler wrote Michener.[34] Despite the prominent endorsements the Stratton bill elicited, the measure perished unceremoniously in committee. Relief would have to wait for a new Congress.

GOING PUBLIC ON THE REFUGEE CRISIS: TRUMAN AND THE COMMITTEE BARONS

After the demise of the Stratton bill, congressional leadership—especially the restrictionist chairs of the Judiciary Committees and the Immigration Subcommittees—were under tremendous pressure to do something about the DP crisis. The Truman White House, joined by a broad array of newspapers, magazines, radio broadcasters, advocacy groups, and luminaries, assailed Congress for failing to consider the Stratton Bill in 1947. The *Washington Post* worried that the failure of lawmakers "to take constructive action on the displaced persons problem will subject the United States to the charge that our professions of democracy and humanitarianism are the variest mockery."[35] The Federal Council of Churches expressed outrage on behalf of a broad coalition of groups favoring refugee relief:

> The failure of Congress at its last session to act upon the Stratton Bill has placed upon the conscience of this nation a great moral burden. 120 national organizations representing the bulk of church, farm, labor, civic, women's, veteran's and other important groups are asking that immediate action be taken.[36]

The coalition's reference to veteran support reflected an important development: the CCDP persuaded the American Legion's National Executive Committee to alter its official stance on DP relief from staunch opposition to tepid support.[37] Congressional nativists increasingly found themselves at odds with most national advocacy groups on the European refugee issue.

Several additional developments further intensified the pressure on congressional leaders regarding the DP crisis. First, officials of the Truman administration alerted both the public and members of Congress of the considerable burdens that would be placed on the federal budget if DPs were not resettled. In particular, they stressed the hefty costs associated with either maintaining existing DP camps in Europe or, alternatively, helping to support DPs if they were released into a precarious German economy. Another argument for enacting special DP legislation advanced by Marshall and other State Department officials was that East European refugees were an important weapon in the Cold War. The notion of extending relief to those escaping Soviet rule had special appeal to congressional conservatives preoccupied with the specter of communist expansion. Finally, the White House and State Department rarely missed an opportunity to assert that the DP problem blocked European and, concomitantly, global postwar recovery. As Marshall warned, inaction on the DP question would "have disastrous effects on the larger problem of the reconstruction of Europe that will alone make possible a peaceful world."[38] In short, congressional nativists had great difficulty blocking refugee relief once it was tied to the twin goals of anticommunism and postwar economic recovery.

During the spring of 1948, House Judiciary Committee restrictionists grudgingly threw their support behind a new plan proposed by Representative Frank Fellows (R-ME) for admitting displaced persons. The Fellows bill was markedly less expansive than the earlier Stratton bill; it reduced proposed DP admissions from 400,000 to 202,000, and stipulated that all DP visas would be "mortgaged" against available quota slots of originating countries in future years. Moreover, DPs were eligible for special visas only so long as they entered the western-controlled zones of Germany or Austria by April 21, 1947. The Fellows bill was quickly reported out of committee and passed by the House soon after its introduction.

In the Senate, two of the most dominant Judiciary Committee members, Pat McCarran (D-NV) and Revercomb forged a bipartisan partnership to craft DP legislation that was more restrictive than the Fellows bill, including an earlier deadline for DPs to enter Allied-controlled territories. The McCarran-Revercomb measure was enacted easily. During conference committee, McCarran and Revercomb accepted the House limit of 202,000 DP visas. In exchange, they secured changes in the House bill's eligibility requirements and preference categories for DP visas that effectively excluded most displaced Jews. For example, the eligibility deadline for entering western zones of Austria or Germany—April 21, 1947—was moved back to December 22, 1945. This earlier deadline barred large numbers of Jewish refugees who fled the Soviet Union, Poland, and other East European countries after 1945. Likewise, Jews also were disadvantaged by a requirement that 30 percent of all DP visas be allocated to persons "previously engaged in agricultural pursuits and who will be employed in the United States in agricultural pursuits." By contrast, the Fellows plan had established preferences for DPs possessing a variety of needed skills and occupational backgrounds, including medicine, education, science, as well as "clothing and garment work." Many Jewish refugees could have secured visas under these original preference categories. Just before adjourning in June, the conference compromise was approved. "It is a close question whether this bill is better or worse than no bill at all," Truman scolded Congress when the 1948 legislation arrived on his desk. Its provisions, he declared, reflected "a pattern of discrimination and intolerance wholly inconsistent with the American sense of justice."[39] Truman only reluctantly signed the Displaced Persons Act of 1948 into law. The 1948 elections enabled the Democratic party to regain control of both houses of Congress, with the new majority including a modest increase in liberal-minded members. The CCDP vigorously lobbied the new Congress to eliminate discriminatory features of the Displaced Persons Act and to increase visa allocations to levels proposed in the original Stratton bill.

Due to the alliance of McCarran and Revercomb, however, the partisan changeover of Congress had little effect on the restrictionist tenor of the Senate Judiciary Committee. For nearly two years, McCarran employed the considerable resources of his committee chairmanship to hold at bay expansive amendments to the Displaced Persons Act. In the House, Celler assailed his Senate counterparts for stalling crucial revisions in the 1948 act and compared its anti-Semitic provisions to Nazi racial policy. "The present law sets up so clearly offensive a pattern of racial and religious discriminations that it bids fair to becoming known as 'America's first Nuremburg law,'" he declared. Nativist legislators no longer spoke plainly of the racial inferiority of particular groups, as they had before the war, but the ethnic and racial targets of exclusion remained unmistakable.

What was more compelling to most of Celler's colleagues, however, was the fact that many "recent refugees" who had fled communist regimes from behind the Iron Curtain were ineligible for DP visas. As the White House reminded them, the 1945 eligibility cutoff date that barred most Jewish refugees also disqualified countless other refugee groups who fled communist territory after that date. Many in Congress understood that the admission of recent escapees of communist rule was an important "weapon in our ideological war against the forces of darkness, the forces of communist tyranny."[40] The 1949 Central Intelligence Agency Act authorized a modest number of special visas to be allocated each year for aliens who were expected to enhance American "national security." The linking of refugee admissions to anticommunist foreign policy objectives hastened a more expansive Displaced Persons Act. In 1950, Congress passed new DP legislation that removed the agricultural preference and moved the cutoff date for DP visa eligibility to January 1, 1949. The ceiling on DP visa allocation also was increased to levels proposed by Stratton three years earlier, although "quota mortgaging" continued apace. Against the backdrop of the Marshall Plan and a new NATO alliance, 400,000 refugees came to the United States under the Displaced Persons Acts of 1948 and 1950.

OLD WINE IN NEW BOTTLES: NATIONAL ORIGINS QUOTAS AND THE MCCARRAN-WALTER ACT

Having achieved special legislation to assist DPs, liberal reformers associated with the CCDP and the National Committee on Immigration Policy set their sights on dismantling national origins quotas. In the immediate postwar years, pro-immigration groups helped defeat several proposals to shut down immigration. They also won some incremental reforms that provided modest cause for optimism. The War Brides Act of 1945 enabled the foreign spouses and children of veterans to gain admission as nonquota immigrants. Likewise, the Fiancés Act of 1946 extended the same nonquota immigrant status to fiancés of American GIs. Subsequent legislation authorized the extension of token quotas for Indians and Filipinos—but not more than one hundred immigrant slots annually. Chinese wives of American citizens also gained nonquota immigrant status. By 1950, Northern Democrats announced their intention to propose an immigration reform package that would replace national origins quotas with a new preference system based on individual skills and unified family units.[41]

Senator McCarran and his restrictionist colleagues looked warily upon these reform ambitions of Northern Democrats, liberal advocacy groups, and the Truman administration. Their strategic response was to seize the initiative by proposing reform legislation that in fact preserved much of the old policy structure, most notably the national origins quota system. Since 1947, the Senate Judiciary Committee had been engaged in a broad investigation of American immigration policy. Prominent committee restrictionists like Revercomb, McCarran, and Eastland saw the investigation as a means of tabling expansive reform proposals until their study was complete. Yet passage of the Displaced Persons Act of 1950 shook the confidence of McCarran and his allies, who saw it as a possible prelude to sweeping immigration reform.[42] To defend the existing policy regime, committee nativists drafted their own reform proposals that in fact retained national origins quotas as the key organizing feature.[43]

McCarran enjoyed a close working relationship with the chair of the House Immigration Subcommittee, Representative Francis Walter (D-PA), who shared his zeal for American isolation and restrictive immigration policies. Together they would capitalize on anticommunist anxieties to steer the Internal Security Act through Congress in 1950. The legislation was a prime artifact of the McCarthy era, one that linked alien threats to widespread American anxieties of communist infiltration at home (see table 7.1). It authorized the exclusion of aliens who were once communists or members of any groups deemed to be "front" organizations for communist expansion. It also subjected to swift deportation any noncitizens living within U.S. borders who belonged to the Communist party or engaged in any activities considered "subversive to the national security." The second Displaced Persons Act (enacted a few months before) was an important victory for Truman's brand of Cold War internationalism. The Internal Security Act offered a very different portrait of how the Cold War could influence American immigration policy, one in which isolationist strains of anticommunism fortified and expanded existing barriers to alien admissions and rights.[44] The tensions between these competing visions would be played out in interbranch struggles for years to come.

This rivalry between isolationist and internationalist visions of immigra-

TABLE 7.1
Public Opinion on Groups "In This Country" Considered "More Likely to Be
Communists Than Others," November 1950

Groups Selected	Public Response (%)
Labor union members	28
Puerto Ricans in the United States	24
Poor people	21
Don't know	19
People in the government in Washington	18
None of them	17
Negroes	14
College students	13
New Yorkers	12
Actors	12
Jews	11
Americans of Italian descent	9
Teachers	8
Americans of Polish descent	7

Source: National Opinion Research Center, November, 1950 survey.

Note: Total does not add up to 100% because those polled were allowed more than one response.

tion control reemerged when three celebrated congressional liberals—
Hubert Humphrey, Lehman, and James Roosevelt—sponsored an ambitious pro-immigration initiative that they associated with civil rights reform at home and democratic leadership abroad. The bill specifically
called for an increase in annual admissions by 100,000, the pooling of
unused annual quota slots, and the recalculating of national origins
quotas on the basis of 1950 census. Their plan also advocated a stronger
emphasis on family reunification, "civil rights and liberties even for
aliens," and the removal of "all racial discriminations from our immigration laws."[45]

McCarran and Walter's own immigration reform initiative affirmed national origins quotas, but called for visa allocations *within each country's
existing quota* to be based on a new preference system emphasizing job
skills and family reunification. With anticommunist vigilance, the McCarran-Walter bill included new exclusionary categories aimed at punishing
political radicalism and social nonconformity. If the principal goal of the
legislation was to preserve national origins quotas as the keystone of the
nation's immigrant admissions policy, its sponsors did their best to characterize their proposal as remedying the most pernicious racial biases in
federal immigration law. These claims were based on a provision abolishing Asian exclusion and the ignominious Asiatic Barred Zone established

in 1924. Yet its replacement was scarcely an improvement: two thousand total annual visas were to be available for all nonwhite immigrants born within an Asian-Pacific Triangle stretching from India to Japan to the Pacific Islands. Tellingly, immigrants from predominantly white Asian countries like Australia and New Zealand were not constrained by this new allocation scheme.

McCarran and Walter sought and won approval for joint House and Senate subcommittee hearings on the rival immigration reform bills, with McCarran serving as chair. This shrewd maneuver was intended to blunt the influence of Celler, the new House Judiciary Committee chair. The McCarran-Walter alliance proved frustrating to liberal immigration reformers, who were marginalized in the joint hearings process. Celler and a young Peter Rodino (D-NJ), both supportive of the Humphrey-Lehman-Roosevelt bill, were often muffled during the hearings.[46] More importantly, McCarran and Walter orchestrated witness lists and testimony to favor their bill. To be sure, a small number of groups like the ADA and ACPFB testified that the bill reflected "politically exploited hysteria and confusion in the country" that sacrificed democratic "concepts of justice and equal treatment."[47] But this was the exception.

Most groups appearing at the joint hearings endorsed the McCarran-Walter package. Prominent veterans and patriotic organizations, including the Veterans of Foreign War (VFW) and the American Legion, said the nation's internal strength depended on severe immigration restriction. Although supportive of liberal efforts to assist European refugees, the AFL unwaveringly backed the McCarran-Walter bill. The AFL Executive Council denounced the Humphrey-Lehman-Roosevelt bill because it promised to undermine "the spirit of the Quota Act of 1924" and "disturb the ethnic equilibrium of this country."[48] Early in 1952, AFL president Walter Mason privately told his Washington lobbyists that the Executive Committee fully supported the *racial* basis for restricting immigrant admissions:

The pooling of unused quotas would be in direct conflict with the national origin principle . . . which seeks to maintain the general racial composition of our population. . . . The effect of pooling of unused quotas would be not only to increase substantially the number of people coming to the U.S. but would, in the course of a generation or so, change the complexion of the population of this nation.[49]

Even the Japanese American Citizens League testified in favor of the McCarran-Walter bill for providing annual visas for Japanese immigrants; the group's ambivalent leadership decided that token quotas were preferable to outright exclusion.[50]

Floor debate on the McCarran-Walter bill was virtually identical in the

House and Senate. Opponents denounced the legislation as "restrictive, exclusionist, and oppressive," claiming that it contradicted the "essence of America—peoples of every ethnic and economic group, of all races and creeds and religions, fused in freedom and working to achieve the great American ideal of equal justice under the law."[51] Critics underscored the disastrous effects the legislation would have on the ideological contest with the Soviet Union, "blackening the name of America all over the world."[52] Senator Lehman reminded colleagues that German radio highlighted national origins quotas in the 1930s "to show that Members of our Congress felt the same way that Nazis did about the . . . superiority of the so-called Nordics."[53] America had won the war, he noted sadly, but the "purely racial and racist theories" endured in national immigration policy. Humphrey assailed restrictionists for ignoring central tenets of liberal democracy. "The key and heart of the democratic philosophy is recognition of the dignity of human kind, and of the brotherhood and fraternity of mankind," he declared.[54]

By design, proponents of the McCarran-Walter bill said almost nothing on the floor about the ethnic and racial biases that so clearly informed the national origins quota system and the Asian-Pacific Triangle proposal. Yet the immigration subcommittees took care in their reports to carefully document how the existing policy regime gave preferential treatment to Northern and Western Europeans (see tables 7.2 and 7.3). And one Idaho representative could not resist admitting during floor debate that on "the question of racial origins—though I am not a follower of Hitler—there is something to it. We cannot tie a stone around its neck and drop it into the middle of the Atlantic just because it worked to the contrary in Germany."[55] But most xenophobic lawmakers followed McCarran's lead in defending broad exclusions in terms of national security, sounding the alarm that "criminals, Communists, and subversives of all descriptions are even now gaining admission into this country like water through a sieve." It was a time-worn theme, but one that had special

TABLE 7.2
Immigrants Admitted, by Region, 1921–1950

Region	1911–20 (prequota)	1921–30	1931–40	1941–50
Northern and western Europe	998,194	1,299,987	200,665	496,569
Southern and eastern Europe	3,370,259	1,154,883	130,477	126,698
Asia	192,559	97,400	15,344	31,780
Africa	8,443	6,286	1,750	7,367

Source: Joint Hearings before the Immigration Subcommittees of the Judiciary Committees, 82d Congress, 1st Session (Washington, DC: Government Printing Office, 1951).

TABLE 7.3

Average Annual Immigration from Europe before and after Establishment of the National Origins Quota System, by Region, 1901–1950

	Average Annual Immigration	
Region	Before Quotas, 1901–20	After Quotas, 1921–50
Northern and western Europe	145,411	66,569
Southern and eastern Europe	473,816	47,069

Source: Based on data in Joint Hearings before the Immigration Subcommittees of the Judiciary Committees, 82nd Congress, 1st Session (Washington, DC: Government Printing Office, 1951).

resonance at a time when 81 percent of Americans agreed that "communists or disloyal people" worked in the State Department and Joseph McCarthy told rapt audiences of menacing internal conspiracies.[56] McCarran and other nativists readily accepted their opponents' claim that the nation had key postwar international responsibilities. But as the United States was "the last hope of Western civilization," they asserted, the country's chief obligation was to guard its domestic security. "If we destroy the internal security of this country by opening the floodgates of unlimited immigration, without screening and without curtailment," McCarran concluded, "we will have destroyed the national security of the United States."[57]

If the McCarran-Walter bill promised to maintain draconian limits on Asian, African, and southern and eastern European immigration, it also implicitly welcomed the continued importation of *returnable* Mexican laborers. Many restrictionist legislators, including McCarran and Eastland, represented regions in which agricultural growers and other business interests relied upon easy access to cheap Mexican guestworkers. Although the AFL pledged support for national origins quotas, it joined other labor organizations of the early 1950s in expressing alarm about a rising tide of illegal Mexican immigration that "depressed wages and destroyed working conditions." In 1951, the AFL complained that the presence of hundreds of thousands of braceros coupled with an estimated 1.5 million undocumented aliens compromised the "security" of American workers. Most legal Mexican guestworkers entered the United States between 1948 and 1951 under regulations issued by the secretary of Labor, who invoked the ninth proviso of the immigration law to appease the labor needs of growers and other employers (see chap. 6). At the behest of organized labor, the Truman administration created a Commission on Migratory Labor in Agriculture to investigate Mexican labor inflows. In

1950, Truman's commission rebuked Congress and administrators for failing to deter illegal immigration or to protect vulnerable Mexican braceros. Nevertheless, McCarran, Eastland, and others tenaciously opposed ending the Bracero Program. Claiming that it would be "unfair to the farmer and the Mexican involved," Southern and Western members won passage of Public Law 78 in 1951, reauthorizing the importation of Mexican guestworkers.[58]

After failing to terminate legal guestworker programs, organized labor and the Truman administration urged Congress to impose legal sanctions on those who illegally smuggled aliens into the country and on employers who intentionally hired illegal aliens. During floor action on the McCarran-Walter bill, liberal senator Paul Douglas (D-IL) proposed just such an employer-sanctions amendment at the behest of labor activists. "In this amendment we are trying to reduce the volume of . . . illegal entries by imposing penalties upon those who knowingly employ illegal entrants," Douglas declared.[59] But McCarran and Eastland successfully defeated the amendment; the final legislation contained language that made it unlawful to transport or harbor illegal aliens, but clarified that "harboring" did not include employment of illegal aliens. This "Texas proviso," as it later became known, highlighted the lengths to which congressional champions of national origins quotas were willing to go to preserve Mexican labor immigration, both legal and illegal. Despite this bitter pill, the AFL continued to endorse the legislation because it sustained restrictive quotas (see table 7.4).

To no one's surprise, Truman refused to sign the McCarran-Walter measure. Instead, he issued a blistering veto message condemning dis-

TABLE 7.4
Interest Coalitions and Immigration Policy, 1952

The Importation of Mexican Guestworkers Should Be	National Origins Quotas Should Be	
	Preserved	Dismantled
Encouraged	American Farm Bureau Federation, southern and western agricultural growers	Low-skill industrial employers
Terminated	American Federation of Labor, veterans' groups, patriotic societies	Congress of Industrial Organizations, American Council for the Protection of Foreign-Born, Americans for Democratic Action

criminatory immigration policies for undermining the nation's anticommunist agenda abroad. To defeat "one of the most terrible threats mankind has ever faced," he proclaimed, the United States entered into a NATO alliance with free European countries including Italy, Greece, and Turkey. "But, through this bill, we say to their people: You are less worthy to come to this country than Englishmen and Irishmen," he noted. Even more "fantastic" was its treatment of Eastern Europeans:

> The countries of Eastern Europe have fallen under the Communist yoke; they are silenced, fenced off by barbed wire and mine fields; no one passes their borders but at the risk of his life. We do not need to be protected against immigrants from these countries; on the contrary, we want . . . to save those who have managed to flee into Western Europe, to succor those who are brave enough to escape from barbarism.[60]

The Democratic Congress was unfazed by Truman's words, overriding his veto by a vote of 278 to 113 in the House and 57 to 26 in the Senate. The measure's enactment owed much to lopsided support from Southern and Western conservatives in both houses (see table 7.5).

The McCarran-Walter Act preserved national origins quotas as the centerpiece of American immigration policy, and continued to impose sharp limits on total annual inflows; only the spouses and unmarried minor children of U.S. citizens were exempted from the numerical ceiling. Northern and western Europeans continued to receive preferential treatment in terms of annual per-country admissions quotas. Among quota immigrants of *each nationality*, special preference was given to those with needed job skills and family connections to American citizens and permanent residents (see table 7.6). In addition, the new law authorized the exclusion or deportation of aliens deemed by government officials to be politically subversive or a national security risk. The act designated a total

TABLE 7.5
Regional Breakdown of the Veto-Override Vote for the McCarran-Walter Act

Region	House of Representatives		Senate	
	Yes	No	Yes	No
Northeast	56	66	8	10
Midwest	96	32	15	8
South	91	3	19	3
Far West	35	12	15	5

Source: *Congressional Record*, June 26, 1952, p. 8225, and June 27, 1952, p. 8267.

TABLE 7.6
The Preference System of the McCarran-Walter Act

Preference among Quota Immigrants of Each Country	*% of Country Quota*
First Preference: Those with special skills or training whose services are beneficial to the U.S., and the spouses of children of such immigrants	50%
Second Preference: Immigrants who are parents of U.S. citizens over 21 and unmarried adult children of U.S. citizens	30%
Third Preference: Immigrants who are spouses and unmarried children of permanent resident aliens	20%
Fourth Preference: Immigrants who are siblings or adult children of U.S. citizens	50% of national quota not used for the first three preferences

of thirty-three classes of persons who were to be denied entry into the country, including homosexuals, epileptics, the "insane" and mentally retarded, those likely to become public charges, and communists and other political radicals. Nonwhite immigrants were assigned token racial and nationality quotas of one hundred per year.

The McCarran-Walter Act also included naturalization provisions that the bill's sponsors viewed as a gesture of egalitarian tokenism akin to the symbolic quotas established for the Asian-Pacific Triangle. While the new law increased language qualifications for naturalization, it also abolished racial tests and marital qualifications for citizenship. The act established that "the right of a person to become a naturalized citizen of the United States shall not be denied or abridged because of race or sex or because such person is married." Restrictionists viewed the measure as a symbolic concession to those concerned about racial or gender equality in the postwar years, but one that posed no real threat to the nation's ethnic makeup, since the vast majority of noncitizens entering the country came from Europe. In subsequent decades, however, this important change in naturalization law would help make Asian and Latin American immigrants an important political force in the United States.

INTERBRANCH STRUGGLE AND THE COLD WAR CAMPAIGN FOR IMMIGRATION REFORM

Truman was undaunted by the ease with which congressional restrictionists overrode his veto. His administration viewed expansive immigration reform as a foreign policy necessity, and it used the ample resources of the modern presidency to pursue it with vigor. Truman had roiled congressional restrictionists in 1945 by issuing an executive order independently admitting European refugees, a practice that subsequent presidents would emulate, using special parole powers ironically codified by the McCarran-Walter Act. His earlier use of the rhetorical presidency to "go over the heads" of national lawmakers to attain special refugee relief legislation on behalf of displaced persons was equally assertive. During his last months in office, Truman made an all-out effort to discredit national origins quotas and to urge a new round of immigration reform. In particular, he established a presidential commission to challenge the racist findings of earlier investigations, and vigorously infused the issue into the 1952 election.

In the final months of the 1952 campaign, Truman toured the country on behalf of the Democratic ticket headed by Senator Adlai Stevenson of Illinois. Significantly, he used this platform to denounce the isolationism and nativism of Republican lawmakers in several well-publicized speeches. He specifically assailed Richard Nixon, Eisenhower's running mate, and other Republican legislators who showed "moral blindness" in their votes for the McCarran-Walter Act. Not surprisingly, Truman made no mention of the prominent role played by conservative Democrats like McCarran, Walter, and Eastland in securing restrictionist legislation. By reaffirming the national origins quota system, he told voters, Republican leadership perpetuated "a philosophy of racial superiority developed by the Nazis, which we thought we had destroyed when we defeated Nazi Germany and liberated Europe." Truman added that Eisenhower's selection of Nixon as a running mate, along with his silence on immigration, reflected isolationist impulses.[61]

Similar attacks on the Republican party were launched by liberals such as Senator Lehman. Before diverse New York crowds, Lehman spoke of "two prominent wings of the Republican party." The first he described as a relatively harmless collection of backward-looking conservatives, an "Old Guard" that still followed the "discredited" laissez-faire liberalism of Harding and Hoover. But he warned that "a much more sinister faction—the faction of McCarthy and Nixon" now controlled the Republican party, scorning decency, racial equality, and civil liberties in fervent pursuit of "the principle of power."[62] For several heated weeks, Democratic politicians led by Truman demanded that the Republican standard-bearer, Dwight D. Eisenhower, clarify his position on the McCarran-Walter Act and its relation to American prestige around the world.

Eisenhower himself had entered the presidential campaign to defeat isolationists within the Republican party and to assure that the presidency was safely in the hands of a seasoned internationalist who could deftly

manage the nation's unprecedented contest with the Soviet Union. Indeed, he candidly said as much to the traveling press corps during the
1952 campaign for the Republican nomination, focusing most of his
wrath on the stalwart Republican conservative Robert Taft: "All right, I'll
tell you why I'm running for the presidency. I'm running because Taft is
an isolationist. His election would be a disaster."[63] Truman's challenges
to the former World War II commander during the general campaign
emboldened Eisenhower to denounce national origins quotas unequivo-
cally, and to further distance himself from the isolationist wing of the
Republican party. In a series of speeches delivered less than a month before election day, Eisenhower pledged support for a new round of immigration reform that "will strike an intelligent, unbigoted balance between
the immigration welfare of America and the prayerful hopes of the un-
happy and oppressed."[64] In dramatic fashion, the retired general read the
names of several veterans of the Korean conflict who had received the
Congressional Medal of Honor and who, because of their ethnic backgrounds, would have been denied entry if they had immigrated under
existing quota limits. Such discrimination was unworthy of America's immigrant past and clearly at cross-purposes with Cold War imperatives, he
contended.[65] Turning the tables on Truman, Eisenhower suggested that
"the McCarran Immigration Law" was "another glaring example of the
failure of [presidential] leadership to live up to our high ideals."[66] Truman's rhetorical campaign goaded the Republican ticket to publicly denounce the national origins quota system.

The Truman administration also made a frontal assault on the national
origins quota system through his Presidential Commission on Immigration and Naturalization. Revisiting subjects originally explored by the
Dillingham Commission, it sponsored new studies on the likely influence of new immigration on American economic, social, and population trends. Its research agenda placed special emphasis on the "contributions of immigrants to the American economy, culture, etc.," the
social value of family reunification, the "role of immigrants in the anticommunist crusade," and the detrimental "effect of racial and national
discriminations."[67]

The commission's work revealed an important shift in the intellectual
convictions of academics and experts engaged in immigration policy debates. As noted earlier, the racial sciences that had flourished in the Progressive Era were rejected in most academic circles by the postwar era.
The commission heard from natural scientists, economists, sociologists,
anthropologists, historians, and political scientists who challenged the eugenicist methodology and findings of the Dillingham Commission and
the House Immigration Committee of the 1920s. In contrast to McCarran's subcommittee report of 1952, commission experts refuted the exis-

tence of innate differences between "old" and "new" immigrants, and offered empirical evidence of the need for increased immigrant admissions to offset future population decline. The commission also held several public hearings on national immigration policy, and invited a variety of pro-immigration groups who had been denied an opportunity to testify before McCarran's joint subcommittee hearings of 1952. Commissioners heard from social workers, clergy, international business owners, lawyers, ethnic group leaders, and politicians, along with prominent scholars, who condemned the quota system.

In its well-publicized report, *Whom We Shall Welcome*, the commission asserted that "the best scientific evidence available today is that there [are] no . . . inborn differences of personality, character, intelligence, or cultural and social traits among races. The basic racist assumption of the national origins system is invalid."[68] Tellingly, Truman's battle with Southern and Western restrictionists in Congress over the McCarran-Walter Act paralleled conflict over African American civil rights; the 1946 Committee on Civil Rights and the 1952 Commission on Immigration and Naturalization offered analogous views on the necessity of eliminating racial barriers in Southern racial policy and federal immigration law. "[W]e cannot be true to the democratic faith of our own Declaration of Independence in the equality of all men," the commission averred, "and at the same time pass immigration laws which discriminate among people because of national origin, race, color or creed." As much as Truman stressed civil rights reform as a critical issue in "world politics," the commission argued that national origins quotas made "a hollow mockery of confident world leadership."[69]

The research and testimony gathered by the commission captured growing expert support for more universalistic admissions standards. It also helped recast public discourse on immigration, drawing attention to the benefits of expanding immigration opportunities. Still, pro-immigration reformers continued to encounter formidable roadblocks in Congress from McCarran, Eastland, Walter, and their restrictionist allies. After the commission issued its report, McCarran intimated that immigration reformers aided the communist cause. "It is a tragic fact that the out-and-out Reds have ready colleagues: the 'pinks' and the well-meaning but misguided 'liberals' and the demagogues who auction the interests of America for alleged minority bloc votes," he lamented. "I shall fight them with the last ounce of my energy."[70]

Whereas postwar civil rights reformers pursued successful legal strategies in the courts to challenge entrenched segregation policies, liberal immigration reformers could expect little support from the federal bench. As in the past, the federal judiciary during the 1950s remained exceptionally deferential to the "political branches" and administrative actors on immigration matters. While the Supreme Court demonstrated little timidity in challenging government authorities on behalf of politically vulnerable groups in these years, it was unwilling to question the McCarran-Walter Act's exclusionary categories or their enforcement. Indeed, the Court stipulated in several controversial cases that the exclusion of noncitizens lay beyond the scope of constitutional protection.[71] Moreover, the admissions decisions of administrators, so long as they were conferred discretionary powers by Congress, were affirmed as due process of law. In *United States ex rel. Knauff v Shaughnessy*, the Court upheld the exclusion of the alien wife of an American veteran without the benefit of a hearing. Administrators told the Court that they had determined her entry to be "prejudicial to the interests of the United States"—a finding based upon confidential evidence that was not disclosed to the alien wife, her husband, or the Court. The Court endorsed broad administrative discretion: "Whatever the procedure authorized by Congress is, it is due process as far as an alien denied entry is concerned."[72]

A few years later, the Court ruled that government officials were entitled to exclude *and incarcerate* an alien who had legally resided in the United States for twenty-five years on the basis of unseen "confidential information." In dissent, Justice Jackson protested, "If the Government has its way he seems likely to be detained indefinitely, perhaps for life, for a cause known only to the Attorney General."[73] During the McCarthy era, however, such concerns for the individual rights of aliens were easily obscured by national security claims. Whereas civil rights reformers pursued a well-designed legal strategy of challenging African American exclusion in the courts, liberal immigration reformers were compelled to look to the White House for policy leadership. As Edward Corsi, the former Ellis Island commissioner and pro-immigration reformer, observed, "The President alone has the power to move us from 'No' to positive actions."[74]

The Eisenhower administration, much as its predecessor had, came to view national origins quotas as an impediment to its foreign policy goals. In particular, it shared Truman's concern that existing restrictions made it arduous for the administration to assist escapees of communist rule behind the Iron Curtain; the White House consistently advocated asylum for these "friends of freedom." Yet Eisenhower faced a significant dilemma in this regard: the expiration of the Displaced Persons Act combined with the rigidity of the quota system provided scant few immigration slots for East European refugees. Drawing on a specific recommendation of Truman's Commission on Immigration and Naturalization, Eisenhower sent a message to Congress in 1953 requesting "emergency" legislation to admit European refugees. General Walter Bedell Smith, the acting secretary of state, told a House committee that refugee relief had "an important impact upon the health and stability of friendly countries in Europe." Congressional inaction, the White House also warned, would "gravely endanger the objectives of American foreign policy."[75] After considerable White House lobbying, Eisenhower's Emergency Migration bill was enacted by Congress as the Refugee Relief Act of 1953, extending 209,000 special visas to European refugees on a non-quota basis.

Shortly after the "emergency" legislation passed, future House Speaker John McCormick alerted Celler that the compromises that were required to secure refugee relief would probably derail more significant pro-immigration reform for many years. "A deal was struck whereby the champions of the McCarran Act got together with men 'on the leadership level' in the Senate, and bought off revision of the McCarran Act in return for support by Senator McCarran of the President's emergency act for admission of . . . refugees," McCormick informed Celler. "The plan of those instituting this legislative blockade is to table in committee all bills filed for revision of the Immigration Act."[76] Whether or not McCarran and his allies indeed held immigration reform hostage to refugee relief, it is clear that strategically situated restrictionists in Congress effectively resisted broad policy change throughout the 1950s.[77]

Nevertheless, Eisenhower did not hesitate to take autonomous executive action on immigration matters when he believed it was warranted—often to the chagrin of congressional committee leaders. One such example was his response to growing public angst, particularly on the West Coast, regarding illegal Mexican immigration. As noted above, many congressional defenders of national origins quotas, including McCarran and Eastland, supported both legal and illegal Mexican immigration in order to curry favor with growers, ranchers, and other employers. Southern and Western legislators were instrumental in sustaining the Bracero Program, discouraging strict INS enforcement along the Mexican border (particularly during harvest season), and blocking Douglas's employer-sanctions amendment in 1952. However, reports of dramatic increases in illegal immigration heightened pressure on national policymakers to respond.[78] Newspaper articles and radio stories provided sensational accounts of the public health risks, criminal activity, exploitation, welfare dependency, and native job displacement that accompanied large-scale illegal immigration. The AFL's Executive Council resolved in 1954 to give "unceasing publicity" to the "wetback problem."[79]

In response to this mounting pressure, Eisenhower dispatched Attorney General Herbert Brownell to southern California in 1953 to investigate the situation. Brownell concluded that the presence of a large population of illegal aliens in the United States hurt the economic well-being and public health of Americans. With White House backing, he urged Congress to enact employer-sanctions legislation similar to that previously proposed by Senator Douglas and labor activists. But congressional supporters of Southwestern growers remained adamantly opposed to such legislation; the employer-sanctions proposal languished in committee.

Frustrated by congressional veto-points, the White House decided to take independent action. It recruited retired General Joseph M. Swing to head the INS in 1954 for the specific purpose of launching a military-style campaign to seize and deport Latino illegal aliens en masse. In a series of dragnet raids in California and across the Southwest in June of 1954, thousands of Mexican aliens (including an undetermined number of legal residents) were rounded up as part of Operation Wetback. INS agents also descended on Midwestern cities like Chicago, where some illegal aliens had obtained industrial jobs. After the operation, the INS reported that more than a million illegal aliens had been summarily shipped back to Mexico. Brownell justified the "drive against illegal Mexican labor" as necessary "to wipe out the disease, criminal activity, juvenile delinquency, and social instability that attends any wetback invasion."[80] The 1955 INS report boasted that "the so-called 'wetback' problem no longer exists. . . . The border has been secured."[81]

Tellingly, beyond the media glare, INS agents allowed many arrested "wetbacks" to remain in the country as legal bracero workers—a process that agents described as being "dried out." In the same period, the AFL argued that distinctions between illegal aliens and braceros were tenuous at best, and challenged the unauthorized recruitment of Mexican labor by federal agents.[82] Such protests fell on deaf ears. Following Operation Wetback, annual bracero admissions more than doubled despite widespread employer violations of wage, hour, safety, and recruitment regulations established by Public Law 78. Growers, ranchers, and other employers of low-skilled workers continued to enjoy an abundant supply of cheap labor. A powerful iron triangle ensured access to temporary Mexican labor, one animated by growers, Southern and Western Immigration Subcommittee chairs, and a malleable INS bureaucracy.[83]

The Eisenhower administration asserted itself once again in 1956 to assist Hungarian refugees who had fled their homeland after the Soviet Union violently ended the week-old government of Imre Nagy. As in the past, the White House found itself struggling to assist East European refugees despite hurdles imposed by the national origins quota system. But rather than request new "emergency" legislation, administration officials focused on a section in the McCarran-Walter Act that authorized the attorney general to admit aliens "temporarily" under emergency conditions.

The "parole powers" section of the law was an afterthought of Congress, intended to provide entry to *individual* aliens who might serve as key witnesses in a criminal prosecution or require "immediate medical attention." Yet Eisenhower instructed his attorney general to employ these extraordinary "parole powers" to admit over 30,000 otherwise inadmissible Hungarian refugees. At the time, Walter and Eastland (who assumed chairmanship of the Senate Judiciary Committee following McCarran's death in 1953) initially expressed sympathy for admitting escapees of Soviet oppression in Hungary. But before long, they grew wary of future executive activism and demanded that the White House "discontinue forthwith the exercise of discretionary power . . . in behalf of Hungarian refugees."[84] Their protest was registered too late; the use of parole powers in 1956 set a precedent that would be employed by presidents many times in later decades to extend asylum to tens of thousands of refugees.

IMMIGRATION POLITICS AND COALITIONAL CHANGE: ORGANIZED LABOR REALIGNS

While national decisionmakers were locked in stalemate over immigration policy during the 1950s, the alignment of organized interests on immigration policy changed markedly. Most significantly, the 1955 merger of the AFL and CIO brought about a momentous and enduring shift in organized labor's role in national immigration politics. For decades, American labor stood at the center of successful political struggles for immigration restriction. A nascent labor movement spearheaded grassroots mobilization for Chinese exclusion in California during the Gilded Age, setting in motion political forces that ultimately produced unprecedented governmental barriers to Asian entry and membership.[85] After an initial period of circumspection, the AFL joined right-wing restrictionist groups in their pursuit of literacy tests and national origins quotas designed to discourage "new" immigration from southern and eastern Europe. Organized labor's deep investment in this anti-immigrant crusade would culminate in several crowning legislative achievements, most notably the 1924 and 1928 Quota Laws. The AFL's commitment to national origins quotas in later years was one reason Roosevelt and New Deal reformers distanced themselves from expansive immigration reform. During the heart of the Cold War, however, rapprochement between member unions of the AFL and CIO would recast attitudes toward immigration in the house of American labor.

The CIO and its affiliated unions were long-time supporters of both refugee relief and the dismantlement of the national origins quota system. As Walter Reuther of the United Auto Workers and CIO explained to Congress in 1955, "many thousands of members of CIO unions themselves immigrated to this country, including Philip Murray, the late President of the CIO."[86] Because of its rich ethnic tradition, he observed, the CIO was insulted by the preferential treatment of northern and western European immigrants and the idea that an "ideal racial composition can be frozen."[87] By contrast, the AFL backed emergency refugee relief but parted with liberal reformers on the subject of permanent quota restrictions, choosing instead to support the postwar immigration agenda of conservative isolationists like McCarran. Yet even before its merger with the CIO, key factions within the AFL embraced a liberalization of the existing policy regime. During the early 1950s, state-level Federations of Labor in Massachusetts, Minnesota, and other Northern states challenged the AFL's position on immigration policy. The ascendance of George Meany to the presidency of the AFL in these years, a labor leader who favored both the AFL-CIO merger as well as liberal immigration reform, was also significant. Meany assumed the helm of the newly merged labor organization in 1955 and promptly purged the AFL's director of legislative affairs, who was a longtime champion of immigration restriction. As one union official recalls, Meany strode into the director's office and declared, "You're out! Get out!"[88] Former liberal House Democrat Andrew Biemiller was named director of the AFL-CIO's new Legislative Office.[89]

Tellingly, the AFL-CIO Executive Committee informed Biemiller's Legislative Office early on that one of its top priorities was to secure immigration reform that increased annual admissions to 250,000 and secured the "abolishment of the national origins quota system entirely." Under Meany's leadership, the AFL-CIO worked closely with other liberal groups in championing expansive immigration reform. In sharp contrast to labor activists of earlier decades, AFL-CIO leaders assailed the intellectual underpinnings of the existing policy structure. "It is a philosophy which condemns *groups* of people, a philosophy which ranks one people as inferior or superior to another," declared AFL-CIO lobbyist Hyman Bookbinder. "It runs contrary to the democratic philosophy that people ought to be judged as *individuals*."[90] Organized labor's defection from the restrictionist camp was a serious blow to postwar nativists, who now depended on well-situated allies in the congressional committee system to guard existing policies from a growing cross-party coalition devoted to reform (see table 7.7).

To bolster support for policy change, American Jewish groups initiated an ambitious campaign to publish and widely distribute pamphlets and books by prominent politicians favoring robust immigration. In *The Stranger at Our Gate*, Hubert Humphrey embraced "the very diversity of the peoples who have made up our immigrant population." Lamenting what he described as "bigoted immigration laws," Humphrey reminded

TABLE 7.7
Shifting Policy Coalitions in American Immigration Politics, 1956

Immigrant Rights Should Be	Immigrant Admissions Should Be	
	Expanded	Restricted
Expanded	Nationality groups AFL-CIO------------------------ Religious organizations Civil liberties groups	---The AFL before 1955
Restricted	Agricultural growers Low-skill industrial Employers	Veterans' groups Patriotic societies

readers that "American democracy has no genealogy. Its family tree is not easily traced."[91] John F. Kennedy's widely read *A Nation of Immigrants*, ghostwritten by his assistant Meyer Feldman, celebrated the country's rich immigrant past and denounced existing policy.[92] Just as new expertise advanced by Truman's commission and fresh empirical studies vindicated expansive immigration reform, works like *A Nation of Immigrants* helped frame a pro-immigration narrative for attentive publics that further eroded the early-twentieth-century "policy paradigm" legitimating quotas.[93]

This period also saw the national Democratic party once again become an ardent champion of immigration, restoring a traditional commitment to expansive alien admissions and rights that was abandoned during the Progressive Era. But whereas the nineteenth-century party drew sharp distinctions between white and nonwhite immigration, contemporary Democratic ideology embraced what Gerring has called "a *Universalist* perspective—the extension of rights to all aggrieved claimants and a general rhetoric of inclusion."[94] The national party's newfound passion for eliminating traces of discrimination based upon race or color made national origins quotas especially suspect to its liberal leadership.

For several years, the national party organization was urged to support major immigration reform by a coalition of liberal groups, including ethnic and religious organizations, labor, prominent academics, business leaders, the ACLU, and civil rights organizations like the NAACP.[95] By the mid-1950s, DNC leaders drafted an internal memo that mapped out an ambitious immigration reform agenda:

1. Elimination of statutory distinctions between native-born and naturalized citizens. All citizens should have equal status before the law.
2. Revision of the discriminatory features of the present law and the elimination of the National Origins Quota System.

3. Extension of more effective emergency immigration opportunities to refugees.[96]

These intraparty developments were reinforced by the 1958 elections, which produced a liberal Democratic majority in the House that was anxious to secure major programmatic innovations in such areas as civil rights, education, medical care for the elderly, social welfare, *and immigration control.* The fact that many liberal House Democrats represented ethnically diverse Northern districts added an electoral incentive for the Democratic Study Group (DSG), a liberal subcaucus of the House Democratic party, to make expansive immigration reform one of its major concerns.

Yet liberal House Democrats, flush with programmatic ambition, were vexed during the late 1950s by structural impediments of committee government, much as Progressive Era reformers were impeded by party government. The DSG was itself an institutional product of this frustration, created to initiate reforms in the House that would expand liberal influence on public policy. Well before the 1958 election gave liberals a majority of Democratic seats in the House, the 1946 election resulted in massive defeats for Northern Democrats and victories for Southern Democratic incumbents (see table 7.8). When Democrats later regained control of Congress , a conservative Southern minority enjoyed greater seniority and thus dominated most standing committees. The entrenched power of southern Democrats enabled them to thwart the egalitarian policy goals of liberal and moderate elements of their own party.[97] Northern legislators proposed a number comprehensive immigration reform bills in the late 1950s, but none survived the committee power structure. Only

TABLE 7.8
Democratic Gains and Losses in Congressional Elections, 1946–1964

Election Year	House Seats	Senate Seats
1946	−55	−12
1948	+75	+9
1950	−29	−6
1952	−22	−1
1954	+18	+1
1956	−2	0
1958	+49	+13
1960	−21	0
1962	−4	+3
1964	+37	+1

Source: Data from Norman Ornstein et al., *Vital Statistics on Congress* (Washington, DC: Congressional Quarterly Press, 1998).

minor amendments to the McCarran-Walter Act, relating generally to refugee relief, were enacted in 1958. In the Senate, liberal Democratic senators warned Majority Leader Lyndon Johnson (D-TX) that the party would lose "the large cities of the North" if it did not dismantle national origins quotas.[98] The Southern minority was unmoved by such arguments. Explaining to Jewish activists why there had been "little progress on immigration reform" in the 1950s, Celler pointed to "a coalition of southern Democrats and midwest Republicans whose opposition is strong and precludes action."

IMMIGRATION AND THE NEW FRONTIER

Since the Second World War, the White House had been the central force behind every successful effort to open the gates—if sometimes only temporarily—for refugees and some immigrant groups. From his opening campaign speech to the National Press Club on January 14, 1960, John Kennedy left no doubt that he envisioned a vigorous chief executive who was to be "the vital center of action in our whole scheme of government." The "central issue" of the 1960 election was not the farm problem, or the defense problem, or any other special policy dilemma. The fundamental question facing American voters, he insisted, was whether they would elect a president equal to the enormous leadership challenges of the Cold War era. "The American Presidency will demand that the president place himself in the very thick of the fight, that he care passionately about the fate of the people he leads," Kennedy proclaimed.[99]

Many liberal reformers, including pro-immigration activists, welcomed Kennedy's vision of energetic presidential leadership. Most liberal reformers had grown weary of the seemingly complacent leadership style displayed by Eisenhower. And their frustration with the veto power of Southern "committee barons" and the "conservative coalition" had reached a boiling point. "Since 1937 the Republican–southern Democratic voting coalition has controlled the basic decisions on legislation dealing with education, social welfare, labor, regulation of business, civil rights, *immigration*, taxes and other economic issues," the AFL-CIO complained. Likewise, the seniority system enabled Southern Democrats to frustrate "such votes as those to authorize an investigation of 'sit down' strikes, on anti-lynching legislation, *alien relief, and immigration measures*" (emphasis added).[100] The House DSG added that presidential activism on immigration policy was sorely lacking in the Eisenhower years. "Promised leadership in correcting this undemocratic and unjust [McCarran-Walter] Act has not been forthcoming from the White House," it told urban ethnics.[101] "Liberal Democrats will work to eliminate the national origins clause from immigration laws."[102]

The 1960 Democratic platform contained a plank calling for national origins quotas to be supplanted by an admissions system based on family reunion, the technical and professional needs of the country, asylum claims, and foreign policy interests. Another plank pledged to end "unfair competition by importation of nearly half a million foreign contract laborers" via the Bracero Program. Like Truman, Kennedy linked the causes of civil rights and immigration reform during his 1960 presidential campaign.[103] His campaign organization also distributed hundreds of thousands of foreign language brochures with messages tailored to Italian, Polish, Hungarian, *and* Latino voters. While committed to terminating the Bracero Program, Kennedy took care to assure Mexican Americans that his administration would consider "your traditions and your language as integral parts of the culture of the United States."[104] Bookbinder gave expression in 1960 to an abiding faith in cultural pluralism and robust immigration:

> The melting pot of America is now more appropriately and accurately described as the "mosaic" of American culture. Assimilation and integration do not mean uniformity. . . . Perhaps even more appropriate than the mosaic, the true image of America is the kaleidoscope. It is a mosaic of human beings that is always changing but encased in a basic framework of freedom, of brotherhood, of tolerance, of creativity. . . . The national origins quota system has no place on the American statute books.[105]

After the 1960 election, the DSG led an all-out effort to revise the House Rules Committee, which managed the flow of legislative traffic. For years the Rules Committee had blocked liberal measures from reaching the floor, thanks to an alliance of four Republican conservatives and two Southern Democrats that often deadlocked the twelve-member committee. As the 1960s began, the DSG narrowly won a reform campaign to enlarge the Rules Committee to fifteen members that gave liberal activists a working majority on the committee. An important structural logjam to liberal reform was removed.

While liberal lawmakers and advocacy groups celebrated this House victory, they soon discovered that the Kennedy administration was reluctant to press their agenda. Immigration reformers, who envisioned "working closely" with the White House after the 1960 election, were especially disappointed when the administration chose not to pursue reform legislation in its first two years. Kennedy and his team were chastened by several factors concerning immigration reform, including the restrictionist tenor of public opinion. But their inaction owed mostly to the enormous resistance they expected to face from James Eastland and from Francis Walter, who served notice early on that they would fight any

Kennedy efforts to dismantle a quota system "based on the image of our own people."[106] In 1961, pro-immigration activists lamented that the Kennedy White House had not mentioned immigration reform in the State of the Union message, had failed to establish a special task group to advance reform, and had retained the hard-nosed General Swing as INS commissioner.[107] In order "to get a basic commitment from the Administration for action as soon as possible," liberal immigration reformers resolved "to demonstrate to the President that the major faiths, the labor movement, and other groups . . . are in support of the humane immigration policies which the President has eloquently enunciated in the past."[108] Despite such efforts, it was not until after Walter's death in 1963 that the Kennedy administration drafted immigration legislation that was introduced to Congress by Celler and Democratic senator Philip Hart.

The administration's bill called for national origins quotas to be phased out over a five-year period, and for the Asian-Pacific Triangle to be abolished immediately. In their place, the White House proposed that immigrants apply for admission under a preference system that reserved 50 percent of visas for persons with needed skills and education, with the other half reserved for relatives of American citizens and permanent residents. The new formula was said to promote "equality and fair play for the people of all nations."[109] But the president's leading immigration adviser, Abba Schwartz, chief of the Bureau of Security and Consular Affairs, soon reported strong resistance at the other end of Pennsylvania Avenue. Eastland, still chair of the Senate Judiciary Committee and its immigration subcommittee, predictably opposed the administration's bill. Just as troubling to the Kennedy White House was the fact that the new chair of the House immigration subcommittee, Representative Michael Feighan (D-OH), was equally obstreperous. Celler, despite chairing the House Judiciary Committee, told Schwartz that he was "helpless" to control Feighan and urged the administration to do what it could to apply pressure on him.[110] Like McCarran and Walter before them, Eastland and Feighan had significant structural clout to derail reform. At the end of 1963, neither immigration subcommittee had even held hearings on Kennedy's immigration bill.[111]

The Kennedy administration enjoyed much greater success in its quest to terminate the Bracero Program. For years, organized labor, religious groups, and welfare organizations protested that imported farm labor hurt U.S. laborers and Mexican guestworkers alike. Federal standards for bracero wages and working conditions were routinely disregarded by employers, they complained. Worse yet, these violations often occurred with the full knowledge of INS and other government officials, thereby creating a system that reformers described as a "broken down . . . state of corruption."[112] After the 1960 election, the AFL-CIO lobbied Congress heavily for the program's termination. The administration and Democratic leaders in Congress lent their support to the effort.

Yet growers and other interests exerted considerable pressure of their own on members of Congress, especially those representing rural agricultural areas. The American Farm Bureau Federation, the National Cotton Council, the United Fresh Fruit and Vegetable Association, the National Beet Growers, ranchers, and other advocacy groups rallied to save the Bracero Program. Several congressmembers made the familiar argument that Southern and Western employers, especially growers of perishable crops, lacked a ready supply of domestic workers. In 1961, compromise legislation was approved that extended the Bracero Program for two years but imposed new protections for U.S. farm laborers. Kennedy reluctantly signed the measure, noting that it was "necessary to protect domestic farm workers."[113] The administration later took steps to lower the number of contracts granted for the importation of Mexican guestworkers (see table 7.9).

TABLE 7.9
Mexican Contract Labor and Legal Immigrant Admissions, 1942–1964

	Mexican Guestworkers Granted Contracts by U.S. Officials	Mexican Immigrants Legally Admitted
1942	4,203	2,378
1943	52,098	4,172
1944	62,170	6,598
1945	49,454	6,702
1946	32,043	7,146
1947	19,632	7,558
1948	35,345	8,384
1949	107,000	8,083
1950	67,500	6,774
1951	192,000	6,153
1952	197,100	9,079
1953	201,380	17,183
1954	309,033	30,645
1955	398,650	50,772
1956	445,197	65,047
1957	436,049	49,154
1958	432,643	26,716
1960	315,846	32,684
1961	291,420	41,632
1962	194,978	55,291
1963	186,865	55,263
1964	177,736	32,967

Source: Data from INS, *Annual Report*, 1943–1964 (Washington, DC: Government Printing Office, 1944–65).

Two years later, growers again called for an extension to the Bracero Program. Their vigorous campaign led one weary Democrat to remark that "in 23 years in Congress, I have never been lobbied by so many high-handed, brazen lobbyists."[114] Nevertheless, the AFL-CIO and the DSG mobilized liberal majorities in both houses against an extension, highlighting the fact that growers had done little to improve the plight of either domestic or imported farmworkers. No longer enjoying the luxury of quietly hammering out guestworker policies in committee rooms, the champions of grower interests struggled to make a persuasive case for extending the Bracero Program. "It is somewhat of a Peace Corps in reverse, you might say," argued Representative Ed Foreman (R-TX) in desperation, "and a new twist on foreign education and assistance."[115] But newly elected representative Henry B. Gonzalez (D-TX), a prominent Mexican American leader who despised the Bracero Program, would hear none of it. "The men who say they love this laborer and who say that they really want to help him are the very ones that will not help him to come here in freedom," declared Gonzalez.[116] If the United States required extra hands to harvest its crops, Gonzalez and other liberal reformers argued, then Latinos should be welcomed as legal immigrants with the opportunity of becoming full members of American society.[117] "If we need the Mexican laborer, why not let him come here in freedom as our parents did and as a free man," he demanded.[118] Gonzalez had effectively linked the concerns of organized labor to Latino civil rights. Grower allies struggled to marshal an adequate response. Moreover, the burden was on enthusiasts of the Bracero Program to secure congressional authorization for another two-year extension. To the delight of labor activists, their bid to renew the guestworker program failed. Significantly, less than a decade after Operation Wetback, lawmakers were unconcerned that the termination of the labor program might spur illegal Mexican immigration. Liberals concentrated instead on fighting off grower campaigns in 1964 and 1965 to revive the Bracero Program.

IMMIGRATION REFORM AND THE GREAT SOCIETY JUGGERNAUT

Some immigration scholars have argued that Kennedy's assassination and Johnson's landslide victory of 1964 "meant the end of the quota system and its replacement by a preference system was virtually inevitable."[119] However, many pro-immigration reformers looked upon Johnson's ascendance to the Oval Office with considerable dread. Johnson had voted without hesitation for the McCarran-Walter Act in 1952 and as Senate majority leader thwarted efforts by Kennedy, Lehman, and others to overhaul the immigration code. During his tenure as the senator from Texas, Johnson also was criticized for placing the "big gas-oil-cattle-sugar interests" of his state ahead of Mexican American civil rights.[120] Whether or not such views were overly harsh, immigration reformers had reason to question Johnson's resolve when it came to dismantling national origins quotas.

Johnson wasted little time in calling on Congress to honor his fallen predecessor by enacting a New Frontier program that included civil rights reform. Exercising enormous political skills, many of which he had mastered as Senate majority leader, Johnson resuscitated a civil rights bill that had languished before Kennedy's death. In his efforts to break the Senate logjam, Johnson successfully bartered with Everett Dirksen, the Senate Republican leader, to secure his endorsement of the bill. As such, one cross-party coalition ended another's age-old blockade against civil rights reform, as the conservative coalition failed to stop passage of the landmark Civil Rights Act on July 2, 1964. The victory signaled a resurgence of executive preeminence as legislative leader.[121] As Sidney Milkis has observed, LBJ "continued—even accelerated—developments of the Kennedy era that accentuated the power and independence of the executive; arguably his administration marked the height of modern presidential leadership."[122]

Rather than relish his civil rights victory, Johnson pressed Congress to pass as many bills as possible in his quest to transcend Roosevelt's New Deal accomplishments. Driven to be "the greatest of them all," he resolved that "there was no time to rest" in pursuit of his Great Society agenda.[123] But if Johnson was tireless in his efforts to realize and surpass Kennedy's New Frontier program, immigration reformers were painfully aware of his silence on the issue that mattered most to them. Sensing retreat, White House officials who worked on immigration reform during Kennedy's tenure urged LBJ to support the dismantlement of national origins quotas. However, Johnson initially resisted the idea when urged by former Kennedy advisers like Meyer Feldman, who were told that immigration was an explosive issue that could hurt other reform plans. He also worried about being assailed for championing the Kennedy immigration bill after having voted for McCarran-Walter Act in 1952.[124] To his own close adviser, Jack Valenti, Johnson voiced grave reservations about backing immigration reform legislation that enjoyed little public support.[125]

Behind the scenes, Feldman and other original Kennedy staffers persuaded Valenti to prevail upon Johnson to expand immigration opportunities.[126] Schwartz secured similar support from Bill Moyers, another of Johnson's close advisers.[127] White House insiders offered several compelling arguments to the president on behalf of immigration reform: Kennedy had described it as "the most urgent and fundamental reform" of his 1963 legislative agenda; Italians, Poles, and Jews were more likely to vote on immigration policy questions than were other mass publics for whom the issue was less salient; national origins quotas hurt American credibility abroad as much as Jim Crowism did; and the persistence of the quota system clearly contradicted Johnson's pledge "to eliminate from this Nation every trace of discrimination and oppression that is based upon race or color."[128] According to Feldman, Johnson ultimately could not escape the linkages between immigration reform and the administration's most prominent foreign policy and civil rights goals. "The President eventually recognized that existing immigration law, and in particular, national origins quotas created many decades before on racist grounds, as inconsistent with civil rights and racial justice," recalls Valenti.[129] Johnson became an eleventh-hour convert to immigration reform.

Once committed to immigration reform, the Johnson administration worked closely with liberal Democrats and moderate Republicans to secure policy innovations that had proven elusive for decades. In his 1964 State of the Union address, Johnson outlined a civil rights agenda that championed for all citizens equal access to public facilities, equal eligibility for federal benefits, an equal chance to vote, and "good public schools" for all children. Then he added, "We must also lift by legislation the bars of discrimination against those who seek entry into our country."[130] Immigration reform had become a prominent element of Johnson's Great Society juggernaut. Kennedy's reform bill was swiftly reintroduced by Hart in the Senate and Celler in the House.

One week after his address, Johnson summoned to the White House members of the House and Senate Immigration Subcommittees, leaders of pro-immigration advocacy groups, and the media. As Eastland and Feighan looked on warily, Johnson went before television cameras to urge lawmakers to make American immigration law more egalitarian. He reminded Congress that every president since Truman believed that existing immigration policies hurt the nation in its Cold War struggle with the Soviet Union. Johnson then invoked the language of Kennedy's inaugural address, urging a meritocratic admissions policy that asked immigrants, "What can you do for our country?" He added that "we ought to never ask, 'In what country were you born?'"[131] On cue, Hart, Celler, Rodino, and other pro-immigration lawmakers praised the bill. When they concluded their statements, Johnson caught Eastland off guard by asking him to address assembled reporters and advocacy groups. Eastland told the gathering that he was prepared to look into the matter "very carefully and very expeditiously."[132]

During the Kennedy years, Eastland refused to hold hearings on any bill intended to revise the system established by the McCarran-Walter Act of 1952. According to Johnson's chief liaison to Congress, Lawrence O'Brien, "It was hard to find Jim Eastland friendly to any measure that was advocated by presidents in the New Frontier–Great Society period."[133]

Yet after a series of tense Oval Office meetings with Johnson in 1964, Eastland surprised Washington insiders by agreeing to temporarily relinquish control of his Immigration Subcommittee to the freshman senator from Massachusetts, Edward Kennedy. As Valenti observed, Eastland "didn't want to fight the President and agreed . . . to go along on this one" after horse-trading, presidential intimidation, and assurances that he could save face by ultimately voting against the measure.[134]

The administration and its allies encountered stronger resistance from Feighan, who initially refused to report the president's bill out of his subcommittee. "He had his own views and he was going to be disruptive procedurally to accomplish his objectives," O'Brien noted. "There's nothing worse than to have a subcommittee chairman, or committee chairman, get his nose out of joint."[135] Throughout 1964, Celler, as chair of the House Judiciary Committee, fought to gain control of a wayward Immigration Subcommittee. The ensuing struggle between Celler and Feighan—as well as pressing battles over civil rights, Medicare, and other issues—postponed action until after the 1964 election.

During the 1964 presidential campaign, Democrats pledged their fealty to Johnson and the Great Society reform program. "Under the leadership of President Johnson, Democrats will continue to work for enactment of the type of progressive legislation that has brought to the American people the most prosperous era in the history of mankind," the House DSG proclaimed.[136] Immigration was featured prominently among the "progressive" reforms promised by House liberals. Republican spokespersons offered some mild challenges to the liberal immigration reform agenda. Barry Goldwater promised to revive the Bracero Program, while his running mate, Representative William Miller (NY), occasionally suggested that immigration reform would produce increased unemployment and welfare dependency.[137] But immigration proved to have little political salience for most of the electorate. Immigration became a significant issue in Robert Kennedy's successful bid for New York's Senate seat, but rarely surfaced in the presidential contest.[138] Only in Northern cities did the Johnson campaign remind ethnic voters that immigration reform would contribute to "building the Great Society."[139]

Shortly after the Democratic electoral windfall of 1964, one liberal lobbyist confessed "a recognition that spread like wildfire among liberal and labor organizations—that the back of the old conservative-Dixiecrat coalition had been broken, but that it might mend again as soon as the next election." As a result, he observed, most liberal reformers believed "we must get everything through in the next 2 years that we need in the next 10."[140] Johnson shared this perspective, embracing a "politics of haste" that led to the passage of eighty of his legislative proposals in 1965 alone.[141] Immigration reform was one of the administration's top priorities for the 89th Congress. Days after the new Congress convened, Johnson sent a special message to Congress again endorsing the dismantlement of national origins quotas. Administration experts testifying before Congress stressed the "urgency" of immigration reform "in terms of our self-interest abroad. In the present ideological conflict between freedom and fear, we proclaim to the world that our central precept is that all are born equal. . . . Yet under present law, we choose among immigrants on the basis of where they are."[142] Others, such as Vice President Hubert Humphrey, drew explicit linkages between the causes of black civil rights and immigration reform. "We have removed all elements of second-class citizenship from our laws by the Civil Rights Act," he declared in several speeches. "We must in 1965 remove all elements in our immigration law which suggest that there are second-class people. . . . We want to bring our immigration law into line with the spirit of the Civil Rights Act of 1964."[143]

While the administration applied rhetorical pressure on congressional restrictionists, it also maneuvered with House Democratic leaders to expand the membership of the immigration subcommittee to neutralize Feighan. For instance, Jack Brooks (D-TX), a Johnson loyalist, was added to the subcommittee as a crucial swing vote.[144] Although Feighan eventually agreed to report legislation abolishing national origins quotas and the Asia–Pacific Triangle, he succeeded in changing the emphasis of the new preference system. Whereas the administration's original proposal placed considerable emphasis on admitting aliens with needed skills and educational backgrounds, Feighan was able to make family reunification the centerpiece of the new immigration system. In particular, he secured four preference categories for family reunification, only two for those possessing needed skills, and one for refugees.

In the Senate, the White House and liberal lawmakers compromised with Dirksen and Sam Ervin (D-SC) on a 120,000 annual ceiling for Western Hemisphere immigration (although no per country limit). As O'Brien explained, "Listen we're not going to walk away from this because we didn't get a whole loaf. We'll take half a loaf or three-quarters of a loaf."[145] In the case of immigration reform, Great Society reformers agreed that the most important goal was to abolish national origins quotas. With stronger emphasis on family unification and new Western Hemisphere limits, the Immigration Reform Act of 1965 passed both houses with large cross-party majorities. In a signing ceremony at the Statue of Liberty, Johnson celebrated the legislation for repairing "a deep and painful flaw in the fabric of American justice."[146]

The new immigration system provided 170,000 visas for immigrants originating in the Eastern Hemisphere (no country was to be allotted more than 20,000 visas), and 120,000 visas for Western Hemisphere im-

TABLE 7.10
The Preference System Established by the Immigration Act of 1965

Preference	Category Description	Number Alloted
Exempt	Spouses, unmarried minor children, and parents of U.S. citizens	no limit
First	Unmarried adult children of U.S. citizens	58,000 (20%)
Second	Spouses and unmarried children of permanent resident aliens	58,000 (20%)
Third	Professionals, especially gifted scientists and artists	29,000 (10%)
Fourth	Married children of U.S. citizens	29,000 (10%)
Fifth	Brothers and sisters of U.S. citizens over age 21	69,600 (24%)
Sixth	Skilled and unskilled workers who fill labor shortage needs	29,000 (10%)
Seventh	Refugees	17,400 (6%)
Total	74% family-based; 20% employment-based; 6% refugees	290,000 (pierceable for immediate family of U.S. citizens)

migrants (no country limit imposed). Spouses, minor children, and parents of American citizens were exempted from these numerical ceilings. All other persons from the Eastern Hemisphere were placed on waiting lists under seven preference categories: 64 percent of visas were reserved for family reunification, 20 percent for needed professionals and unskilled workers, and 6 percent for refugees (see table 7.10). Significantly, liberal reformers sought to mollify reluctant colleagues by assuring them that the new system would principally benefit Europeans with family ties in the United States. "Since the people of Africa and Asia have very few relatives here, comparatively few of them could immigrate from those countries," Celler explained. Johnson officials made similar assertions.[147] However forthright these predictions were, immigration trends would follow a very different trajectory under the new system.

CONCLUSION

The Second World War transformed America's orientation toward the world, making its national security interests so intimately tied to global affairs that the nation no longer had the luxury of turning inward. The United States emerged from the war as an uneasy superpower locked in tense struggle with the Soviet Union, a rivalry that cast long shadows on how American political leaders addressed such diverse policy concerns as education, civil rights, social welfare, and defense.[148] The Cold War profoundly shaped the nature of national political conflict over immigration in the postwar decades, giving modern presidents and congressional liberals new incentives to expand immigration opportunities and conservative lawmakers an interest in using entrenched committee power to actively defend existing quota restrictions. Anti-immigrant "committee barons" adeptly seized upon Cold War insecurities to reinvigorate a nativist policy regime, and for a time their strategy effectively frustrated nonincremental reform. Their capacity to thwart major policy change came easily in a fragmented American political system intended to make coordinated action elusive.

Tellingly, the demise of the national origins quota system came only at the zenith of the Great Society, when an extraordinary convergence of pro-immigration developments propelled an opening of the gates. In the final analysis, the expansive turn of national immigration policy in 1965 sprang from a familiar set of order-shattering forces: new international pressures, shifting group alliances, fresh expertise, and institutional change. Eugenicist narratives that powerfully validated literacy tests, Asian exclusion, and national origins quotas during the early-twentieth century fell into intellectual disrepute after the war, largely due to their intimate association with Nazi racism. In their wake, a new generation of academic experts and bureaucratic specialists structured the terms of official immigration debate by embracing robust admissions as beneficial to the country; in the process, they recast the policy implications of scientific government. Equally important, Cold War competition with the Soviet Union bestowed broad powers on the American presidency and in turn created new imperatives for postwar executives to pursue expansive immigration reform. The emergent postwar policy narrative linked expansive immigration opportunities to Cold War imperatives, a new civil rights zeitgeist, and sustained economic prosperity. By the late 1950s, organized labor's defection from the restrictionist camp and a growing bloc of liberal congressional Democrats signaled the gathering political momentum for pro-immigration reform.

Yet the institutional supports for a restrictionist policy regime were not easily surmounted. The national origins quota system persisted under the watchful eye of conservative committee barons until 1965, when immigration reformers made the most of what Jeff Fishel has described as "a structural responsiveness in the policy-making process that was ripe for effective presidential leadership in helping forge agenda breakthroughs."[149]

Although the Immigration Act of 1965 was a watershed in the development of American immigration policy, its most prominent sponsors did their best to downplay the law's significance in their public discourse. National policymakers were well aware that the general public was opposed to increases in either the volume or diversity of immigration to the United States.[150] Senator Edward Kennedy, one of the bill's principal stewards, assured skeptics that the reform "would not inundate America with immigrants from any one country or area or the most populated and economically deprived nations of Africa and Asia."[151] Even Lyndon Johnson, who was never one to understate his programmatic achievements, spoke of the law in moderate tones. "This bill we sign today is not a revolutionary bill," he remarked at the 1965 signing ceremony. "It does not affect the lives of millions. It will not reshape the structure of our daily lives."[152]

In truth, the policy departures of the mid-1960s dramatically recast immigration patterns and, concomitantly, the nation. Annual immigrant admissions increased sharply in the years after the law's passage. Yet its most profound impact was on the ethnic makeup of newcomers, as "chain migration" of family members under the new preference system led to unprecedented levels of Third World immigration to the United States in subsequent decades. Indeed, Asian and Latin American arrivals would comprise three-quarters of legal alien admissions in the 1970s and 1980s, and currently represent 80 percent of all new arrivals. The Bracero Program's termination and new caps on Western Hemisphere immigration both contributed to new waves of illegal entries, creating public policy dilemmas that bedevil national political leaders to the present day. The 1965 law also established refugee admissions as a formal policy priority in U.S. immigration law, with refugees defined as those escaping communist regimes or the Middle East. However, the number of refugees seeking relief soon outstripped the 10,200 refugee preference limit, leading subsequent presidents to use their parole powers to admit large numbers of Cuban, Vietnamese, and other refugee groups. Policy innovations of the 1960s would open the gates to a stream of immigration that was unprecedented in the nation's history. These demographic shifts in American immigration inspired both a new restrictionist movement as well as broad and enduring popular support for decreasing immigration in subsequent years. As the next chapter illuminates, future policy choices were to be deeply influenced by the legacies of an immigration regime forged in the postwar era.

CHAPTER EIGHT

The Rebirth of American Immigration

THE RIGHTS REVOLUTION, NEW RESTRICTIONISM, AND POLICY DEADLOCK

THE UNITED STATES has not always been a country of immigration. During the decades in which the national origins quota system flourished, immigration was highly restricted. The Hart-Celler Act of 1965 marked a decisive turnaround in national policy and helped breathe life into new era of mass immigration. Not only did annual legal immigration grow sharply after 1965, but an unprecedented majority of newcomers came from Asia, Latin America, and the Caribbean (see fig. 8.1). At the same time that refugee admissions and family preferences and exemptions spurred legal immigration from nontraditional sending countries, European admissions fell to less that 20 percent of legal admissions during the 1970s.[1] These demographic trends were reinforced in the same decade by increased flows of illegal immigrants. In short, the policy initiatives of New Frontier and Great Society reformers, pursued at a time of modest inflows, ushered in a new wave of large-scale immigration.

In the nineteenth century, expansive policy outcomes were reinforced by the large number of white male newcomers who easily became voting citizens and who commanded sufficient electoral and partisan clout to guard expansive immigration policies. New immigrants and kindred ethnics after 1965 ostensibly had similar opportunities to protect their policy interests. Section 311 of the McCarran-Walter Act of 1952 established that "the right of a person to become a naturalized citizen of the United States shall not be denied or abridged because of race or sex or because such person is married." Yet Mexican and other Latin American immigrants naturalized at very low rates during the 1970s. According to various scholars, the post-1960s expansion of individual and group rights meant that the incentives for newcomers to naturalize and vote were quite small in the 1970s when compared to nineteenth-century imperatives.[2] As Schuck and Smith observed:

The law . . . increasingly speaks of individuals' "rights," the language of entitlement, rather than of their "interests," the language of policy and accommodation. Moreover, the law increasingly emphasizes the

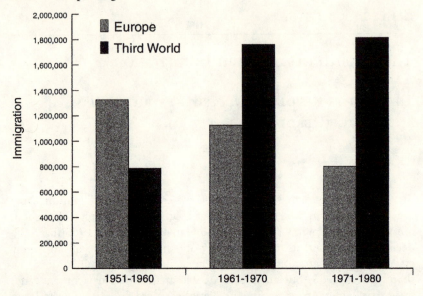

Fig. 8.1. European and Third World Immigration to the United States in the Postwar Decades (Source: *INS Statistical Yearbook, 2000* [Washington, DC: Government Printing Office, 2000])

values of equality, group interest, and nondiscrimination. . . . And it is welfare state membership, not citizenship, that increasingly counts. Political membership uniquely confers little more than the right to vote and the right to remain here permanently; the former is used by only a bare majority of eligible voters, while the latter, although undeniably valuable, is problematic for only a minority of legal aliens.[3]

In short, the post-1960s "rights revolution" gave immigrants fewer reasons to become citizens. Naturalized voters and parties were no longer the political lifeblood of expansive immigration policies.

What, then, sustained broad immigration opportunities in the 1970s despite economic "stagflation," growing public disquietude about the size and diversity of alien inflows, and new organized opposition to robust admissions? Applying our familiar explanatory framework, this chapter points to structural veto-points that derailed restrictionist proposals; geopolitical considerations that propelled special refugee admissions; and coalitional and ideological legacies of the civil rights movement that reinforced expansive policies. Few issues were more prominent than illegal immigration. But from 1966 to 1976, efforts to discourage unauthorized entries were stymied by a tenacious Senate Judiciary Committee chair and an aging "iron triangle." Even after the demise of this subgovernment, new Latino ethnic lobbies and rights-oriented arguments hindered employer sanctions and deportation initiatives. When refugee numbers outstripped the Hart-Celler Act's preference levels, presidents motivated by foreign policy concerns took independent action to provide asylum for more refugees. Significantly, human rights advocates in Congress pressed administrations to admit additional refugees who fled persecution but did not meet certain national geopolitical interests. Finally, increases in the volume and diversity of legal immigration amidst domestic economic woes gave rise to a new restrictionist movement comprised of environmentalists, population control activists, and cultural protectionists. Popular restrictionist proposals were hamstrung by new ethnic lobbies, a post–civil rights era sensitivity of policymakers to claims that new restrictive initiatives were racially inspired efforts to exclude nonwhite Asians and Latinos, and dilatory tactics of congressional Democratic leaders. The result was strategically designed policy inertia.

The Hart-Celler Act recast the politics of immigration control in another way. In the years following its passage, a new issue pluralism was institutionalized. That is, political struggles over how to regulate alien admissions and rights were increasingly compartmentalized into distinctive policy realms governing refugee and asylee relief,[4] illegal immigration, and legal immigration. This chapter examines each of these realms in turn.

GEOPOLITICS AND HUMAN RIGHTS: CONGRESS, THE PRESIDENCY, AND REFUGEE POLICY

The seventh preference of the Hart-Celler Act reserved roughly 10,000 visas annually for refugees who escaped persecution in "any Communist or Communist-dominated country or area." Many lawmakers hoped that setting aside special visas for refugee admissions would make it unnecessary for presidents to invoke emergency parole powers to admit large numbers of refugees outside of the regular system. Lest there be any doubt of their intentions, both the Senate and House Judiciary Committees stated in their 1965 reports that the parole provisions of the Immigration and Naturalization Act of 1952 had not been administered "in accordance with the original intention of the drafters of that legislation." It called on executives to act only in "emergency, individual, and isolated situations, such as the case of an alien who requires medical attention, *and not for the immigration of classes or groups outside the limit of the law*" (emphasis added).[5]

Legislative attempts to limit executive "parole" authority were dashed even before the ink had dried on the 1965 reform. At the Hart-Celler Act's signing ceremony, carefully staged at the base of the Statue of Liberty, Lyndon Johnson triumphantly announced that he had directed the attorney general to parole all Cubans who fled the Castro regime for the United States.[6] The parole program, which became known as the Freedom Flight Program, reflected the continuing belief of presidents and the U.S. foreign policy establishment (starting with Truman and Eisenhower) that targeted refugee relief could serve as a means of discrediting communist regimes. Significantly, Congress affirmed these Cold War commitments with passage of the Cuban Adjustment Act of 1966. This law treated all Cubans as refugees entitled to settle in the United States. As implemented over the next three decades, it allowed hundreds of thousands of Cubans to be admitted expeditiously, granted special financial assistance unavailable to other newcomers, and permitted them to adjust their status to legal permanent residents after one year.

The Nixon administration strongly supported the Freedom Flight Program begun by Johnson. It is hardly surprising, then, that the Nixon White House used the parole to enable between 40,000 to 60,000 Czechoslovakians visiting the country on travel permits to remain after the Soviet Union invaded Prague in 1968. Another 12,000 Czech refugees were admitted from abroad. Nevertheless, the Nixon administration's willingness to employ the parole authority of the attorney general to assist refugees fleeing communist regimes had its limits. For instance, Henry Kissinger and other advisers were unwilling to sacrifice the policy of detente on behalf of Jews facing Soviet persecution. As Kissinger pressed William Safire and Robert Haldeman, "How would it be if Brezhnev comes to the United States with a petition about the Negroes in Mississippi?"[7]

Across Pennsylvania Avenue, however, an unlikely coalition of liberal and conservative legislators championed the use of executive parole authority to assist Jewish refugees from the Soviet Union. Whereas past presidential use of parole powers to admit refugees beyond the boundaries of applicable law drew fire from congressional restrictionists, the New Congress of the 1970s often criticized the executive branch for not doing enough *to broaden* refugee relief. The Nixon White House was assailed by both conservative anticommunists and liberal human rights advocates in Congress for its silence on asylum for Soviet Jews. When the United States and Soviet Union reached a trade agreement in 1972, Senator Henry Jackson and Representative Charles Vanek generated strong support for making open emigration a condition for granting trade benefits to communist nations. To cool these tempers, the Nixon administration assured Congress that it would not attempt to lower trade barriers without their approval, while the Soviet Union removed obstacles to emigration. When Congress finally passed the Trade Reform Act of 1974, it also enacted the Jackson-Vanek amendment.

The powerful coalition of Cold War anticommunists and human rights liberals also spurred large Indochinese refugee admissions. Michael Teitelbaum writes of a shared sense of "moral obligation" among policymakers after the failed U.S. intervention in Vietnam. "State Department officials with deep personal involvement in Vietnam policies were among those strongly advocating generous admissions from that country," he notes.[8] As Saigon fell in the spring of 1975, the United States rescued more than 130,000 Vietnamese, Cambodians, and Laotians. Although these refugee admissions were supported broadly by members of Congress, some resistance was expressed by Representative Joshua Eilberg, chair of the House Immigration Subcommittee. But while he pointed to rising unemployment and a Gallup poll indicating that 54 percent of Americans opposed the new parole program, leaders of both parties praised Ford for providing refugee relief. Large congressional majorities enacted legislation extending legal residency, resettlement assistance, language and vocational training, and medical care for Indochinese refugees.

During the Carter administration, ethnic lobbies, civil rights and religious groups, organized labor, and liberal politicians rallied behind the executive use of parole authority to assist large numbers of Indochinese "boat people." A Citizen's Committee on Indochinese Refugees, led by Leo Cherne of the International Rescue Committee and Bayard Rustin of the A. Philip Randolph Institute, organized advocacy efforts on behalf of Indochinese refugees throughout the decade. Ninety of the country's most prominent African American leaders also voiced strong support for rescuing Indochinese refugees in an open letter to the White House and Congress in 1978. "Through our arduous struggle for civil, political, and economic rights in America, we have learned a fundamental lesson: the battle against human misery is indivisible," they wrote. "If our government lacks compassion for these dispossessed human beings, it is difficult to believe that the same government can have much compassion for America's black minority, or for America's poor."[9] Speaking for the AFL-CIO, George Meany offered similar ideological reasons for affirming generous refugee policies. "Unemployment is not the only thing that the labor movement cares about," he said. "We care about suffering human beings everywhere."[10] Beyond strategic alliances with ethnic lobbies, these interests shared an ideological commitment to the human rights of necessitous strangers. By the late-1970s, Carter invoked parole powers annually to help Indochinese refugees.

While liberal human rights advocates found common ground with conservative Cold Warriors in their support for generous refugee admissions on behalf of Jews escaping Soviet territory and displaced Indochinese, they called for more expansive refugee and asylee policies. In their view, the fundamental problem with existing policies was that they granted relief almost exclusively to those escaping communist countries. Democrats like Representative Donald Fraser argued that the promotion of human rights "is both morally imperative and practically necessary."[11] Other congressional liberals, such as Senator Kennedy and Representatives Robert Drinan and Shirley Chisholm, protested that countless Chilean, Haitian, Filipino, and South Korean refugees fleeing regime persecution were virtually ignored. Chisholm and the Black Caucus were particularly concerned that of the roughly 30,000 Haitians who sought asylum in the United States between 1972 and 1980, fewer than fifty received asylum.[12] Battles between the Carter White House and the Black Caucus over Haitian asylees were particularly bitter. Similar to Republican administrations, Carter officials insisted that Haitians fled dire economic conditions rather than political repression and warned that grants of relief might trigger a flood of Haitian asylum seekers to U.S. shores. By contrast, many liberal lawmakers yearned for a universal asylum process for persecuted aliens, one that transcended the dictates of the Cold War and geopolitics. The refugee and asylum policies of the Reagan and Bush presidencies would intensify these ideological conflicts in the 1980s.

ILLEGAL IMMIGRATION AND THE INERTIAL POWER OF AN AGING SUBGOVERNMENT

Illegal immigration inspired more media attention, public concern, and remedial efforts by national policy elites than did any other migratory issue of the 1970s. In the decade after Operaton Wetback, apprehensions of illegal aliens never exceeded 100,000 annually. Following the end of the Bracero Program and the implementation of a new Western Hemisphere ceiling, however, apprehensions rose steadily to more than one million per year by the late 1970s (see table 8.1).[13] Congressional activists, Republican and Democratic presidents, and organized labor all seized upon employer sanctions legislation to resolve the perceived illegal immigration crisis.

Organized labor had expressed alarm about Mexican labor inflows for decades. The termination of the Bracero Program in 1964 was led by the AFL-CIO, which loathed the importation of temporary Mexican workers to harvest seasonal crops at low wages and under poor working conditions. Yet the end of the Bracero Program did not stem Mexican labor recruitment. Instead, the program's demise combined with new Hart-Celler limits on Western Hemisphere immigration sent Mexican labor inflows underground, where they soon thrived and expanded.

Union leaders had worried a great deal about illegal immigration in the past. Delegates at AFL conventions as early as 1950 endorsed "the immediate enactment of legislation to bar the illegal entries of aliens . . .

TABLE 8.1
Undocumented Aliens Apprehended and Deported, 1961–1980

	Number	Year	Number
1961	88,823	1971	420,126
1962	95,758	1972	505,949
1963	88,712	1973	655,968
1964	86,597	1974	788,145
1965	110,371	1975	766,600
1966	138,520	1976	875,915
1967	161,608	1977	1,046,215
1968	212,057	1978	1,057,977
1969	283,557	1979	1,076,418
1970	345,353	1980	910,361
1961–70	1,608,356	1971–80	11,883,328

Source: Immigration and Naturalization Service, Statistical Yearbook (Washington, DC: Government Printing Office, 1990).

and further that such legislation provide a criminal penalty for employers who hire such labor."[14] It was at labor's behest that Senator Douglas proposed an employer sanctions amendment to the McCarran-Walter Act, only to be frustrated when McCarran and Eastland inserted a "Texas proviso" that insulated employers of undocumented aliens from any legal sanction. In the decade after the Eisenhower administration initiated Operation Wetback of 1954, the issue of illegal immigration virtually disappeared from the public agenda. INS leadership confidently told Congress that the problem of illegal immigration had been resolved, a claim that seemed to be borne out by the low numbers of annual apprehensions of undocumented aliens along the Mexican-American border.[15] At the time illegal immigration was increasing in the late-1960s, the U.S. share in world markets was in decline and inflation threatened domestic prosperity. Against this backdrop, union leaders renewed their call for employer sanctions and stepped-up border control.

Congressional liberals led the assault on illegal immigration. At Senate hearings on the problem in 1969, Walter Mondale (D-MN) warned that if the federal government did not "stop that hemorrhaging . . . along the Texas border and along the California border," domestic labor protection and antipoverty campaigns would be compromised.[16] Pro-labor liberals long disdained the cozy relationship between growers, the INS, and Southern and Western committee chairs in Congress—an alliance that granted employers access to a steady supply of cheap and exploitable Mexican workers. The postwar campaign against temporary worker pro-

grams and illegal immigration, then, was considered a fundamentally liberal cause.

The progressive character of fighting illegal immigration was confirmed
for many liberal Democrats by the struggle of Cesar Chavez and his Farm
Workers Association (FWA) to win decent wages and working conditions
for Mexican-American agricultural workers. When Chavez and the FWA
organized a grape-pickers' strike in Delano, California, in 1965, it soon
was heralded as a new movement for Mexican American civil rights.
Grape pickers were joined on the picket line by student protesters, clergy,
national labor leaders, as well as members of the Congress on Racial
Equality (CORE) and the Student Nonviolent Co-ordinating Committee
(SNCC).[17] The campaign to organize farmworkers focused attention on
undocumented aliens who were being imported by growers to break the
grape-pickers' strike. In 1968, Chavez urged Senator Robert Kennedy
(D-NY) and others to pressure INS officers "to remove Wetbacks (illegal
entrants) . . . who are being recruited and imported to break our strike."[18]
At congressional hearings and in publications, Chavez and the United
Farm Workers, a new AFL-CIO affiliate that succeeded the FWA, assailed
the INS for doing little to discourage illegal immigration during harvest
season.[19]

During the early 1970s, the AFL-CIO's Legislative Department secured broad support in the House for employer sanctions legislation.
Employer sanctions appealed to many liberal Democrats because they
promised to discourage illegal entries by targeting unscrupulous employers rather than resorting to mass deportation campaigns that threatened civil liberties abuses of Latino citizens and legal permanent residents. If employers could be dissuaded from hiring undocumented aliens,
so the argument went, fewer foreign workers would be drawn illegally
across national borders by the magnet of American jobs. The AFL-CIO's
Andrew Biemiller worked closely with House Democrats on employer
sanctions legislation, forming a particularly strong alliance with Peter
Rodino (D-NJ), chair of the House Judiciary Committee's Subcommittee on Immigration.[20] Biemiller and Rodino agreed that in an increasingly
liberal and reform-minded Congress, the employer sanctions proposal
was "an idea whose time has come."[21] In 1971, Rodino's subcommittee
held extensive hearings on illegal immigration across the country.

At hearings held in California, Colorado, and Texas, the subcommittee
was urged by state politicians, labor organizations, civil rights groups,
and even religious service agencies to enact employer sanctions. "Cold
statistics emphasize the urgency of a change in the federal government
policy toward illegal entry," stated Leonard Carter, the NAACP's Western regional director. In Los Angeles alone, he estimated, "the poor have
been deprived of 100,000 jobs for which they might qualify."[22] The U.S.

Commission on Civil Rights heard similar testimony from urban African American leaders that black youth were losing jobs to illegal immigrants. At the subcommittee's Texas hearings, witnesses from the U.S. Catholic Conference and the League of United Latin American Citizens (LULAC) also endorsed employer sanctions. Albert Armendariz, a former LULAC president, pointed out that "all illegal aliens, all 3 million of them, are certainly in . . . unfair competition with the minorities in this country and certainly the Mexican American is in competition with the Mexican."[23] Yet Armendariz and other Latino witnesses also supported an amnesty program for undocumented aliens already residing in the country, noting that vigorous internal enforcement would violate the civil rights of many Mexican Americans.[24] At the investigation's close, Rodino and his colleagues concluded that undocumented aliens were "depriving Americans of jobs" amidst high unemployment. They also worried that illegals were consuming federal welfare benefits that might otherwise assist poor citizens and legal aliens.[25]

Support for employer sanctions legislation, however, was not universal. For example, the Mexican American Political Association informed the George McGovern presidential campaign in 1971 that it expected the Democratic party to disband the INS Border Patrol and to create an open United States–Mexican border. It also demanded voting rights and welfare benefits for all Mexicans residing in the United States, regardless of legal status.[26]

During House debate in 1972 over employer sanctions, Herman Badillo (D-NY), Edward Koch (D-NY), and Edward Roybal (D-CA) opposed Rodino's employer sanctions bill on the grounds that it would lead to discriminatory hiring practices against Hispanics, Asians, and anyone who might appear or sound foriegn.[27] As problems associated with "bankrupt economic policies and soaring unemployment" intensified, Badillo sadly noted, it was little wonder that Republican and Democratic leadership targeted illegal aliens as "popular scapegoats" for the country's economic disquietude.[28] Despite these protests, a steady stream of House liberals—including Rodino, Celler, and Gonzalez—linked sanctions to the postwar struggle against the Bracero Program and worker exploitation. Rodino's bill ultimately passed easily with modest Republican and broad Democratic support.

The Rodino bill languished in the Senate, where Eastland refused to allow the Judiciary Committee and Immigration Subcommittee he chaired to take action. A cotton grower with strong ties to Southern agricultural interests, Eastland represented a long line of influential Southern and Western lawmakers who supported a cheap and "returnable" labor supply from Mexico.[29] Although the Bracero Program's termination in 1964 ended the legal importation of Mexican guestworkers, it did not dissolve the iron triangle that existed between Eastland, INS officials, and Southwestern growers.

General Joseph Swing's tenure at the helm of the INS during the Eisenhower years helped to alter the agency's poor border enforcement reputation, ushering in high-profile crackdowns like Operation Wetback. By contrast, Swing's successor, Raymond Farrell, and his associate commissioner, Edward Loughran, preferred to maintain a low profile for the INS. Even as annual apprehensions of illegal immigrants soared in the late 1960s, INS leadership downplayed the problem. Indeed, Farrell and Loughran never complained to Congress or the White House about insufficient funds. "They went trotting to Congress each year, asking for minimal appropriations and telling everyone that there was no real illegal alien problem," one INS official later recounted. "They didn't want to rock the boat."[30] Other INS officials alleged that Eastland forged an alliance with the Farrell-Loughran administration, one that encouraged lax border enforcement and cooperation on INS staff appointments. As John Crewdson put it, "Eastland . . . controlled the agency's top appointments, in return for protecting the INS from meddlers, reformers, and other outside interference."[31] While liberal reformers in Congress opened the policy process in a variety of issue areas, Eastland tenaciously presided over an increasingly anachronistic subgovernment that remained a crucial veto-point for employer sanctions initiatives.

The House Immigration Subcommittee reintroduced Rodino's employer sanctions measure in 1973. Early in the session, Roybal again denounced the bill as discriminatory toward Mexican Americans and other "non-Anglo" groups.[32] Biemiller privately assured House Democrats that "the argument that the bill discriminates unfairly against Mexicans and Mexican-Americans . . . is without foundation."[33] When the Rodino bill reached the floor, some opposition was mounted by an unlikely coalition of liberals concerned about potential discrimination and Southwestern members committed to providing cheap foreign labor to growers, ranchers, and other employers.[34] Nonetheless, the 1973 employer sanctions bill once more won easy approval in the House, passing by a margin of 297 to 63.[35]

The measure never made it out of Eastland's Immigration Subcommittee. The AFL-CIO leadership and House Democrats fumed. In a tersely worded statement on illegal immigration, the AFL-CIO Executive Council assailed Eastland:

His intransigence has blocked all efforts to erect barriers to importation and employment of low-paid foreign workers at the expense of American workers. The AFL-CIO demands that Senator Eastland abandon his effort to impose a new "bracero" program. . . . We call for prompt, final Congressional action.[36]

Yet Eastland was undaunted by media pressure and the protests of unions and liberal colleagues. Instead, he simply insisted that he could not obtain the necessary quorum to hold hearings. Numerous members and staffers of the Judiciary Committee refute this claim.[37] "Democrats on the Judiciary [Committee] desperately wanted hearings," one committee staffer recalls, "but Eastland flat out refused to activate the immigration subcommittee following the '65 Act. It is almost unbelievable, but he did not hold a single hearing on immigration from the '60s to 1977."[38]

As illegal immigration inspired growing media attention and public concern during the 1970s, Farrell's administration at the INS came under fire for lax enforcement at the nation's borders. Farrell soon resigned amid increased oversight by House members, while Loughran, his chief lieutenant, found refuge as staff director of Eastland's Immigration Subcommittee.[39] To reinvigorate the INS, Nixon went outside the "normal routine" to select former Marine Corps general Leonard Chapman, a manager in the mold of General Swing.[40] In contrast to Farrell, Chapman worked hard to create a sense of urgency about illegal immigration. He actively encouraged increased media coverage of the problem, warning that as many as 12 million undocumented aliens were filling domestic jobs and overburdening the welfare state.[41] Predictably, Chapman simultaneously requested big increases in the INS budget so as to redress personnel shortages along the two-thousand-mile United States–Mexican border.[42]

While Eastland continued to hold employer sanctions hostage in the Senate, the illegal immigration problem assumed new prominence during the Ford presidency. In 1975, Ford created a special interagency committee, the Domestic Council Committee on Illegal Immigration, to investigate the scope of the problem and formulate a policy response. Former officials point to two principal reasons why the White House mobilized on the issue. The committee's executive director recalls:

> First, the administration felt it had to have a position to respond to Rodino's initiative and there was some disquiet that it had taken no position. Second, there was a fiscal concern. General Chapman made substantial requests for increases in the INS budget. The OMB and others . . . saw the Domestic Council as a way to explore employer sanctions as an alternative way.[43]

In its final 1976 report, the committee observed that little reliable, "quantified" evidence existed regarding the size of the undocumented population or its impact on American society.[44] But in explaining why illegal immigration must be discouraged, it appealed to values beyond traditional economic and cultural anxieties. Indeed, it placed special emphasis on the rule of law and equal rights: "People who are underground . . . cannot be protected from abuse on the job or from landlords, discrimination, disease, or crime; they may avoid education for children, and they are unable or reluctant to assert political or legal rights," the report stressed. "Thus there is the possibility of a substantial underclass which must avoid the legitimate institutions and government of the society in order to survive."[45] This was not the familiar rhetorical assault on illegal aliens who take American jobs, consume public benefits, and promote crime and disease. Illegal immigration's dangers lay not only with its disregard for the rule of law, its economic impact on poor citizens, or the burdens it placed on "society's infrastructures," but also with its propensity to create a vulnerable subclass anathema to post-1960s notions of nondiscrimination and individual rights.

As expected, the Domestic Council urged Ford to "aggressively pursue legislation [imposing] penalties for employers who knowingly hire aliens not authorized to work."[46] To the delight of the Office of Management and Budget and other fiscal hawks, the report made no mention of expanding INS resources. Indeed, the report cautioned against an internal enforcement campaign like that of Operation Wetback. "Massive deportation is both inhumane and impractical," the council concluded, without specifying how policymakers should deal with the large number of illegal aliens residing in the country.[47] Even Chapman, who served on the council's steering committee, agreed that mass deportation campaigns were ill advised. Such an effort, he warned members of Congress, might require "police state" tactics "abhorrent to the American conscience."[48] But as Ford's Domestic Council endorsed employer sanctions, Rodino and other legislative activists recognized new barriers to reform.

"BUILDING COALITIONS IN THE SAND": NEW GROUPS AND ELUSIVE MAJORITIES

When Rodino's subcommittee began to investigate illegal immigration in the early 1970s, few Latino organizations had offices in Washington.[49] Moreover, the most prominent Mexican American leaders who did testify before the subcommittee were closely tied to groups that opposed illegal immigration: Chavez's UFW, the AFL-CIO, and LULAC. Whereas labor groups worried that undocumented aliens would be used by employers to break strikes and depress wages, LULAC's old guard saw illegal immigration as an obstacle to Mexican American integration. With a membership of upwardly mobile professionals, LULAC leaders hoped to distance the Mexican American community from its immigrant identity. As Benjamin Marquez notes, "they were concerned with such questions as political accommodation and cultural assimilation, the issues of the U.S. citizen."[50]

The interest group system, however, was far from static. Numerous scholars note an explosion of organized interests in Washington during the 1970s, especially of citizens groups and ethnic lobbies inspired by the civil rights movement.[51] Particularly important for immigration politics was the rise of new Mexican American and other Hispanic groups with fresh political orientations, resources, and policy goals. Between 1973 and 1976, eight national Latino organizations established offices in Washington with support from government contracts and private grants.[52] Their links to the civil rights movement were unmistakable. These groups would eventually argue that employer sanctions could expose Hispanics to job discrimination and other civil rights infringements. Strikingly, they did more than balance the positions of UFW and LULAC leaders; they persuaded them to oppose sanctions.

One of the most important new groups was the Mexican-American Legal Defense and Education Fund (MALDEF), an organization modeled after the NAACP's Legal Defense Fund. Indeed, the NAACP LDF executive director Jack Greenberg was instrumental in helping MALDEF become incorporated in 1968 with Ford Foundation support. As envisioned by its founders, the group was to empower Mexican Americans by pursuing litigation strategies like those of the NAACP LDF in the postwar era. Ford Foundation president McGeorge Bundy drew a close connection: "In terms of legal enforcement of civil rights, American citizens of Mexican descent are now where the Negro community was a quarter-century ago."[53] Bundy's conclusions were reinforced by a Civil Rights Commission study in the early 1970s which suggested that Mexican Americans were routinely denied equal protection of the law.[54] MALDEF looked to the courts for relief, but its initial litigation efforts yielded little success. In *San Antonio v Rodriguez* (1973), for example, it lost a monumental Supreme Court decision on public school funding.[55] In the aftermath of *Rodriguez*, MALDEF devoted new resources to cases involving the legal rights of Mexican aliens. Emboldened by these litigation efforts, it quickly assumed a more active role in lobbying Congress on immigration matters.

Other national Latino organizations mobilized to influence immigration policymaking. The National Council of La Raza (NCLR), also established in 1968 with a startup grant from the Ford Foundation, moved its headquarters to Washington in 1973 and devoted new resources to lobbying on immigration policy generally and employer sanctions specifically.[56] Although founded in 1929, LULAC waited until the 1970s to create a legislative office in Washington. This development captured an important shift in the leadership and political orientation of an organization that once spurned partisanship and ethnic lobbying as unpatriotic.[57] As LULAC's old guard made room for younger activists in the 1970s, the once-restrictive organization opened its membership beyond English-speaking citizens to all "Hispanics residing in the United States." In turn, its advocacy efforts expanded to include the political interests of all Latinos living in the country, regardless of citizenship status.

These new Hispanic lobbies vigorously opposed employer sanctions. Likewise, Latino leaders who once called for crackdowns on illegal immigration disavowed their early support for sanctions. In 1975, Chavez and the UFW were persuaded by Latino groups to oppose only undocumented workers who engaged in strikebreaking activities. The UFW also announced new support for a generous amnesty program.[58] The same year, the International Ladies Garment Workers Union (ILGWU) served notice that it was campaigning to unionize illegal aliens because of their enduring presence in the garment industry. ILGWU officials publicly explained that their new policy toward undocumented workers reflected an inability on the part of the federal government "to do anything about illegal immigrants."[59] Among prominent Latino labor groups, only the AFL-CIO's Labor Council for Latin American Advancement (LCLAA) remained stridently opposed to illegal immigration.

While Mexican American advocates attempted to mobilize civil rights groups against employer sanctions, they faced potential opposition from a coalition of African American groups that traditionally viewed illegal aliens as competitive with poor blacks for jobs and public benefits. Indeed, African American leaders had long expressed concern about the negative effects of immigrant labor on native-born blacks. "Every hour sees the black man elbowed out of employment by some newly arrived immigrant whose hunger and whose color are thought to give him a better title to the place," Frederick Douglass wrote of European newcomers of the 1860s.[60] Stanley Lieberson's study of job competition in expanding urban labor markets of the late-nineteenth century suggests that new immigrants often were preferred over blacks who had migrated from the South.[61] Although essentially shut out of immigration policy debates during the Progressive Era, many African American opinion leaders endorsed Chinese exclusion and European restriction in the early-twentieth century. As the *Washington Colored American* urged in 1902: "Negro labor is native labor and should be preferred to that of the off-scourings of Europe and Asia. Let America take care of its own."[62] During the Great Depression, African American newspapers joined those favoring Mexican exclusion and applauding mass deportations of Latinos. As one journalist asked rhetorically, "If the million Mexicans who have entered the country have not displaced Negro workers, whom have they displaced?"[63]

During the 1970s, African American leaders sounded similar themes on illegal immigration. In the early 1970s, the NAACP and other African American groups joined organized labor in supporting employer sanctions. Newspaper columnist William Raspberry wrote of how immigration—and illegal immigration in particular—hurt the economic prospects of African Americans.[64] To be sure, African American leaders such as Shirley Chisholm voiced early opposition to employer sanctions because of their potentially corrosive effects on Latino civil rights. But many shared the view of the AFL-CIO that illegal immigration benefited American employers at the expense of working-class and poor citizens.

Employer sanctions were but one issue over which Hispanic and African American groups clashed in the 1970s. Tensions surfaced over coverage of the Voting Rights Act, federal jobs programs, and public education.[65] The Leadership Conference on Civil Rights (LCCR), formed in the 1960s to link civil rights groups, heard from members throughout this period who worried that such conflicts could profoundly hurt the coalition. "There seems to be a strain, even outright competition, among various minority groups and civil rights organizations resulting in too little for too many emerging groups," the executive director of the Japanese American Citizens League warned in 1975. "I think this is something that we collectively have to deal with because we all . . . lack empowerment in this system."[66]

Over the course of the decade, however, African American and Hispanic groups averted open conflict by forging new alliances on voting rights, education, antipoverty programs, and other issues.[67] Instrumental in this regard was a Working Committee on the Concerns of Hispanics and Blacks formed in the 1970s by presidents of the National Urban Coalition and the NCLR. Its avowed purpose was "to encourage cooperation and joint action by the two largest U.S. minority groups."[68] The committee brought together the NAACP, the National Urban Coalition, the Urban League, the NCLR, LULAC, and other groups. While it found common ground on many issues, illegal immigration continued to polarize African American and Hispanic leaders. NCLR meeting minutes capture the conflict well:

Hispanics are very much opposed to employer sanctions since these would lead to civil rights violations [and] give employers an excuse for discriminating against Hispanics. Black leaders feel that the undocumented workers coming into this country are definitely taking jobs from unskilled Blacks. As one national Black organization official put it, "It all boils down to jobs." . . . Many Black leaders, although not all, argue that employer sanctions are the only way to curb undocumented immigration and job displacement.[69]

Despite these differences, meeting participants reached compromise on several important issues. There was strong agreement that undocumented aliens residing in the country should be eligible for citizenship, that the INS Border Patrol should not be enhanced, and that guestworker programs should be opposed. African American leaders expressed sympathy with Hispanic concerns that a beefed-up Border Patrol might lead to "more cases of police brutality." Likewise, they endorsed an amnesty program that would allow Hispanic families to remain together, noting that they faced "the same problem when their family members were separated during times of slavery."[70] Within Congress, members of the Black and Hispanic Caucuses also worked to avoid conflict over immigration control.[71] In coming years, national African American leaders increasingly supported the efforts of their Latino counterparts to block employer sanctions and to secure amnesty for undocumented aliens.

The policy subgovernment that Eastland guarded during his long tenure as judiciary committee chair unraveled with Farrell's resignation. But Rodino and other employer sanctions proponents well understood by the mid-1970s that the large House majorities that once supported reform were now elusive thanks to powerful opposition from an odd coalition of growers and Hispanic groups. To the dismay of congressional Democratic leaders, however, the Carter administration wasted little time in proposing a comprehensive plan for addressing illegal immigration in August 1977. Warnings from Labor and Justice Department officials that the White House needed to bring "constituency groups on board" and approach Congress "with an open mind" went unheeded.[72] The Carter plan included four key provisions: (1) stiff civil fines and eventual criminal prosecution of employers who engaged in a "pattern or practice" of hiring undocumented aliens; (2) use of the Social Security card as the designated identification document for employee eligibility; (3) beefed-up Border Patrol forces at the Mexican border; and (4) an amnesty program granting permanent resident alien status for all aliens living in the country prior to 1970.[73] The Carter bill was introduced swiftly in the House and Senate, and Attorney General Griffin Bell even persuaded Eastland to hold one day of subcommittee hearings on the measure after heated negotiations on judicial appointments.[74]

Carter's employer sanctions legislation of 1977 galvanized opposition from growers, new Latino lobbies, and other groups. Shortly after the Carter proposal was announced, the NCLR issued a memo listing its "public policy and legislative priorities," with "immigration" at the top, followed by "unemployment," "bilingual education," and "welfare reform."[75] NCLR lobbyists helped form an Ad Hoc Coalition on Immigration including MALDEF, LULAC, the ACLU, church lobbies, and lawyers groups to devise a program of "coordinated lobbying and other strategic legislative work" against the Carter bill.[76] Coalition members assailed employer sanctions because "some employers, who harbor prejudices against Mexican Americans and other ethnic Americans, would use the provision as justification for their discriminatory practices."[77] Coalition lobbyists also denounced Carter's proposed amnesty program because it limited eligibility for permanent legal residency to undocumented aliens who had resided in the United States prior to 1970. No "reliable factual data or analysis," they added, demonstrated that undocumented aliens had a detrimental impact on American society.[78]

The Carter plan became hopelessly mired in conflicts between congressional defenders of organized labor, growers, Hispanics, and other social interests. Tellingly, Kennedy and Rodino had been caught off guard by Carter's proposal on illegal immigration, even though their bills served as the basis of his package. "It was vintage Carter—no consultation with outside groups, no consultation with Congress," a key congressional staffer recalls. "It was a mess and wasn't going anywhere, which is exactly what we would have told the President had we been brought in ahead of time."[79] To the frustration of congressional Democrats, the Carter White House had failed to recognize a growing Mexican American presence in immigration politics—one that transformed employer sanctions into one of the party's most divisive issues.

LEGAL IMMIGRATION AND ITS DISCONTENTS:
THE RISE OF A NEW RESTRICTIONIST MOVEMENT

When the 1970s began, the new admissions policies established by the Hart-Celler Act elicited little political controversy. Some Irish American groups and politicians did protest that under the new preference system, only about a thousand visas were available annually for Irish immigrants. John Collins of the American Irish National Immigration Committee described the situation to the House Immigration Subcommittee as a "problem of discrimination," since most Irish immigrants lacked family ties and job skills necessary to gain preference under the 1965 system.[80] But when a handful of Irish American legislators introduced legislation to extend special visas to Irish immigrants, the bill was defeated by those who worried that the remedial action would be perceived as racist.[81] As one prominent lobbyist summed up the prevailing view, "the effort by several Irish congressmen to help Irish specifically would amount to a back-door reinstitution of the national origins quota system."[82] Significantly, Irish American groups and politicians expressed no interest in reducing existing levels of immigration.

This was not true of environmental and population-control advocates, who organized in opposition to U.S. legal immigration policies throughout the decade and who would become the foot soldiers of a new restrictionist movement. Many of these activists were first mobilized by findings of the Commission on Population Growth and the American Future. Established by Nixon in 1969 shortly after Paul Ehrlich's best-selling *The Population Bomb* sparked policy debate (promising a catalytic effect not unlike Upton Sinclair's *The Jungle* or Rachel Carson's *Silent Spring*), the commission was chaired by John D. Rockefeller III. Immigration was but one of the issues examined by the commission, but its investigations between 1970 and 1972 left little doubt that immigration was an important source of population growth.[83] Even excluding population growth due to illegal immigration, the Rockefeller Commission reported in 1972, annual immigration since 1965 (about 400,000 per year) was said to be more than twice that of the 1924–65 period. Another set of figures presented by the commission troubled opponents of population growth even more: Legal immigration accounted for 16 percent of annual U.S. population growth in 1970, 18 percent in 1971, and 23 percent in 1972.[84] The commission considered recommending a reduction of the legal-immigrant flow by 10 percent each year, with the purpose of cutting it in half by the end of five years. But most commissioners "felt that the contribution made by immigration to the Nation outweighed other considerations."[85] Its only specific policy suggestion on immigration was unanimous support for legislation "which will impose civil and criminal sanctions on employers of illegal border-crossers."[86] Yet the language of the Rockefeller Commission's final report was provocative. "We regard population growth . . . as an intensifier or multiplier of many problems impairing the quality of life in the United States. Tightening up certain areas of immigration, eliminating others, and keeping still others may help buy the precious time we need to put our house in order."[87]

For some environmental and population-control activists associated with such groups as the Sierra Club and Zero Population Growth (ZPG), these findings underscored the need for immigration restriction. Significantly, the commission and most national environmental and population-control groups were reluctant to embrace the restrictionist cause. But others were less reticent. "In some quarters, there are rumblings of a desire for new changes in immigration law," noted one activist, "a desire motivated not by prejudice but by concerns for the environment, dwindling resources and the quality of our lives."[88] Gerda Bikales, future head of U.S. English, explained in a 1977 edition of *National Parks and Con-*

servation Magazine that many environmentalists now saw "the swelling stream of immigrants" as a direct source "population pressures on our natural resources."[89] But for several new restrictionist leaders, the dangers immigration posed to the nation's environmental health could not be separated from the ethnic origins of Third World newcomers. One of the spearheads of new restrictionism, John Tanton, former ZPG president and chair of the Sierra Club's population committee, explained that his early concerns about post-1965 immigration reflected a devotion to preserving "an American culture." Indeed, Tanton described environmental protection as a distinctively Western tradition likely to be compromised by post-1965 immigration:

> The cultural values that led to the conservation ethos that's typified by the Sierra Club . . . are values that are characteristic of American society. We could probably trace their roots back through Western civilization. If we look at the conservation ethic of some of the countries from which large numbers of immigrants are coming, we don't find the same sort of respect for the land and our fellow creatures that has developed here. We certainly don't see this in many of the southeastern Asian cultures or in Latin America.[90]

In 1979, Tanton and Roger Connor, a young environmental lawyer, formed the Federation for American Immigration Reform (FAIR). As early literature explained, "FAIR is needed now because immigration is out of control and unchecked immigration complicates the solution to every important problem before the country."[91] FAIR and other new restrictionist groups could point to illegal immigration, increased refugee admissions, and family exemptions to the legal preference system as sources of soaring alien inflows. Beyond environmental and population impacts of renewed mass immigration, restrictionists also hoped to seize upon the economic costs of newcomers as a means of broadening their coalition. "We had potential allies from America's own domestic, if not underclass, at least disadvantaged," FAIR board member Otis Graham, Jr., recalls. "We were sure that the black community was taking it on the chin from unbridled Third World manpower pouring into the country."[92] But in a lengthy meeting at the NAACP's Washington office on a quiet weekend afternoon, one in which FAIR and NAACP participants entered through separate doors, African American leaders ultimately rejected FAIR's overtures.[93] For restrictionists eager to distance themselves from the racist agenda of Progressive Era nativists, an important political ally was lost.

Within Congress, Joshua Eilberg used his clout as chair of the House Immigration Subcommittee to champion placing Western Hemisphere countries under the same per-country limits that operated for the Eastern

Hemishpere. In 1976, Congress amended the 1965 law to establish a 20,000-person annual limit for each country of the Western Hemisphere. Representative James Scheuer, chair of the House Select Committee on Population, held a series of hearings examining the social perils associated with rising immigration. By 1978, he was urging colleagues to authorize the deportation of any immigrant who received welfare within five years of their initial entry.[94] More radically, Senator Walter Huddleston (D-KY) called for major reductions in legal immigration and an end to the 1965 law's exemptions for immediate family members. Huddleston worked closely with FAIR and other restrictionist groups, which helped his office draft restrictive immigration bills.[95]

Immigration restriction grew increasingly popular over the course of the 1970s. Illegal immigration, perhaps the most visible migratory issue of the decade, highlighted the porousness of U.S. borders. Dramatic increases in INS apprehensions and deportations of undocumented aliens were seen as evidence that illegal immigration had reached crisis levels (see table 8.4).[96] Moreover, legal immigration soared to 4.5 million in the 1970s, the largest total since the second decade of the twentieth century. Along with illegal immigration, expansive refugee admissions and family preferences and exemptions established in 1965 spurred a new era of mass immigration. What most Americans noticed was that the latest wave of immigrants was dominated by Asian, Latin American, and Caribbean newcomers. As the *Christian Science Monitor* warned, "the challenge lies not only in numbers. It involves also the digesting into the U.S. mainstream of a vast segment of the population much of which sees itself as both linguistically and culturally different."[97] Anxieties about Third World immigration were exacerbated by economic "stagflation" at the start of the decade and a recession at its end. Demographic shifts and economic downturns sharpened anti-alien feelings among ordinary citizens; opinion polls indicated that most Americans believed that too many illegal *and legal* immigrants were entering the country.[98]

Democratic leaders in Congress had little interest in pursuing immigration reform in this political climate. Rodino was pessimistic about the chances of winning majority support for a new employer sanctions bill in the late-1970s, and he joined others in privately predicting the swift demise of Carter's plan. Edward Kennedy, who became chair of the Senate Judiciary Committee after Eastland's retirement, was instrumental in securing the 1965 reform and strongly opposed new restrictions on legal immigration. As he considered a run for the presidency in 1980, Kennedy also distanced himself from employer sanctions proposals that pitted two important Democratic constituencies against one another: organized labor and ethnic lobbies. Kennedy was not alone on this score. "No Northern Democrat in his right mind wanted to choose between civil rights groups and the AFL-CIO," one prominent congressional staffer observed.[99] New efforts by Huddleston and FAIR to secure reductions in legal admissions, seemingly affirmed by broad public support for sweeping restrictions, made pro-immigration liberals like Rodino and Kennedy even more resistant to immigration reform. Against this backdrop, congressional Democratic leaders considered dilatory tactics. "The name of the game was to ride things out until cooler heads prevailed," one pro-immigration lawmaker recalls.[100] Democratic leaders ultimately persuaded Congress and the White House to form the Select Commission on Immigration and Refugee Policy (SCIRP) in 1978 for the purpose of studying the controversial illegal immigration problem and all other facets of immigration and refugee policy and issuing specific recommendations for future reform. Significantly, Kennedy and others saw the Select Commission as more than a political way station. Indeed, they hoped the new commission would broker an effective compromise package on illegal immigration while renewing support for robust legal immigration.[101] The new commission would in fact profoundly shape immigration reform in the 1980s.

CONCLUSION

After decades of restriction, the post-1965 policy regime helped breathe life into a new era of large-scale immigration. As David Reimers aptly put it, America was again "the golden door" for hundreds of thousands of immigrants.[102] As in the past, significant shifts in the volume and ethnicity of newcomers inspired popular resistance and the rise of a new restrictionist movement in national politics. But the legacy of the civil rights movement was unmistakable in the care with which new restrictionists distanced themselves from the ethnic and racial arguments of Progressive Era nativists, instead offering environmental, economic, and population control rationales for stemming alien inflows. If voting by immigrants and kindred ethnic groups was crucial to sustaining broad immigrant admissions and rights in the nineteenth century, it had little impact on the maintenance of expansive policies in the 1970s. To begin with, naturalization and voting rates among Latino newcomers were quite low. Schuck and Smith theorize that a line of post-1965 judicial decisions weakened immigrant naturalization and voting rates by extending broad rights to aliens regardless of their citizenship status, thereby removing incentives to secure those rights through electoral means.[103] In *Graham v Richardson*, for example, the Supreme Court invalidated statutes restricting noncitizen access to welfare benefits and asserted that legal distinctions between citizens and aliens were inherently suspect under the equal protection clause of the Fourteenth Amendment.[104]

Both the expansion of alien rights and the sensitivity of new restrictionists to charges of racism provide some indication that the rebirth of mass immigration in the 1970s was fueled by ideological, coalitional, institutional, and geopolitical forces far removed from ordinary citizens. Refugee admissions consistently outstripped the annual levels set by the Hart-Celler Act during the late 1960s and the 1970s. Presidents frequently employed their parole authority as an effective means of expanding refugee relief to discredit communist regimes or to meet moral obligations following failed Cold War campaigns in Cuba and Vietnam. Congressional majorities routinely supported executives in their efforts to significantly increase refugee resettlement numbers, quickly enacting legislation that provided legal permanent residency and special assistance programs for refugees. Significantly, an unlikely coalition of liberal and conservative lawmakers sometimes pressed the White House to resettle *more* refugees in the name of advancing anticommunism and human rights. While most of the general public opposed generous refugee resettlement programs in these years, the strongest disagreements over refugee and asylum policies in Washington were between those who wanted to expand refugee admissions on behalf of people fleeing communist regimes and those who wanted to expand admissions on the basis of more universal and humanitarian criteria. Little wonder that refugee numbers grew markedly after 1965.

Illegal immigration was a prominent issue on the public agenda throughout the 1970s, but a decisive policy response proved elusive. In 1954, Eisenhower claimed independent executive authority to launch a massive military and police roundup of undocumented aliens. Operation Wetback resulted in the expulsion of hundreds of thousands of Mexican and Latin American aliens who were said to have entered the country without authorization. Two decades later, executive branch officials firmly rejected such an operation as inhumane and impractical in light of its likely intrusion upon the civil rights of Hispanic permanent resident aliens and citizens. Employer sanctions legislation was the preferred solution of labor groups and many liberal politicians in this period, but Eastland's aging subgovernment and his stranglehold on the Senate Judiciary Committee were insurmountable institutional veto-points until the mid-1970s. After the demise of these structural barriers, pro-labor champions of employer sanctions encountered formidable resistance from important new Mexican American and Hispanic lobbies whose unshakable opposition to employer sanctions hopelessly divided Democratic politicians and liberal advocacy groups. The fact that these new ethnic lobbies offered potent arguments about the ethnic and racial discrimination that sanctions would encourage at the workplace raised strong ideological conflicts for the American Left. The House majority coalitions that resoundingly endorsed Rodino initiatives in the early-1970s were now a chimera. Political fragmentation is a defining feature of American politics, but many observers suggested a new atomization emerged in this period. "The materials out of which coalitions might be built simply do not exist," Anthony King wrote in 1978. "Building coalitions in the United States today is like building coalitions in the sand."[105] This was particularly true for employer sanctions proposals. In the realm of illegal immigration, political stalemate was the order of the day.

Porous national borders, expanded refugee admissions, and the changing face of legal immigration collectively inspired growing popular disquietude about the latest wave of newcomers and the existing policy regime. But immigration policymaking was well insulated from mass publics. As Theodore Lowi observed, the United States now had a two-tiered democracy, with socialism for the organized and capitalism for the unorganized.[106] Yet even as environmentalists, population-control activists, and cultural protectionists formed new national organizations to campaign for immigration restriction initiatives, the political processes favoring a decidedly pro-immigration policy regime were overwhelming.

CHAPTER NINE

Two Faces of Expansion

THE CONTEMPORARY POLITICS OF IMMIGRATION REFORM

THE PAST QUARTER-CENTURY witnessed remarkable transformations in how the United States governs immigrant admissions and rights. Initially, American policymakers focused their attention in these years on a problem that seemed to highlight the extent to which national borders had become porous and inadequately regulated: illegal immigration. By the close of the millennium, however, the entire structure of U.S. immigration and of refugee and immigrant policies had been recast by significant federal legislation, independent executive actions, and judicial rulings. Sweeping policy changes of this period were achieved in both good and bad economic times, always during divided government, and despite the fact that congressional and White House officials dreaded the issue because of the contentious and unpredictable politics it routinely inspired. "We always felt like we were walking across a political minefield when it came to immigration," one congressional leader recalls. "But we understood that something which speaks to so many fundamental concerns—jobs, health, crime, racial fairness, civil liberties, trade, foreign relations, you name it—isn't going to go quietly into the night."[1] Indeed, not since the early-twentieth century has immigration reform been such a regular focus of conflict and change in American politics.

When the 1980s began, the chances for attaining *any* major policy innovations seemed a tall order after years of political stalemate. The prospects for enacting *pro-immigration* reforms were slimmer still. The American public, convinced that the country had lost control of its borders, readily embraced harsh crackdowns on illegal immigration, significant reductions in legal immigration and refugee admissions, and limits on public benefits for aliens residing in the country.[2] "Americans are beset with anxieties, for which aliens now, as in the past, provide convenient scapegoats," political scientist Elizabeth Hull noted in the early 1980s. "Exacerbating their anxiety . . . is fear that the country's assimilative capacities [are] overtaxed, or indeed, that its character [is] imperilled by the preponderance of non-white, Spanish-speaking newcomers."[3] Republican and Democratic policymakers alike saw little room for expansive immigration reform. Rodino's chief adviser on immigration policy grimly told reporters in 1980 that "liberal legislation in the immigration field" was a pipe dream.[4] Republican senator Alan Simpson (WY), a prominent figure in immigration politics over the next two decades, shared this view and privately reminded colleagues the same year that Americans were "offended" by immigration policies that made them "the sugar daddies of the world."[5] The conventional wisdom in Washington in the early 1980s was that immigration reform was certain to fall under the spell of either inertial or restrictionist forces.[6] "The main public concerns driving immigration politics during the 1980s—especially the tide of illegal immigration and the recessions that struck at the decade's beginning and end—should have generated powerful pressures to *restrict* immigration," Peter Schuck observes.[7]

Legal immigration in fact soared in the 1980s, reaching levels unseen since the record inflows of the first decade of the twentieth century. Illegal immigration, always hard to pin down statistically, brought hundreds of thousands of additional newcomers to U.S. soil. Moreover, the major policy innovations adopted by national political actors from 1980 to 1990 were not only less restrictive than originally expected, but they dramatically increased immigration opportunities. To be sure, national immigration law and administration in this period were unkind to particular foreigners, including persons infected with the AIDS virus and asylum-seekers fleeing Haiti, El Salvador, Guatemala, and other noncommunist countries. This was not a new open-door era (indeed, there never was such a time in our national development). But in historical comparison to earlier policy regimes, the immigration controls established from 1980 to 1990 were decidedly *expansive* for alien admissions and rights. U.S. efforts to govern international migration in this period capture this trend well.

Illegal immigration remained the focus of considerable media attention and public alarm in the 1980s (in one Roper poll, over 90 percent of respondents endorsed "an all-out effort to stop" unauthorized entries).[8] But the polarizing politics it inspired among national policymakers and interest groups delayed official action until passage of the Immigration Reform and Control Act of 1986 (IRCA). The measure established employer sanctions and provided the INS Border Patrol with new resources. But as we shall see, the odds were stacked against the efficacy of employer sanctions in curbing illegal immigration at the outset. A reliable identification system of employee eligibility, crucial to the effective functioning of employer sanctions, was derailed during protracted legislative wrangling. This was compounded by the fact that administrative implementation of sanctions was relatively weak. Illegal immigration flowed unabated after 1986. While IRCA's enforcement mechanisms were quite limited in discouraging unauthorized entries, the law's expansive features were striking: the largest amnesty program for undocumented aliens of any country to date, a seasonal agricultural program that granted laborers opportunities to become permanent residents and citizens, and new anti-discrimination rights for aliens at the workplace. When executive officials attempted to exclude certain undocumented alien groups from IRCA's amnesty program, pro-immigration groups won judicial vindication of more generous amnesty regulations. Whereas national officials once responded to worrisome illegal immigration by launching dragnet raids and mass deportation campaigns (like Operation Wetback), IRCA ultimately conferred legal status to roughly 3 million undocumented aliens.

Refugee admissions and grants of asylum also grew sharply in the 1980s. The 1980 Refugee Act was designed by Congress to regularize the resettlement of refugees from third countries. It increased annual refugee admissions to 50,000 and empowered the president to exceed the annual limit in emergency situations. The act also routinized public assistance and legal permanent residency for refugees, and initiated a new asylum adjudication process. Finally, it adopted a new definition of "refugee" to include those fleeing varied forms of political, racial, or religious persecution—not just those escaping communist regimes. Within months of the Refugee Act's signing, the so-called Mariel Boatlift brought more than 125,000 Cubans to Florida. It was the first (and largest) of many waves of asylum-seekers who arrived on U.S. soil claiming need of protection from persecution. Throughout the decade, refugee and asylum policies would be the subject of significant struggle between the federal executive, legislative, and judicial branches. At issue were sharp disagreements about whether refugee and asylum benefits should be based on Cold War criteria or more universal standards. This conflict was never decisively resolved, and those pressing for more universal criteria often failed to secure relief for Haitians, Salvadorans, Guatemalans, homosexuals, and other asylum-seekers. But if the decade started with calls for reducing refugee admissions, the 1980 act clearly established a more generous annual admissions ceiling. The new ceiling was frequently exceeded in the 1980s, as more than one million refugees and asylum-seekers were admitted as permanent residents during the decade, while additional asylum-seekers received temporary protected status.

At the start of the 1990s, national officials left little doubt that they supported a decidedly pro-immigration policy regime when they rallied behind sweeping legislation designed to substantially increase legal immigrant admissions. The Immigration Act of 1990, the most important reform of the legal admissions system in the contemporary period, raised annual immigration levels by 40 percent. Equally significant, national policymakers affirmed family- and employment-based preferences that they explicitly recognized as advancing record inflows from Asia, Latin

America, and the Caribbean for the foreseeable future. The expansiveness of the 1990 reform stood in juxtaposition with the preferences of most ordinary citizens, who favored *reductions* in annual legal admissions when the law was enacted.

All this seemed to change in the mid-1990s, as California politics became consumed by efforts to limit public benefits for aliens and a new set of congressional reformers pressed for sharp restrictions of immigrant admissions and rights. Many scholars have assumed that the 1994 election ushered in a major retrenchment of the nation's immigration policies and signaled a new era of American nativism.[9] California's Proposition 187, a measure aimed at excluding undocumented aliens from various social services, including educational benefits for undocumented children, sailed to a landslide victory that year. The election also installed a firm Republican majority in both houses of Congress, one whose leadership was enamored by the notion of courting native-born voters in key electoral states by supporting sharp restrictions of annual immigration and alien rights. Immigration and welfare reforms of 1996 seemed to confirm this policy shift, as noncitizens were newly denied eligibility for major social welfare benefits, certain rights of judicial appeal, and other membership claims. Yet Schuck reminds us that limitations on the procedural rights of aliens were successful "in hitting only the easy targets: undocumented aliens, visa violators, and criminals."[10] More striking is the fact that those provisions of 1996 immigration reform legislation dedicated to scaling back legal admissions were soundly defeated on the House and Senate floors. Shortly thereafter, Republican lawmakers and office seekers joined Democrats in either celebrating immigration or treading lightly on the issue.[11] "We had a period in which the direction of the party was to try to restrict immigration," then-senator Spencer Abraham (R-MI) said in 1999. "Those days are over."[12]

How do we explain national immigration and refugee policies of the past two decades that dramatically expanded alien admissions at a time when most Americans favored sizable reductions? The fact that national officials expected increased immigration opportunities to mainly benefit nonwhite newcomers of Third World origins—defying both public anxieties about immigration demographics and older Gilded Age and Progressive Era traditions of excluding those of unfamiliar racial or ethnic makeup—only deepens the puzzle. Finally, how can we account for why the dominance of modern restrictionists in the policymaking process was so short-lived (1994–96) or why their policy achievements were so modest? This chapter addresses these questions by analyzing those forces of contemporary American politics that have fueled immigration policy choices and outcomes that are, as Gary Freeman puts it, "largely expansive and inclusive."[13]

Two kinds of politics have promoted robust immigrant admissions and rights in the United States over time: one rooted in immigrant enfranchisement and competitive democratic elections, the other in the insulation of elite decisionmakers from mass publics. The first kind of politics shaped pro-immigration policies in the United States for much of the nineteenth century. The second kind animated new refugee admissions and passage of the landmark Hart-Celler Act in the postwar era. Pro-immigration policies of the contemporary period have been fueled by *both* kinds of expansive politics. From the Refugee Act of 1980 to the Immigration Act of 1990, the policy choices of national officials were molded by several forces well insulated from the preferences of ordinary citizens: an ideological convergence of liberal and conservative politicians and interest groups in favor of immigration; the dominance of pro-immigration expertise in the findings of national commissions and other governmental bodies; and international pressures such as global trade competition and foreign policy commitments. Later Republican-led efforts to adopt anti-immigrant measures as a winning political issue, however, had the unintended consequence of spurring naturalization and electoral mobilization of new immigrants and kindred ethnic groups. Popular democratic supports for pro-immigration policies were being built anew, with the path-dependent processes that shaped national immigration policy in the nineteenth century receiving fresh life. To begin this inquiry into contemporary American immigration politics, let us turn to efforts in the early 1980s to reform U.S. refugee policy.

The Refugee Act of 1980 and the Mariel Boatlift

During the late 1970s, refugee admissions were frequently more generous than most Americans preferred. Between 1975 and 1979 alone, 300,000 Indochinese refugees were admitted under executive paroles.[14] A handful of congressional restrictionists called for new limits on these presidential actions, which consistently produced refugee admissions seven to ten times greater than the annual refugee ceiling set by the Hart-Celler Act. Against this backdrop, Kennedy and Rodino, with White House support, proposed a major overhaul of U.S. refugee and asylum law. The chief impetus for reform was the ad hoc manner by which Indochinese refugees were admitted under presidential paroles, something that troubled Congress for decades. But the principal innovations offered in the reform bill reflected none of the parsimony favored by the general public and a new restrictionist movement. Instead, the sponsors of the Refugee Act of 1980 set out to regularize large-scale refugee admissions and resettlement programs.[15]

The refugee bill specifically called for the refugee category of the visa preference system established in 1965 to be abolished. In its place, re-formers proposed that the annual "normal flow" ceiling for refugee ad-missions (with successful applicants screened and selected overseas) be increased to 50,000 and that such admissions no longer be counted to-ward the overall annual immigration ceiling. Visas reserved for refugees under the seventh category were to be reallocated to family-based immi-gration categories, with refugee admissions subsequently treated as a spe-cial and distinct category lying beyond the immigration preference sys-tem. Moreover, reformers endorsed an annual process of consultation between the White House and relevant congressional committees in or-der to allow for larger annual ceilings when necessary (they were rou-tinely negotiated at higher levels in later years) and to set refugee relief priorities for different regions of the world. The bill also endorsed a bet-ter-funded and more universal public/private system for providing reset-tlement and welfare assistance to refugees. Sponsors advocated the cre-ation and funding of a U.S. Coordinator for Refugee Affairs and a new agency, the Office of Refugee Resettlement, to be housed within the Department of Health, Education, and Welfare. Another provision al-lowed all refugees to be awarded legal permanent residency after only one year of probationary status; existing law conferred such status on an ad hoc basis and typically after two years of probationary residence.[16]

One particularly significant provision of the refugee bill was a proposal to change the definition of "refugee" to embody more universal language consistent with the 1951 U.N. Refugee Convention and its 1967 Refu-gee Protocol (which the United States endorsed in 1968). For years, human rights organizations and congressional liberals criticized the exist-ing definition as narrowly dominated by Cold War criteria. The new pro-posed definition reached beyond the anticommunist agenda: "Any per-son who is outside of any country of such person's nationality . . . and who is unable or unwilling to return to . . . that country because of per-secution on account of race, religion, nationality, membership in a partic-ular social group, or political opinion." Further language codified a legal duty of *nonrefoulement*, the duty of U.S. officials to not return a refugee to any country where the attorney general determined that "such alien's life or freedom would be threatened" on the basis of characteristics that would qualify her as a refugee under the 1951 Refugee Convention. As Gil Loescher and John Scanlan note, "Congress was concerned that the definition emphasize the humanitarian and nondiscriminatory aspects of the legislation, remove the ideological and geographic bias which charac-terized previous U.S. law, and conform closely to international stan-dards."[17]

The Refugee Act of 1980 ultimately passed by narrow majorities. The strongest resistance to the bill came from House Republicans upset by the generous provision of public assistance for refugee resettlement.[18] Despite high inflation and double-digit unemployment, the first comprehensive refugee law in the nation's history was unquestionably expansive. The major innovations it codified were largely driven by elite foreign policy and humanitarian commitments far removed from popular preferences. The act also reflected the increasing institutionalization of issue pluralism in national immigration politics in which different migratory streams—legal, illegal, and refugee inflows—were being decoupled and compartmentalized in the policymaking process. If the 1980 reform regularized large-scale refugee admissions on an annual basis and enhanced resettlement assistance, its more universal definition of "refugee" made little difference in the 1980s. Executive branch officials continued to place a heavy preference on admitting refugees fleeing communist countries. But the new definition and consultation process invited significant interbranch struggle over refugee policy in coming years. Nevertheless, the ensuing conflict was quite different from that of the post–World War II era. Whereas the postwar debate pitted officials who wanted to admit persons displaced by the war or fleeing communist regimes against those who wanted to shut the gates, most contemporary officials took for granted that large-scale annual refugee admissions were desirable. The struggle among modern policymakers has reflected differences over *who* should benefit from generous refugee relief.

The Refugee Act of 1980 focused almost exclusively on policies for screening and selecting refugees living overseas, typically in refugee camps, for resettlement in the United States. Yet the act also included procedures for allowing asylum claims by any alien who met the refugee definition and was "physically present in the United States or at a land border or port of entry, irrespective of such alien's status." However, the law further stipulated that discretion to grant asylum to claimants rested with the attorney general. This new system of asylum adjudication was overwhelmed within month's of the act's passage, as Fidel Castro's mass expulsion of Cubans from Mariel Harbor saturated the Florida coast with more than 125,000 asylum-seekers during the spring and summer of 1980. A minority of the migrants who came to the United States during the Mariel Boatlift were violent criminals released from jail by the Castro regime to join the exodus. Thousands of Haitian boat people arrived on American shores during the same period. The Carter administration struggled to respond to the politics of mass asylum. While some of these Marielitos were immediately resettled, thousands were detained in military camps around the country. Domestic immigrant rights and civil liberties groups offered legal representation to asylum-seekers. As the U.S. government tried to cope with an unprecedented backlog of asylum claims, it vowed to never again permit a mass exodus from Cuba to occur.[19] The same year, more than 200,000 Indochinese and other refugee groups were resettled in the United States despite intensified public alarm about alien inflows after the Mariel Boatlift.

Framing a Pro-Immigration Policy Paradigm: SCIRP and the Reform Agenda

At the same time as policymakers revised refugee law and tried to cope with the demands of mass "first" asylum, the Select Commission on Immigration and Refugee Policy (SCIRP) was in the final stages of its work. Created to avert a political backlash against immigration and to quiet intraparty battles over employer sanctions in the late 1970s, SCIRP ultimately played a significant role in immigration politics of the 1980s by advancing a "policy paradigm" that helped frame reform choices and official narratives for over a decade. The influence of the Dillingham Commission on immigration policy during the early-twentieth century rested largely in its legitimacy among most political actors of the day as an impartial investigative and problem-solving body. In similar fashion, SCIRP's original sponsors promised that their panel would offer broad expertise and prudent policy recommendations capable of resolving the political impasse over illegal immigration and other international migration issues. As they put it, the new commission would produce "an objective and thorough study of current immigration law and practice—a review that is beyond the capacity and scope of a single agency of the Executive branch or a committee of Congress."[20] SCIRP chair, Father Theodore Hesburgh, president of Notre Dame University and former head of the Civil Rights Commission, and its staff director, Brandeis professor Lawrence Fuchs, were committed to elevating ideas and policy proposals forceful enough to transcend partisan and special interests. SCIRP's composition included four public members, four Cabinet secretaries, and eight congressional members, many of whom belonged to ethnic and racial groups that the Dillingham panel once described as inferior immigrant stock. In addition to Hesburgh, the public members included a Cuban American AFL-CIO official, a Japanese American assistant to Los Angeles mayor Tom Bradley, and a Mexican American judge. Several congressional members, most notably Kennedy and Simpson, who forged an unlikely partnership over time, were key players in immigration-reform politics of later years.

The Dillingham Commission and SCIRP contrasted sharply in membership, staffing, research approach, and general perspective on immigration. While most Dillingham members and staff were predisposed to embrace eugenicist notions of racial hierarchy and restrictive policies, their SCIRP counterparts stressed the importance of racial nondiscrimination and other civil-rights values in formulating immigration policy. At a time when the Third World origins of most newcomers provoked a familiar angst among native-born citizens, commissioners like Patricia Roberts Harris, Health and Human Services secretary and a prominent African American leader, asserted that "the issue of race will be neither implicit nor explicit in the decisions on source."[21] During many meetings, commissioners like Rose Ochi, whose Japanese American parents were interned during World War II, Judge Cruz Reynosa, whose father was deported in one of the mass expulsions of Mexicans during the 1930s, and Hesburgh, who recalled his work on the Civil Rights Commission, frequently emphasized the importance of racial equality and alien rights in national immigration policy. These concerns deeply informed SCIRP research and proposals.

While the Dillingham Commission mirrored public anxieties about new immigrants and offered pseudoscientific validation for them, SCIRP members were determined to distance the policy debate from popular "emotions" and "demagoguery" on the issue.[22] At early meetings, Kennedy expressed his hope that SCIRP might play a role akin to Truman's presidential commission by providing "definitive information" and "enlightened" reform proposals that would elevate immigration policymaking beyond mass-based appeals for "retrograde legislation."[23] Fuchs later noted that "the central strategy was to take xenophobia, race, and even economic conflict out of the debate." Over roughly two years, SCIRP staff pored through the research findings of various social scientists and other immigration specialists, sponsored fresh research, and held twelve public hearings across the country. In 1981, it issued a final report on its findings and recommendations, *U.S. Immigration Policy and the National Interest.*

The SCIRP report, like the Dillingham findings of another era, helped frame policymakers' basic assumptions about the effects of international migration on the United States and the key problems associated with alien inflows. It also gave expert and nonpartisan validity to specific policy solutions. Members of Congress reverently and frequently cited SCIRP's research and recommendations in subsequent legislative debates. Four key ideas advanced by SCIRP helped set an expansive tone for immigration policymaking over the next decade. First, the commission repeatedly affirmed that robust lawful immigration was, in Hesburgh's words, "a positive force in American life."[24] More specifically, the SCIRP report emphasized that robust immigrant and refugee admissions reflected *national interests*, not U.S. generosity. This was a direct response to those who claimed that Americans had succumbed to "compassion fatigue" with respect to welcoming newcomers. The report asserted that immigration was economically beneficial to the country, showing that new arrivals were hardworking, entrepreneurial, and less likely than citizens to draw social welfare benefits. "They create as well as take jobs," Hesburgh summarized the commission staff's economic research. "In the aggregate they contribute to economic growth and productivity." SCIRP pointed to other national interests served by pro-immigration policies, such as the social benefits of reuniting families and the foreign policy imperatives for admitting refugees. In short, SCIRP's final report highlighted that "lawful immigration is useful in every important respect."[25]

Second, SCIRP promoted the notion that illegal immigration was a serious problem in need of control *before* legal immigration could be expanded. Although commission staff found that specialists disagreed about the economic impact of illegal inflows, the final report was unequivocal about their adverse impact on American society. Unauthorized entries created a vulnerable shadow population that had few incentives to report crimes, health problems, or exploitation by employers. The presence of large numbers of undocumented aliens "undercut the principle that all who live and work in the U.S., regardless of ethnicity, should have fundamental rights."[26] SCIRP members also worried that illegal immigration encouraged a disregard for the rule of law: "illegality erodes confidence in the law generally, and immigration law specifically."[27] Only by taking steps to close the back door, the SCIRP report concluded, could the front door be opened wider.[28] As such, most commissioners and staff endorsed the familiar scheme of employer sanctions and enhanced Border Patrol forces. To make sanctions effective, it also proposed a national identification card as the linchpin of a secure and universal system of employee eligibility. SCIRP's portrayal of illegal immigration as an urgent problem ensured that the issue would be a prominent feature of the public agenda despite its lack of appeal for most national politicians. The commission's linkage between controlling unauthorized entries and expanding legal immigration helps explain why Congress addressed illegal immigration problems in 1986 before turning its attention to legal immigration reform in 1990. Yet national policymakers ultimately would not make effective illegal immigration control a precondition for broadening legal immigration opportunities. Ironically, then, SCIRP's contrasting portraits of illegal and legal immigration had the more lasting effect of helping to *decouple* these two migratory streams in national politics. While restrictionists attempted to fuse illegal immigration control and sharp reductions in legal admissions, SCIRP's distinction between beneficial legal and deleterious illegal inflows predominated throughout the 1980s and 1990s.

Third, SCIRP affirmed a three-track system of legal admissions based on family reunification, recruitment of independent immigrants with needed job skills, and refugee admissions. The 1981 report emphasized that each of these tracks served vital national interests and urged expansions in annual visa allotments. It was a blueprint that shaped the terms of legal immigration reform in later years.

Finally, as already noted, adherence to notions of racial justice and civil rights values was a theme that deeply informed SCIRP's pro-immigration policy paradigm. SCIRP studies suggested that Asian, Latin American, and Caribbean newcomers were making valuable contributions to American society and were being assimilated as easily as earlier ethnic groups. Commissioners agreed that the nation's immigration policies should be nondiscriminatory in terms of race, ethnicity, and religion—extending principles of universalism and due process to selection, enforcement, and naturalization procedures. Reflecting their concern for alien rights, SCIRP members rejected the notion of a large-scale guestworker program on the grounds that it would create a captive and exploitable labor force. In similar fashion, all sixteen commissioners agreed on a generous amnesty or legalization program for undocumented aliens residing in the country; all were eager to extend full membership to persons "living in the shadows of American life" and unwilling to risk the civil liberties abuses associated with mass deportation efforts of the past.[29]

The immigration reforms adopted in 1986 and 1990 largely codified the central ideas advanced by the Hesburgh Commission. Only a few years after Kennedy and Rodino proposed a new commission intended to forestall a popular political backlash against immigration, SCIRP refocused elite political debate in a decidedly expansive direction. The social knowledge and policy alternatives endorsed by SCIRP, like the findings of its Progressive Era predecessor, enjoyed special intellectual and bipartisan credibility in the policymaking process. But if Dillingham Commission findings reinforced popular nativism of the day, SCIRP did little to alter public preferences for restriction. "As a general rule, the American public . . . has been negative toward the admission of immigrants and refugees to the United States," Hesburgh observed in 1981. "It is the most human thing in the world to fear strangers."[30] SCIRP's main audience, however, lay within Washington, where its policy agenda resonated across partisan lines.

STALEMATE REDUX: THE POLARIZING POLITICS OF ILLEGAL IMMIGRATION CONTROL

As SCIRP finished its work, Hesburgh and Fuchs successfully courted media attention and editorial endorsements for the commission's "close the back door and open the front door" formula. Meeting with various editorial boards, SCIRP leaders hoped to spur Congress to act on its reform package. Two lawmakers were particularly eager to make their mark as immigration reformers. One was Simpson, who persuaded Judiciary Committee chair Strom Thurmond to place him at the helm of a long-dormant immigration subcommittee. As both Simpson and his key staffers recall, the young senator believed that "if you want to go anywhere in Washington, you've got to learn a policy area and put your stamp on it."[31] On the House side, Romano Mazzoli, a moderate Kentucky Democrat with ties to Father Hesburgh, agreed to chair the Judiciary's immigration subcommittee at Hesburgh's urging. "Most people who wish to become players in Washington must become specialists," notes James Q. Wilson.[32] Simpson and Mazzoli, early in their legislative careers, intended to do just that.

Early in 1982, Simpson and Mazzoli together drafted and introduced omnibus legislation on illegal and legal immigration. Its provisions for illegal immigration control incorporated many of SCIRP's recommendations for a mix of employer sanctions and amnesty, and both lawmakers took pains to associate their bill with the respected commission. But they departed from the SCIRP agenda by also proposing legal immigration reform that placed immediate relatives under a 425,000 annual cap, all but eliminated visas for brothers and sisters of U.S. citizens, and increased admissions for an "independent" category of skilled workers. When the bill reached the floor, Simpson beat back amendments by Jesse Helms (R-NC) to scuttle the amnesty program and by S. I. Hayakawa (R-CA) to secure a one-million-per-year guestworker program. The Senate ultimately passed the measure with relative ease. Republicans were in the majority for the first time in two decades, and most followed Judiciary chair Thurmond's urging to take their cues on immigration reform from Simpson.

The Simpson-Mazzoli bill went nowhere in the House. As one House member put it, "the roadblock to getting legislation certainly wasn't the public mood which favored action. It was fierce resistance from an unbelievable variety of groups with clout on the Hill."[33] A broad coalition of business interests organized to defeat the measure, from grower interests and the U.S. Chamber of Commerce to the National Association of Manufacturers and the Business Roundtable. The Chamber of Commerce's Christopher Lewis complained that a law requiring "government's permission before a U.S. citizen can accept a job and before an employer can hire that U.S. citizen is both extremely costly and unworkable."[34] Opposition from interest groups of the Left was equally strong. "I would dance with the devil if I had to, to see this bill not pass," declared MALDEF's Antonia Hernandez.[35] A core of liberal advocacy group leaders representing key ethnic and civil rights lobbies, the ACLU, religious groups, and a new immigrant rights organization, the National Immigration Forum, held regular strategy meetings on how to derail employer sanctions and restrictions on legal admissions. "Our mission was to carry out the equivalent of legislative guerrilla warfare," one of the working group organizers explains. "We were willing to do whatever it took to make sure sanctions and new limits on the fifth preference never saw the light of day."[36] Eliminating the fifth preference, for adult siblings, was particularly galling to Asian American and Latino groups, who argued that Simpson's emphasis on an "Anglo" understanding of the nuclear family ignored the importance of extended family in other cultures.[37] Many House Democrats, led by the Hispanic and Black Caucuses, worked closely with liberal advocacy groups to defeat the Simpson-Mazzoli bill in 1982. At their urging, the Rules Committee permitted virtually unlimited floor amendments on the measure. Opponents amended the bill to death as the House session drew to a close; Edward Roybal (D-CA), a Hispanic Caucus leader, alone proposed more than two hundred amendments.

In truth, the Simpson-Mazzoli initiative also met resistance from both the House Democratic leadership and the Reagan administration. Simpson liked to remind fellow politicians that the Washington establishment was "surrounded on all four sides by reality"—a reality in which the American people were "offended" by an immigration and refugee policy that made them "the sugar daddies of the world."[38] But not all Americans were equally opposed to new immigration; well-educated professionals in higher income brackets were less likely to favor immigration restriction than other citizens (a trend that has continued to present; see table 9.1). The gap between elite and mass opinion toward immigration was especially wide between national political actors and restive publics outside the Washington beltway. For very distinct ideological reasons, many prominent Democratic and Republican officials were lukewarm

TABLE 9.1
Support for Decreased Immigration, 1980–1996

	Percentage Supporting Decrease		
Demographic Group	*1980*	*1986*	*1996*
Education			
Less than high school	79	56	74
College	44	41	49
Income Level			
Less than $15,000	76	58	65
More than $50,000	42	44	54

Sources: Roper Center, University of Connecticut, 1980 Poll; CBS News/*New York Times*, Monthly Poll, June 1986, September 1996.

about illegal immigration control and enthusiastic about large-scale legal immigration.

Employer sanctions were originally a liberal cause championed by organized labor and its congressional allies. But once ethnic lobbies and civil rights groups protested that sanctions would produce job discrimination against all who looked or sounded foreign, the question of illegal immigration control hopelessly divided liberal interest groups and Democratic politicians. Even after SCIRP placed its expert, bipartisan imprimatur on a sanctions-amnesty package, House Speaker Thomas "Tip" O'Neill and his Democratic leadership team continued to view employer sanctions reform as a dangerously polarizing issue for the party. Hispanic lawmakers warned O'Neill that Reagan officials might veto an illegal immigration control bill to curry favor with Latino voters.[39] There were other reasons House Democratic leaders opposed the Simpson-Mazzoli bill. Most liberal advocacy groups and House members favored a more generous amnesty or legalization program for undocumented aliens and strongly opposed new restrictions on legal immigration. The pro-immigration impulses of the Left were richly informed by a universal rights zeitgeist that gained ascendance among progressive Democrats in the postwar era. After midcentury, John Gerring writes, "the organizing theme of Democratic ideology changed from an attack against special privilege to an appeal for inclusion. Party leaders rewrote the Democratic hymnbook; Populism was out, and Universalism was in."[40] These ideological commitments were prominent in the postwar liberal assault on national origins quotas. Once Asians, Latin Americans, and Caribbeans benefited from a new visa preference system, most liberal political actors welcomed new openings for immigrants whose race or national origins long disadvantaged them in U.S. immigration law. "Racist policies denied these people the right to enter freely for most of our history," one liberal House member said. "We can't justify slamming the door just as they're getting their fair chance to settle here. Didn't the civil rights movement mean anything?"[41]

The political ascendance of Ronald Reagan and his supporters in 1980 invigorated a strain of American conservatism that celebrated large-scale immigration and temporary worker programs. During his 1980 presidential campaign, Reagan endorsed the notion of a North American free trade zone in which goods, services, technology, *and workers* could move freely across U.S., Canadian, and Mexican borders. Key members of the campaign team recall that Reagan, who had strong ties to California growers, originally was persuaded that the best way to redress illegal immigration was to create an open border with Mexico. "The answer to our problem," he told Texas voters, was to welcome Mexican laborers "for whatever length of time they want to stay."[42] This perspective drew intellectual inspiration from conservative economics and free-market philosophies of the 1970s and 1980s that disavowed immigration restrictions as unwelcome fetters on the free movement of persons in a competitive global economy. Economists like George Gilder assailed efforts to reduce immigration as "economically self-destructive," warning that many of the nation's greatest "entrepreneurial feats" never would have happened "without the crucial contributions of labor, ingenuity, and industrial daring of a new generation of immigrants."[43] For those enamored with laissez-faire economics and "regulatory relief," the Simpson-Mazzoli bill seemed laden with burdensome and inefficient government controls.

Some Reagan officials shared Simpson's view of illegal immigration as a potent threat to national sovereignty. The most influential of these law-and-order conservatives was Attorney General William French Smith, a trusted friend of the president, who argued that the country had "lost control of its borders" and that tougher border enforcement, employer sanctions, and national identification cards were necessary to restore "faith in our laws."[44] But an early White House task force on illegal immigration, created in response to the SCIRP report, demonstrated strong resistance within the administration to new control mechanisms.[45] Edwin Gray, director of the White House Office of Policy Development, warned that "establishing penalties for employers who hired illegal aliens would increase Federal regulation of the workplace at a time when Mr. Reagan says he has a mandate to reduce Government regulation."[46] Other White House officials noted that sanctions were "opposed by the business community as undue regulation and government interference."[47] Some task force members argued against illegal immigration controls because they "would disrupt an established pattern of employment" that provided employers "access to a low-skilled and relatively low-cost workforce."[48] Most agreed that national identification cards "would invade the privacy of individuals and threaten civil liberties."[49] When Smith pressed the matter at a Cabinet meeting, Reagan sat quietly as Interior Secretary James Watt issued a blistering assault. "I would like to suggest another way that I think is better," Watt proclaimed. "All we have to do is tattoo an identification number on the inside of everybody's arm!"[50]

Faced with media pressure and polls showing broad public concern about illegal immigration, the Reagan administration tepidly advanced its own reform plan. It revealed how reluctantly the administration approached illegal immigration control; employer sanctions penalties were significantly watered down in the plan and the national identity card scheme was jettisoned altogether.[51] The proposal also demonstrated that the Reagan administration generally welcomed low-skilled foreign workers but was relatively uninterested in extending broad civil, social, and political rights to them; the plan called for a large temporary farmworker program while placing stringent limits on who was eligible for amnesty (Office of Management and Budget director David Stockman and others worried about the costs of making large numbers of legalized aliens eligible for public benefits).[52] The White House ultimately expended little political capital on the plan. The internal task force report on illegal immigration presaged the administration's diffidence. "Given the difficulties that can be expected," it noted, White House action "may be more detrimental to domestic standing than living with the current situation."[53]

The same year that Simpson-Mazzoli went down in defeat, the Supreme Court issued a landmark ruling affecting undocumented aliens in the case of *Plyler v Doe*. The decision prevented the state of Texas from denying a public education to undocumented school-age children. In writing for the majority, Justice William Brennan noted that the equal protection clause of the Fourth Amendment "extends to anyone, citizen or stranger, who is subject to the laws of the state." The ruling did not absolve undocumented adult aliens of entering the country illegally, stressing instead that "innocent children" should not be made victims of their parents' unlawful behavior. Significantly, the Court opinion also highlighted the hypocrisy of de facto federal policies that permitted the country to benefit from the labor of illegal aliens but denied them the most elemental rights of membership. "This situation raises the specter of a permanent caste of undocumented resident aliens," Brennan wrote, "encouraged by some to remain here as a source of cheap labor, but nevertheless denied the benefits our society makes available to citizens and lawful residents."[54] It was a stinging indictment of federal inaction.

Simpson and Mazzoli reintroduced their reform bill in 1983. It again passed easily in the Senate with one amendment that was approved 63 to 33 over Simpson's objections: a provision requiring INS agents to have search warrants before raiding an open field. Its adoption was an indication of the political influence grower interests enjoyed within both parties. In the House, the measure was hamstrung by a sequential referral process that enabled committees with rival concerns to claim jurisdiction. On the Agriculture Committee, grower lobbyists worked closely with two members, Leon Panetta (D-CA) and Sid Morrison (R-WA), both of whom represented districts with a great many perishable crop businesses. Together they advanced an annual 300,000-person temporary worker program to assist growers. Liberal Democrats on the Education and Labor Committee endorsed new civil rights protections for legal aliens against job bias that might result from enactment of employer sanctions. Specifically, one amendment called for the creation of a Justice Department agency to investigate and prosecute workplace discrimination against legal aliens.[55] The Energy and Commerce Committee supported broad health-care benefits for aliens who received amnesty. Finally, Judiciary Committee members led by Rodino worked to make the bill less restrictive. Barney Frank (D-MA), for instance, won an expansion of the amnesty program.

As House committees wrangled over the bill, O'Neill announced that it would not be considered on the floor. When proponents of the measure reminded the Speaker that action was overwhelmingly favored by the public, O'Neill put the matter plainly: "I don't deal in polls here. I deal in politics. I deal with votes on the House floor."[56] And Democratic votes remained deeply divided. To reporters, O'Neill demurred that "no constituency" existed for illegal immigration control, adding coyly that it "had not been mentioned to me as a priority."[57] Other members of the House Democratic leadership team explained that they tabled the bill only after learning that the White House intended to "score a political coup" by vetoing employer sanctions legislation in an attempt to attract Hispanic voters in 1984.[58]

If divided government contributed to stalemate on controversial policy change, it also could spur action when media pressure, public opinion, and partisan rivals endorsed tough choices. Shortly after O'Neill sounded the death knell for immigration reform in 1983, Attorney General Smith held a news conference in which he assailed the Speaker for stonewalling on an issue of vital importance. O'Neill's explanations, he intoned, were "grievously wrong." The media sounded similar refrains. The *New York Times*, for example, castigated House Democrats for allowing special interests to prevail over the national interest. One of its headlines read: "The Speaker and the Big Wink."[59] Members of the House Democratic leadership team now worried about how their partisan rivals might exploit these charges of delay and inaction.[60] In November, O'Neill told reporters that the House would take up illegal immigration control in early 1984.

OVERCOMING GRIDLOCK

When the House reconvened in 1984, a number of young legislative entrepreneurs from key committees worked behind closed doors to harmonize conflicting versions of the Simpson-Mazzoli bill. With the blessing of party leaders such as O'Neill and Rodino, junior members like Charles Schumer (D-NY) and Howard Berman (D-CA) of the Judiciary Committee and Panetta of the Agricultural Committee took the lead in trying to fashion a compromise package. Bill Richardson (D-NM) of the Hispanic Caucus distanced himself from the dilatory tactics of Roybal and met quietly with various reform-minded colleagues to iron out differences. During the 1970s, the diffusion of power in Congress allowed policy entrepreneurship and innovation to flourish—reflecting what Burdett Loomis described as an "emphasis on the individual as captain of his or her own political fate."[61] By the 1980s, however, Congress was said to have entered a "postreform" era in which "fiscal and revenue issues" gave rise to a more disciplined and centralized legislative environment in which policy entrepreneurship was less likely.[62] Yet the difficult choices posed by illegal immigration control elevated activist members who were adept at bridging differences between polarized factions. Berman, Schumer, Panetta, and others were in turn eager to shape a compromise reform package. As one of the key junior House member explains, "Basically, since most of the older hands steered clear, this was a golden opportunity to roll up my sleeves and get some results. You can get a lot of respect around here for cracking tough nuts like immigration."[63]

Like the Social Security rescue of 1983 and the Tax Reform Act of 1986, closed-door negotiations among major legislative players were crucial to hammering out a House reform package opposed by organized interests (a process R. Douglas Arnold calls "breaking the chain of traceability," and Anthony King, "collusion of elites").[64] In June 1984, the House narrowly approved a patchquilt bill including employer sanctions, an expansive amnesty program, a 350,000 annual farmworker program, new antidiscrimination rights for aliens not covered by the Civil Rights Act (an amendment by Barney Frank), and federal reimbursement of states for costs related to legalizing undocumented aliens. As lawmakers readied for conference committee negotiations, White House officials expressed their reticence to support the measure. Simpson responded by demanding a private meeting with the president. In a tense gathering at the Oval Office, Simpson and Attorney General Smith urged Reagan to back reform. Influential Reagan advisers attending the meeting, such as James Baker, Edwin Meese, and Stockman, remained skeptical. But Simpson and Smith reminded Reagan that presidential resistance would not compare favorably with the House Democratic leadership's decision to permit action on a problem that continued to trouble the mass electorate and the media. Since Smith held a press conference criticizing O'Neill for stonewalling, it was noted, political fallout for the White House might be severe if it helped obstruct reform. Reagan closed the meeting by assuring Simpson he would sign the bill if federal reimbursement and the Frank amendment were limited.[65] When Senate and House conferees were unable to agree on these White House terms, illegal immigration again died.

Undaunted, Simpson proposed new legislation as Congress convened in 1985. "The problem of illegal immigration has not gone away," he told colleagues. "I have been shot down on that issue many times, but never by an armor-piercing bullet."[66] Simpson's new bill looked quite different from its predecessors. To win greater cooperation from pro-immigration colleagues, he dropped all matters related to legal immigration. Simpson also made changes that appeased business and employer interests, including voluntary employer verification of worker eligibility and the elimination of criminal penalties for repeated employer violations. Key business lobbies endorsed the measure as a tolerable alternative. As the Business Roundtable's Samuel Maury noted, "We have agreed to accept the employer sanctions provision as long as Congress does not place an undue burden on employers."[67] The Simpson bill also called for a "triggered legalization" program that extended amnesty to undocumented aliens only after it was shown that employer sanctions curbed unauthorized entries. Before reaching the Senate floor, grower organizations lobbied both sides of the aisle vigorously. "We knew legislation wasn't going to be put off indefinitely," one grower lobbyist recalls, "so we pushed for a useful amendment."[68] The National Council of Agricultural Employers, the American Farm Bureau Federation, and other grower interests hired Robert Strauss, former Democratic party chair, and James Lake, a Reagan fund-raiser, to bolster bipartisan support for a new farmworker program.[69] When Simpson's illegal immigration control bill passed the Senate, for a third time, in September 1985, it included an amendment permitting the admission of 350,000 foreign guestworkers to harvest perishable crops for up to nine months a year.[70]

In the House, Rodino and Mazzoli worked together on their own reform package. Gone were most of the "guerrilla tactics" pursued by ethnic, civil liberties, and immigrant rights groups in previous years. "We realized that even our closest friends in Congress . . . were getting restless to do *something*," recalls one ethnic lobbyist. "Most of us decided to change strategy to get items that were important to us into a bill that we despised." Interest group uncertainty about the nature of closed-door negotiations was a key force driving this shift to satisficing strategies.[71] The Rodino-Mazzoli bill looked nothing like its Senate counterpart. The House version included a sunset provision on employer sanctions, reinserted Frank's antidiscrimination provision, and offered far more generous terms of amnesty for illegal aliens. Expansive features of the bill overshadowed more modest efforts to discourage illegal immigration. Rodino also supported efforts by Berman, Panetta, and Schumer to quietly devise a farmworker program that satisfied growers while meeting union demands for worker protection. Their compromise plan provided temporary resident status for up to 350,000 aliens who resided in the United States for three years and worked in agriculture for at least ninety days of each of those years. With an additional year of farm labor, these aliens were eligible for permanent legal residency. Aliens who did farm labor for ninety days between May 1985 and May 1986 also were eligible for temporary residency, which could be upgraded to permanent residency after two additional years of agricultural work. A third category of replenishment workers extended permanent residency to those who did farm labor for five years. Behind closed doors, Senators Simpson, Howard Metzenbaum (D-OH), Paul Simon (D-IL), and Pete Wilson (R-CA) privately reached agreement with House members on the farmworker package. On the House floor, sponsors reminded colleagues of SCIRP's urgings for a strong but humane response to the illegal immigration problem. The Rodino-Mazzoli bill prevailed 230 to 166, with Democrats supporting the bill by a margin of 168 to 61 and Republicans opposing 105 to 62. Many pro-immigration members were swayed by warnings of an anti-immigrant backlash if some reform legislation were not enacted. "What's going to happen if we don't act is that a psychology will develop that says, 'Don't let anybody in,'" Rodino cautioned.[72]

During the conference, House Democrats agreed to scrap a sunset provision on employer sanctions in exchange for a Kennedy proposal requiring the General Accounting Office and Congress to evaluate the sanctions' impact on job discrimination in three years. Simpson accepted Frank's antidiscrimination provisions, dropped "triggered legalization," and assented to the more generous House amnesty cutoff date (undocumented aliens living in the country prior to January 1, 1982, were qualified for legal permanent residency and citizenship). Reimbursement to the states for costs associated with legalizing illegal aliens was capped at $1 billion over four years. Finally, the House farmworker package was adopted as a compromise between grower labor interests and liberal demands for worker protection. The conference report passed in both houses and was signed into law as the Immigration Reform and Control Act of 1986. "Lazarus was raised from the dead at least ten times," remarked a central congressional staffer on IRCA's improbable survival.[73]

IRCA was propelled by several forces. The Hesburgh Commission underscored the urgency of the illegal immigration problem and of giving intellectual and bipartisan credibility to a reform package of employer sanctions and amnesty that was embraced by the media and other opinion leaders. Congressional entrepreneurs pressed for compromise legislation behind closed doors, creating a sense of momentum that compelled business, ethnic, and civil rights groups to pursue satisficing strategies on a measure they opposed. Finally, in an era of divided government, both the House Democratic leadership and the Reagan White House were eager to avoid blame for killing an illegal immigration control initiative endorsed by SCIRP, the media, and the general public. The end product reflected a remarkable evolution. When employer sanctions were first proposed in the early-1970s, sponsors were strictly concerned with discouraging illegal immigration and punishing unscrupulous employers. IRCA's employer sanctions provisions, however, were watered down during legislative wrangling. Most notably, no secure identification system for employee eligibility was established. Time would reveal that IRCA's most significant legacy was an amnesty program that enabled roughly 3 million undocumented aliens to gain legal permanent residency in the United States. Originally designed as a restrictive enforcement measure, IRCA proved to be surprisingly expansive in both design and effect. FAIR president Roger Connor, one of the most prominent voices of the restrictionist movement, described IRCA in 1986 as a major defeat for his cause: "We wanted a Cadillac, we were promised a Chevy, and we got a wreck."[74] As we shall see, administrative and judicial processes soon reinforced the limited reach of employer sanctions and the expansiveness of legalization programs.

SHIFTING THE BATTLEGROUND: ADMINISTRATIVE POLITICS AND JUDICIAL ACTIVISM

Almost from the outset, the odds were stacked against employer sanctions working effectively to curb illegal immigration. The absence of a reliable identification system for verifying employee eligibility made it relatively easy for undocumented aliens to evade detection at the workplace. Soon after IRCA's enactment, an underground industry of fraudulent documents flourished in Mexico and the United States, enabling illegal aliens to obtain work with ease. In addition, a dizzying array of tasks and missions assigned to the INS were complicated by IRCA's contrasting sanctions and amnesty provisions. One INS official complained that it is "increasingly difficult to know what you're working on because there's so much you should be working on. We're like a cat on a hot tin roof."[75]

The Reagan and Bush administrations were less than zealous in their enforcement of employer sanctions. Few Reagan officials welcomed employer sanctions and even fewer favored their rigorous enforcement at a time when *deregulation* was the watchword of the executive branch. "We got here to get government off the backs of hard-working businessmen, not to add to their burdens," one Reagan official explained.[76] As a pro-immigration free marketer, Reagan himself was inclined to celebrate the uninhibited flow of workers across national borders. The INS tended to enforce employer sanctions with considerable forbearance toward offenders. "The differences between legalization and employer sanctions in terms of openness of rule making and the generosity of implementation were like night and day," recounts a prominent immigration lawyer who represented both legalization applicants and employer interests. "Legalization was very adversarial. But when it came to employers, they were very easygoing and cooperative."[77] According to administration officials interviewed, Alan Nelson, the INS commissioner during the Reagan and

Bush years, was encouraged to pursue a policy of "least employer resistance" by stressing business education over penalties. IRCA authorized a 70 percent increase in the INS budget, with an annual $100 million earmarked for employer sanctions enforcement. Tellingly, $34 million was spent on enforcing sanctions fiscal year 1987, $59 million in fiscal year 1988, and below $30 million annually in ensuing years.[78]

From his perch on the Senate immigration subcommittee, Simpson pressed the Reagan and Bush administrations to take a harder line on employer sanctions. Yet despite his clout as Republican minority whip, Simpson made little headway during either Republican presidency. "Even when we direct the Administration to do such things as 'study' the employer sanctions verification system and develop a more secure system, if necessary, we get no action unless we continually hammer away," he complained in 1991.[79] Few other lawmakers were in fact troubled by lax enforcement of employer sanctions. Indeed, the most vigorous congressional oversight of sanctions focused on whether they should be repealed because they unfairly burdened small business (led by Orrin Hatch) or engendered increased job discrimination against legal aliens and citizens who appear or sound foreign (led by Kennedy). Concerns about workplace bias were heightened by a 1990 General Accounting Office investigation that suggested sanctions indeed produced increased job discrimination.[80] Even the AFL-CIO, long the most ardent advocate of employer sanctions, made little effort to press for stronger enforcement of employer sanctions. Instead, AFL-CIO president Lane Kirkland joined fellow members of the Leadership Conference on Civil Rights in lobbying for more vigorous enforcement of job antidiscrimination protections for Latinos, Asians, and legal aliens.[81] Few conservative politicians, most of whom embraced "regulatory relief" and open markets, or their liberal counterparts, dedicated to universal rights and inclusion, worried about employer sanctions. Dampened briefly after IRCA's enactment, illegal immigration soon returned to peak levels of the pre-reform era (see table 9.2).[82]

During the same period, Reagan officials set out to restrict the number of amnesty grants that were issued under IRCA. For many law-and-order conservatives, such as Representative Bill McCollum (R-FL), IRCA legalization programs were offensive because they seemingly rewarded aliens who engaged in illegal behavior. But within the Reagan administration, the greatest concern was the potential budgetary costs posed by granting legal status to large numbers of undocumented aliens. Reimbursement of states for health care and educational costs of legalized aliens was an immediate issue, but fiscal conservatives also were disquieted by the fact that legalized aliens would become eligible for welfare benefits after five years. As early versions of IRCA were debated in Congress, the White

TABLE 9.2
Estimated Undocumented Alien Population in the United States, by Countries of Origin, 1996

Country	Number
Mexico	2,700,000
El Salvador	335,000
Guatemala	165,000
Canada	120,000
Haiti	105,000
Philippines	95,000
Honduras	90,000
Nicaragua	70,000
Total	5,000,000

Source: U.S. Statistical Abstract, 1997 (Washington, DC: Government Printing Office, 1998).

House urged its allies to contain the potential costs of legalization by "rolling back eligiblity dates and deferring welfare eligibility." A central goal of the Reagan administration was "to ensure that [amnesty] provisions are appropriately limited."[83]

In IRCA's final language, however, provisions on the legalization program called for generous terms of amnesty and for an implementation process that encouraged broad participation. Knowing that many aliens would be afraid of applying for amnesty at an INS office, the law allowed community organizations trusted by undocumented populations to serve as "qualified designated entities" (QDEs) for helping aliens in the application process. In the House Judiciary Committee report on IRCA, liberal Democrats took care to spell out their expectations of how the amnesty program should be implemented. "Unnecessarily rigid demands for proof of eligibility for legalization could seriously impede the success of the legalization effort," the report noted. "Therefore, the Committee expects the INS to incorporate flexibility into the standards for legalization eligibility . . . taking into consideration the special circumstances relating to persons previously living in this country." Its legislative intent was to see "that the legalization program should be implemented in a liberal and generous fashion."[84]

Under IRCA, the Reagan Justice Department was required to extend amnesty to illegal aliens who could demonstrate evidence of having entered the country illicitly before January 1, 1982. In 1987, the INS published final eligibility rules for IRCA's legalization program in the *Federal Register*. Pro-immigration advocacy groups, including the American Immigration Lawyers Association (AILA), NCLR, and the National Immigration Forum, viewed the rules as restrictive in intent. Specifically, they contested what they saw as overly rigorous eligibility standards for "timely filing," "continuous residence," and "known to the government" as well as exclusion of those "likely to become a public charge."[85]

Controversy over the "timely filing" requirement focused on illegal aliens who were apprehended after IRCA was enacted. According to the law, when illegal aliens were issued deportation orders, they had thirty days in which to file legalization applications. However, if the deportation order came after IRCA's passage but before the amnesty program officially began, the law allowed for the alien to file an application during the program's first month. INS rules narrowed the window of opportunity, requiring all aliens apprehended between IRCA's enactment and the program's start six months later to meet the thirty-day requirement. Based on this standard, the INS denied applications from all aliens who failed to apply within thirty days of INS apprehension—despite the fact that these aliens had not been issued a deportation order. Pro-immigration advocates immediately filed a national class-action suit challenging this application of the "timely filing" requirement, leading the INS to reopen the applications of these aliens.[86]

IRCA also stipulated that amnesty eligibility required that an alien's unlawful status was "known to the government" on or before January 1, 1982. Ignoring criticisms made during the rule-making process, the INS definition of "known to the government" became "known to the INS." This standard was justified on the grounds that only the attorney general was empowered to decide that an alien's status was "unlawful."[87] It was a stringent standard of eligibility. As Susan Gonzalez Baker notes, "an applicant who came to the U.S. in 1980 on a student visa and worked for pay, in violation of the visa restrictions, all the while filing tax returns and showing up on an employer's payment records to the Social Security Administration, did not qualify as 'known to the government.' Such an applicant would be denied the legalization benefit."[88] After immigrant-rights groups successfully challenged the rule in regional suits against the INS, a national class-action suit was filed in 1988. The resulting *Ayuda, Inc. v Meese* decision proved to be a major victory for advocacy groups pressing for generous terms of amnesty. A federal district court vacated application denials based on the INS's "known to the government" rule, stipulating that the standard could be met by any federal agency record that indicated an alien's unlawful status as of January 1, 1982.[89] An INS rule requiring "continuous lawful presence" in the United States from IRCA's passage until the date of application also was successfully attacked in the courts, where looser standards allowing for "brief, casual, and innocent" departures from the country were established.[90] INS efforts to deny amnesty applicants deemed "likely to become a public charge" also lost in court.[91] At the end of the day, implementation politics helped enervate employer sanctions while making amnesty benefits easier to obtain.

Republican presidents also clashed in the 1980s with pro-immigration lawmakers and groups over refugee admissions and asylum claims. Like other conservatives, Reagan saw refugee policy as an important instrument in the nation's struggle against the Soviet Union's "evil empire." Indeed, his speeches frequently alluded to the U.S. asylum tradition as a potent symbol of American freedom versus Soviet repression. As Reagan proclaimed in his 1980 Republican convention acceptance speech, "Can we doubt that a Divine Providence placed this land, this island of freedom, here as a refuge for all those people who yearn to breathe freely: Jews and Christians enduring persecution behind the Iron Curtain, the boat people of Asia . . . the freedom fighter of Afghanistan?"[92] As much as Cold Warrior presidents before him, Reagan continued a postwar policy of admitting large numbers of refugees fleeing communist regimes. Democratic lawmakers and liberal interest groups generally supported the Justice Department's favorable treatment of refugees and asylees from Nicaragua, Cuba, the Soviet Union, Afghanistan, Eastern Europe, and Southeast Asia. But at annual consultation hearings in Congress, they protested that the administrative practices of the Reagan and Bush years biased refugee and asylum policy in favor of escapees from communist and anti-American regimes and against most others (see table 9.3). When the Reagan administration refused to grant asylum to those fleeing Central America, church groups around the country formed a "sanctuary movement" to shelter illegal entrants from El Salvador, Nicaragua, and

TABLE 9.3
Immigrants Admitted as Permanent Residents under the Refugee Acts, 1981–1990

Country of Birth	1981–90 Total	Regime Type Escaped From
Vietnam	324,453	Communist
Laos	142,964	Communist
Cambodia	114,064	Communist
Cuba	113,367	Communist
Soviet Union	72,306	Communist
Iran	46,773	Anti-American
Poland	33,889	Communist
Romania	29,798	Communist
Afghanistan	22,946	Communist
Ethiopia	18,542	Communist

Source: INS, Statistical Yearbook, 1991 (Washington, DC: Government Printing Office, 1992).

Guatemala, many of whom were targeted for deportation. House Democrats led by Rules Committee chair Joe Moakley attempted to grant "extended voluntary departure" (EVD) protections to Salvadoran and other Central American asylum-seekers by writing it into the Rodino-Mazzoli bill in 1985, but the provision was later sacrificed in conference when the White House threatened to veto IRCA if EVD was not struck.[93] In 1987, the House adopted legislation to extend temporary asylum to 500,000 Salvadorans, which later failed in the Senate.

To the chagrin of liberals intent upon advancing the universal criteria of the 1980 Refugee Act, congressional Democrats had little success in trimming White House discretion over refugee admissions and asylum policy. Reagan officials openly questioned the wisdom of the UN *refugee* definition adopted in the act and made little effort to adhere to it. Attorney General Edwin Meese confessed that he "found it difficult to accept the view that the refugee law and the asylum rules permitted no distinction between aliens fleeing communist and non-communist countries."[94] Meese later issued a controversial order extending asylum to those claiming to have escaped regimes where they were pressured to have abortions, to be sterilized, or to limit the size of their families. Humanitarian, religious, and ethnic organizations enjoyed some success in challenging administration policies in the federal courts. Groups like the Lawyer's Committee for Human Rights offered evidence that fewer than 1 percent of Haitians, Guatemalans, and Salvadorans were granted asylum in the 1980s.[95] Republican administrations defended these results on the grounds that most Central Americans and Haitians left their homelands for economic rather than political reasons.[96] While higher courts generally upheld the detention and interdiction policies of the decade, federal judges were far more inclined to overturn administrative denials of asylum requests. Moreover, successful asylum litigation could lead to favorable out-of-court settlements for thousands of asylum-seekers.[97] Conservative and liberal policy activists alike supported broad refugee admissions, but they clashed bitterly over who was most deserving of refugee and asylum benefits. It was an issue that would resurface in the politics of legal immigration reform.

WIDENING THE GATES: THE IMMIGRATION ACT OF 1990

When the 1980s began, SCIRP took pains to separate the deleterious effects of illegal inflows from what it described as the enormous benefits of legal immigration. The intent of its conceptual distinctions between these two migratory streams was to highlight the need for both effective illegal immigration control *and* expansive legal admissions, a clear retort to restrictionists who used a broad brush to portray all forms of immigration as corrosive to American interests. But if SCIRP recommended a linkage between closing the back door and opening the front door wider, many lawmakers were eager in the late-1980s to separate not only the effects but also the regulation of illegal and legal immigration. Although the elusive control problems associated with unauthorized entries and mass asylum persisted at the decade's close, most members of Congress happily shifted their attention to legal immigration reform. In 1988, Kennedy and Simpson cosponsored legislation that would dramatically recast the rules and priorities of legal immigration. The omnibus bill called for a firm cap on the annual number of visas available to legal immigrants and refugees (Simpson's goal) while substantially increasing the annual ceiling for admissions to 590,000 (Kennedy's goal). Kennedy and Simpson also were concerned with revising the existing preference system to provide new openings for particular immigrant groups.

During the 1980s, Kennedy and other Northeastern politicians were lobbied heavily by Irish American groups to secure changes in legal immigration rules favorable to Irish nationals. An Irish Immigration Reform Movement, backed by a variety of Irish American associations, organized in this period to protest family-based preferences because they were said to "disadvantage" would-be Irish immigrants who lacked close family ties to U.S. citizens and permanent residents. During the bruising horse-trading over IRCA, Irish American groups won a controversial two-year program to distribute an additional 10,000 visas to foreign nationals of countries "adversely affected" by the 1965 preference system. In 1987, Kennedy's immigration subcommittee heard from prominent Irish American politicians, including Boston mayor Raymond Flynn and Senator Daniel Patrick Moynihan (D-NY), on the plight of would-be Irish immigrants. "Fairness is at issue here," Moynihan intoned. Invoking language usually reserved for civil rights debates, Kennedy inserted a curious provision in the 1988 bill providing special visa set-asides for Irish foreign nationals.

Under the constraints of a firm immigration cap, Simpson hoped to expand immigration opportunities for immigrants possessing desirable job skills and education. As early as 1982, Simpson expressed sympathy to groups like the Business Roundtable and various firms, who argued that global economic competition made it imperative for U.S. businesses to have access to the world's most skilled workers.[98] International pressures on immigration policy increasingly reflected not only Cold War geopolitics and traditional foreign policy concerns, but also the perceived demands of promoting U.S. fortunes in global trade. In 1988, Simpson called for a firm cap on legal immigration and new openings for immigrants with needed job skills.

Kennedy and Simpson merged their interests in Irish nationals and skilled workers under a so-called independent category which would distribute "points" to foreign applicants based on education, job skills, English language fluency, and "source-country diversity"—the latter a euphemism for allocating points to foreign nationals from Ireland and others who did not benefit from family-based preferences. To make room for this independent category under the proposed cap, the bill limited the number of visas allocated to the 1965 law's second preference for spouses and minor children of legal resident aliens and restricted its fifth preference to never-married siblings of U.S. citizens. The existing fifth preference provided visas to brothers and sisters of American citizens, as well as to the spouses and children of those siblings. While Kennedy said the new category would promote "diversity" by setting aside visas for countries "under-represented" in the existing system, Latino and Asian groups scored the plan as hostile to nonwhite newcomers. But ethnic lobbies had little time to mobilize opposition in the Senate, where the Kennedy-Simpson bill passed easily.

In the House, most Democrats refused to support the bipartisan compromise that sailed through the Senate. As a key Democratic staffer put it, "For generations we only admitted white, European immigrants, and then, after Asians and Latin Americans finally have an opportunity to get in, there's this proposal to limit their numbers. We simply weren't going to support something so racially biased."[99] Instead, House Democrats momentarily appeased Irish American lobbies and other ethnic groups by offering a special lottery for foreign nationals from countries "adversely affected" by the existing preference system. With the active encouragement of Latino, Asian, and immigrant rights groups, the Senate bill died in the House.

Beyond the legislative realm, the American Immigration Lawyers Association (AILA) led by Warren Leiden fashioned its own strategy toward legal immigration reform, one that richly informed the actions of most pro-immigration interest groups in coming months. Legal immigration reform placed AILA in a potentially awkward position. It had long-standing ties with Asian, Latino, immigrant rights, and religious groups that defended family-based immigration tooth and nail. Yet AILA also represented multinational firms and other business interests that supported Simpson's plan to increase employment-based immigration. "We realized that if each side thought of immigration reform as a zero-sum game in which visas for one group were seen as a loss for the other, there would be an ugly fight and someone would lose," Leiden recalls. "The solution was to work together to make the pie bigger."[100] Shuttling between various groups, Leiden and his allies persuaded each side to support increases in *both* employment-based and family-based immigration.[101] In order to harmonize the "business" and "family" coalitions, as they became known to policy community insiders, it was critical to defeat Simpson's plan for a firm cap on legal immigration.

Kennedy and Simpson teamed up again in 1989 to sponsor an omnibus reform bill that closely resembled their 1988 package. In contrast to the previous year, however, their proposal came under heavy bipartisan fire during Judiciary Committee markups. Strikingly, Kennedy's proposal for "diversity" visas to benefit Irish immigrants and others elicited no response. As in the past, he clothed the diversity program in egalitarian rhetoric, promising that it would "create a level playing field for all nations."[102] But Simpson's plan to alter the second and fifth preferences for family-based admissions was assailed on the Left by Paul Simon, who was working closely with Asian, Latino, and immigrant rights groups to defend family-based visa levels, and on the Right by Orrin Hatch, who aligned himself to both the "family" and "business" coalitions. "I am not being ethnically evil," Simpson told colleagues. "I have yet to see, under our definition in this country of a nuclear family, how that includes brothers and sisters of U.S. adult citizens."[103] But Simpson's limits on the second and fifth preferences lost in committee.

Simon also led a bipartisan attack on distributing points for English-language ability. "You know, my grandparents came over here from Italy and they settled in Vermont and neither one of them spoke English," Patrick Leahy (D-VT) said. "Yet they started a granite business and became one of the bigger employers in the small town they are in."[104] Other senators offered similar testimonials. An amendment to strike the English point preference was affirmed by a lopsided 12 to 2 committee vote, with only Kennedy and Simpson opposed. Strong bipartisan opposition to Simpson's firm cap on legal immigration also surfaced. "I have strong reservations about the cap," declared Arlen Specter (R-PA). "From the point of view of our national welfare, we could use a lot more immigrants." Hatch warned Simpson that he should expect "potential danger ahead" for his proposed cap.[105] While Democrats spoke of the benefits of reuniting families, Republicans emphasized the contributions of immigrant workers to American economic competitiveness. Both pro-immigration liberals and conservatives highlighted the findings of SCIRP, various economists, and a new study sponsored by the Labor Department, *Workforce 2000*, that suggested the United States might face a serious labor shortage in the future—especially among skilled laborers desperately needed by U.S. firms in a global marketplace.[106] After gutting English fluency points and alterations in the second and fifth preferences, the Judiciary Committee reported the bill.

Before reaching the Senate floor, Kennedy, Simon, and Simpson quietly negotiated a compromise package that melded their respective family, diversity, and skills emphases. Their joint statement on the proposal struck a decidedly pro-immigration tone:

We believe this compromise bill is a balanced attempt to serve the national interest; it preserves the immigration rights of those who have close family connections in this country; it stimulates immigration from earlier sources of immigration to our country that have contributed so much to America in the past; and it promotes the entry of those who are selected specifically for their ability to contribute their needed skills and talents to the development of our country.[107]

Proponents of the bill also took care on the Senate floor to link their proposal to SCIRP recommendations on legal immigration as well as to new expert research by economists and other specialists on the need for a more ambitious and flexible system of skills-based admissions. The only significant revisions of the bill on the floor were designed to expand immigration opportunities. Hatch and Dennis DeConcini (D-NM) garnered sixty-two votes for an amendment allowing the annual legal ceiling to be "pierced" to admit immediate relatives of U.S. citizens, thereby defeating Simpson's goal of a firm cap. The Senate also approved a proposal to grant stays of deportation for relatives of aliens legalized under IRCA. Another amendment raised the annual legal immigration ceiling from a proposed 590,000 to 630,000. The pro-immigration measure passed with broad cross-party support. The strong bipartisan majority reflected a crucial ideological convergence of liberal and conservative politicians and interest groups in favor of making large-scale legal immigration even larger.

In the House, a new immigration subcommittee chair, Bruce Morrison (D-CT), envisioned an even more expansive reform package. Morrison, an energetic junior member with strong liberal credentials, won control of the subcommittee after Mazzoli was ousted by Judiciary Committee Democrats who resented his eagerness to cooperate with Republicans. The fact that Morrison was catapulted into the position with limited immigration expertise highlighted the extent to which an increasingly partisan House rewarded members who demonstrated the right combination of entrepreneurial ambition and party loyalty. Morrison pursued a logrolling strategy for legal immigration reform, one meant to satisfy the policy preferences of Democratic colleagues and key labor, business, and ethnic interest groups favoring increased admissions. The "old American political system," Wilson reminds us, distributed tangible benefits such as free land, pensions, and subsidies to various clients. In modern American politics, he observes, success is more often measured in favorable rules rather than funds. At a time of budget austerity, legal immigration reform seemed to provide Morrison and his colleagues with a unique form of distributive politics that carried few apparent costs—namely, the allocation of visas.[108]

In 1990, Morrison introduced his own Family Unity and Employment

Opportunity Act. Similar to its Senate counterpart, the Morrison bill set aside special "diversity" visas for Irish and other foreign nationals "adversely affected" by the 1965 preference system. Responding to demands of business groups, the measure also embraced a more flexible and expanded system of employment-based admissions for temporary and permanent workers. But because these preferences troubled organized labor, Morrison and other Democrats also proposed that employers pay a head tax for each skilled immigrant they hired under the new system, with revenues targeted for retraining domestic workers. Asian, Latino, Italian, and other ethnic lobbies joined with immigrant rights and religious organizations to secure support from Morrison to significantly expand family-based admissions (a cause championed by Democrats like Berman). The Morrison plan also called for a "family fairness" program to grant amnesty to the immediate relatives of undocumented aliens who were legalized under IRCA. At Moakley's behest, the bill extended stays of deportation to Salvadoran asylum-seekers whose claims were denied by the Reagan and Bush Justice Departments. Finally, Morrison's bill deleted categories established by the McCarren-Walter Act of 1952 that denied entry to aliens based on ideology and sexual preference, a matter raised by Frank and gay and lesbian rights groups.[109] In October 1990, the House approved the Morrison bill.

The Bush administration said little about legal immigration reform initially. Labor secretary Elizabeth Dole privately scolded the White House for failing "to hammer out an Administration position."[110] When it finally did weigh in on the immigration reform process late in 1990, it took cues from Simpson and denounced the Morrison bill for imposing no sound limits on legal immigration. Simpson himself threatened to filibuster the selection of Senate conferees unless the immigration reform bill included new efforts to curtail illegal immigration, lower overall numbers for legal immigration, set a firm annual cap, make cutbacks in family-based visa preferences, and set limits on a new amnesty program.

White House support for Simpson's position proved fleeting. Reflecting the enthusiasm with which most free-market conservatives greeted the House bill's expansive employment-based system, the *Wall Street Journal* praised Morrison's bill for its potential contributions to U.S. economic growth. Its editorial pages hailed "Democrats for Vitality," while criticizing Bush officials for allowing "Stonewall Simpson" to derail expansive immigration reform.[111] Other pro-immigration conservatives reminded the administration and Congress of a 1989 General Accounting Office report linking American economic health to robust immigration. "Increasing immigration to meet the needs of the U.S. economy may help increase its international competitiveness, solve labor problems associated with low birth rates, and deal with weaknesses in the education of young U.S. workers," GAO experts concluded.[112] In response, Michael Boskin, a leading spokesperson for the Bush White House on economic affairs, soon offered public assurances of the administration's strong support for increased employment-based admissions.[113]

Bush officials also felt heat from ethnic lobbies and other groups favoring broader opportunities for family-based immigration. Top advisers worriedly discussed the political fallout of the administration's support for Simpson's efforts to scale back family-based admissions. As one internal memorandum noted:

> It requires constant vigilance against the charge that the Administration supports retreating from or is insensitive to this nation's traditional commitment to the institution of the family—and the President's strong pro-family stance. Could raise the ire of the Asian and Hispanic communities. . . . The greatest danger may be our identification with those whom the press calls the immigration "restrictionists" or "exclusionists."[114]

A late-1990 meeting with Asian leaders and lobbyists confirmed for Bush officials the need to support expansive legal immigration reform. As one adviser put it, "How could any president, let alone President Bush, oppose an immigration package so closely identified with economic growth and family values?"[115] At the eleventh hour, the Bush administration went public in support of increasing both family- and employment-based admissions.

With conference action delayed by Simpson's threatened filibuster, Kennedy tried to sway him by promising not to sign any conference report that the Wyoming senator found unacceptable. Simpson relented. As they had in 1986, conferees held lengthy meetings behind closed doors to craft a compromise. During negotiations, conferees agreed on a Kennedy proposal to increase annual legal admissions to 700,000 for the first three years and to 675,000 thereafter. A new amnesty program was approved for the immediate family of undocumented aliens legalized under IRCA. Simpson's proposal for a firm cap was scuttled; the annual ceiling on legal admissions could be "pierced" whenever the number of citizens' immediate relatives exceeded the cap. Family-based visas were not only unscathed, but modestly expanded; employment-based visas were increased substantially. A permanent diversity program for Irish and other foreign nationals was approved. Special immigration opportunities were extended to foreign nationals of Hong Kong and Tibet. Under Frank's stewardship, conferees also agreed to dismantle ideological and sexual preference exclusions established by the McCarran-Walter Act.

In exchange for conceding these modest reforms, Simpson secured a few modest proposals for discouraging illegal immigration. Conferees agreed to enhanced resources for border enforcement and a pilot program in three states testing a more secure driver's license for verifying employee eligibility in conjunction with employer sanctions. Simpson and Representative Bill McCollum (R-FL) also won a provision limiting the legal rights of criminal aliens facing deportation. Yet one volatile issue remained unresolved as conferees concluded negotiations: Moakley's proposal for extending "temporary protected status" to Salvadoran asylum-seekers for thirty-six months. When the White House telephoned to inform conferees that the president would veto the measure if it included Salvadoran relief, Moakley refused to budge. Instead, a bargain was struck whereby Salvadoran asylum-seekers would be granted stays of deportation for eighteen rather than thirty-six months. "This turkey gets more feathers every day," Simpson quipped in disgust.[116]

When conferees emerged from their last closed-door meeting, they hailed their package as a triumph for "cultural diversity," "family unity," and "job creation." The conference agreement secured swift passage in the Senate, 89 to 8. But it ran into unexpected opposition on the House floor, where the Hispanic Caucus challenged Simpson's pilot program for a more secure identification card linked to employer sanctions. Drawing analogies to South African passbooks and U.S. slave certificates, Esteban Torres (D-CA) argued that a new identification card invited civil rights abuses.[117] Alarmed by this development, Frank met with Simpson late in the evening to request that he drop his pilot program. Once again, Simpson relented. With the Hispanic Caucus satisfied, the House passed the conference package 264 to 118. Praising the Immigration Act of 1990 for fostering stronger families and national economic competitiveness, Bush signed the omnibus measure into law (see table 9.4). It was in part the product of an influential pro-immigration policy paradigm initiated by SCIRP and sustained by experts for most of a decade. The pressures associated with international trade and economic competition also helped propel xenophilic reform. But perhaps most important, the Immigration Act of 1990 reflected an insulation of the policymaking process from restrictive-minded publics, one in which the ideological convergence of liberal and conservative politicians and organized interests in favor of expanding immigration opportunities framed policy outcomes (see table 9.5).

REAWAKENING POPULAR POLITICS: RESTRICTIONISM AND ITS DISCONTENTS IN THE 1990S

As national political leaders turned their attention to new issues in the early 1990s, a handful of lawmakers worked with FAIR and other restrictionist groups on new legislation to crackdown on illegal immigration

TABLE 9.4
The Immigration Preference System Established by the 1990 Act

Preference Category	Visa Allocation, 1992–94		Visa Allocation, After 1994	
Family-based immigration	520,000	(74%)	480,000	(71%)
Immediate family members of U.S. citizens or legal residents	239,000	(39%)	254,000	(38%)
1st Preference: Unmarried adult children of U.S. citizens	23,400	(3%)	23,400	(4%)
2d Preference: Spouses and unmarried children of legal residents	114,200	(16%)	114,200	(17%)
3d Preference: Married adult children of U.S. citizens	23,400	(3%)	23,400	(4%)
4th Preference: Brothers and sisters of adult U.S. citizens	65,000	(9%)	65,000	(10%)
Nonpreference: Spouses and children of aliens granted amnesty under IRCA	55,000	(8%)	0	(0%)
Employment-based immigration	140,000	(20%)	140,000	(21%)
1st Preference: Workers with special talents or skills	40,000	(6%)	40,000	(6%)
2d Preference: Workers with advanced degrees or technical expertise	40,000	(6%)	40,000	(6%)
3d Preference: Workers with needed job skills, professionals, and others	40,000	(6%)	40,000	(6%)
4th Preference: Special immigrants and religious workers	10,000	(1%)	10,000	(1%)
5th Preference: Immigrants who invest at least $1 million and hire ten or more native workers	10,000	(1%)	10,000	(1%)
Diversity immigration	40,000	(6%)	55,000	(8%)
Total	700,000	(100%)	675,000	(100%)

and to reduce legal immigration to 300,000 annually. Their proposals went nowhere, garnering fewer than sixty supporters in both houses of Congress.[118] But outside the Washington Beltway, FAIR and other restrictionist groups set about to build strong grass-roots opposition to immigration in key receiving states like California, Texas, and Florida.[119] In California, a low-budget organization called Save Our State (SOS) was formed by local restrictionist leaders and former INS officials like Harold Ezell. Its central purpose was to promote Proposition 187 to deny illegal aliens and their children welfare benefits, nonemergency health care, and

TABLE 9.5
Alien Admissions and Rights (Contemporary Coalitions)

Alien Rights Should Be	Alien Admissions Should Be	
	Expanded or Maintained	Restricted
Expansive	1. **Cosmopolitans** Edward Kennedy Howard Berman Xavier Becerra Ethnic groups; human rights and religious groups; AFL-CIO; National Immigration Forum; American Immigration Lawyers Association	2. **Nationalist Egalitarians** Barbara Jordan Alan Simpson Richard Lamm A. Philip Randolph Institute; population control and environmental groups
Restrictive	3. **Free-Market Expansionists** Ronald Reagan Spencer Abraham Richard Armey American Farm Bureau Federation; Business Roundtable, National Association of Manufacturers; CATO Institute	4. **Classic Exclusionists** Patrick Buchanan Edward Gallegly Peter Brimelow Federation for American Immigration Reform; California Save Our State movement

public education. As one SOS leader explained, "It made sense to target the most objectionable recipients first—illegals. Then we could put the issue of too much legal immigration on the table."[120] California governor Pete Wilson (R) threw his support behind Proposition 187, calling for wholesale restrictions on immigrant access to public benefits in his reelection bid. As he struggled to survive a serious statewide economic slump and related budget shortages, Wilson decried what he claimed was a $4.8 billion expenditure the previous year for health, welfare, education, and criminal justice costs of legal and illegal immigrants. Ethnic, religious, and educational organizations in the state vigorously opposed Proposition 187, and they drew upon prominent Democrats like Jesse Jackson and Republicans such as William Bennett and Jack Kemp to denounce the measure. But Wilson's staunch backing of Proposition 187 made it a partisan issue, especially when the state Republican party added its endorsement.[121]

Popular support for restricting immigration also seemed to intensify across the country by 1994. Of course, public resistance to large-scale immigration and ambivalence toward new immigrant groups has been a hallmark of public opinion polling since at least the 1940s.[122] But immigration restriction seemed to not only gain in popularity in 1994 (roughly 65 percent favored major reductions in legal admissions),[123] but its salience for the general public also appeared to surge. When ordinary citizens were asked which issues mattered most to them in the 1994 election, 20 percent placed illegal immigration at the top of their lists; the most common answers were crime at 33 percent and welfare reform at 28 percent.[124] Another poll conducted just before the election found that 72 percent of respondents saw mass immigration as a "critical threat" to the "vital interests of the United States."[125] Jack Citrin and his colleagues found that voters were increasingly connecting immigration to negative economic experiences and economic uncertainty in the two elections after 1992.[126] Events like the 1994 bombing of the World Trade Center in New York City by Islamic terrorists, who had gained entry to the United States with relative ease, heightened public tension over international migration.

When the dust settled on a contentious California race in November, Wilson won reelection and Proposition 187 carried the state with 59 percent of the vote. As restrictionists in various Southern and Western states prepared to replicate the substance and success of Proposition 187, the measure was immediately enjoined by a federal court that held that its denial of public education to the children of undocumented aliens was unconstitutional. If judicial intervention blunted popular assaults on immigrant rights at the state level, a dramatic changing of the guard in Congress seemed to offer new opportunities for restrictionist policy innovations supported by large majorities of the public. For the first time since 1952, the Republican party gained control of both houses of Congress. Simpson assumed leadership of the Senate Immigration Subcommittee, while Lamar Smith (R-TX), a restrictionist who had been cut out of the policymaking process by Morrison in 1990, became Immigration Subcommittee chair on the House side. Both of these lawmakers envisioned a fresh round of restrictive immigration reform to limit legal admissions, to make immigrants ineligible for welfare benefits, and to finally curb illegal immigration. In the House, a considerable number of Republican members were eager to support tighter controls over illegal flows and cuts in legal immigrant admissions and welfare rights. The Republican delegations of California and Texas were particularly dogged in urging Speaker Newt Gingrich (R-GA) to facilitate restrictive reform. Many Republican lawmakers, mobilized by the success of Proposition 187 and opinion poll trends, became convinced that immigration restriction could be used effectively as a "wedge" issue to win crucial blue-collar Democratic voters (especially in key battleground states like California and Florida).[127] Gingrich responded to intraparty pressures by creating a special task force on immigration reform chaired by Elton Gallegly, a California Republican known for his hard line on illegal immigration and legal immigrant welfare eligibility. Senate majority leader Robert Dole (R-KS) joined many fellow partisans in supporting immigration curbs, appearing on television to decry the unfair immigration costs imposed on California, Florida, and Texas, and to denounce policymakers "not willing to protect our borders."[128] Immigration defenders poised themselves for a formidable restrictionist assault.

The Commission on Immigration Reform (CIR), established by the 1990 act, offered additional institutional openings to restrictionists. Led by former representative Barbara Jordan (D-TX), CIR membership included pro-immigration and restrictionist figures. Jordan herself supported legal immigration and extensive immigrant rights to welfare and other public benefits, while calling for tougher enforcement against illegal entries, which subverted the legal admissions system. This was a position quite similar to the one adopted by SCIRP a decade before. But whereas Hesburgh presided over a commission dominated by pro-immigration members, Jordan had to broker compromises between distinct camps (with commissioners like Morrison and Leiden on the one side and SOS activists like Ezell on the other). Moreover, the Jordan Commission heard testimony and addressed topics, such as the influence of newcomers on poor African Americans, that encouraged more circumspect conclusions about the benefits of immigration. The Jordan Commission's 1994 report on illegal immigration focused on making employer sanctions more effective through the creation of a computerized registry for verifying worker eligibility using data provided by the INS and Social Security Administration.[129] It issued a new report on legal immigration one year later that endorsed large-scale admissions but called for modest cuts in annual visa numbers and the elimination of the fifth preference for extended family members of U.S. citizens.[130] Anxious not to be outflanked on the immigration issue in California and other states by its partisan and institutional rivals, the Clinton administration praised the nation's immigrant tradition while endorsing the recommendations of the Jordan Commission. The White House also took a hard line on mass asylum, clarifying that Cuban and Haitian boat people intercepted at sea would not be allowed to enter the United States; this marked a significant break from three decades of treating all Cuban escapees as refugees.[131]

Recognizing the importance of expertise in contemporary policymaking, restrictionists looked for specialists and research to challenge the prevailing policy paradigm concerning the benefits of immigration. The relatively young Center for Immigration Studies (CIS), a think tank located in Washington, generated a steady stream of scholarly reports and studies that supported a restrictive policy agenda. Founded in 1985 with the support of FAIR, which had grown weary of research it believed was unduly biased in favor of robust immigration, the CIS provided expertise during the 1990s that complimented the policy ambitions of Lamar Smith and restrictive lawmakers. Anti-immigration activists also pointed to work by social scientists such as Rice University's Donald Huddle and Cornell's Vernon Briggs, Jr., for evidence that the existing immigration system was seriously flawed.[132] But these efforts to recast the intellectual convictions of the Washington immigration policy community had limited success; the most influential government and academic studies tended to reaffirm SCIRP's earlier conclusion that expansive legal immigration served the national interest (a finding echoed by the CIR reports). As restrictionist Chilton Williamson, Jr., lamented in the 1990s, a pro-immigration policy paradigm was accepted and advanced by most national politicians in both parties, "most of the establishment and business press and all of the major television networks; numerous columnists, the academy, the federal bureaucracy . . . [and] the liberal, radical, neoconservative, and libertarian journals of opinion."[133]

Still, a general audience read popular books by authors like Peter Brimelow and Roy Beck that offered dire portraits of how contemporary mass immigration would devastate U.S. economic, social, and political life.[134] Their sensational accounts of immigration-driven decline were reminiscent of the apocalyptic passages of Josiah Strong's *Our Country*, written more than a century earlier. In the same period, William Buckley's *National Review* began to print blistering conservative critiques of expansive immigration policies. But conservatives were hardly of one mind on immigration. Many continued to positively associate robust immigration with free markets, entrepreneurial newcomers, and Ronald Reagan's vision of the nation as a "beacon of hope" for those oppressed under communist and other regimes. Others argued that any reform that provided fewer visas for reuniting families was anathema to a conservative pro-family agenda.[135] Dick Armey (R-TX) was one of several prominent figures of the House Republican leadership team who vigorously defended expansive legal immigration. Tellingly, the Gallegly task force established by Gingrich skirted legal immigration conflicts by confining its recommendations to illegal flows and public benefits for immigrants. The panel endorsed increased Border Patrol resources, pilot programs for verification of worker eligibility, tougher sanctions for those using fake documents or knowingly hiring undocumented aliens, and expedited procedures for removing aliens (including asylum-seekers) who entered the country without authorization. Hoping to draw from the success of Proposition 187, the task force also called for denying educational benefits to the children of undocumented aliens.

Lamar Smith had a far more ambitious restrictionist agenda in mind when the Republican 104th Congress convened in 1995, and his immigration subcommittee wasted little time in holding hearings and drafting reform legislation. But as he devised a blueprint for restricting legal immigration and toughening enforcement against illegal immigration, AILA and immigration defenders like Rick Swartz, founder of the National Immigration Forum, worked to rebuild the incongruous coalition of business, ethnic, religious, labor, libertarian, and civil rights groups that had fueled the 1990 expansions in family- and employment-based visas. John Juddis aptly dubbed this revived coalition of odd bedfellows the "huddled elites."[136] Of these coalition members, Republican politicians were particularly uneasy about various businesses that relied on skilled and unskilled immigrant labor. As Microsoft lobbyists chastised restrictionists for missing "the point that to succeed in foreign markets, you need foreign personnel," the National Association of Manufacturers warned that "this country is not producing the workers we need to be globally competitive."[137] Employers of unskilled workers also made their presence felt on Capitol Hill. During a meeting with lobbyists for the National Restaurant Association, an organization whose large membership relied heavily on unskilled alien workers, Gingrich offered assurances that he had no intention of cutting their supply to immigrant labor.[138] Occupational visas were emerging as a "third rail" for Republican lawmakers.

Smith's immigration reform bill, as reported by the full House Judiciary Committee, reflected these interest-group pressures. The initiative included provisions for reducing legal immigration, constricting immigrant access to public benefits, strengthening enforcement against illegal immigration at the border and at the workplace, expediting the deportation of criminal aliens, limiting the adjudication of asylum claims, and extending refugee relief to those escaping regimes with coercive population-control policies. In terms of legal admissions, Smith's bill called for three preference categories: family-based, employment-based, and humanitarian. Family-based entries were reduced from 480,000 to 330,000 annually by eliminating preferences for siblings and adult children. Hoping to allay resistance from business groups and fellow partisans, Smith left unscathed employment-based immigration. Finally, a 70,000 annual cap was proposed for humanitarian admissions including refugees, asylees, and other immigrants deserving special relief. But a proposal by Smith to gut the diversity category failed in committee action, where Schumer succeeded in drawing bipartisan support for saving it.[139]

The full committee markup of Smith's bill revealed important political alignments. Not surprisingly, a clear partisan divide emerged in this committee on provisions that threatened the substantive and procedural rights of legal aliens, such as expediting deportations and limiting access to social welfare programs. Yet there was broad consensus across party lines on efforts to strengthen enforcement against illegal immigration, and some indication that more than a few Republicans were uncomfortable with Smith's proposal to shrink legal admissions. Fearful that employer groups and free-market Republicans would oppose his bill, Smith cut a deal with business lobbyists before the Judiciary Committee vote that left employment-based visas untouched in exchange for their support.[140] It was a shrewd strategy intended by Smith to divide the powerful family-business coalition that had propelled the 1990 expansions and derailed subsequent efforts to enact restrictionist policies. Even when Smith deftly took occupational visas out of the mix, however, the Judiciary Committee's exceptionally partisan Republicans broke ranks to support Schumer's restoration of the diversity category and quarreled over limiting family preferences.

On the Senate side, Simpson's subcommittee drafted legislation with provisions on illegal immigration enforcement and limits on alien eligibility for public benefits that closely resembled the House bill. It also included new limits on legal admissions; but unlike Smith's plan, its restrictions took their heaviest toll on employment-based immigration. The Simpson bill proposed reducing occupational visas from 140,000 to 90,000 annually and assessing a fee of $10,000 on employers for each skilled immigrant worker hired (family-based immigration was reduced by 30,000 annually). In addition, Simpson called for restrictions on the asylum process and a firm cap of 50,000 annual refugee admissions. But the refugee cap never survived subcommittee markup, as every senator but Simpson backed a Kennedy amendment striking it. While business groups like Microsoft, the U.S. Chamber of Commerce, and NAM brokered a deal with Smith in the House, they had strong incentive to join with ethnic, religious, and immigrant rights groups of the Left in their efforts to defeat legal immigration reform in the Senate. As in 1990, a potent Left-Right alliance of organized interests championed expansive legal immigrant admissions. Amid fierce lobbying, the full Senate Judiciary committee voted to split legal and illegal reform by a 12 to 6 margin. The "split-the-bill" amendment was adeptly shepherded by Michigan Republican Spencer Abraham; six of ten Republicans deserted Simpson to pass the amendment.

These committee patterns reflected broader political trends in Washington. As GOP leaders recognized, pro-immigration and restrictionist conservatives were most unified behind proposals to scale back alien rights to various social welfare benefits and procedural due process claims. Whereas the Republicans' 1994 Contract with America said nothing about restricting immigration, it offered clear proposals to deny Medicaid, Supplemental Security Insurance (SSI), Aid to Families with Dependent Children, and Food Stamps to legal immigrants. Some Republican politicians such as Simpson and Senator Nancy Kassebaum (R-KS) opposed these efforts, but they were outliers on the alien rights issue.[141] Free-market defenders of immigration in the Reagan mold celebrated newcomers who were hardworking and economically self-sufficient, not those who relied upon the government for financial support. As Gingrich proclaimed on the House floor, "Come to America for opportunity. Do not come to America to live off the law-abiding American taxpayer."[142] "Immigration yes, welfare no" was the slogan that caught fire among pro-immigration conservatives on Capitol Hill and in the halls of think tanks like the CATO Institute. The failure of many legal aliens to naturalize also struck various conservatives as disloyal and unpatriotic. "If they don't want to pledge their allegiance to the United States," Gallegly averred, "they shouldn't be eligible for food stamps."[143] By contrast, liberal Democrats defended the rights of aliens to receive public benefits and procedural justice as passionately in the 1990s as they had in previous decades.

As was the case in the 1980s, neither Republican nor Democratic leaders wanted to appear lax in their response to unpopular illegal immigration; the failure of IRCA to address the problem only served to intensify "blame-avoidance" strategies in an era of divided government. During California town meetings early in his presidency, Clinton took pains to assure restive citizens that his administration was working to curb illegal immigration. He also quickly endorsed the Jordan Commission's recommendations for rigorous enforcement against illegal immigration during the 1994 midterm election year. In 1995, Berman introduced an administration bill, the Immigration Enforcement Improvements Act, which sought to codify tough measures to discourage surreptitious entries. Like the Hesburgh Commission almost two decades before, both moderate and liberal Democrats drew sharp distinctions between the virtues of legal immigration and the perils of undocumented flows. Indeed, former SCIRP staff director Lawrence Fuchs advised the White House to rhetorically highlight the enormous contributions of legal immigrants "who play by the rules."[144] In keeping with their fealty to civil rights, most Democratic politicians opposed Proposition 187 and Gallegly's efforts to deny educational benefits and birthright citizenship to the children of undocumented aliens. But fighting illegal immigration had become a valence issue that attracted strong bipartisan support, one that Gingrich and the Republican 104th Congress failed to translate into a partisan triumph.

The decoupling of legal immigration reform from illegal immigration control efforts was a major victory for the Left-Right coalition of interest groups determined to protect expansive family and occupational admissions. As organized interests mobilized effectively against the legal reform plans of the Smith and Simpson bills, the Clinton White House shifted away from its earlier position in favor of the Jordan Commission's call for modest visa reductions and flatly disavowed any legal restrictions. Republicans proved equally unwilling to reduce legal admissions, as William Kristol, Kemp, Bennett, and other respected conservative voices argued that immigration restriction contradicted the GOP's celebration of global markets, individual opportunity, and families. Even the Christian Coalition mobilized against legal immigration reform because "scaling back the ability of Americans to reunite with their families will not improve national security, and could severely damage the American family."[145]

In the wake of the pro-immigration coalition's victory in Senate Judiciary Committee action, the battle over legal immigration restriction shifted to the House floor in March 1996. There, Berman and two pro-immigration conservatives, Sam Brownbeck (R-KS) and Dick Chrysler (R-MI), offered an amendment to gut the Smith bill's legal immigration provisions. In a chamber defined by partisan estrangement, the amendment was carried by a cross-party majority (75 Republicans deserted Smith on legal reform). By contrast, a Gallegly amendment to deny public education to undocumented children carried with a party-line vote. The final version of the Smith bill, now largely an enforcement measure targeting undocumented aliens, visa violators, and criminal aliens, passed by a lopsided 333 to 87 vote. On April 15, Simpson's illegal immigration reform initiative reached the Senate floor. In a last-ditch effort to achieve legal restrictions, Simpson offered an amendment that would impose a temporary five-year reduction in family-based immigration. By focusing on family admissions, he hoped to gain support from business groups and Republican colleagues who opposed his original plan. The effort proved quixotic, as 40 Republicans and 40 Democrats voted against the amendment. Simpson's illegal immigration bill ultimately passed, 97 to 3. The Illegal Immigration Reform and Immigrant Responsibility Act (IIRIRA) made its way to conference committee.

The final version of IIRIRA enhanced the federal government's ability to guard national borders, tightened asylum procedures, limited immigrant access to public benefits, required U.S. financial sponsors for new-comers, and established stringent provisions for criminal and undocu-mented aliens. Under a firm threat of presidential veto, the Gallegly amendment modeled after Proposition 187 was struck in conference ne-gotiations. But in the heat of a national campaign, legislation primarily designed to get tough on illegal immigration was hard to resist for politi-cians of either party. IIRIRA passed easily in both houses and was signed into law the last week of September. Although anything but expansive, this new enforcement law was a pyrrhic victory for restrictionists. "Your hopes of reining in uncontrolled immigration were dashed," FAIR told voters. "[I]n the end, Congress sold out to the special interests."[146]

Welfare reform was another product of party competition in a presi-dential election year that had important consequences for immigrants. The Personal Responsibility and Work Opportunity Act of 1996 barred noncitizens from a broad set of federal benefits programs. President Clin-ton told the press that he was offended by the legislation's harshness toward legal immigrants, but that he chose to sign the reform package because of his devotion to fundamentally restructure the larger welfare system. Together, the immigration and welfare reform laws marked a re-trenchment of the legal protections and social entitlements that legal and undocumented aliens could claim. It was a triumph for free-market ex-pansionists, who allied with pro-immigration liberals to sustain unprece-dented legal admissions and with anti-immigrant conservatives to trim alien substantive and procedural rights. The outcomes of 1996 suggested that large-scale immigration would flow into the United States uninter-rupted for the foreseeable future, and that those who arrived would enjoy fewer membership rights until they acquired citizenship.

The maintenance of expansive legal admissions in the 1990s captured a two-tiered democracy that allowed pro-immigration politicians and inter-est groups to insulate past policy achievements from popular restriction-ism. Indeed, this insulation of the policymaking process was crucial to the resilience of an expansionist policy regime that reflected what Gary Free-man has described for other contexts as a kind of "bilateral influence in which small and well-organized groups intensely interested in a policy develop close working relationships with those officials responsible for it."[147] The result was an elite-driven form of pro-immigration policy re-production animated by interest group influence, dominant expertise, and the ideological and foreign policy commitments of state actors.

Yet the new Republican Congress that came to power in 1995 was unmistakably caught up by the popular wave of anti-immigrant politics that seemed to wash over the country between 1994 and 1996. House Republican efforts to replicate the Proposition 187 in national legislation captured their responsiveness to public anxieties about newcomers, as did new reforms cracking down on illegal immigration and cutting immigrant welfare rights. "When Prop 187 passed," Frank Sharry of the National Immigration Forum recalls, "the consensus was that immigrants don't vote and the people who do vote are angry about immigration."[148] In 1995, several prominent Republican congressional leaders expressed optimism behind closed doors that the immigration issue would cost Democrats some important blue-collar votes.[149] At the start of the 1996 election, Pete Wilson made immigration control a prominent feature of his short-lived presidential campaign; Pat Buchanan assailed Third World immigration as a source of economic and cultural insecurity at home; and Bob Dole, the eventual Republican standard bearer, associated himself with the stringent immigration enforcement measures then working their way through Congress.[150] The1996 Republican platform pledged support for national legislation barring children of undocumented aliens from public schools. In the later stages of the election, however, Dole and other Republican candidates took heed of new reports that immigrants and kindred ethnic groups had become energized by political restrictionism. But it was too late for backpedaling.

REVIVING IMMIGRANT DEMOCRACY

The results of the 1996 election left little doubt about two crucial facts: immigrants comprised the nation's fastest growing voting bloc and Democrats were the immediate beneficiaries of their unexpected electoral clout. Naturalization rates soared after 1995, as record numbers of aliens became naturalized citizens (see fig. 9.1). More than one million people naturalized in 1996 alone. At the same time that unprecedented numbers of aliens petitioned for naturalization in the wake of mid-1990s restrictions on public benefits for noncitizens, President Clinton instructed the INS to implement the so-called Citizenship USA initiative of 1995. In the words of the agency, the initiative "was designed to streamline the naturalization process and greatly increased naturalizations during 1996."[151] Meanwhile, voter registration among Latinos grew by 1.3 million, or 28.7 percent, between 1992 and 1996; the percentage of Latinos on the voter rolls rose from 59 percent of those eligible in 1992 to 65 percent in 1996. These increases reflected both naturalizations and new interest in politics among Latinos angered by anti-immigrant measures.[152] Significantly, various studies and polls indicate that a majority of Mexican Americans and other Latinos favored reductions in legal immigration.[153] But in various surveys, Latino citizens supporting immigration restriction expressed resentment toward cutbacks in public benefits for aliens and other initiatives targeting immigrants for exclusion.[154] Enfranchised immigrants and kindred ethnic groups made their displeasure clear at the vot-

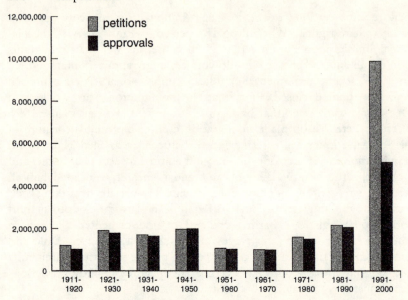

Fig. 9.1. U.S. Naturalization Petitions and Approvals, 1911–2000 (Source: *INS Statistical Yearbook, 2000* [Washington, DC: Government Printing Office, 2000])

ing booth. Mexican Americans turned out in record numbers, and the Latino Democratic vote went from 60 to 72 percent between the 1992 and 1996 presidential elections. Asian Americans, a smaller yet important swing bloc, increased their support for the Democratic ticket in the same years from 29 to 43 percent. Even traditionally Republican Cuban Americans showed a greater inclination to vote Democratic in 1996. Dole became the first Republican presidential candidate to lose Florida since Gerald Ford in 1980.

These trends were even more striking in the pivotal electoral state of California. Latinos increased from 8 to 10 percent of the state's electorate between 1992 and 1996. In the 1996 presidential elections and the 1997 Los Angeles city elections, Latino voter turnout percentages exceeded non-Latino voter turnout. Clinton garnered 71 percent of the Latino vote in 1996, and immigrant voters were credited with helping Democrats reclaim control of the California House the same year (where Latinos served as the new Speaker and floor leader). Robert Dornan (R-CA), who found himself ousted from his congressional seat by Democrat Loretta Sanchez, protested that unqualified immigrant voters handed him defeat.[155] "For the first time in 20 years there was no whining about the paltry turnout of Latino voters," the *Los Angeles Times* noted. "Thank God and Pete Wilson, not necessarily in that order.[156]

As naturalization numbers in 1997 topped the previous year's levels, Republican lawmakers and candidates swiftly backed away from the anti-immigrant politics of the mid-1990s. In 1997, Congress restored SSI to many immigrants who lived in the country before the 1996 law was enacted. The same year, lawmakers adopted a new amnesty program for more than 400,000 Central American refugees. Eligibility for food stamps was also restored the following year. To the surprise of many observers, most states with large immigrant populations have used their new authority over alien benefits to provide broad assistance to immigrants. Proposition 187 was first enjoined and then nullified by federal judges; California governor Gray Davis (D), who received 78 percent of the Latino vote in his 1998 campaign, had little incentive to appeal the ruling to higher courts. As the 2000 presidential election neared, both national and state organizations of the Republican party drew up plans to attract new Asian and Latino voters, emboldened by party strategists who warned that "if we're only getting 25 percent of the Hispanic vote, you wait three, four presidential elections, and we'll be out of business."[157] George W. Bush was hailed by the party establishment as the ideal candidate to court new immigrant voters in 2000, and he reminded Latino voters throughout the campaign that he "rejected the spirit of Prop 187," opposed "English only" proposals, and refused "to bash immigrants" in the mid-1990s.[158] For his part, Al Gore assured immigrant voters of Democratic plans to restore welfare benefits stripped away by a Republican Congress in 1996 and vowed to support expansive legal immigration. At the start of the new millennium, an outgoing Democratic president coordinated with Republican lawmakers on new legislation that permitted expansions in annual admissions of skilled foreign workers. They also collaborated on the Legal Immigration and Family Equity Act, which its sponsors expected to extend legal status to an estimated 1.5 million undocumented aliens who obtained sponsorship from an employer or an immediate relative with citizenship or a green card.

The restrictionist movement that appeared so menacing to policymakers in the mid-1990s ultimately reawakened an expansionist politics rooted in immigrant enfranchisement and competitive democratic elections. Ironically, several important anti-immigrant measures fueled this revival. The McCarran-Walter Act of 1952 introduced changes in the nation's naturalization laws that, more than 150 years after the first naturalization rules were adopted, made nonwhite newcomers eligible for full membership in the American polity. More than four decades later, Proposition 187, IIRIRA, and welfare reform motivated record numbers of new immigrants and kindred ethnics to make the most of their naturalization opportunities and voting rights. The unintended consequence of these restrictive laws is a new generation of foreign-born voters, who, like European newcomers more than a century before, have created fresh electoral incentives for national politicians to guard expansive immigration policies.

CHAPTER TEN

Conclusion

A closed country is a dying country.

—Edna Ferber

All the ills of democracy can be cured by more democracy.
—Alfred E. Smith (borrowing from a philosopher, John
Dewey, as politicians are sometimes wont to do)

IMMIGRATION IS A powerful and elemental leitmotif of American national development. Other modern nations, including Argentina, Australia, Canada, and France, share parallel histories with the United States as countries of immigration.[1] Yet Americans are perhaps unusual to the degree that they have woven immigration narratives and iconography into their collective cultural identity. While there are numerous countries that have been deeply affected over time by alien inflows, it is telling that so many contemporary Americans like to think of the United States as a distinctive "nation of immigrants." Most celebrate their immigrant origins at the same time as their political leaders pay tribute to previous waves of newcomers who built the nation. Immigration myths are integral to how Americans define themselves as a people: "a nation of sojourners in a nation itself on a journey," as David Jacobson recently put it.[2] Equally compelling for many Americans is the notion that theirs is a "chosen, redeemer nation," promoting universal human rights principles and serving as a special haven for the world's poor and oppressed.[3] The concept of a nation of immigrants, albeit cliché, has become an almost sacred fixture of American national identity.

However, at the same time as Americans reify immigration traditions and myths, they remain profoundly ambivalent about the immigrant present and future. As in the past, sustained mass immigration promises to alter the nation's cultural identity, to challenge its capacities for territorial control, to fuel economic transformation while frustrating particular redistributionist goals, and to recast the form and substance of democratic politics in the United States. Philosophically, new immigration raises crucial tensions in American thought between a devotion to universal principles first articulated in the Declaration of Independence and yearnings for democratic self-determination in a bounded civic community. Political theorists such as Joseph Carens argue that well-guarded national borders are arbitrary, discriminating among individuals on the basis of accidental territorial birthright rather than any justifiable moral criteria. Liberal universalist principles, he concludes, vindicate open borders.[4] On the other hand, many theorists contend that meaningful democratic self-legislation most often occurs among members of a bounded community.[5] "An important role of a people's government, however arbitrary a society's boundaries may appear from a historical point of view," John Rawls notes, "is to be the representative and effective agent of a people as they take responsibility for their territory and its environmental integrity, as well as for the size of their population."[6] For the United States, new immigration underscores a crucial philosophical tension between universalist principles and the right of a national citizenry to self-determination. Whereas universalism threatens the quality and character of democratic citizenship within bounded civic communities, the official choices of those communities often have significant implications for those living outside their borders.

Of course, far more practical issues have consumed U.S. immigration politics over time. One of the most compelling effects of immigration to the United States has been its capacity to introduce change into a political system renowned for its seemingly unshakable stability. Ultimately, national struggles over immigrant admissions and rights have been fueled by conflict over the fate of prevailing social, economic, and political orders. As fresh waves of immigration have transformed the demographics of American democracy, conditions of entry and exit have assumed great significance for natives uneasy about the arrival of new and potentially rival stakeholders in national life.

A darker tension at the heart of many immigration policy battles in American political development has pitted universalist ideals against potent traditions of ethnic and racial hierarchy. As previous chapters illustrate, the arrival of large numbers of immigrants of ethnic, racial, linguistic, or religious identity distinct from that of the American majority has routinely elicited popular hostilities and new restrictionist movements. Moreover, the creation and long tenure of immigration policies that systematically excluded Asians and southern and eastern Europeans on explicitly racist grounds underscore the extent to which inegalitarian ideologies have indeed had a powerful hold on U.S. politics and government. The restrictionist regimes that were constructed in the late-nineteenth and early-twentieth centuries breathed life into literacy tests, a so-called Asiatic Barred Zone, and a durable national origins quota system, which cannot be brushed aside as fleeting historical exceptions to a dominant liberal tradition.

Accordingly, scholars such as Roger Daniels, Desmond King, Gwendolyn Mink, Juan Perea, Rogers Smith, and Ronald Takaki believe the politics of immigration control reveals a more insidious side of American civic culture, one that privileges notions of ascriptive exclusion and racial hierarchy.[7] These scholars are deeply critical of what might be called the "triumphant liberalism" school, which contends that the strength of the nation's founding ideology, rooted in liberal democratic principles, has meant that inegalitarian practices and beliefs could not ultimately withstand the slow but determined historical progress of liberal universalism. In a brilliant articulation of the "multiple traditions approach," for example, Smith challenges the received wisdom of Alexis de Tocqueville, Louis Hartz, and others that a hegemonic liberal tradition rules the U.S. political culture. Instead, he argues, American political thought and practice has been shaped by rival civic ideologies in perpetual contest with one another for preeminence. "The overall pattern," he contends, is "one of fluctuation between more consensual and egalitarian and more ascriptive and inegalitarian arrangements."[8]

The immigration policy regimes that have emerged over the course of American political development certainly lend credence to the kind of fluctuation Smith describes. Moreover, there is ample evidence today that what Smith calls "illiberal, undemocratic traditions of ascriptive Americanism" are alive and well, whether from the political appeals of Patrick Buchanan to the overwrought writings of *Forbes* and *National Review* editor Peter Brimelow. Brimelow's widely read *Alien Nation* sounds apocalyptic refrains that our strikingly similar to Josiah Strong's popular anti-Catholic and anti-immigrant *Our Country* of the late-nineteenth century. "These new immigrants are from completely different and arguably incompatible cultural traditions," Brimelow writes of the so-called "browning of America."[9] The demise of the national origins quota system in 1965, he laments, "triggered a renewed mass immigration, so huge and so systematically different than anything that had gone before as to transform—and ultimately, perhaps, even to destroy—the one unquestioned victor of World War II: the American nation, as it had evolved by the middle of the twentieth century."[10]

Moreover, ordinary citizens remain at best uneasy about newcomers. As David Moore observed in a review of Gallup polls conducted in recent years, "Substantial numbers of Americans, often more than a majority, have wanted to see immigration reduced and even halted, expressed concerns about the economic and cultural consequences of admitting more foreigners to this country, and said it is a bad thing for the country that in the past decade the percentage of foreign-born residents in the United States has increased significantly."[11] In particular, most respondents believe new immigrants worsen the quality of public schools, the crime situation, and taxes. They remain evenly divided on the effects of recent arrivals on the economy in general, politics and government, and social and moral values.[12] As in the past, the intensity of popular support for decreasing immigration has been strong over the past decade, while support for widening the gates remains negligible. Whether registered in the rise of movements dedicated to building fresh barriers to new arrivals or the restrictionist policy preferences of mass publics, native anxieties associated with shifts in the volume and demographic composition of immigration continue to fuel national struggles over alien admissions and rights.

If nativist traditions and popular resistance to newcomers (not necessarily the same) have been recurrent features of American immigration politics over time, the distinctive policy regimes that emerged from these struggles reflect important variations. Indeed, the national immigration policies that rest at the heart of this study reveal strikingly different outcomes, from the exclusionary literacy tests and national origins quota system inspired by early-twentieth-century eugenics movement to the explicit expansion of immigration opportunities for a broader portion of humanity under the Immigration Act of 1990. To understand why the United States has advanced contrasting immigration policies during distinctive periods of its history requires what Theda Skocpol describes as "a broader, organizationally grounded analysis of American political development."[13] It demands careful attention to how institutional arrangements of the national state and party system interact with privileged expertise, changing coalitions of interest groups, and international threats in the policymaking process.

The multiple-traditions approach helps explain the ideological foundations for restrictionist policy regimes to privilege northern and western Europeans for most of the twentieth century. It also helps account for the surges in popular resistance to new immigration that have emerged in nearly every era, often informed by racial fears and animosities expressed from Madison Grant to Peter Brimelow. Yet those who focus on the resilience of nativist and racist traditions in American political life provide us with few insights about the origins and development of expansionist policy regimes. For example, most of the choices of insulated U.S. political elites since the 1960s reflect a clear trend toward intentionally expansive immigration policies. In this regard, scholars such as Lawrence Fuchs and Charles Kesler, who emphasize the unfolding promise of liberal universalist ideals in the American national development, are more successful in illuminating crucial secular historical developments—such as the liberalization of naturalization law in the 1950s—that *institutionalize* certain liberal democratic gains and reinforce expansionist trends. Each approach, then, tends to reify a distinctive conception of how historical processes shape political outcomes; whereas the triumphant liberalism school places special emphasis on secular changes and historical trajectories, the multiple traditions approach tends to highlight cyclical processes and enduring forces.

The historical-institutionalist analysis employed in this study was designed to offer a more robust theoretical conception of the temporal processes underlying immigration policymaking in the United States. At the close of his classic investigation of American nativism, John Higham eloquently reminds us of the importance of both cyclical patterns and secular changes. "History may move partly in cycles but never in circles," he notes. "With every revolution some new direction opens, and some permanent accretion is carried into the next phase."[14] However, if one of the pathologies of contemporary political science is that it often comes to misleading conclusions based on the restricted time horizons of most researchers, as Paul Pierson suggests, it is fair to ask what analytical gains are to be had by a historical turn in the social sciences.[15] Our historically rooted investigation of the politics of immigration control provides some clues, uncovering path-dependent processes, elemental forces underlying critical junctures in immigration policymaking, recurrent processes, and political legacies of past policy decisions that reveal themselves only over long stretches of time.

The explanatory power of timing and sequencing is undeniable in the path-dependent processes that emerged at the beginning and end of this analysis. At the start, as we have seen, national political leaders chose both a tolerant, laissez-faire admissions policy and easy terms of naturalization for European newcomers. Initial decisions were made in a period characterized by low immigration and strong demands for laborers to feed the nation's economic and territorial development. The eventual impact of these policy decisions was an unprecedented flow of new European immigration into the United States. In response, nativist politics blossomed in the form of new anti-immigrant and anti-Catholic movements. Yet expansive European immigrant admissions and rights flourished throughout the nineteenth century, fueled by the positive feedbacks of business constituencies reliant upon immigrant labor as well as parties-in-government attentive to influential immigrant and ethnic voting blocs. Chinese settlers, arriving in smaller numbers and denied access to the ballot box, were unable to generate the same self-reinforcing processes that promoted expansive policies for European immigration until the Progressive Era.

In the latter decades of the twentieth century, these familiar path-dependent forces dramatically reemerged. Against the back drop of Cold War competition and a "second reconstruction" for African Americans, national origins quotas were dismantled in the 1960s in favor of new immigration rules primarily designed to reunite families and admit refugees.[16] When unparalleled numbers of Asian and Latin American immigrants took advantage of these openings, new restrictionist movements and politicians called for policy change. But when reform came between 1980 and 1990, the result was an even greater expansion of immigration opportunities. At least in part, these reforms reflected the extent to which earlier admissions policies created new business and ethnic constituencies for large-scale immigration. But in the mid-1990s, new threats to immigrant admissions and rights spurred Latino naturalization and voting. Politicians who flirted in 1995 and 1996 with appealing to restriction-minded native voters soon backpedaled; the positive feedbacks of immigrant labor and enfranchisement reinvigorated an expansionist policy regime. As Mark Twain once quipped, "History never repeats itself, but it often rhymes."

Path-dependent arguments have clear limitations. In their weakest forms, they near the shoals of teleology when they advance a minimalist focus on how certain paths are "locked in."[17] Likewise, path-dependent accounts of critical junctures or turning points across history are typically impoverished, pointing to external disturbances and contingencies that offer little analytical promise for our understanding of crucial moments of change.[18] The immigration policy crossroads carefully studied in the foregoing chapters offer some important insights about the nature and underlying processes of major political and policy change in America. In contrast to the neat trajectories of path-dependence, significant turning points in national politics and policy tend to reflect a rather inelegant convergence of forces. This study highlights four interlocking processes (changing institutional opportunities and constraints, shifting expertise, international threats, and interest group coalitions) that have driven the demise of aging immigration policy regimes and the creation of new ones. Given that the national political system was designed with a formidable set of veto-points to frustrate major political and policy departures, it should not surprise us that those rare historical moments in which new political and policy orders are founded in American politics often require the convergence of several forces at once. This historically oriented research approach of course raises problems for parsimonious theory-building. But as Albert Hirschman asks of us, "Is it not in the interest of social science to embrace complexity, be it at some sacrifice of the claim of predictive power?"[19]

One promising means of taming critical junctures for more systematic analysis is to focus, as Kathleen Thelen suggests, on the breakdown of "specific reproduction mechanisms" that animate and sustain given political or policy trajectories.[20] In this study, for instance, the rise of the national origins quota system in the 1920s was propelled at least in part by a Progressive Era assault on traditional nineteenth-century partisan and electoral processes that undergirded and reinforced expansive European immigration. The breakdown of these processes provided "political space" for a more insulated policymaking process to emerge, one driven by committee barons, scientific government, and national security imperatives that advantaged nativist reformers. In turn, the capacity of post–World War II immigration reformers to use this insulated process to produce policies at odds with the nativist goals of its Progressive Era architects suggests that innovators sometimes can rework the logic of a preexisting system for their own purposes.[21]

Historically rooted policy research also illuminates recurrent processes to which Higham was attentive. The politics of immigration control reveals patterned native reactions to "new immigration," the repeated emergence of odd liberal and conservative bedfellows in national struggles, and the capacity of certain electoral processes to produce expansive policy outcomes in different times. Analyzing politics and policy over long stretches of history allows us to identify important patterns and secular developments that are not overdetermined by the present.

Finally, broader time horizons help us fully appreciate E. E. Schattschneider's famous insight that "new policies create a new politics."[22] The political impacts of expansive immigration policy over time offer a compelling illustration. Policies that facilitated the entry of large numbers of "new" immigrant groups have routinely left a deep imprint on American political life. These newcomers can reshape the American electorate, and with it the electoral calculations of officeholders as well as the political fortunes and programs of political parties. They often form organized ethnic lobbies that place new pressures on policymakers, and they can alter the membership and preferences of existing interests such as organized labor. In short, expansive policies have introduced new power claimants to American politics who, over time, have challenged the political clout of earlier arrivals. This historically revealed process, like others just described, highlights the analytic benefits of extending the time horizons of our research.

Today, American admissions policies extend broad immigration opportunities to a diverse set of would-be settlers. Two powerful political processes, one rooted in the insulation of elite decisionmakers from mass publics and the other in immigrant voting blocs and competitive democratic elections, are likely to fortify these expansive policies for some time. Yet the uneasy status of immigrant rights in the modern American polity reminds us that a disturbingly thin vision of immigrant incorporation still has a hold on many policymakers. The outcomes of 1996 immigration and welfare reforms were a triumph for free-market conservatives, who allied with pro-immigration liberals to sustain large-scale legal admissions and with anti-immigrant conservatives to rollback alien civil and social rights. It reminds us of American liberalism's inhospitality to the kind of social rights T. H. Marshall associated with modern democratic citizenship, and of the capacity of Lockean traditions to produce disquieting inequalities. After all, mass immigration is often more compatible with a nineteenth-century brand of laissez-faire capitalism than with decidedly modern conceptions of distributive justice. As Susan Jonas and Suzie Dod Thomas observe, "Taken together, what the most recent [1996] acts indicate is that the representatives of the American people want a low-paid, compliant and easily exploitable immigrant labor force, with no basic democratic rights."[23]

However, it is significant that new immigrants did not sit quietly on the sidelines as these events unfolded. Instead, they employed the most crucial democratic rights that were preserved in the aftermath of the 1996 acts. Their ability to do so could be traced to an older legal innovation never intended to court radical change: The McCarran-Walter Act of 1952 removed racial and gender barriers from American naturalization law, considered at the time a small concession to liberal reformers by Cold War restrictionists who expected nonwhite immigration to be negligible in later years. The transformative potential of this innovation, like that which established easy naturalization for white European men long before, became evident only with the large waves of new immigration that followed several decades later. Yet whereas European arrivals were swiftly incorporated into the robust electoral and partisan politics of nineteenth-century American life, contemporary Third World newcomers encountered a modern U.S. polity in which many citizens were politically inactive and distrustful of government. By the 1990s, critics of multiculturalism wrote wistfully about earlier immigrant assimilation traditions and fretfully about low naturalization rates and the diminution of American citizenship.[24] In the wake of Proposition 187 and the 1996 welfare and immigration reforms, however, record numbers of new immigrants sought citizenship and access to the voting booth to recover their former rights. This new generation of enfranchised immigrants, like European newcomers of the nineteenth century, has created strong electoral incentives for national political leaders to adopt expansive policies toward future arrivals. Their political efficacy once more highlights the powerful interaction of politics and policy over time. It also allows us to end on a hopeful note. If we are lucky, new immigrants may do much more than give new life to the nation's troubled cities and graying labor force. They may demonstrate that participatory democracy and partisan competition still have vibrant possibilities in American politics.

The Sample of Interviewees

AN IMPORTANT PORTION of the case study research presented in chapter 8 relies upon interviews with a variety of political actors who participated in and/or possessed special knowledge about the immigration policymaking process between 1965 and 1998. Although the individuals who agreed to be interviewed do not comprise a representative sample, they *do* offer a wide range of perspectives and vantage points from which to view national immigration politics and policy in recent decades. Interviewees include present and former members of Congress, congressional staffers, White House advisers, executive department officials, select commissioners, interest group leaders and lobbyists, immigration lawyers who initiated or participated in litigation concerning asylum claims and immigrant rights, and journalists.

Interviews were "semistructured" in the sense that they were shaped by a set of topics and open-ended questions I designed to elicit as much information as possible from respondents based on their privileged access to the policymaking process. Most topics and questions that I raised during these exchanges were not presented in a precise order or with identical wording. However, certain questions were systematically asked of each of these interviewees for comparative purposes, and of a subset of interviewees who shared similar access to particular events (for example, those who participated in closed negotiations between lawmakers, in White House deliberations and decisionmaking, or in coalition-building activities among advocacy groups). Still, in general the semistructured format of these interviews provided room for subject elaboration and followup questions that were less likely highly standardized exchanges.[1]

Nearly all of the interviews were conducted in person; eighteen interviews were conducted by telephone.[2] The length of interviews ranged from roughly twenty minutes to three hours; most lasted forty-five minutes to one hour. The vast majority of interviews were conducted with the understanding that respondents would remain anonymous, with the exception of a few key actors who were willing to be identified and quoted directly.

Table A.1 below summarizes both the number of individuals who granted interviews for this study and the positions they held with relevance to contemporary immigration policymaking. Because some interviewees held several relevant positions, the number of interviews per position exceeds the total number of interviews conducted.

TABLE A.1
Sample of Interviewees by Position

Position of Interviewee	Number
Congressional actors	46
Senators	5
House members	19
Congressional staffers	22
Executive branch officials	42
White House advisers/staff	17
Office of Management and the Budget	1
Council of Economic Advisers	1
Justice Department officers	11
Immigration and Naturalization Service	7
Labor Department officers	3
State Department officers	2
State-level officials	8
California	3
Florida	1
Texas	2
New York	2
Commission members and staff	13
Select Commission on Immigration and Refugee Policy	7
Commission on Immigration Reform	6
Interest-group leaders and lobbyists	34
Immigration single-issue groups	4
Ethnic/civil rights groups	11
Labor groups	6
Business groups/grower lobbies	8
Human rights/civil liberties/religious groups	5
Journalists	4
Immigration lawyers	6
TOTAL	123

Notes

CHAPTER ONE: INTRODUCTION

1. Oscar Handlin, *The Uprooted*, 2d ed. (Boston: Little, Brown, and Co., 1973), p. 2.

2. See, for example, Michael Walzer, "The Distribution of Membership," in Peter Brown and Henry Shue, eds., *Boundaries: National Autonomy and Its Limits* (Totowa, NJ: Rowman and Littlefield, 1981), pp. 1–36; Michael Walzer, *Spheres of Justice* (New York: Basic Books, 1983), chap. 2; Mark Gibney, *Strangers and Friends* (Westport, CT: Greenwood Press, 1986); Daniel Tichenor, "Immigration and Political Community in the United States," in Amitai Etzioni, ed., *New Communitarian Thinking* (Charlottesville: University Press of Virginia, 1995), pp. 259–79; and David Jacobson, "Introduction: An American Journey," in *The Immigration Reader* (Oxford: Blackwell, 1998).

3. John F. Kennedy, *A Nation of Immigrants*, (New York: Harper and Row, 1964). The Meyer Feldman Oral History transcript, John F. Kennedy Library, Boston, as well as interviews conducted by the author strongly suggest that Meyer Feldman was the ghostwriter for at least much of the manuscript.

4. There were regulatory structures and policies in existence in various states. For a superb debunking of the myth of open borders in the nineteenth century, see Gerald Neumann, "The Lost Century of American Immigration Law (1776–1875)," *Columbia Law Review* 93, no. 8 (1993): 1833–1901.

5. See the thoughtful essays in Juan Perea, ed., *Immigrants Out! The New Nativism and the Anti-Immigrant Impulse in the United States* (New York: New York University Press, 1997); Susanne Jonas and Suzie Dod Thomas, eds., *Immigration: A Civil Rights Issue for the Americas* (Wilmington, DE: Scholarly Resources, 1999); and David Reimers, *Unwelcome Strangers: American Identity and the Turn against Immigration* (New York: Columbia University Press, 1998).

6. Alejandro Portes, "Immigration Theory for a New Century," *International Migration Review* (1997): 817.

7. For example, see Sven Steinmo and Kathleen Thelan, eds., *Structuring Politics* (New York: Cambridge University Press, 1992); Peter Hall, *Governing the Economy: The Politics of State Intervention in Britain and France* (New York: Oxford University Press, 1986); G. John Ikenberry, "Conclusion: An Institutional Approach to American Economic Policy," in G. John Ikenberry, David Lake, and Michael Mastanduno, eds., *The State and American Foreign Economic Policy* (Ithaca: Cornell University Press, 1988); James March and Johan Olsen, "The New Institutionalism: Organizational Factors in Political Life," *American Political Science Review* 78, no. 3 (September 1984): 734–49; Theda Skocpol, *Protecting Soldiers and Mothers: The Political Origins of Social Policy in the United States* (Cambridge: Harvard University Press, 1992); Sven Steinmo, *Taxation and Democracy: Swedish, British, and American Approaches to Financing the Welfare*

State (New Haven: Yale University Press, 1993); Margaret Weir, *Politics and Jobs: The Boundaries of Employment Policy in the United States* (Princeton: Princeton University Press, 1992).

8. Seymour Martin Lipset, *The First New Nation* (New York: W. W. Norton, 1979); and John Kingdon, *America the Unusual* (New York: St. Martin's Press, 1999), pp. 58–64.

9. Ira Katznelson, *Liberalism's Crooked Circle* (Princeton: Princeton University Press, 1996); Rogers Smith, *Civic Ideals: Conflicting Visions of Citizenship in U.S. History* (New Haven: Yale University Press, 1997).

10. The first quote is from A. Lawrence Lowell to Henry Cabot Lodge, August 9, 1910, Immigration Restriction League Files, Joseph Lee Papers, Box 1 Massachusetts Historical Society, Boston; the second is from Hubert Humphrey, Jr., "The Stranger at Our Gate," pamphlet distributed by the Public Affairs Committee of the American Jewish Commitee, January 1954, copy located in the Papers of the American Federation of Labor, AFL-CIO Department of Legislation, Box 27, Folder 14, George Meany Memorial Archives of the AFL-CIO.

11. Louis Hartz, *The Liberal Tradition in America* (New York: Harcourt Brace, 1955); Samuel Huntington, *American Politics: The Promise of Disharmony* (Cambridge: Harvard University Press, 1981); Rogers Smith, "Beyond Tocqueville, Myrdal, and Hartz: The Multiple Traditions in America," *American Political Science Review* 87 (1993): 549–66; and Smith, *Civic Ideals*.

12. Again, for an excellent account of historical institutionalism in political science, see Steinmo and Thelan, *Structuring Politics*.

13. Richard McCormick, "Walter Dean Burnham and 'The System of 1896,'" *Social Science History* 10 (1986): 245.

14. E. E. Schattschneider, *The Semi-Sovereign People* (New York: Holt, Rinehart and Winston, 1960).

15. The ideological convergence of liberals and conservatives in U.S. immigration politics is discussed in Daniel Tichenor, "The Politics of Immigration Reform in the United States, 1981–1990," *Polity* 26 (1994): 333–62; and more recently by Kenneth Lee, *Huddled Masses, Muddled Laws* (Westport, CT: Praeger, 1998).

16. On causal stories, see Deborah Stone, *Policy Paradox*, 2d ed. (New York: W. W. Norton, 1997), pp. 188–208.

17. Schattshneider, *Semi-Sovereign People*, p. 68.

18. Stephen Skowronek, *Building a New American State: The Expansion of National Administrative Capacities, 1877–1920* (New York: Cambridge University Press, 1982), p. 27.

CHAPTER TWO: THE POLITICS OF IMMIGRATION CONTROL

1. Gary P. Freeman, "Modes of Immigration Politics in Liberal Democratic States," *International Migration Review* 29, no. 4 (Winter 1995): 881–902; and Gary P. Freeman, "Rejoinder," *International Migration Review* 29, no. 4 (Winter 1995): 909–13.

2. E. E. Schattschneider, *The Semi-Sovereign People* (New York: Holt, Rinehart and Winston, 1942).

3. Rita Simon and Susan Alexander, *The Ambivalent Welcome: Print Media, Public Opinion, and Immigration* (Westport, CT: Praeger, 1993), p. 244.

4. Alejandro Portes and Ruben Rumbaut, *Immigrant America: A Portrait*, 2d ed. (Berkeley and Los Angeles: University of California Press, 1996), p. 270.

5. John Higham, *Strangers in the Land: Patterns of American Nativism, 1860–1925* (New York: Atheneum, 1966), esp. pp. 3–11.

6. Freeman, "Modes of Immigration Politics."

7. David Mayhew, "Presidential Elections and Policy Change: How Much of a Connection Is There?" in Harvey Schantz, ed., *American Presidential Elections* (Albany: State University of New York Press, 1996), p. 176. See also David Mayhew, *Divided We Govern* (New Haven: Yale University Press, 1991).

8. Mayhew, "Presidential Elections and Policy Change."

9. Brimley Thomas, *Migration and Economic Growth* (Cambridge: Cambridge University Press, 1973); and George Borjas, *Friends or Strangers* (New York: Basic Books, 1990). For a critical perspective of this approach, which highlights the importance of social networks, see Portes and Rumbaut, *Immigrant America*.

10. See, for example, James Hollifield, *Immigrants, Markets, and States: The Political Economy of Postwar Europe* (Cambridge: Harvard University Press, 1992); Freeman, "Modes of Immigration Politics"; Rogers Brubaker, "Comments," *International Migration Review* 29, no. 4 (Winter 1995): 903–8. and Alexander Saxton, *The Indispensable Enemy: Labor and the Anti-Chinese Movement in California* (Berkeley and Los Angeles: University of California Press, 1971).

11. For a good synopsis of this model, see Freeman, "Rejoinder."

12. See Jonathon Hughes, *American Economic History* (Gleview, IL: Scott, Foresman, and Co., 1983), pp. 451–66.

13. See George Soule, *Prosperity Decade* (New York: Rinehart and Company, 1947), pp. 290–93; and Robert A. Divine, *American Immigration Policy, 1924–1952* (New York: Da Capo Press, 1972).

14. *Congressional Record* (December 4, 1928), p. 20.

15. Soule, *Prosperity Decade.*

16. Author's anonymous interviews with lawmakers and key legislative staffers (see appendix for summary of elite interview research); and Tichenor, "The Politics of Immigration Reform in the United States, 1981–1990," *Polity* 26 (1994): 333–62.

17. Michael LeMay, *From Open Door to Dutch Door* (New York: Praeger, 1987), p. xv.

18. For an excellent summary and critique of this literature, see Keith Fitzgerald, *The Face of the Nation* (Stanford, CA: Stanford University Press, 1996), chap. 2.

19. Manuel Castells, "Immigrant Workers and Class Struggles in Advanced Capitalism: The West European Experience," *Politics and Society* 5 (1975): 33–66; Michael Burroway, "The Functions and Reproduction of Migrant Labor," *American Journal of Sociology* 81 (1976): 1050–87.

20. Robert Dahl, *Who Governs?* (New Haven: Yale University Press, 1961), p. 23.

21. Roger Daniels, *Asian America: Chinese and Japanese in the United States*

since 1850 (Seattle: University of Washington Press, 1988); and Charles J. Mc-Clain, *In Search of Equality: The Chinese Struggle against Discrimination in Nineteenth-Century America* (Berkeley and Los Angeles: University of California Press, 1994).

22. Keith Fitzgerald aptly notes that neither pluralists nor neo-Marxists can fully account for the development of American refugee policy. Unfortunately, he fails to draw justifiably similar conclusions about their shared limitations in explaining policies regarding legal and illegal immigration. Fitzgerald, *The Face of the Nation*.

23. LeMay, *From Open Door to Dutch Door*; Castells, "Immigrant Workers"; and Burroway, "The Functions."

24. Tichenor, "The Politics of Immigration Reform in the United States."

25. Theda Skocpol, "The Origins of Social Policy in the United States: A Polity-Centered Analysis," in Lawrence Dodd and Calvin Jillson, eds., *The Dynamics of American Politics: Approaches and Interpretations* (Boulder, CO: Westview Press, 1994), p. 196. See also Theda Skocpol, *Protecting Soldiers and Mothers* (Cambridge: Harvard University Press, 1992).

26. Jack L. Walker, Jr., *Mobilizing Interest Groups in America* (Ann Arbor: University of Michigan Press, 1991).

27. For an incisive discussion and critique of the values literature and approach, see Margaret Weir, *Politics and Jobs* (Princeton: Princeton University Press, 1992), pp. 13–14.

28. Lawrence H. Fuchs, *The American Kaleidoscope* (Middletown, CT: Wesleyan University Press, 1990).

29. Rogers Smith, *Civic Ideals: Conflicting Visions of Citizenship in U.S. History* (New Haven: Yale University Press, 1997).

30. Walter Dean Burnham, *Critical Elections and the Mainsprings of American Politics* (New York: W. W. Norton, 1970), pp. 10, 27.

31. Ibid.; Arthur M. Schlesinger, Sr., *Paths to the Present* (New York: Macmillan, 1949); V. O. Key, "A Theory of Critical Elections," *Journal of Politics* 17, no. 3 (1955); Jerome Clubb, William Flanigan, and Nancy Zingale, *Partisan Realignment* (Beverly Hills, CA: Sage, 1980); and Paul Kleppner, *Continuity and Change in Electoral Politics, 1893–1928* (Westport, CT: Greenwood Press, 1987), pp. 239–49.

32. Richard McCormick, "Walter Dean Burnham and 'The System of 1896,'" *Social Science History* 10 (1986): 245.

33. Martin Sklar, "Periodization and Historiography," *Studies in American Political Development* 5 (1991): 179.

34. Smith, *Civic Ideals*, p. 7.

35. See, for example, Kitty Calavita, *Inside the State: The Bracero Program, Immigration, and the INS* (New York: Routledge, 1992); Aristide Zolberg, "Matters of State: Theorizing Immigration Policy," in *Becoming American, America Becoming* (New York: Russell Sage, forthcoming); Alejandro Portes, "Immigration Theory for a New Century," *International Migration Review* (1997): 817; Hollifield, *Immigrants, Markets, and States*; and Tichenor, "The Politics of Immigration Reform in the United States."

36. Aristide Zolberg, "Matters of State: Theorizing Immigration Policy," in *Becoming American, America Becoming*.

37. Sven Steinmo, *Taxation and Democracy* (New Haven, CT: Yale University Press, 1993), p. 12.

38. Hollifield, *Immigrants, Markets, and States*; Calavita, *Inside the State*; and Tichenor, "The Politics of Immigration Reform."

39. Schattschneider, *Semi-Sovereign People*.

40. Skocpol, *Protecting Soldiers and Mothers*, p. 54.

41. Ira Katznelson, "Rethinking the Silences of Social and Economic Policy," *Political Science Quarterly* 101 (1986): 307–25; Stephen Krasner, "Approaches to the State," *Comparative Politics* 16 (January 1984): 223–46; Stephen Lukes, "Introduction," in *Power* (New York: New York University Press, 1986), 15–16; Key, "A Theory of Critical Elections"; Burnham, *Critical Elections*.

42. Karen Orren and Stephen Skowronek, "Beyond the Iconography of Order: Notes for a 'New Institutionalism,'" in Dodd and Jillson, *The Dynamics of American Politics: Approaches and Interpretations*, pp. 311–32.

43. Roger Davidson, "The Presidency and Congressional Time," in James Thurber, eds., *Rivals for Power* (Washington, DC: Congressional Quarterly Press, 1996), pp. 19–44.

44. For example, James Gimpel and James Edwards argue that Congress has long assumed primacy in American immigration policymaking. However, a careful historical treatment of immigration policymaking reveals that different governmental institutions have played a commanding role in immigration politics in distinctive eras of our political development. Moreover, special emphasis on congressional immigration politics obscures crucial interbranch processes that shape government actions in this policy realm. *The Congressional Politics of Immigration Reform* (Boston: Allyn and Bacon, 1999).

45. Anonymous interview with the author, May 1995.

46. Morton Keller, *Regulating a New Society: Public Policy and Social Change in America, 1900–1933* (Cambridge: Harvard University Press, 1994), p. 222.

47. Michael Walzer, *Spheres of Justice: A Defense of Pluralism and Equality* (New York: Basic Books, 1983), especially the chapter "Membership."

48. Frederick Douglass is quoted in Adrian Cook, *The Armies of the Streets* (Lexington: University Press of Kentucky, 1974), p. 205. See also Lawrence Fuchs, "The Reactions of Black Americans to Immigration," in Virginia Yans-McLaughlin, ed., *Immigration Reconsidered: History, Sociology, and Politics* (New York: Oxford University Press, 1990), pp. 293–314.

49. The views of both labor leaders will be discussed extensively in chapter 5.

50. Richard Lamm and Gary Imhoff, *The Immigration Time Bomb* (New York, 1985).

51. Gimpel and Edwards, *Congressional Politics of Immigration Reform*, pp. 216–21.

52. Alexander Hamilton, *Papers on Public Credit, Commerce, and Finance*, ed. Samuel McKee (Indianapolis, IN: Bobbs-Merrill, 1957), pp. 194–95.

53. Andrew Carnegie, *Triumphant Democracy; or, Fifty Years of the Republic* (New York, 1887), pp. 34–35.

54. Lowell is quoted in Keller, *Regulating a New Society*, p. 230.

55. Peter Brimelow, *Alien Nation* (New York: Random House, 1995).

56. These views will be discussed and documented at length in chapter 5.

57. Walker, *Mobilizing Interest Groups in America*, pp. 29–31.

58. Ann Costain, *Inviting Women's Rebellion: A Political Process Interpretation of the Women's Movement* (Baltimore: Johns Hopkins University Press, 1992).

59. Karen O'Connor and Lee Epstein, "A Legal Voice for the Chicano Community," *Social Science Quarterly* 65 (June 1984): 248–49.

60. See Daniels, *Asian America*; and Charles J. McClain, *In Search of Equality*.

61. McClain, *In Search of Equality*.

62. LeMay, *From Open Door to Dutch Door*, p. 120.

63. J. David Greenstone, *Labor in American Politics* (Chicago: University of Chicago Press, 1977), p. 69.

64. Ibid.

65. Max Weber, "The Social Psychology of World Religions," in *From Max Weber: Essays in Sociology*, ed. H. H. Gerth and C. Wright Mills (New York: Oxford University Press, 1946), p. 280.

66. Peter Hall, *Governing the Economy* (New York: Oxford University Press, 1986); Weir, *Politics and Jobs*; Martha Derthick and Paul Quirk, *The Politics of Deregulation* (Washington, DC: Brookings Institution Press, 1990).

67. Judith Goldstein, "The Impact of Ideas on Trade Policy: The Origins of U.S. Agricultural and Manufacturing Policies," *International Organization* 43, no. 1 (Winter 1989): 71. Others suggest that the foreign policy influence of ideas is still more profound; see Edward Rhodes and Mark Shulman, "Explaining American Strategic Adjustment," in Peter Trubowitz, Edward Rhodes, and Emily Goldman, eds., *The Politics of Strategic Adjustment* (New York: Columbia University Press, 1998), p. 18.

68. I borrow this term from Peter Hall, *Governing the Economy*.

69. Desmond King, *In the Name of Liberalism* (New York: Oxford University Press, 1999).

70. James Morone writes of "scientific government" as a central element of Progressive era politics in America. *The Democratic Wish: Popular Participation and the Limits of American Government* (New York: Basic Books, 1990), chap. 4.

71. See for example Dietrich Rueschemeyer and Theda Skocpol, "Conclusion," in *States, Social Knowledge, and the Origins of Modern Social Policies* (Princeton: Princeton University Press, 1996), p. 310.

72. Ibid.

73. See Deborah Stone "Causal Stories and the Formation of Policy Agendas," *Political Science Quarterly* 104 (1989): 281–301.

74. E. E. Schattschneider assumed that expanding the scope of conflict to bring broader audiences into the policy process would produce results that favor mass publics over special interests. However, this study reaffirms the conclusion of Darrell West and Burdett Loomis that "conflict expansion does not necessarily redound to the benefit of the general public." As West and Loomis demonstrate, organized interests can effectively construct powerful narratives in highly visible policy struggles. See *The Sound of Money: How Political Interests Get What They Want* (New York: W. W. Norton, 1998), pp. 43–44.

75. Bartholomew Sparrow, *From the Outside In: World War II and the American State* (Princeton: Princeton University Press, 1996), p. 7.

76. Doug McAdam, "On the International Origins of Domestic Political Op-

portunities," in Anne Costain and Andrew McFarland, eds., *Social Movements and American Political Institutions* (Totowa, NJ: Rowman and Littlefield, 1998), pp. 251–67.

77. Higham, *Strangers in the Land.*

78. Daniel J. Tichenor, "Traditions of American Reform," *International Issues* 38 (April 1995): 45–62.

79. Stone, "Causal Stories."

CHAPTER THREE: IMMIGRANT VOTERS IN A PARTISAN POLITY

1. James Bryce, *The American Commonwealth*, 3d ed. (New York: Macmillan, 1895), 2:5.

2. John Higham, *Strangers in the Land* (New York: Atheneum, 1974), p. 97.

3. Paul David, "Clio and the Economics of QWERTY," *American Economic Review*, 75:332–37; Brian Arthur, *Increasing Returns and Path Dependence in the Economy* (Ann Arbor: University of Michigan Press, 1994); Margaret Weir, *Politics and Jobs: The Boundaries of Employment Policy in the United States* (Princeton: Princeton University Press, 1992); Paul Pierson, *Dismantling the Welfare State? Reagan, Thatcher, and the Politics of Retrenchment* (Cambridge: Cambridge University Press, 1994); and John Kingdon, *America the Unusual* (New York: St. Martin's Press, 1999).

4. John Gerring, *Party Ideologies in America, 1828–1996* (New York: Cambridge University Press, 1998), pp. 111–16.

5. Ibid., p. 69.

6. Stephen Krasner, "Sovereignty: An Institutional Perspective," *Comparative Political Studies* 21:66–94.

7. See Higham, *Strangers in the Land*, pp. 108–9.

8. Lawrence Fuchs provides one of the richest accounts of the distinctive colonial traditions toward immigration and assimilation. *The American Kaleidoscope* (Middletown, CT: Wesleyan University Press, 1990), chap. 2.

9. John Garrity and Peter Gay, eds., *The Columbia History of the World* (New York: Harper and Row, 1972), pp. 669–73.

10. Benjamin Franklin, "Observations Concerning the Increase of Mankind," (1751) in Leonard Labaree, ed., *The Papers of Benjamin Franklin* (New Haven: Yale University Press, 1961), 4:234.

11. Thomas Jefferson, "Notes on the State of Virginia" (1781), in Merrill Peterson, ed., *The Portable Thomas Jefferson* (New York: Penguin Books, 1988), pp. 123.

12. His arguments concerning immigrant acculturation stand in sharp contrast with those of his contemporary Michael-Guillaume-Jean de Crevocoeur in the latter's *Letters from an American Farmer* (1782). In what Roger Daniels describes as "a product of French romanticism," Crevocoeur insisted that immigrants swiftly became full-fledged Americans who left behind all their "ancient prejudices and manners" in favor of a new culture and government. See Roger Daniels, "What Is an American?: Ethnicity, Race, the Constitution, and the Immigrant in Early American History," in David Jacobson, ed., *The Immigration Reader: America in a Multidisciplinary Perspective* (London: Blackwell, 1998), pp. 29–30.

13. Thomas Paine, *Common Sense and Other Political Writings*, ed. Nelson Adkins (Indianapolis, IN: Bobbs-Merrill Co., 1953), pp. 21–23.

14. Quoted in Patrice Higgonet, *Sister Republics: The Origins of French and American Republicanism* (Cambridge: Harvard University Press, 1988), p. 20.

15. See Maldwyn Allen Jones, *American Immigration* (Chicago: University of Chicago Press, 1960), p. 79.

16. Franklin's letter is published in *The Papers of Benjamin Franklin* 2:467–77.

17. Quoted in Peter S. Onuf, *Statehood and Union* (Bloomington: Indiana University Press, 1987), p. 18.

18. James Madison, *Notes of Debates in the Federal Constitutional Convention of 1787* (Athens: Ohio University Press, 1966), pp. 418–22; Jones, *American Immigration*, pp. 80–81; see also James Kettner, *The Development of American Citizenship, 1608–1870* (Chapel Hill: University of North Carolina Press, 1978).

19. Madison, *Notes of Debates*.

20. *Ibid.*

21. Seymour Martin Lipset, "Why No Socialism in the United States?" in Seweryn Bialer and Sophis Sluzar, eds., *Sources of Contemporary Radicalism* (Boulder, CO: Westview, 1977), p. 86; Seymour Martin Lipset, *The First New Nation* (New York: W. W. Norton, 1979), p. 58; and Kingdon, *America the Unusual*, pp. 58–64.

22. Madison, *Notes of Debates in the Federal Constitutional Convention*, pp. 418–22.

23. Kettner, *The Development of American Citizenship*, pp. 26–27; and Fuchs, *The American Kaleidoscope*, pp. 14–15.

24. The quote is from the Pennsylvania Convention, December 4, 1787 in John Kaminski and Gaspare Saladino, eds., *Commentaries on the Constitution: The Documentary History of the Ratification of the Constitution* (Madison: State Historical Society of Wisconsin, 1981), 8:477. In Massachusetts, Pennsylvania, Virginia, New York, and other states, xenophilic views concerning the virtues of robust European immigration were prevalent in newspapers and state conventions. "Behold America with extended arms, inviting the numerous, oppressed and distressed inhabitants of Europe," one Massachusetts observer noted. "[O]ur woods and waste lands will become at once valuable, and in great demand . . . arts and sciences will be cultivated with redoubled ardour—every kind of business will increase—and in a word, this continent will soon become, under the new government, the delight and envy of the European world." See "One of the People," *Massachusetts Centinel*, October 17, 1787, in Kaminski and Saladino, *Commentaries* 8:394–95. In Pennsylvania, some delegates to the state convention argued that expansive European immigration was consistent with "the first command given by the Deity to man, increase and multiply." His enthusiasm for immigration was intimately linked with notions of manifest destiny: "We are representatives, sir, not merely of the present age, but of future times; not merely of the territory along the seacoast, but of regions immensely extended westward." Proceedings of the Pennsylvania Convention, December 4, 1787, in *Commentaries* 8:477. Perhaps indicative of broad support for immigration among state delegates, Virginia proponents of the Constitution argued that the proposed gov-

ernment would encourage new immigration. Madison himself noted that large-scale European immigration "will depend on the degree of security provided . . . for private rights and public order" by a strengthened national government. James Madison to George Nicholas, May 17, 1787, in *Commentaries* 9:809. Praise for the Constitution's facilitation of expansive European immigration during the ratification process was voiced in many conventions and newspapers: Proceedings of the Pennsylvania Convention, December 14, 1787, p. 477; *Philadelphia Gazetteer*, August 22, 1787, in *Commentaries* 9:189; B. A. True American, *Massachusetts Centinel*, September 29, 1787, in *Commentaries* 9:267; Marcus, *New York Daily Advertiser*, October 15, 1787, p. 383; "One of the People," *Massachusetts Centinel*, October 17, 1787, in *Commentaries* 9:392–95; An American, *Pennsylvania Gazette* (Virginia paper), May 21, 1787, in *Commentaries* 9:838.

25. Of course, John Jay's *Federalist* No. 2 suggested that Americans were in fact quite homogenous, or at least many have suggested that he dreamed as much. "Providence has been pleased to give this one connected country, to one united people; a people descended from the same ancestors, speaking the same language, professing the same religion, attached to the same principles of government, very similar in their manners and customs." Yet the United States was already far more diverse than he suggested. It is likely that his hyperbole concerning American cultural homogeneity was motivated at least in part as an effort to minimize ethnic and religious differences that might imperil the Constitution's ratification. A similar spirit can be detected in the Declaration of Independence, which wistfully described Americans as "one people."

26. Letters of Agrippa, *Massachusetts Gazette*, December 28, 1787, in Herbert Storing, ed., *The Complete Anti-Federalist* (Chicago: University of Chicago Press, 1981), 4:85–86.

27. The Preamble of the Constitution promises that the new government will "provide for the common defence." Alexander Hamilton discusses the central government's role in guarding against foreign threats in *Federalist* No. 23, in *The Federalist Papers*.

28. Donald Horowitz, "Immigration and Group Relations in France and America," in Donald Horowitz and Gerard Noiriel, eds., *Immigrants in Two Democracies: French and American Experience* (New York: New York University Press, 1992).

29. Jones, *American Immigration*, pp. 64–65; and William S. Bernard, "A History of U.S. Immigration," in Richard Easterlin, ed., *Immigration: Dimensions of Ethnicity* (Cambridge: Harvard University Press, 1980), p. 81.

30. Daniels, "What Is an American?" pp. 44–47.

31. See Kettner, *The Development of American Citizenship*.

32. Jones, *American Immigration*, p. 85.

33. For a rich account of the Alien and Sedition Acts and partisan struggles of this period, see John C. Miller, *Crisis in Freedom* (Boston, 1952); and James M. Smith, *Freedom's Fetters: Alien and Sedition Laws* (Ithaca: Cornell University Press, 1956).

34. Thomas Jefferson to George Flower, in *The Writings of Thomas Jefferson*, ed. A. A. Lipscomb and A. E. Bergh (New York, 1903), 15:139–42. James Mad-

ison emphasized both the economic and humanitarian appeal of generally open immigration and easy naturalization; see his "Speeches in the First Congress," in *The Writings of James Madison*, ed. Gaillard Hunt (New York, 1904), 5:436–37; and "Population and Emigration," *National Gazette*, November 21, 1791, also in *Writings of James Madison* 6:65.

35. *Massachusetts' Federalist Columbia Sentinel*, January 20 and January 23, 1802. The *Columbia Sentinel* ran a fascinating series on "naturalization," warning of the dangers of sharing "all the privileges of citizens" with immigrants. It asserted that "the destruction of the ancient republic [of Rome] . . . may be attributed to the addition of foreigners to all rights of the city. . . . If, then, naturalization destroyed Roman liberty, may we not fear for that of America?" Other Federalists, however, favored efforts to conciliate naturalized voters.

36. Ibid.

37. Alexander Hamilton, *Papers on Public Credit, Commerce, and Finance*, ed. Samuel McKee (New York: Liberal Arts Press, 1957), pp. 194–95.

38. David Hackett Fischer, *The Revolution of American Conservatism: The Federalist Party in the Era of Jeffersonian Democracy* (New York: Harper and Row, 1965), p. 164; Thomas J. Curran, *Xenophobia and Immigration, 1820–1930* (Boston: Twayne Publishers, 1975), p. 20.

39. Ray Billington, *The Protestant Crusade, 1800–1860: A Study of the Origins of American Nativism* (New York: Macmillan, 1938); Marshall Smelser, "The Federalist Era as an Age of Passion," *American Quarterly* 10 (Winter 1958): 301–19; and David Bennett, *The Party of Fear* (New York: Vintage Books, 1995), pp. 22–23.

40. Billington, *Protestant Crusade*; D. Montgomery, "The Shuttle and the Cross: Weavers and Artisans in the Kensington Riots of 1844," *Journal of Social History* 5, no. 4 (Summer 1972): 411–46; Richard Maxwell Brown, "Historical Patterns of Violence in America," in Hugh Davis Graham and Ted Robert Gurr, eds., *Violence in America* (New York: New American Library, 1969), pp. 49–70.

41. Samuel Morse, *Foreign Conspiracy against the Liberties of the United States* (New York: American Protestant Society, 1844), see pp. 59–73.

42. Bennett, *Party of Fear*, pp. 48–50; Charles McCarthy, *The Antimasonic Party: A Study of Antimasonry in the United States, 1827–1840*, in American Historical Association, *Annual Report for 1902* (Washington, DC: Government Printing Office, 1903) 1:367–83; and Lee Benson, *The Concept of Jacksonian Democracy* (Princeton: Princeton University Press, 1970),pp. 19–21.

43. Quoted in Bennett, *Party of Fear*, p. 54.

44. See Jones, *American Immigration*, pp. 142–44.

45. Bennett, *Party of Fear*, p. 51.

46. Charles Hamilton, *Lincoln and the Know-Nothing Movement* (Washington, DC: Public Affairs Press, 1954), pp. 1–2; Curran, *Xenophobia and Immigration*, pp. 40–41.

47. *Guide to U.S. Elections*, 2d ed. (Washington, DC: Congressional Quarterly Press, 1985), pp. 329–66.

48. Hamilton, *Lincoln and the Know-Nothing Movement*, p. 2; and Bennett, *Party of Fear*, p. 59.

49. Samuel F. B. Morse, "Imminent Dangers to the Free Institutions of the United States" (New York: E. B. Clayton, 1853), pp. 70–71.

50. See E. P. Hutchinson, *Legislative History of American Immigration Policy, 1798–1965* (Philadelphia: University of Pennsylvania Press, 1981), pp. 16–44.

51. On Jeffersonian and Jacksonian political philosophies, see Robert M. Johnstone, Jr., *Jefferson and the Presidency* (Ithaca: Cornell University Press, 1978); Forrest McDonald, *The Presidency of Thomas Jefferson* (Lawrence: University Press of Kansas, 1976); Marvin Myers, *The Jacksonian Persuasion* (Stanford, CA: Stanford University Press, 1957); Sidney Milkis and Michael Nelson, *The American Presidency* (Washington, DC: Congressional Quarterly Press, 1994), pp. 89–143.

52. Gerald Neumann, "The Lost Century of American Immigration Law (1776–1875)," *Columbia Law Review* vol. 93, no. 8 (December 1993): 3–115.

53. *Mayor of New York v. Milne*, 36 U.S. (11 Pet.) 102. See also Bernard Schwartz, *A History of the Supreme Court* (New York: Oxford University Press, 1993), pp. 77–79.

54. Lucy Salyer, *Laws Harsh as Tigers* (Chapel Hill: University of North Carolina Press, 1995), p. 4.

55. William Bernard, "A History of U.S. Immigration Policy," in Easterlin, *Immigration*, pp. 82–85.

56. Kitty Calavita, *U.S. Immigration Law and the Control of Labor, 1820–1924* (New York: Harcourt Brace Jovanovich, 1984), p. 21.

57. See Martin Shefter, "Party, Bureaucracy, and Political Change in the United States," in Louis Maisel and Joseph Cooper, eds., *Political Parties: Development and Decay* (Beverly Hills, CA: Sage Publications, 1978); Richard P. McCormick, *The Second American Political System: Party Formation in the Jacksonian Era* (New York: Norton, 1966); and Theda Skocpol, *Protecting Soldiers and Mothers: The Political Origins of Social Policy in the United States* (Cambridge: Harvard University Press, 1992), pp. 71–75.

58. Leon E. Aylsworth, "The Passing of Alien Suffrage," *American Political Science Review* 25, no. 1 (February 1931): 114–16.

59. Jones, *American Immigration*, p. 154; see also Louis DeSipio and Rodolfo O. de la Garza, *Making Americans, Remaking America* (Boulder, CO: Westview Press, 1998), pp. 73–75.

60. Clay is quoted in Richard Shenkman, *Presidential Ambition* (New York: HarperCollins, 1999), p. 217.

61. Morse, "Immigrant Dangers to the Free Institutions," p. 72.

62. *A Complete Guide to the Messages and Papers of the Presidents* (New York: Bureau of National Literature, 1897), 4:1894.

63. Lee, *The Origins and Progress of the American Party in Politics*, pp. 26–27.

64. Bennett, *Party of Fear*, pp. 105–16.

65. *New York Tribune*, November 16, 1853.

66. Douglass is quoted in Eric Foner, *Free Soil, Free Labor, Free Men: The Ideology of the Republican Party before the Civil War* (New York: Oxford University Press, 1970), p. 238.

67. Ibid.; see also J. B. McMaster, "Riotous Career of Know-Nothings," *Forum*, 17:534.

68. Fuchs, *American Kaleidoscope*, p. 41.

69. Bennett, *Party of Fear*, p. 115.

70. Harry Carman and Reinhard Luthin, "Some Aspects of the Know-Nothing Movement Reconsidered," *South Atlantic Quarterly* 39 (April 1940): 211; Allen Nevins, *Ordeal of the Union* (New York: Scribner's, 1947); W. Darrell Overdyke, *The Know-Nothing Party in the South* (Gloucester, MA: Peter Smith, 1968).

71. Overdyke, *The Know-Nothing Party in the South*, p. 1.

72. *American Crusader*, Boston, July 12, 1854, quoted in *Reports of the Select Commission on Immigration and Refugee Policy* (Washington, DC: Government Printing Office, 1981), 39:13.

73. Michael Holt, "The Antimasonic and Know-Nothing Parties," in Arthur Schlesinger, Jr., ed., *History of U.S. Political Parties* (New York: Chelsea House, 1973), pp. 575–620; Bruce Maizlish, "The Meaning of Nativism and the Crisis of the Union: The Know-Nothing Movement in the Antebellum North," in Bruce Maizlish and John Kushma, *Essays on American Antebellum Politics, 1840–1860* (College Station: Texas A&M Press, 1982), pp. 169–72.

74. Quoted in Maizlish, "The Meaning of Nativism," p. 171.

75. Ibid.

76. *Congressional Globe*, 34th Congress, 1st Session, pp. 350, 979, and 1409.

77. Ibid., pp. 568 and 2188.

78. Hutchinson, *Legislative History of American Immigration Policy*, p. 622.

79. For a brilliant account of the Republican party's free labor ideology, see Foner, *Free Soil, Free Labor, Free Men*. Stephen Maizlish argues persuasively that nativism of the Know-Nothings could be neatly reconciled with the free labor ideology of the Republicans; see "The Meaning of Nativism," pp. 173–74.

80. Joel Silbey, *The Partisan Imperative* (New York: Oxford University Press, 1985), pp. 110–15.

81. Hamilton, "Lincoln and the Know-Nothing Movement," pp. 4–5.

82. Foner, *Free Soil, Free Labor, Free Men*, p. 234.

83. Charles Sumner, "Political Parties and Our Foreign-Born Population," speech at a Republican Rally in Faneuil Hall, Boston, November 2, 1855, in *The Works of Charles Sumner* (Boston: Lee and Shepard, 1873), pp. 63, 73, 74.

84. Ibid., p. 78.

85. Ibid.

86. Maizlish, "The Meaning of Nativism," pp. 192–98.

87. Ibid.

88. Republican Senator Oliver Morton proclaimed that the nation's "invitation" to the world cannot and ought not be limited or controlled by race or color," quoted in "The Views of the Late Oliver P. Morton," Senate Miscellaneous Document no. 20, 44th Congress, 2d Session. Many Republican leaders including Abraham Lincoln, expressed hostility for the Know-Nothing movement on cosmopolitan grounds. Ralph Waldo Emerson expressed his faith in ethnic and cultural diversity by advocating what he described as a "smelting pot theory":

I hate the narrowness of the Native American Party. . . . Well, as in the old burning of the Temple of Corinth, by the melting and intermixture of silver and gold and other metals, a new compound more precious than any, called

Corinthian brass, was formed; so in this continent—asylum of all the nations—
the energy of Irish, Swedes, Poles, and Cossacks, and all the European tribes—
of the Africans, and of the Polynesians, will construct a new race, a new religion, a new state.

Emerson is quoted in *The Journals and Miscellaneous Papers of Ralph Waldo
Emerson*, ed. Ralph Orth and Alfred Ferguson (Cambridge: Harvard University
Press, 1971), pp. 299–300.

89. Jones, *American Immigration*, pp. 161–69.

90. 1860 Republican National Platform, sec. 14, quoted in Thomas McKee,
The National Conventions and Platforms of All Political Parties, 1789 to 1905
(Baltimore: Friedenwald, 1906), p. 115.

91. For evidence of Lincoln's political overtures toward Know-Nothing voters,
see Hamilton, "Lincoln and the Know-Nothing Movement," pp. 9–10. Yet privately, Lincoln wrote the following in response to the stunning successes of the
American Party during the 1850s: "Our progress in degeneracy appears to me to
be pretty rapid. As a nation, we began by declaring 'all men are created equal.'
We now practically read it 'all men are created equal, *except negroes*.' When the
Know-Nothings get control, it will read 'all men are created equal, except negroes, *and foreigners, and catholics*.' When it comes to this I should prefer em-
igrating to some country where they make no pretense for loving liberty." See
Lincoln to Joshua Speed, August 24, 1855, in Roy P. Basler, ed., *The Collected
Works of Abraham Lincoln*, (New Brunswick, NJ: Rutgers University Press,
1953), 4:320–23.

92. Abraham Lincoln, "Speech to Germans in Cincinatti, Ohio," in *Collected
Works* 4:202–3.

93. LeMay, *From Open Door to Dutch Door*, p. 35.

94. C. Erickson, *American Industry and the European Immigrant, 1860–1885*
(Cambridge: Harvard University Press, 1957), p. 8.

95. Quoted in Ella Lonn, *Foreigners in the Union Army and Navy* (Baton
Rouge: Louisiana State University Press, 1952), p. 420.

96. LeMay, *From Open Door to Dutch Door*, p. 24.

97. McKee, *The National Conventions*, p. 126.

98. An Act to Encourage Immigration, c. 246, 13 Stat. 385 (1864); *Congressional Globe*, 38th Congress, 1st session, app., pp. 1–2.

99. Quoted in Maurice Davie, *World Immigration* (New York: Macmillan,
1936), p. 82.

100. Abraham Lincoln, "Annual Message to Congress," in *Collected Works*
8:141.

101. Calavita, *U.S. Immigration Law*, pp. 36–38; Erickson, *American Industry*, p. 7.

102. McKee, *National Conventions*, pp. 133, 139. See also LeMay, *From Open
Door to Dutch Door*, p. 34.

103. Neumann, "The Lost Century of American Immigration Law."

104. Ibid.

105. *Henderson v Mayor of New York*, 92 U.S. 259, 1875. For an overview of
events leading up to the Supreme Court rulings, see Roy Garis, *Immigration
Restriction* (New York: Macmillan, 1928).

106. *Henderson v Mayor of New York.*

107. Hutchinson, *Legislative History of American Immigration Policy,* pp. 396–404.

108. Jones, *American Immigration,* pp. 250–51; Andrew Carnegie, *Triumphant Democracy* (New York, 1887), pp. 34–35; Higham, *Strangers in the Land,* p. 44.

109. Rowland Berthoff, "Southern Attitudes toward Immigration, 1865–1914," *Journal of Southern History* 17 (1951): 329–36.

110. Rutherford B. Hayes to Carl Schurz, September 15, 1876, in Carl Schurz *Speeches, Correspondence, and Political Papers of Carl Schurz* (New York: G. P. Putnam's Sons, 1913), 6:338–39.

111. For example, see the Democratic platform of 1884, in McKee, *National Conventions,* pp. 206–7.

112. Hutchinson, *Legislative History of American Immigration Policy,* p. 79.

113. Marian Smith, "Overview of INS History," in George Kurian, ed., *A Historical Guide to the U.S. Government* (New York: Oxford University Press, 1998); and Sharon Masanz, "The History of the Immigration and Naturalization Service," Select Commission on Immigration and Refugee Policy, Congressional Research Service, Library of Congress, 96th Congress, 2d sess., (Washington, DC: Government Printing Office, 1980), p. 7.

114. *Congressional Record,* 48th Congress, 1st session, 1884, pp. 5349–64.

115. Ibid., p. 5349.

116. Ibid., p. 5350.

117. The Democratic National Committee, *The Campaign Textbook of the Democratic Party* (New York: Democratic National Committee, 1884), pp. 295–96.

118. Ibid., p. 49.

119. 26 Stat. 1084.

120. The federal immigration bureaucracy, established in 1891, did not acquire the title of Bureau of Immigration until 1895. See Smith, "Overview of INS History."

121. Quoted in Higham, *Strangers in the Land,* pp. 54–55.

122. Josiah Strong, *Our Country* (Cambridge: Harvard University Press, Belknap Press, 1963). The Librarian of Congress described the book, one of the most widely read of the time, as rivaling *Uncle Tom's Cabin* in the intensity of its reception.

123. Ibid., pp. 41–58.

124. Richard Jensen, *The Winning of the Midwest: Social and Political Conflict, 1888–1896* (Chicago: University of Chicago Press, 1971), p. 188.

125. W.H.J. Traynor, "Policy and Power of the APA," *North American Review,* 162 (June 1896): 663; and Humphrey Desmond, *The APA Movement* (1912; reprint, New York: Arno Press and *New York Times,* 1969).

126. Richard Wheatly, "The American Protective Association," *Harper's Weekly,* October 27, 1894; Desmond, *The APA Movement,* p. 27; and Donald Kinzer, *An Episode in Anti-Catholicism: The American Protective Association* (Seattle: University of Washington Press, 1964). The APA was by no means the only organization devoted to patriotism and limiting Catholic influence in these

years. The National League for the Protection of American Institutions surfaced in 1889 to defend public education and political institutions, and "to prevent all sectarian or denominational appropriations of public funds." Its officers were prominent figures, including college presidents, former and future members of the U.S. Supreme Court, business leaders such as J. Pierpont Morgan and Cornelius Vanderbilt, and political luminaries like Rutherford B. Hayes. These patriotic societies, or self-described "American organizations," preoccupied with public education, national unity, and "true Americanism," anticipated the expansive Americanization movement that emerged on the eve of the First World War; see Kinzer, *An Episode in Anti-Catholicism*, p. 56.

127. Kinzer, *An Episode in Anti-Catholicism*, p. 45.

128. Humphrey J. Desmond, *The APA Movement* (Washington, DC: New Century Press, 1912), p. 27.

129. For a colorful account of Cleveland's willingness to pander to immigrant voters to win office, see Richard Shenkman, *Presidential Ambition* (New York: HarperCollins, 1999), pp. 211–24.

130. *Century Magazine* (May 1896).

131. Traynor, "Policy and Power of the APA," p. 663.

132. Paul Kleppner, *The Cross of Culture: A Social Analysis of Midwestern Politics, 1850–1900* (New York: Free Press, 1970), pp. 252–53.

133. Ibid., p. 223.

134. Jensen, *The Winning of the Midwest*, p. 233.

135. Kinzer, *An Episode in Anti-Catholicism*, p. 144.

136. Jenson, *The Winning of the Midwest*; Kinzer, *An Episode in Anti-Catholicism*.

137. William McKinley, "No Compromise with the Demagogue," Columbus, OH, June 17, 1891; and McKinley, "The Ohio Campaign of 1891," Niles, OH, August 22, 1891, in McKinley, *Speeches and Addresses of William McKinley: From His Election in Congress to the Present Time* (New York: D. Appleton and Company, 1893), pp. 524 and 539.

138. Jensen, *The Winning of the Midwest*, pp. 155–56.

139. McKinley, "The Ohio Campaign of 1891," p. 547.

140. McKinley, "No Compromise with the Demagogue," p. 525.

141. Norman Ornstein, Thomas Mann, Michael Malbin, and John Bibby, *Vital Statistics on Congress, 1982* (Washington, DC: American Enterprise Institute, 1983).

142. On the Ohio APA's flap with McKinley over Catholic employees, see Kinzer, *An Episode in Anti-Catholicism*, pp. 119–20. Jensen details McKinley's herculean efforts on behalf of Republican candidates during the 1894 election in *The Winning of the Midwest*, p. 286.

143. Kinzer, *An Episode in Anti-Catholicism*, p. 224.

144. Ibid., p. 77

145. See Stanley L. Jones, *The Presidential Election of 1896* (Madison: University of Wisconsin Press, 1964), p. 143.

146. Ibid.

147. See the Republican National Committee, *The Republican Campaign Textbook of 1896* (Washington, DC: Republican National Committee, 1896).

148. Ibid.

149. William McKinley is quoted in Jensen, *The Winning of the Midwest*, p. 291.

150. Gwendolyn Mink, *Old Labor and New Immigrants in American Political Development: Union, Party, and State, 1875–1920* (Ithaca: Cornell University Press, 1986), p. 141.

151. Harold W. Stanley and Richard G. Niemi, *Vital Statistics on American Politics*, 2d ed. (Washington, DC: Congressional Quarterly Press, 1990), pp. 102–6; *Guide to U.S. Elections*, 2d ed. (Washington, DC: Congressional Quarterly Press, 1985), pp. 329–66.

152. For a discussion of "direct democracy" and Progressive political thought, see Sidney Milkis and Daniel Tichenor, "'Direct Democracy' and Social Justice," *Studies in American Political Development* 8 (Fall 1994): 282–340; on the Progressive movement's reverence for "scientific government," see James Morone, *The Democratic Wish* (New York: Basic Books, 1990), pp. 115–23.

153. See the Constitution of the Immigration Restriction League, May 31, 1894, and Annual Reports of the Executive Committee of the Immigration Restriction League, 1894–99, original copies of which may be found in two collections: The Immigration Restriction League Papers, Prescott F. Hall Collection, Houghton Library, Harvard University; and the Joseph Lee Papers, Immigration Restriction League Files, Massachusetts Historical Society, Boston.

154. Annual Reports of the Executive Committee of the IRL.

155. Press Statement Issued by the IRLeague, Lee Papers, Box 3.

156. Annual Report of the Executive Committee of the IRL for 1896, January 11, 1897, IRL Papers, Hall Collection.

157. Nelson Polsby, "The Institutionalization of the U.S. House of Representatives," *American Political Science Review* 62 (1968): 144–68; and Morton Keller, *Affairs of State: Public Life in Late-Nineteenth-Century America* (Cambridge: Harvard University Press, 1977), pp. 301–7.

158. The phrase "little legislatures" was actually coined by Senator George Frisbie Hoar (R-MA), but was made famous in Woodrow Wilson, *Congressional Government: A Study in American Politics* (Boston: Houghton, Miflin and Co., 1885), p. 103.

159. Rhoda Yale, "Immigration Evils," *Lippincott's Monthly Magazine*, August 1896, p. 231.

160. Richard Mayo-Smith, "Control of Immigration: Do We Need Immigrants?" *Political Science Quarterly* 3, no. 2 (June 1888): 219.

161. Ibid., p. 220.

162. Richard Mayo-Smith, *Emigration and Immigration: A Study in Social Science* (New York: Charles Scribner's Sons, 1890), p. 290.

163. George Gunder, "Restriction of Immigration," *Lecture Bulletin of the Institute of Social Economics* (November 1, 1901): 81–83.

164. Robert A. Woods, "Traffic in Citizenship," *Americans in Process: A Settlement Study* (Boston: Houghton Mifflin and Co., 1903), pp. 148–49.

165. Edward A. Ross, "Naturalized Immigrants and Political Leaders," in *The Old World in the New* (New York: Macmillan, 1913), pp. 266–76.

166. Ibid.

167. Francis Walker, "Immigration and Degradation," *Forum* 11 (August 1891): 643.

168. Ibid., p. 644.

169. Francis Walker, "Restriction of Immigration," *North American Review* 67 (June 1896); reprinted as IRL Publication no. 33, March 1902, p. 447.

170. Walker's lecture comments are quoted by the IRL in its Publication no. 33, which featured the MIT economist's public statements on immigration restriction (p. 450 n. 2, IRL Papers, Hall Collection.

171. Nancy Stepan, *The Idea of Race in Science: Great Britain, 1800–1960* (Hamden, CT: Archon Books, 1982); Thomas Gosset, *Race: The History of an Idea in America* (New York: Schocken Books, 1965); Elazar Barkan, *The Retreat of Scientific Racism* (New York: Cambridge University Press, 1992).

172. Charles Darwin, *The Descent of Man* (New York, 1888), p. 142.

173. Stepan, *The Idea of Race in Science*, pp. 111–16.

174. Higham, *Strangers in the Land*, p. 96.

175. Henry Cabot Lodge, "The Restriction of Immigration," *North American Review* (January 1891): 32–34.

176. Henry Cabot Lodge, "The Census and Immigration," *Century Illustrated Monthly Magazine*, October 1891, pp. 732 and 738.

177. The founders of the IRL were a small group of Harvard-trained professionals living in the Boston area. The organization grew quickly, establishing new League offices and membership in other states. The membership rolls of the IR League soon included prominent academics; dozens of college and university presidents were persuaded to serve as honorary vice presidents, including: A. Lawrence Lowell, president of Harvard University; William DeWitt Hyde, president of Bowdoin College; David Starr Jordan, president of Stanford University; James T. Young, director of the Wharton School of Finance; Richard MacLaurin, president of the Massachusetts Institute of Technology; Henry Garfield, president of Williams College; E. B. Craighead, president of Tulane University; John Commons, Richard Ely, William Ripley, and many others, see the Annual Reports of the Executive Committee of the IRL, 1894–1906, IRL Papers, Hall Collection. For later evidence of academic support for these theories, see the petition for immigration restriction from college and university presidents, *Congressional Record*, February 4, 1914, H3029–32. Representative John L. Burnett (D-AL), chairman of the House Immigration and Naturalization Committee, boasted that "not only President Lowell, but nearly all members of the departments of history and economics at Harvard are in favor of restriction; and the same is true of professors . . . at Yale University" (p. H3032).

178. IRL, Annual Report of the Executive Committee for 1894, January 14, 1895; and article II of the Constitution of the IRL, May 31, 1894; Annual Reports of the Executive Committee, 1894–1903, IRL Papers, Hall Collection.

179. See Annual Reports from January 14, 1894; January 13, 1896; January 11, 1897; and January 10, 1898, Annual Reports of the Executive Committee, 1894–1903, IRL Papers, Hall Collection.

180. William E. Chandler, "Shall Immigration Be Suspended?" *North American Review* (January 1893): 220–27.

181. Barbara Miller Solomon, *Ancestors and Immigrants* (Cambridge: Harvard University Press, 1956), pp. 78–79; and Higham, *Strangers in the Land*, p. 101.

182. Minutes of the Executive Committee of the IRL meeting, January 10, 1898, note that Lodge urged the League to send to each member of Congress the AFL's resolution favoring restriction, letters, and other such material; Records of the Executive Committee of the IRL, vol. 1; Henry Cabot Lodge to Prescott Hall, November 30, 1896, Correspondence files of the IRL, Box 4, Hall Collection.

183. This involvement is recalled by Joseph Lee to "Mrs. Moors," August 9, 1917, IRL Files, Lee Papers, Box 3.

184. The bills also prescribed the nature of the text that would be used in the test: passages of the Constitution, roughly five lines in length, in the native language of the immigrant.

185. Annual Report of the Executive Committee of the IRL for 1896, Hall Collection.

186. The text of Lodge's speech was reprinted in the *New York Times*, March 17, 1896, p. 3.

187. Henry Cabot Lodge, "Speech on Immigration Restriction, from *Congressional Record*, March 16, 1896, reprinted in Edith Abbott, ed., *Immigration: Select Documents and Case Records* (New York: Arno Press, 1969), pp. 192–93.

188. Chandler's interview with the press was covered by the *New York Times*, November 19, 1896, p. 1.

189. Senator Charles Gibson (D-MD) was particularly outspoken regarding the literacy test and its links to anti-Catholic nativism. See the *New York Times*, May 15, 1896, p. 3.

190. Higham, *Strangers in the Land*, p. 104.

191. Richard Bartholdt and conference of German American societies to members of Congress, Senate Committee on Immigration and Naturalization, National Archives, Record Group 46.

192. Joseph Senner, "Immigration from Italy," *North American Review* 162 (1896): 651.

193. Calavita, *U.S. Immigration Law*, p. 93.

194. *Proceedings of the Annual Convention of the American Federation of Labor, 1894* (Bloomington, IL, 1905), p. 47; and *Proceedings, 1896*, pp. 81–82.

195. Grover Cleveland, "Veto Message," *Immigration: Documents and Case Records*, p. 199.

196. O. P. Austin, "Is the New Immigration Dangerous to the Country?" *North American Review* 178 (1904): 570.

197. Shenkman, *Presidential Ambition*, p. 219.

198. Paul Kleppner, *Continuity and Change in Electoral Politics, 1893–1928* (New York: Greenwood Press, 1987), pp. 201–3.

199. *New York Times*, January 8, 1898, p. 11.

200. Walter Fleming, "Immigration to the Southern States," *Political Science Quarterly* 20, no. 2 (June 1905): 278–94; Walter Fleming, "Immigration and the Negro Problem," *World Today* 12 (1907): 96–97; Raymond Griffiss, "Encouraging Immigration to the South;" *Proceedings of the Social Science Association* (Boston: Damrell and Upham, 1906), chap. 4; Bert James Loewenberg, "Efforts of

the South to Encourage Immigration, 1865–1900," *South Atlantic Quarterly* 33 (1934): 365–67; and Rowland Berthoff, "Southern Attitudes toward Immigration, 1865–1914," *Journal of Southern History* 17, no. 3 (August, 1951): 328–60.

201. *New York Times*, March 3, 1898, p. 5.

202. Ibid.

203. Ibid.

204. Carl Schurz's letter is quoted in the *New York Times*, March 3, 1898, p. 5.

205. William McKinley's letter of acceptance was reprinted in the *Republican Text Book for the Campaign of 1898* (Washington, DC: Republican Congressional Committee, 1898), p. 202.

206. Ibid.

207. Higham, *Strangers in the Land*, pp. 108–9.

208. Samuel McCall to Immigration Restriction League Executive Committee, February 17, 1898, IRL Correspondence, Box 4, Hall Collection,

209. *Congressional Record* 31:4988.

210. See Theodore Roosevelt to William Williams, June 23, 1902; Williams to Roosevelt, June 24, 1902; and special memos "Former Assistant Commissioner McSweeney" and "The Privilege Holders" prepared by William Williams, all in 1902 Scrapbook, William Williams Papers, New York Public Library; August 2 and 6, 1897 entries, Bureau of Immigration, Record of Correspondence, 1891–1903, Record Group 85, National Archives; and Thomas Pitkin, *Keepers of the Gate* (New York: New York University Press, 1975), pp. 16, 27, and 37.

CHAPTER FOUR: CHINESE EXCLUSION AND PRECOCIOUS STATE-BUILDING IN THE NINETEENTH-CENTURY AMERICAN POLITY

1. Morton Keller, *Affairs of State: Public Life in Late-Nineteenth-Century America* (Cambridge: Harvard University Press, 1977); Stephen Skowronek, *Building a New American State: The Expansion of National Administrative Capacities, 1877–1920* (New York: Cambridge University Press, 1982); Theda Skocpol, *Protecting Soldiers and Mothers: The Political Origins of Social Policy in the United States* (Cambridge: Harvard University Press, 1992).

2. Skowronek, *Building a New American State*, pp. 19–24.

3. Skocpol clarifies that the American spending state she analyzes was "precocious in terms of the usual presumption of an absence of federal involvement in social welfare before the New Deal, and precocious in terms of how the United States around 1900 compared to other Western nations" (66). Part 1 of *Protecting Soldiers and Mothers* is devoted to fleshing out what Skocpol calls "a precocious social spending regime" (pp. 63–151).

4. Ibid., esp. pp. 67–101.

5. See Theodore Lowi's salutary work on "distributive," "regulatory," and "redistributive" public policies in Lowi, "American Business, Public Policy, Case-Studies, and Political Theory," *World Politics* 16 (July 1964): 677–715.

6. A Memorial to Congress from the Anti-Chinese Convention of California, March 8, 1886, Record Group 233: Records of the U.S. House of Representa-

tives, Petitions and Memorials, 49th Congress, HR49A-H9.1, Chinese Immigration, February 17–March 11, 1886, Congressional Records Collection, National Archives, Record Group 223, Washington, DC.

7. Most immigration policy scholars have ignored the role of the state and governmental institutions in accounting for policymaking processes and ultimate outcomes. Important salutary work has been done in this area, however, by Kitty Calavita, *Inside the State* (New York: Routledge, 1992); Keith Fitzgerald, *The Face of the Nation* (Stanford, CA: Stanford University Press, 1996); James Hollifield, *Immigrants, Markets, and States* (Cambridge: Harvard University Press, 1992); Daniel Tichenor, "The Politics of Immigration Reform in the United States," *Polity* 26 (Spring 1994): 333–62; Aristide Zolberg, "Matters of State: Theorizing Immigration Policy," in *Becoming American, America Becoming* (New York: Russell Sage Foundation, forthcoming).

8. The statement was made by Henry Cabot Lodge, quoted in the *New York Times*, March 17, 1896, p. 3.

9. The State Department's Philip Jessup hailed the national origins quota system and sweeping Asian exclusion as crucial steps by the national state toward "the pleasing possibility of Nordic supremacy." See Jessup, "Some Phases of the Administration and Judicial Interpretation of the Immigration Act of 1924," *Yale Law Journal* 35 (1925–26): 705.

10. Elmer Sandmeyer, *The Anti-Chinese Movement in California* (Urbana: University of Illinois Press, 1973), p. 16.

11. Governor John McDougall as quoted in Alexander McLeod, *Pigtails and Golddust* (Caldwell, ID: Caxton Press, 1947), p. 64.

12. *People v Hall* 4 Cal. 399 (1854).

13. For instance, see the majority report and extensive testimony in *Report of the Joint Special Committee to Investigate Chinese Immigration*, 44th Congress, 2d Session, Senate Report no. 689 (Washington, DC: Government Printing Office, 1877). A good overview of Californians' attitudes about race in regard to Chinese immigrants is provided by Luther W. Spoehr, "Sambo and the Heathen Chinese: Californians' Racial Stereotypes in the Late 1870s," *Pacific Historical Review* 42, no. 2 (May 1973): 185–204.

14. Reginald Horsman, *Race and Manifest Destiny: The Origins of American Racial Anglo-Saxonism* (Cambridge: Harvard University Press, 1981), p. 182.

15. Ibid., pp. 278–79.

16. *People v Hall* 4 Cal. 399 (1854).

17. Roger Daniels, *Asian America: Chinese and Japanese in the United States since 1850* (Seattle: University of Washington Press, 1988), pp. 33–34.

18. "Letter from Nubia," *Frederick Douglass' Paper*, April 6, 1855, reprinted in *Racism, Dissent, and Asian Americans from 1850 to Present: A Documentary History*, ed. Philip S. Foner and Daniel Rosenberg (Westport, CT: Greenwood Press, 1993), pp. 210–11.

19. Charles Beard and Mary Beard, *The Rise of American Civilization* (New York: Macmillan, 1941), 2:245; Alexander Saxton, *The Indispensable Enemy: Labor and the Anti-Chinese Movement in California* (Berkeley and Los Angeles: California University Press, 1971); Gwendolyn Mink, *Old Labor and New Immigrants in American Political Development: Union, Party, and State, 1875–1920* (Ithaca: Cornell University Press, 1986), pp. 71–112.

20. Daniels, *Asian America*, pp. 33–34.

21. Sandmeyer, *Anti-Chinese Movement* pp. 40–56; and Mink, *Old Labor and New Immigrants*, pp. 73–80.

22. As cited in R. Hal Williams, *The Democratic Party and California Politics, 1880–1896* (Stanford, CA: Stanford University Press, 1973), p. 7.

23. See, for example, B. F. Washington, "Will Find His Level," *San Francisco Examiner*, January 26, 1866; and testimony of Henry George and Albert Winn, in *Report of the Joint Committee to Investigate Chinese Immigration*, 44th Congress, 2d Session (Washington, DC: Government Printing Office, 1877), pp. 280–85, and 321–22.

24. Sandmeyer, *Anti-Chinese Movement*, pp. 40–57; and Mink, *Old Labor and New Immigrants*, 72–81.

25. H. C. Bennett, "Chinese Labor: A Lecture, Delivered before the San Francisco Mechanics' Society, in reply to the Hon. F. M. Pixley, San Francisco, California, May, 1870," reprinted in Philip S. Foner and Daniel Rosenberg, eds., *Racism, Dissent, and Asian Americans from 1850 to the Present: A Documentary History* (Westport, CT: Greenwood Press, 1993), pp. 169–72.

26. Lucile Eaves, *A History of California Labor Legislation* (Berkeley and Los Angeles: University of California Press, 1910), p. 6.

27. A week before the 1856 election, a young Republican newspaper in California, the *Marysville Daily Herald*, attempted to win votes by arguing that Democratic plans to extend slavery into Western territories would sacrifice exclusively white settlements:

> I call that the nigger party which labors to put niggers (and slaves—the worst class of niggers) into possession of every foot of territory that property belongs to the free white citizens of the country; which exerts itself now in Kansas and elsewhere, to put down and drive out free white men. . . . I am down on niggerism, and opposed to any party which is its tool, and for this reason I oppose the Democratic as the only real nigger party.

Quoted in Gerald Stanley, "Racism and the Early Republican Party: The 1856 Presidential Election in California," *Pacific Historical Review* 43, no. 2 (May 1974): 187. Stanley shows that California's early Republican party offered a different variant of a "white man's party," one that advocated not racial progress but an exclusion of African Americans from the Far West (pp. 171–87).

28. See Winfield F. Davis, *History of Political Conventions in California, 1849–1892* (Sacramento: California State Library, 1893), pp. 85–109; and Ronald C. Woolsey, "The Politics of a Lost Cause: 'Seceshers' and Democrats in Southern California during the Civil War," *California History* (Winter 1990–91): 372–83.

29. As cited in Sandmeyer, *Anti-Chinese Movement*, pp. 43–44.

30. See Charles McClain, *In Search of Equality: The Chinese Struggle against Discrimination in Nineteenth-Century America* (Berkeley and Los Angeles: University of California Press, 1994), pp. 25–29.

31. See the platforms and official statements of the Republican Party of California in Davis, *History of Political Conventions in California*, pp. 241–56, 306–8.

32. Eric Foner, *Free Soil, Free Labor, Free Men: The Ideology of the Republican Party before the Civil War* (New York: Oxford University Press, 1970), p. 78.

33. Ibid., pp. 234–38.

34. Burlingame Treaty, July 28, 1868, in *Report of the Special Committee to Investigate Chinese Immigration*, 44th Congress, 2d Session (Washington, DC: Government Printing Office, 1877), pp. 1182–83.

35. Ibid.

36. Mark Twain, "The Treaty with China," *New York Tribune*, August 9, 1868.

37. Wendell Phillips, "The Chinese," *National Standard*, July 30, 1870.

38. *Official Proceedings of the National Republican Conventions of 1868, 1872, 1876, and 1880* (Minneapolis, MN.: Charles W. Johnson, 1903), p. 60.

39. As cited in Cheryl L. Cole, "Chinese Exclusion: The Capitalist Perspective of the *Sacramento Union*, 1850–1882," *California History* 58, no. 1 (Spring 1978): 32.

40. Ibid.

41. Keller, *Affairs of State*, p. 249.

42. Davis, *History of Political Conventions in California*, pp. 241–65.

43. Ibid., pp. 252–73.

44. Democratic Resolutions of 1867, reprinted ibid., p. 265.

45. *San Francisco Examiner*, July 13, 1867.

46. See Sandmeyer, *Anti-Chinese Movement*, pp. 40–56.

47. Alfred Barstow of the National Union Republican Party, State Central Committee of California, to William E. Chandler, Secretary of the Republican National Committee, July 10, 1868, William Eaton Chandler Papers, Container 6, Manuscripts Division, Library of Congress.

48. Ibid.

49. Davis, *History of Political Conventions in California*, p. 293.

50. Ibid., pp. 307–8.

51. E. P. Hutchinson, *Legislative History of American Immigration Policy, 1798–1965* (Philadelphia: University of Pennsylvania Press, 1981), p. 56.

52. *Congressional Globe*, July 4, 1869, reprinted on July 4, 1870, p. 5150.

53. *Congressional Globe* July 4, 1870, pp. 1549–52.

54. *Ibid.*, July 4, 1870, pp. 1554–55, 1571.

55. *Daily Alta*, July 4, 1870.

56. Frederick Douglass to Charles Sumner, July 6, 1870, Correspondence Files, no. 51, Papers of Charles Sumner, Houghton Library, Harvard University.

57. Ibid.

58. Sandmeyer, *Anti-Chinese Movement*, p. 174.

59. *In re Ah Fong*, 1 F. Cas. (1874) 213, 216–18. Interestingly, the California delegation nominated Justice Field for president at the 1868 Democratic Convention, praising him for "stand[ing] up like a wall of fire against the encroachments of Radical domination." *Official Proceedings of the National Democratic Convention, held at New York, July 4–9, 1868* (Boston: Rockwell and Rollins, Printers, 1868), p. 142.

60. *Henderson et al. v Mayor of New York et al.* and *Commissioners of Immigration v North German Lloyd*, 92 U.S. 259 (1875); and *Chy Lung v Freeman*, 92 U.S. 275 (1875).

61. *Congressional Record*, May 1, 1876, p. 2856.

62. Hutchinson, *Legislative History of American Immigration Policy*, p. 59.

63. *The Campaign Textbook of the Democratic Party: A Summary of the Leading Events in Our History under Republican Administration* (New York, 1876), p. 87.

64. *Official Proceedings of the National Democratic Convention* (St. Louis, MO: Democratic Party, 1876), pp. 94–99.

65. Davis, *History of Political Conventions in California*, p. 357.

66. *Official Proceedings of the National Republican Conventions of 1868, 1872, 1876, and 1880*, p. 281.

67. Ibid., p. 284.

68. Ibid., p. 283.

69. Ibid., p. 282.

70. *Official Proceedings of the National Republican Conventions of 1868, 1872, 1876, and 1880*, pp. 279–86.

71. *Congressional Record*, May 1, 1876, p. 2858.

72. *Congressional Record*, July 6, 1876, p. 4419.

73. Senate, *Report of the Joint Special Committee to Investigate Chinese Immigration*, Report 689, 44th Congress, 2d Session, 1877, pp. 666–88.

74. Ibid.

75. Ibid., p. 289.

76. Ibid., pp. iii–viii.

77. See Daniel Cornford, "The California Workingmen's Party in Humboldt County," *California History* (June 1987): 131.

78. Article 1, section 17; Article 2, section 1; and section 19 of the California Constitution adopted in 1878–79; See *Debates and Proceedings of the Constitutional Convention of the State of California*, ed. E. B. Willis and P. K. Stockton (Sacramento, 1881), pp. 1510–11, 1519.

79. Mink, *Old Labor and New Immigrants*, pp. 98–101.

80. National Labor Union to the Committee on Foreign Affairs, Record Group 236, Records of the U.S. House of Representatives, 42d Congress, Petitions and Memorials, HR42A-H5.1, Congressional Records Collection, National Archives, Washington, DC.

81. Daniels, *Asian America*, pp. 33–52.

82. The Chinese Equal Rights League to Members of the House of Representatives, December 30, 1892, Record Group 233, Records of the House of Representatives, Petitions and Memorials, HR52A-H7.4, Congressional Records Collection, National Archives, Washington, DC.

83. See the essays in Sucheng Chan, ed., *Entry Denied: Exclusion and the Chinese Community in America, 1882–1943* (Philadelphia: Temple University Press, 1991).

84. See David L. Anderson, "The Diplomacy of Discrimination: Chinese Exclusion, 1876–1882," *California History* 52, no. 1 (Spring 1978): 32–45.

85. John F. Morgan, "The Political Alliance of the South and the West," *North American Review* (March–April 1878): 309–22.

86. William Lloyd Garrison to the *New York Tribune*, February 17, 1879.

87. Mink, *Old Labor and New Immigrants*, p. 111.

88. Cornford, "California Workingman's Party," p. 139.

89. Davis, *History of Political Conventions in California*, pp. 377–86, 396–400; Ralph Kauer, "The Workingmen's Party of California," *Pacific Historical Review* 13, no. 2 (1944): 278–81; and Williams, *The Democratic Party and California Politics*, pp. 16–19.

90. *Diary and Letters of Rutherford B. Hayes*, ed. Charles Richard Williams (Ohio State Historical Society, 1924), 3:525–26.

91. Anderson, "The Diplomacy of Discrimination," pp. 32–45.

92. *The Campaign Textbook: The Republican Party Reviewed—Its Sins of Commission and Omission* (New York: National Democratic Committee, 1880), pp. 258–63.

93. "The Chinese Must Go," *New York Times*, February 26, 1880, reprinted in *Foner and Rosenberg, Racism, Dissent, and Asian Americans*, p. 107.

94. Hutchinson, *Legislative History of American Immigration Policy*, p. 76.

95. Senate Executive Document, no. 148, 47th Congress, 1st Session, p. 24.

96. Davis, *History of Political Conventions in California*, p. 442.

97. Sandmeyer, *Anti-Chinese Movement*, pp. 93–94.

98. *Daily Alta*, March 3, 1882, as cited in Sandmeyer, *Anti-Chinese Movement*, p. 93.

99. Hutchinson, *Legislative History of American Immigration Policy*, pp. 78–81.

100. *Daily Alta*, April 8, 1882, p. 1.

101. Davis, *History of Political Conventions in California*, p. 429.

102. Hutchinson, *Legislative History of American Immigration Policy*, p. 83.

103. Daniels, *Asian America*, pp. 60–66; and Robert Wynne, "Reaction to the Chinese in the Pacific Northwest and British Columbia, 1850–1910" (Ph.D. diss., University of Washington, 1964).

104. Anti-Chinese Memorial adopted by the Anti-Chinese Convention in California, March 10, 1886, in Davis, *History of Political Conventions in California*, pp. 484–85.

105. Daniels, *Asian America*, pp. 56–57.

106. Sandmeyer, *Anti-Chinese Movement*, p. 101.

107. Daniels, *Asian America*, pp. 56–57.

108. Platforms of the California Republican and Democratic parties in Davis, *History of Political Conventions in California*, pp. 540–45.

109. Hutchinson, *Legislative History of American Immigration Policy*, pp. 104–5.

110. *Appeal of the Chinese Equal Rights League to the People of the United States for Equality of Manhood* (pamphlet) (New York: Chinese Equal Rights League, 1892), pp. 2–3, reprinted in Foner and Rosenberg, *Racism, Dissent, and Asian Americans*, pp. 118–19.

111. Charles McClain and Laurene Wu McClain, "The Chinese Contribution to the Development of American Law," in Chan, ed., *Entry Denied*, pp. 19–20; Daniels, *Asian America*, pp. 60–61.

112. John Torpey, *The Invention of the Passport* (New York: Cambridge University Press, 2000), p. 100. See also Mary Roberts Coolidge, *Chinese Immigration* (New York: Arno Press, 1969), pp. 209–33.

113. This was the view of early-twentieth-century historian Robert Glass Cle-

land, as cited by McClain, *In Search of Equality*, p. 2. Other scholars recently have challenged the conventional wisdom of Chinese political inaction. See Daniels, *Asian America*; and the essays in Chan, *Entry Denied*.

114. McClain and McClain, "The Chinese Contribution to the Development of American Law," pp. 4–5.

115. McClain, *In Search of Equality*, pp. 3–4.

116. *Chae Chan Ping v United States*, 130 U.S. 581 (1889); *Nishimura Eiku v United States*, 142 U.S. 651 (1892); *Fong Yue Ting v United States*, 149 U.S. 698 (1893).

117. *Chae Chan Ping v United States*, 130 U.S. 581 (1889).

118. Ibid., p. 606.

119. Ibid., pp. 606, 609.

120. *Nishimura Eiku v United States*.

121. Ibid., p. 659.

122. Ibid., p. 660.

123. *Fong Yue Ting v United States*, 149 U.S. 698 (1893).

124. Ibid., p. 730.

125. Ibid.

126. Lucy Salyer, "'Laws as Harsh as Tigers': Enforcement of the Chinese Exclusion Laws, 1891–1924," in Chan, *Entry Denied*, pp. 64–65, and 72–75.

127. I am principally referring here to Rogers Smith's "multiple traditions" arguments; *Civic Ideals: Conflicting Visions of Citizenship in U.S. History* (New Haven: Yale University Press).

128. In this regard, see Karen Orren, "Structure, Sequence and Subordination in American Political Culture," and Rogers Smith, "Response to Karen Orren," *Journal of Policy History* no. 4: 470–489.

129. Keller, *Affairs of State*, pp. 238, 285.

130. Skowronek, *Building a New American State*, pp. 39–42.

131. Skocpol, *Protecting Soldiers and Mothers*, chapter 2.

132. See *Plessy v. Ferguson* 163 U.S. 537 (1896), pp. 551–52; *Williams v. Mississippi* 170 U.S. 213 (1898); and C. Vann Woodward, *The Strange Career of Jim Crow* (New York: Oxford University Press, 1974).

133. William Riker, "Federalism," in Fred Greenstein and Nelson Polsby, eds., *Handbook of Political Science* (Reading, MA: Addison-Wesley, 1975), p. 154.

134. For a rich account of the power of "illiberal traditions" in American political culture during the late-nineteenth-century, see Rogers Smith, "Beyond Tocqueville, Myrdal, and Hartz: The Multiple Traditions in America," *American Political Science Review* 87, no. 3 (September 1993): 549–66.

135. Charles Price, *The Great White Walls Are Built* (Canberra: Australian National University Press, 1974), p. 237.

136. Stephen Skowronek and Karen Orren postulate that institutions founded with different logics produce political incongruities and collisions that alter the developmental pathway of each. See Karen Orren and Stephen Skowronek, "Beyond the Iconography of Order: Notes for a 'New Institutionalism,'" in Lawrence Dodd and Calvin Jillson, eds., *The Dynamics of American Politics: Approaches and Interpretations* (Boulder, CO: Westview Press, 1994), pp. 311–32.

CHAPTER FIVE: PROGRESSIVISM, WAR, AND SCIENTIFIC POLICYMAKING

1. The economic and social dislocations of the late-nineteenth century are discussed in many important works, including Ronald Wiebe, *The Search for Order, 1877–1920* (New York: Hill and Wang, 1967); and Morton Keller, *Affairs of State: Public Life in Late-Nineteenth-Century America* (Cambridge: Harvard University Press, 1977).

2. Austin Phelps, "Introduction," in *Our Country* by Josiah Strong (Cambridge: Harvard University Press, 1963).

3. Notes of Joseph Lee, 1907, Joseph Lee Papers, Box 1, 1907 Folder IRL Files, Massachusetts Historical Society, Boston.

4. Peter G. Filene, "An Obituary for the Progressive Movement," *American Quarterly* 22 (1970): 20–34; Daniel T. Rodgers, "In Search of Progressivism," *Reviews in American History* (December 1982): 114–23; on policy contradictions of the era, see Eileen McDonagh, "The 'Welfare Rights State' and the 'Civil Rights State': Policy Paradox and State Building in the Progressive Era," *Studies in American Political Development* 7 (Fall 1993): 225–74.

5. Rodgers, "In Search of Progressivism."

6. Robert DeC. Ward to Joseph Lee, December 3, 1905, Lee Papers, Box 1, 1905 Folder.

7. Ronald M. Peters, Jr., *The American Speakership: The Office in Historical Perspective* (Baltimore: Johns Hopkins University Press, 1990), p. 51; and Randall Strahan, "Thomas Brackett Reed and the Rise of Party Government," in Roger Davidson, Susan Webb Hammond, and Raymond Smock, eds., *Masters of the House* (Boulder, CO: Westview Press, 1998), pp. 33–62.

8. Peters, *The American Speakership*, p. 51.

9. This chapter will provide extended discussion of efforts by presidential candidates to curry favor with immigrant voters in the 1912 election. Yet such concerns would inform campaigns throughout the early-twentieth century. Even after the outbreak of the First World War, Republican party strategists in 1916 published tolerant, pro-immigration statements by their candidate, Charles Evans Hughes, which they thought would appeal to the foreign-born population. For example, party literature highlighted this quote by Hughes: "No true American begrudges anyone his pride of ancestry. . . . We are proud of the fact that in this we are not dependent on any one influence, or any one source of strength; but we have gathered together the best of all, and we represent in our American life the talents and the aptitudes of all of humanity." See the Republican National Committee, *The Republican Campaign Text-Book* (1916), pp. 141–41. And at the height of restrictionist nationalism in the 1920s, the Immigration Restriction League's Washington office complained that President Warren G. Harding had adopted a cautious "Sphinx attitude": "I do not hear of . . . any postition on his part." See James Patten to Joseph Lee, March 31, 1921, Lee Papers, Box #4, 1921 Folder. Thus, restrictionists tended to encounter either fervent White House opposition or presidential silence.

10. The phrase is drawn from Stephen Skowronek, *Building a New American State: The Expansion of National Administrative Capacities, 1877–1920* (New York: Cambridge University Press, 1982), pp. 24–47.

11. Clifton J. Child, *The German-Americans in Politics, 1914–1917* (New York: Arno Press, 1970); and John Higham, *Strangers in the Land: Patterns of American Nativism, 1865–1925* (New York: Atheneum, 1966), pp. 123–24.

12. Gwendolyn Mink, *Old Labor and New Immigrants in American Political Development: Union, Party, and State, 1875–1920* (Ithaca: Cornell University Press, 1986), pp. 152–54.

13. Higham, *Strangers in the Land*, pp. 123–24.

14. "Statement of the National Liberal Immigration League," *Reports of the Immigration Commission* (New York: Arno Press and *New York Times*, 1970), 41:329–33.

15. Lincoln Steffens, *Shame of the Cities* (New York: Hill and Wang, 1957), pp. 2–6.

16. See Jane Addams, *The Second Twenty Years at Hull-House* (New York: Macmillan, 1930), pp. 12–27; Jane Addams, "Social Justice through National Action," speech delivered at the Second Annual Lincoln Day Dinner of the Progressive Party, New York, February 12, 1914, Jane Addams Papers, File 136, Reel 42, Swarthmore College.

17. Jane Addams, "Recent Immigration: A Field Neglected by the Scholar," *Educational Review* 29 (March 1905): 245–63.

18. In its Annual Report of 1897, the IRL Executive Committee notes that numerous contacts were made with "the various bodies composing the American Federation of Labor, calling their attention to the advantages of the illiteracy test." Annual Report of the Executive Committee of the Immigration Restriction League of 1897, January 10, 1898, IRL Papers, Prescott Hall Collection, Houghton Library, Harvard University.

19. Terence V. Powderly, *Thirty Years of Labor, 1859–1889* (New York: Augustus Kelley Publishers, 1967), p. 219. On the Knights' broad-based organizing and commitment to ethnic diversity, see also Kim Voss, *The Making of American Exceptionalism: The Knights of Labor and Class Formation in the Nineteenth Century* (Ithaca: Cornell University Press, 1993), pp. 169–70.

20. American Federation of Labor, "A Sketch of the American Federation of Labor: Its Origin and Progress," May 1, 1904, St. Louis Exposition, 1904, Samuel Gompers Papers, George Meany Memorial Archives, Silver Spring, MD.

21. Samuel Gompers, *Seventy Years of Life and Labor: An Autobiography* (New York: E. P. Dutton and Co., 1937), pp. 153–54, 158.

22. Ibid., pp. 157–58.

23. Mink, *Old Labor and New Immigrants*, pp. 165–66.

24. Ibid., p. 158.

25. "Immigration Referred," *American Federationist* 3, no. 12 (February 1897): 257; and Gompers, *Seventy Years of Life and Labor*, pp. 159–60.

26. For instance, at the height of restrictionist legislative success in the late 1910s and 1920s, the AFL maintained a close working relationship with Representative Albert Johnson (R-WA), chair of the House Immigration Committee, despite his being a Republican. During the 1926 election, William Green, president of the AFL, notified the Washington State Federation of Labor that "Johnson was instrumental" to the restrictionist cause, and that the AFL's Washington lobbyists "kept in daily touch with him." In 1930, Green again urged members

of organized labor in Johnson's district to support him: "Let it not be after the primaries that Labor did not stand by a true friend." See William Green to William Short, August 12, 1926, and William Green to all Organized Labor in the Third Congressional District of Washington, August 21, 1930, both in AFL, AFL-CIO Department of Legislation Papers, George Meany Memorial Archives, Box 79, Folder 69: Albert Johnson, Silver Spring, MD. See also Samuel Gompers to Albert Johnson, March 28, 1921, and Johnson to Gompers, February 18, 1922, in the same file.

27. For example, see Legislative Record of James Michael Curley on Measures of Interest to Labor, AFL, AFL-CIO Dept. of Legislation Papers, Box 67, File 2: James Michael Curley.

28. See W. A. Gates, secretary of state of California Board of Charities and Corrections, to Joseph Lee, vice-president of the IRL, December 6, 1905; and Lee to James Patten, November 28, 1910, both in IRL Files, Lee Papers, Box 1.

29. Rowland Berthoff, "Southern Attitudes toward Immigration, 1865–1914," *Journal of Southern History* 17 (1951): 328–29. Some Southern leaders suggested that European immigrants were better workers than African Americans and expressed hope that foreigners in fact would hasten the black exodus. "Side by side with negroes," observed one Southern commentator, "the Italians have proved their superiority as farm laborers." See Walter Fleming, "Immigration to the Southern States," *Political Science Quarterly* 20, no. 2 (June 1905): 292.

30. *Proceedings of the Southern Interstate Immigration Convention Held at Montgomery, Alabama* (Montgomery, 1888); *Proceedings of the Southern Interstate Immigration Convention Held at Augusta, Georgia* (Augusta, 1894).

31. Speech of General R. A. Cameron, *Proceedings of the Southern Interstate Immigration Convention, Montgomery, Alabama*, pp. 16–17. Attending the convention were representatives from Alabama (10), Arkansas (7), Florida (4), Georgia (12), Kentucky (13), Louisiana (8), Missouri (16), North Carolina (11), New Mexico (3), South Carolina (9), Tennessee (12), Texas (13), and Virginia (12) (see p. 21).

32. Berthoff, "Southern Attitudes toward Immigration," p. 342.

33. James Patten, "The Immigration Problem and the South," *Business Magazine* 15 (March 1906): 118.

34. During one Southern tour, Patten proudly informed the IRL Executive Committee that "on our side" were the "most important men in the South." See Robert DeC. Ward to Joseph Lee, January 4, 1907, Lee Papers, Box 1.

35. Robert DeCourcey Ward, "Immigration and the South," *Atlantic Monthly*, October 1905, 616.

36. *Congressional Record*, 59th Congress, 1st session, December 18, 1905, pp. 650–55.

37. F. M. Simmons, "Immigration," Speech in the Senate, February 16, 1907, copy in the speech files of the IRL, Hall Collection, p. 11.

38. "Resolution of the Legislature of Virginia," February 14, 1908; see also "Resolutions adopted at Tampa, Florida," February 13, 1908, Records of the IRL, Hall Collection, Box 4.

39. A. Lawrence Lowell to Henry Cabot Lodge, August 9, 1910, IRL Files, Lee Papers, Box 1.

40. Notes of Joseph Lee, 1907, Lee Papers, Box 1.

41. Theodore Roosevelt to the Immigration Restriction League, March 26, 1896, Hall Collection, Box 4.

42. Theodore Roosevelt to Henry Cabot Lodge, March, 1897, in *Selections from the Correspondence of Theodore Roosevelt and Henry Cabot Lodge, 1894–1918* (New York: Charles Scribner's Sons, 1925), 1:251.

43. E. P. Hutchinson, *Legislative History of American Immigration Policy, 1798–1965* (Philadelphia: University of Pennsylvania Press, 1981), pp. 127–28.

44. John R. Commons, "Immigration and Its Economic Effects," in U.S. Industrial Commission, *Reports of the Industrial Commission on Immigration* (New York: Arno Press, 1970), p. 303.

45. Ibid., p. 310.

46. Commons, "Immigration and Its Economic Effects," pp. 314–15.

47. E. Dana Durand, "General Statistics of Immigration and Foreign-Born Population," in *Reports of the Industrial Commission on Immigration*, p. 282.

48. Hutchinson, *Legislative History of American Immigration Policy*, pp. 132–33.

49. Lewis Gould, *The Presidency of Theodore Roosevelt* (Lawrence: University Press of Kansas, 1991), pp. 140 and 259.

50. *San Francisco Chronicle*, February 23, 1905; and John P. Young, "The Support of the Anti-Oriental Movement," *Annals of the American Academy of Political and Social Science* (July–December 1909): 229–230.

51. Roger Daniels, *Asian America: Chinese and Japanese in the United States since 1850* (Seattle: University of Washington Press, 1988), pp. 107–19.

52. *Correspondence of Theodore Roosevelt and Henry Cabot Lodge* 2:158.

53. See W. A. Gates, secretary of state of California Board of Charities and Corrections, to Joseph Lee, vice president of the IRL, December 6, 1905; and Lee to James Patten, November 28, 1910; IRL Files, Lee Papers, Box 1.

54. Patten to Lee, March 17, 1906, Lee Papers, Box 1.

55. Ibid.

56. Gompers, *Seventy Years of Life and Labor*, p. 171.

57. *Congressional Record*, May 22, 1906, 40:7230.

58. Concerning pressure on Cannon, see the form letters sent by the Council of Jewish Women to Cannon; Barlow Furniture Company to Joseph G. Cannon, February 1, 1907; and resolutions from the Hebrew Relief Society, Sons and Daughters of Zion, and others, in the Papers of the House Committee on Immigration and Naturalization, 59th Congress, Record Group 233, Box 347, National Archives.

59. Scott William Rager, "Uncle Joe Cannon: The Brakeman of the House," in Roger Davidson and Susan Webb, eds., *Masters of the House: Leadership over Two Centuries* (Boulder, CO: Westview, 1998), p. 68.

60. Wilson, *Congressional Government*, p. 103.

61. During House debate over the Reed Rules, Cannon vigorously defended the notion that a majority party-in-government should be able to pursue the popular will without minority obstructionism. As he argued on February 10, 1890, on behalf of the "disappearing quorum" rule change: "If I must choose between the 'tyranny' of a constitutional majority, responsible people, or the 'tyr-

anny' of an irresponsible minority of one, I will stand by the Constitution and our form of government, and so act as to let the majority rule." See Rager, "Uncle Joe Cannon," p. 66. Cannon's life and career are discussed in L. White Busbey, *Uncle Joe Cannon: The Story of a Pioneer American* (New York: Henry Holt, 1927); Blaire Bolles, *Tyrant from Illinois* (New York: W. W. Norton, 1951); William Rea Gwinn, *Uncle Joe Cannon: Archfoe of Insurgency* (New York: Bookman, 1957).

62. Rager, for instance, argues that the Cannon "court" was oblivious to "the warning signs that a significant shift in the political attitudes of their colleagues in Congress and the public was occurring." "Uncle Joe Cannon," p. 68. While this claim has considerable validity, it is telling that Cannon and his lieutenants recognized that they did not have firm control over the House Republican Caucus.

63. Ibid.

64. *New York Times*, June 26, 1906; *New York World*, June 26, 1906; *Congressional Record*, June 25, 1906, pp. 9429–51.

65. Papers of the Legislative Department of the AFL/AFL-CIO, Container 67, Folder 12. Lobbyists of other restrictionist groups drew similar conclusions. The Junior Order of United American Mechanics, for instance, protested that "Old Joe only managed to substitute the Commission . . . after coercion, browbeating, a rule not allowing a recorded vote, etc. and then only by a majority of 9, many members having been driven off the floor." Legislative Department of the Junior Order of United American Mechanics to John J. Weitzel, December 27, 1909, Lee Papers, Box 1.

66. These newspaper accounts were reprinted in a pamphlet, "The Orignal Insurgency" (New York: New York Immigration League, n.d.), copy in AFL, AFL-CIO Legislative Department Papers, Box 67, Folder 12.

67. Marshall to Daniel Guggenheim, February 9, 1907; see also Marshall to Governor Carroll P. Page, February 1, 1907; Marshall to Judge M. Warley Platzek, February 4, 1907; John Fox (president of the National Democratic Club) to Platzek, February 5, 1907; Marshall to Platzek, February 5, 1907; Marshall to Honorable Edward Lauterbach, February 9, 1907, all in Louis Marshall Papers, Box #1, Folder: 1907, American Jewish Historical Society, Waltham, MA.

68. Senator William P. Dillingham to Governor Carroll P. Page, February 1, 1907, Marshall Papers, Box 1, Folder: 1907.

69. Gompers, *Seventy Years of Life and Labor*, p. 162.

70. Gould, *The Presidency of Theodore Roosevelt*, pp. 259–61.

71. Obscured by the fierce conflict surrounding the literacy test was national legislation in 1907 that captured how hostility toward aliens was blended with strong inegalitarian traditions encountered by American women. In the Act of 1855, Congress promoted "family unity" by extending citizenship to all alien wives of American men. As one sponsor reported, "this act provides that where an American citizen marries a woman—a foreigner—that by the act of marriage itself the political character of the wife shall at once conform to the political character of the husband." Although this legislation made women's citizenship status dependent on that of their husbands, sponsors hailed it as generous to alien women. Its negative implications for women acquiring independent citizenship

status became more apparent when gender inequalities and nativist impulses combined to produce the Act of 1907. This enactment stripped citizenship from American women who married foreigners. When challenged in the courts as a case of involuntary expatriation, thereby depriving American women of liberal consent, the Supreme Court asserted that these women granted consent by voluntarily entering into marriage with alien men. An incisive analysis of this neglected subject is provided in Virginia Sapiro, "Women, Citizenship, and Nationality: Immigration and Naturalization Policies in the United States," *Politics and Society* 13, no. 1 (1984): 1–26. The Supreme Court case is *Mackenzie v Hare*, 239 U.S. 299.

72. Roosevelt is quoted by Oscar Handlin, *Race and Nationality in American Life* (Boston: Little, Brown, and Co., 1957), p. 100.

73. For a superb study of the rise of expertise in modern social policymaking, see Desmond King, *In the Name of Liberalism* (New York: Oxford University Press, 1999).

74. James Morone, *The Democratic Wish: Popular Participation and the Limits of American Government* (New York: Basic Books, 1990), p. 115.

75. Deitrich Rueschemeyer and Theda Skocpol, *States, Social Knowledge, and the Origins of Modern Social Policies* (Princeton: Princeton University Press, 1996).

76. The concept of "policy paradigms" is developed by Peter Hall in *Governing the Economy* (New York: Oxford University Press, 1986) and in "Policy Paradigms, Social Learning, and the State," *Comparative Politics* 25 (1993): 275–96. See also Deborah Stone's incisive treatment of policy "stories" in *Policy Paradox: The Art of Political Decision Making* (New York: W. W. Norton, 1997). In a similar vein, Darrell West and Burdett Loomis carefully examine how organized interests struggle to shape "policy narratives" in *The Sound of Money* (New York: W. W. Norton, 1999).

77. Max Kohler to Simon Wolf, September 27, 1910, Max James Kohler Papers, Box 1, "Board of Delegates on Civil Rights, of American Hebrew Congregations" folder, American Jewish Historical Society.

78. Robert DeC. Ward to Joseph Lee, February 17, 1907, Lee Papers, Box 1; The IRL Executive Committee to A. Lawrence Lowell, August 4, 1910, Lee Papers, Box 2. See also Prescott Hall to James Patten, February 4, 1907, Lee Papers, Box 1; and Barbara Miller Solomon, *Ancestors and Immigrants* (Cambridge: Harvard University Press, 1956), p. 197.

79. Hall to Patten, February 4, 1907, Lee Papers, Box 1.

80. Solomon, *Ancestors and Immigrants*, p. 152.

81. *Reports of the Immigration Commission: Abstracts of Reports of the Immigration Commission* (Washington, DC: Government Printing Office, 1911), 1:23–46.

82. *Reports of the Immigration Commission* 1:42.

83. *Reports of the Immigration Commission: Immigrants in Cities, I*, vol. 26 of *Reports of the Immigration Commission* (New York: Arno Press and the *New York Times*), 4–5.

84. *Reports of the Immigration Commission: The Children of Immigrants in Schools*, 13:77–79.

85. Handlin, *Race and Nationality in American Life*, p. 103.

86. Higham, *Strangers in the Land*; Rogers Smith, *Civic Ideals: Conflicting Visions of Citizenship in U.S. History* (New Haven: Yale University Press, 1997), pp. 423, 467.

87. William Z. Ripley, *The Races of Europe: A Sociological Study* (New York: D. Appleton and Co., 1889), pp. 103–4, and 534–36. See also William Z. Ripley, "Race Progress and Immigration," *Annals of the American Academy of Political and Social Science* (August 1909): 130–38. Elsewhere, Ripley suggested that immigrants could be described generally as "dark in the southern half" of Europe, "and blonde at the north." "Races in the United States," *Atlantic Monthly* December 1908, p. 745.

88. *A Dictionary of Races of Reports of the Immigration Commission*, vol. 5 (New York: Arno Press and the *New York Times*, 1970), p. 4.

89. James Patten to Robert DeC. Ward, November 14, 1910, Lee Papers, Box 2.

90. Patten to Joseph Lee, January 3, 1910, Lee Papers, Box 2.

91. Patten to Lee, December 8, 1910, Lee Papers, Box 2.

92. Lee to Henry Cabot Lodge, December 13, 1910, Lee Papers, Box 2.

93. Patten to Lee, December 11, 1910, Lee Papers, Box 2.

94. Cyrus Adler to Mayer Sulzberger, December 14, 1909, in *Cryus Adler: Selected Letters*, ed. Ira Robinson (New York: Jewish Publication Society of America, 1985), 1:76.

95. See Louis Marshall to President Woodrow Wilson, February 26, 1913, Marshall Papers, Box 1, 1913 folder, which discusses Hourwich's research challenging the Dillingham Commission's work.

96. Cyrus Sulzberger, "Is Immigration a Menace?" Address at the Thirty-Ninth Annual Conference of Charities and Corrections, Cleveland, June 12, 1912 (American Jewish Committee Publication, New York, 1912), Marshall Papers, Box 1, 1912 folder.

97. Norris is quoted in Rager, "Uncle Joe Cannon," p. 74.

98. See "What the Referendum Will Do," *American Federationist*, April 1895, p. 26; and "Let the People Rule," *American Federationist* (April 1896).

99. Gompers, *Seventy Years of Life and Labor*, pp. 171–72.

100. See James Patten to Joseph Lee, November 10, 1910; Patten to Lee, February 1, 1911, Lee Papers, Box 2.

101. Jack London, *Valley of the Moon* (New York, 1913), pp. 102–3; and Jack London, *The Mutiny of the Elsinore* (New York, 1914), pp. 197–201. "No prominent easterner exhibited such wildly contradictory attitudes as Jack London," notes John Higham, "a radical champion of social justice for exploited and submerged classes who was forever glorifying the ruthlessness of supermen and master races." *Strangers in the Land*, pp. 174–75.

102. William Williams memo of October 21, 1902, Official Papers, William Williams Collection, New York Public Library, New York. See also the Williams memo on efficiency (September 1903) and his celebration of "economical and sociological" expertise concerning immigration, Williams to Theodore Roosevelt, February 8, 1903.

103. William Williams, "Immigration Should Be Restricted," published article in the Williams Scrapbooks, 1902, Williams Collection.

104. Williams explains his independent order in a letter to the Trans-Atlantic Passenger Conferences, May 31, 1904, Williams Papers. Regarding ethnic group reaction to these administrative barriers, see Esther Panitz, "In Defense of the Jewish Immigrant (1891–1924)," in Abraham Karp, ed., *The Jewish Experience in America* (Waltham, MA: American Jewish Historical Society, 1969).

105. Thomas Pitkin, *Keepers of the Gate* (New York: New York University Press, 1975), p. 43.

106. Frank P. Sargent to William Williams, October 6, 1902, Williams Papers.

107. See Naomi Cohen, "The Public Career of Oscar Straus" (Ph.D. diss., Brandeis University, 1698), p. 260.

108. Robert DeCourcey Ward to Joseph Lee, February 17, 1907, Lee Papers, Box 1.

109. Pitkin, *Keepers of the Gate*, p. 54.

110. Cohen, "The Public Career of Oscar Straus," p. 261.

111. Higham, *Strangers in the Land*, pp. 189–90.

112. On the importance of Jane Addams and Frances Kellor in the Progressive party movement of 1912, and on Roosevelt's respect for Addams and other women social workers, see Sidney Milkis and Daniel J. Tichenor, " 'Direct Democracy' and Social Justice: The Progressive Party Campaign of 1912." *Studies in American Political Development* 8 (Fall 1994): 282–340.

113. "A Contract with the People," Platform of the Progressive party, adopted at its First National Convention, August 7, 1912, Progressive Party Publications, 1912–16, Theodore Roosevelt Collection, Houghton Library, Harvard University.

114. Woodrow Wilson, *History of the American People* (New York, 1902), 5:212–13.

115. "Wilson on Immigration," *Progressive Bulletin*, September 16, 1912, p. 5, in the Progressive Party Publications.

116. Progressive National Committee, *First Quarterly Report of the Progressive National Service*, March 31, 1913, Jane Addams Papers, File 136, Microfilm reel 42.

117. Mink, *Old Labor and New Immigrants*, p. 225; Higham, *Strangers in the Land*, p. 190.

118. William Howard Taft to A. Lawrence Lowell, November 5, 1913, Correspondence Files of the IRL, Prescott Hall Collection, Box 4.

119. Arthur Link, *Woodrow Wilson and the Progressive Era, 1910–1917* (New York: Harper and Row, 1954), p. 35; Milkis and Nelson, *The American Presidency: Origins and Development, 1776–1990*, (Washington, DC: Congressional Quarterly, 1999), pp. 219–28.

120. Augustus Gardner to Lee Friedman, November 29, 1913, Marshall Papers.

121. Henry Goldfogle to Louis Marshall, December 21, 1913, Marshall Papers.

122. *New York Times*, January 27, 1915; on IRL efforts to capture the women's clubs, see Joseph Lee, "Immigration and Women's Clubs," notes for IRL, n.d.; and Lee to Mrs. Tilton, February 1, 1923, Lee Papers, Box 4, 1922 Folder.

123. Madison Grant to Prescott Hall, July 6, 1914; and Grant to Hall, December 13, 1914; Correspondence Files of the IRL, Hall Collection, Box 4.

124. *New York Times*, January 27, 1915.

125. Higham, *Strangers in the Land*, pp. 192–93.

126. Woodrow Wilson, "The Literacy Test Condemned," in Oscar Handlin, ed., *Immigration as a Factor in American History* (Englewood Cliffs, NJ: Prentice-Hall, 1959), pp. 187–88.

127. The most authoritative account of segregation in the federal executive branch is provided by Desmond King, *Separate and Unequal: Black Americans and the U.S. Federal Government* (Oxford: Oxford University Press, 1995).

128. Child, *German-Americans in Politics*.

129. Theodore Roosevelt, *Fear God and Take Your Own Part* (New York: George Doran Co., 1916), pp. 55–57, see also 104–9 and 361–63.

130. This Progressive effort to impose government "order" and "efficiency" over the immigrant assimilation process is captured in Frances Kellor, *The Federal Administration and the Alien: A Supplement to Immigration and the Future* (New York: George Doran Co., 1921), esp. pp. 30–35.

131. For example, see Ann Rhodes, "Americanization through Women's Organizations," *Immigrant in America* 2, no. 1 (April 1916): 71–72; the *Annual Report of the North American Civil League for Immigrants* (Boston: National Office of the North American Civic League for Immigrants, 1916), pp. 2–4; "A Reply to Willa Cather," *The Immigrant: Monthly Bulletin of the Department of Immigrant Aid of the National Council of Jewish Women* 4, no. 7 (March 1925): 1–3. An excellent overview of the Americanization movement is provided by John F. McClymer, "The Federal Government and the Americanization Movement, 1915–1924," *Prologue: The Journal of the National Archives* 10, no. 1 (Spring 1978): 23–41.

132. Frank Trumbell, "Report of the Committe on Immigration of the Chamber of Commerce of the United States of America, *Immigrant in America* 2, no. 1 (April, 1916): 32–33; and McClymer, "The Federal Government and the Americanization Movement," pp. 29–35.

133. McClymer, "The Federal Government and the Americanization Movement," pp. 36–38.

134. Ibid.

135. I draw these phrases from Theodore Roosevelt, "Americanism," an address delivered before the Knights of Columbus, Carnegie Hall, New York, October 12, 1915, Theodore Roosevelt Collection.

136. See Frances Kellor, "Americanization," *Immigrant in America Review* (March 1915): 15; and Theodore Roosevelt, "Americanization Day Speech," *Immigrant in America Review* (September 1915): 23.

137. Woodrow Wilson, "The Meaning of Citizenship," reprinted in *Americanization: Technic of Race-Assimilation* (New York: H. W. Wilson Company, 1920), pp. 78–79.

138. Willa Cather is quoted in "A Rely to Willa Cather," *The Immigrant: Monthly Bulletin of the Department of Immigrant Aid of the National Council of Jewish Women* 4, no. 7 (March 1925): 1–3.

139. Horace M. Kallen, "The Meaning of Americanism," *Immigrant in America* 1, no. 4 (January 1916): 17.

140. Quotes throughout this paragraph are drawn from Prescott F. Hall, secretary, Executive Committee of the IRL, Boston, "Immigration and the World War," *Annals of the American Academy of Political and Social Science* (January 1921), reprinted as Publications of the Immigration Restriction League no. 76, Hall Collection.

141. House Report 95 (64-I), p. 2.

142. Louis Marshall, address to the New York University Forum, February 20, 1914, Marshall Papers, Box 2.

143. Jane Addams, "Statement against the Literacy Test," reprinted in "The Injustice of the Literacy Test," pamphlet published by the Hebrew Immigrant Aid Society, 1916, Marshall Papers, Box 2.

144. Prescott Hall to Joseph Lee, March 11, 1917, Lee Papers, Box 3.

145. Executive Commmittee to Members of the League, February 22, 1917; and Publications of the IRL no. 69, May 3, 1918, both in Lee Papers, Box 3.

146. William Preston, *Aliens and Dissenters: Federal Supression of Radicals, 1903–1933* (Cambridge: Harvard University Press, 1963); and Louis Post, *The Deportations Delirium of 1920* (Chicago, 1923).

147. Stephen C. Mason, "The Proposal to Suspend Immigration," reprinted in Edith Phelps, ed. *Selected Articles on Immigration* (New York: H. W. Wilson Company, 1920), p. 213.

148. William S. Bernard, *Immigration Policy: A Reappraisal* (New York: Harper and Bros., 1950), p. 19.

149. Hutchinson, *Legislative History of American Immigration Policy*, pp. 171–75.

150. Harding is quoted in John Gerring, *Party Ideologies in America, 1828–1996* (New York: Cambridge University Press, 1998), p. 112.

151. Republican National Committee, *Official Report of the Proceedings of the Seventeenth Republican National Convention*, Chicago, June 8–12, 1920 (New York: Tenny Press, 1921), p. 32.

152. Warren Harding, Republican Acceptance Speech, July 22, 1920, in *Speeches of Senator Warren G. Harding of Ohio* (Republican National Committee, 1920), p. 25. The IRL described Harding as "the first real restrictionist in the White House." James Patten to Tompkins McIlvaine, February 27, 1922, Lee Papers, Box 4, 1922 Folder.

153. "Immigration Restriction Essential to Americanization," Publications of the Immigration Restriction League no. 74, March 1920, copy in Hall Collection.

154. Handlin, *Immigration as a Factor*, p. 132.

155. Prescott F. Hall, "Immigration Restriction and World Eugenics," *Journal of Heridity* (March, 1919).

156. Edward A. Ross, "Racial Consequences of Immigration," in Phelps, *Selected Articles on Immigration*, p. 121.

157. IRL Executive Committee to Franklin MacVeagh, September 18, 1922; and Report of the Executive Committee of the Immigration Restriction League,

June 15, 1923; both in Franklin MacVeagh Papers, Container 31, Manuscript Division, Library of Congress; and *Analysis of America's Melting Pot*, Hearings before the House Committee on Immigration and Naturalization, 67th Congress, (Washington, DC: Government Printing Office, 1923), pp. 725–831.

158. James Patten to Tompkins McIlvaine, February 27, 1922, Lee Papers, Box 5.

159. For example, see Fiorella La Guardia to Max Kohler, February 9, 1924, Kohler Papers, Box 3, House of Representatives Folder.

160. *Congressional Record*, April 8, 1924.

161. Richards M. Bradley to Joseph Lee, July 12, 1927, Lee Papers, Box #5.

162. Barry D. Karl, *The Uneasy State* (Chicago: University of Chicago Press, 1983), p. 12. See also Richard McCormick, *The Party Period and Public Policy: American Politics from the Age of Jackson to the Progressive Era* (New York: Oxford University Press, 1986); and Don Kirshner, "The Ambiguous Legacy: Social Justice and Social Control in the Progressive Era," *Historical Reflections* 2 (1975): 69–88.

163. *New Republic*, June 1916.

164. Matthew Frye Jacobson, *Whiteness of a Different Color* (Cambridge: Harvard University Press, 1998).

165. Smith, *Civic Ideals*.

166. King, *In the Name of Liberalism*, p. 34.

167. Ellis Cose, *A Nation of Strangers* (New York: William Morrow, 1992).

168. On "mechanisms of reproduction" and their capacity to account for profound institutional and policy changes that elude path-dependent analyses, see Kathleen Thelen, "Historical Institutionalism in Comparative Politics," in *Annual Review of Political Science* 2 (Palo Alto, CA: Annual Reviews, 1999), 2:369–404; and James Mahoney, "Path Dependence in Historical Sociology," *Theory and Society* 29 (2000): 510–57.

169. Paul Pierson, "Increasing Returns, Path Dependence, and the Study of Politics," *American Political Science Review* 94 (June 2000): 263.

170. See Ruth Berns Collier and David Collier, *Shaping the Political Arena* (Princeton: Princeton University Press, 1991), chap. 1.

171. Brian Balogh, "Reorganizing the Organizational Synthesis," *Studies in American Political Development* 5 (1991): 119–72; and John Kingdon, *America the Unusual* (New York: Worth Publishers, 1999), p. 43.

172. Demarest Lloyd to Joseph Lee, May 17, 1928, Lee Papers, Box 5.

CHAPTER SIX: TWO-TIERED IMPLEMENTATION

1. For example, see Annual Report of the Executive Committee, 1927, Immigration Restriction League, December 31, 1927, IRL Papers; and "Mexican Standards or American Standards," April 1927, both in Lee Papers Box 4; "Bourbons of Business," IRL Bulletin no. 25, November 22, 1927, Lee Papers; William Green to All Organized Labor in Washington, August 21, 1930, AFL-CIO Dept. of Legislation Papers, Box 79, Albert Johnson folder; and Thomas Pitkin, *Keepers of the Gate* (New York: New York University Press, 1975).

2. Peter Novick, *The Holocaust in American Life* (New York: Houghton-Mifflin, 2000), p. 52.

3. The literal translation of *bracero* is "arm man," and its nearest English analogue might be "field hand" or "farmhand."

4. John Torpey, *The Invention of the Passport* (New York: Cambridge University Press, 2000), p. 121.

5. IRL, Annual Report of the Executive Committee for 1895, January 13, 1896, IRL papers, Prescott Hall Collection, Box 4, Houghton Library, Harvard University.

6. Louis Marshall to Governor Carroll, January 28, 1907, Marshall Papers, Box 1, 1907 Folder, American Jewish Historical Society, Waltham, MA.

7. See Adolph Sabath's attack on William Williams, *Congressional Record*, August 27, 1912, p. 13149; Simon Wolf to Max Kohler, February 9, 1910, Board of Delegates on Civil Rights of American Max Kohler Papers, Box 2, Hebrew Congregations folder, American Jewish Historical Society; Kohler, "Administration of Our Immigration Laws," *Editorial Review* (August 1911), reprinted in Max Kohler, *Immigration and Aliens in the United States* (New York: Bloch Publishing, 1936), pp. 49–69; Pitkin, *Keepers of the Gate*, pp. 111–18.

8. See transcript of investigation minutes of the Senate Immigration Committee, May 21, 1893, William E. Chandler Papers, Box 90, Manuscript Division, Library of Congress.

9. Robert DeC. Ward to Joseph Lee, February 17, 1907, Lee Papers, Box 1; see also Oscar Straus to Robert Watchorn, June 21, 1907, Oscar Straus Papers, Manuscripts Division, Library of Congress.

10. Reuben Fink, "Visas, Immigration, and Official Anti-Semitism," *Nation*, June 22, 1921, p. 870.

11. "Suspension of Immigration," *Survey*, December 18, 1920, pp. 416–17, and Fink, "Visas, Immigration, and Anti-Semitism," p. 872.

12. Laughlin to Johnson, October 18, 1924, Papers of the House Committee on Immigration and Naturalization, Record Group 233, Box 343, National Archives, Washington, DC.

13. Laughlin to Johnson, February 1, 1924, ibid.

14. Pitkin, *Keepers of the Gate*, p. 140.

15. James J. Davis to the White House, April 12, 1923, Joseph Lee Papers, Massachusetts Historical Society, Boston.

16. Fink, "Visas, Immigration, and Anti-Semitism," p. 870.

17. Ibid., p. 871.

18. Ibid.

19. J. P. Cotton, acting secretary of state, to Diplomatic and Consular Officers, September 15, 1930, Diplomatic Serial no. 992, Kohler papers, Box 3, Department of State Folder.

20. Morris Waldman, secretary of the American Jewish Committee, to the Executive Committee, May 8, 1933, Kohler Papers, Box 1.

21. I. M. Rubinow to Max Kohler, August 22, 1933, Kohler Papers.

22. Telegram to State Department from Joint Council of the American Jewish Committee and B'nai B'rith, ca. 1933, and Max Kohler to American Jewish Committee, December 21, 1933, Kohler Papers.

23. *New York Times*, March 22, 1933.

24. Roger N. Baldwin to Kohler, August 7, 1933, Kohler Papers.

25. ACLU to the president, September 7, 1933, Kohler Papers.

26. Kohler to Alfred Cohen, president of B'nai B'rith, September 22, 1933, Kohler Papers.

27. I. M. Rubinow to Kohler, August 22, 1933, Kohler Papers.

28. Kohler to Wilbur Carr, June 3, 1933, Kohler Papers.

29. I. M. Rubinow to Kohler, August 22, 1933, Kohler Papers.

30. Press Conference no. 6, March 24, 1933, *Complete Presidential Press Conferences of Franklin D. Roosevelt* (New York: Da Capo Press, 1972), 1:77.

31. Kohler to Alfred Cohen, president of B'nai B'rith, September 22, 1933, Kohler Papers.

32. Pitkin, *Keepers of Gate*, p. 164.

33. *Report of the Ellis Island Committee* (New York: J. S. Ozer, 1971).

34. Robert A. Divine, *American Immigration Policy, 1924–1952* (New Haven: Yale University Press, 1957), p. 94.

35. Thomas J. Murphy, supervisor, Immigration and Naturalization Service, U.S. Department of Labor, "American Consular Procedure and Technical Advisers in Immigration Work," Lecture no. 9, April 2, 1934, p. 2, National Archives, Record Group 85, Washington, DC.

36. *New York Times*, April 18, 1933.

37. Edward Corsi, *In the Shadow of Liberty: The Chronicle of Ellis Island* (New York: Macmillan, 1935), p. 95.

38. Rubinow, secretary of B'nai B'rith, to Kohler, December 27, 1933, Kohler Papers.

39. Divine, *American Immigration Policy*, p. 94.

40. Ibid., p. 93.

41. Stephen Wise, *Challenging Years: The Autobiography of Stephen Wise* (New York: G. P. Putnam's Sons, 1949), p. 239.

42. *Proceedings of the 53rd Annual Convention of the American Federation of Labor, 1933* (Washington, DC, 1933), p. 103.

43. Martin Dies, "Nationalism Spells Safety," *National Republic*, March 1934, p. 2.

44. *Congressional Record*, June 26, 1935, p. 10229.

45. *New York Times*, November 26, 1938.

46. *New York Times*, May 4, 1934.

47. *New York Times*, May 7, 1934.

48. *New York Times*, August 12, 1934.

49. *New York Times*, March 25, 1938.

50. *Complete Presidential Press Conferences of Franklin D. Roosevelt*, Press Conference no. 445, March 25, 1938, 11:249–50.

51. *Fortune*, May 1938, discussed in Rita Simon, *Public Opinion and the Immigrant* (Lexington, MA: Lexington Books, 1985), p. 33.

52. Novick, *The Holocaust in American Life*, p. 52.

53. Committee on the Judiciary, U.S. Senate, *History of the Immigration and Naturalization Service*, 96th Congress, 2d Session, Committee Print, December 1980, p. 43.

54. Frances Perkins to Cornelia Bryce Pinchot, December 21, 1939, Frances Perkins Papers, 1939 Correspondence File, General Records of the Labor Department, Record Group 174, National Archives, Washington, DC.

55. David Wyman, *The Abandonment of the Jews* (New York: Pantheon Books, 1984), p. 72.

56. American Federation of Labor, *Proceedings of the Annual Conventions*, 1939 bound volume, p. 678, George Meany Memorial Archives, Silver Spring, MD.

57. Divine, *American Immigration Policy*, p. 101.

58. W. C. Roberts, Memorandum on Immigration Bill, April 13, 1938, AFL-CIO Legislative Dept. Papers.

59. "The Fortune Survey," *Fortune*, April 1939, p. 102.

60. Wyman, *Abandonment of the Jews*, pp. 89 and 91.

61. *Ibid.*, p. 92.

62. Ibid., pp. 119–20.

63. *Press Conference no. 645, May 21, 1940, in Roosevelt Presidential Press Conferences* 15:352.

64. Assistant Secretary of State Breckenridge Long to State Department officials Adolf Berle and James Dunn, June 26, 1940, in David Wyman, ed., Barring the Gates to America (New York: Garland, 1990), p. 2.

65. Margaret Jones, American Friends Service Committee, November, 1940, to Clarence Pickett, executive secretary of the AFSC, in Wyman, *Barring the Gates*, p. 3.

66. Wyman, *The Abandonment of the Jews*, p. 71.

67. David Wyman, "Introduction," in *Barring the Gates*, pp. v–vi.

68. Perkins, Memorandum Regarding Reverend Sally Rosenfelder, March 3, 1939; see also State Department to Frances Perkins, March 11, 1939; both in Frances Perkins Papers, National Archives, Washington, DC.

69. Frances Perkins letter of May 15, 1939, Perkins File, 1939 Correspondence File, Record Group 174, National Archives, Washington, DC.

70. "Report to the Secretary on the Acquiescence of This Government in the Murder of the Jews," prepared by Randolph Paul and associates of the Foreign Funds Control Unit, Treasury Department, January 13, 1944, in David Wyman, ed., *America and the Holocaust: Showdown in Washington* (New York: Garland, 1990), p. 238.

71. Morgenthau reports that Breckenridge asked to speak privately with him after catching wind of the Treasury findings. During the conversation, Morgenthau candidly observes that he and his staff had little reason to doubt that Breckenridge was the most anti-Semitic official in the State Department. At the end of the conversation, Morgenthau says, "Breck, the United States of America was created as a refuge for people who were persecuted the world over, starting with Plymouth. That was the concept of the United States and as Secretary of the Treasury for one hundred and thirty-five million people—I am carrying this out as Secretary of the Treasury, and not as a Jew." See December 20, 1943, transcript of a meeting, "Jewish Evacuation," between Treasury Secretary Henry Morgenthau, Jr., and his staff, in Wyman, *Showdown in Washington*, pp. 166–67.

72. Henry Morgenthau, Jr., "Personal Report to the President," January 16, 1944, in Wyman, *Showdown in Washington*, p. 499.

73. U.S. Bureau of Immigration, *Annual Report of the Commissioner-General of Immigration to the Secretary of Commerce and Labor* (Washington, DC: Government Printing Office, 1904), p. 105.

74. Senate Committee on the Judiciary, *History of the Immigration and Naturalization Service*, 96th Congress, 2d Session, Committee Print, December 1980, p. 14.

75. Ibid., p. 21.

76. Mark Reisler, *By the Sweat of Their Brow: Mexican Immigrant Labor in the United States* (Westport, CT: Greenwood Press, 1976), pp. 2–7.

77. U.S. Immigration Commission, *Reports of the Immigration Commission: Abstracts* (Washington, DC: Government Printing Office, 1911), 1:691.

78. Ibid.

79. Reisler, *By the Sweat of Their Brow*, p. 27.

80. William B. Wilson, secretary of the Department of Labor, to Representative John L. Burnett, chair of the Committee on Immigration and Naturalization, May 31, 1917, copy in Lee Papers.

81. Reisler, *By the Sweat of Their Brow*, p. 40.

82. Bulletin No. 7, Immigration Restriction Leagues, January 5, 1927 to IRLs of New York and Boston from Washington Office.

83. Annual Report of the Executive Committee, 1927, IRL, December 31, 1927, IRL Papers, Houghton Library, Harvard University.

84. Reisler, *By the Sweat of Their Brow*, pp. 156–57.

85. "Mexican Standards or American Standards," April 1927, Lee Papers, Box 4; "Bourbons of Business," IRL Bulletin no. 25, November 22, 1927, Lee Papers.

86. Reisler, *By the Sweat of Their Brow*, p. 175.

87. Divine, *American Immigration Policy*, p. 59.

88. Reisler, *By the Sweat of Their Brow*, p. 201.

89. Undated notes, Kohler Papers, Box 5, Immigration Notes Folder.

90. Demarest Lloyd to Joseph Lee, May 17, 1928; Lee Papers.

91. Ward to Lee, May 17, 1928, Lee Papers, Box 5.

92. IRL, Executive Committee Bulletin no. 12, June 1, 1928, IRL Papers, Houghton Library, Harvard University.

93. John H. Clark, U.S. commissioner of Immigration, "Surreptitious Entry of Aliens," undated, Record Group 233, Box #487, Records of the House of Representatives, HR 66A-F18.3, Committee on Immigration and Naturalization—Transcripts and General Correspondence.

94. U.S. Department of Labor, Fiscal Year 1922 Annual Report (Washington, DC: Government Printing Office, 1923), p. 13.

95. Senate Committee on the Judiciary, *History of the Immigration and Naturalization Service*, p. 36.

96. U.S. Department of Labor, Bureau of Immigration, *Annual Report of the Commissioner-General of Immigration to the Secretary of Labor, 1928* (Washington, DC: Government Printing Office, 1928), p. 3.

97. James Patten to Frank H. Kinnicutt, February 6, 1928, Lee Papers.

98. Green to All Organized Labor in Washington, August 21, 1930.

99. American Federation of Labor, *Proceedings of the Annual Conventions*, 1930 bound volume, p. 334, Meany Archives.

100. Reisler, *By the Sweat of Their Brow*, p. 215.

101. Senate Committee on the Judiciary, *History of the Immigration and Naturalization Service*, p. 37.

102. American Federation of Labor, Proceedings of the Annual Conventions, 1934 bound volume, p. 550, Meany Archives.

103. U.S. Department of Labor, *26th Annual Report of the Secretary of Labor, 1938* (Washington, DC: Government Printing Office), pp. 95–96.

104. Kitty Calavita, *Inside the State: The Bracero Program, Immigration, and the INS* (New York: Routledge, 1992), pp. 6–7.

105. Arthur Altmeyer, executive director of the War Manpower Commission, to Claude R. Wickard, secretary of Agriculture, Memo on Proposed Agreement for the Importation of Mexican Workers, July 29, 1942, Box 35, Folder 26 on Mexican Labor, AFL-CIO Dept. of Legislation Papers.

106. Senate Committee of the Judiary, *History of the Immigration and Naturalization Service*, p. 51.

107. American Federation of Labor, *Proceedings of the Annual Convention*, 1942 bound volume, Meany Archives.

108. Mexican Workers Resolution, *Daily Proceedings of the Second Constitutional Convention of the Congress of Industrial Organizations*, October 10–13, 1939, San Franciso.

109. Calavita, *Inside the State*, p. 33.

110. Ibid., p. 35.

CHAPTER SEVEN: STRANGERS IN COLD WAR AMERICA

1. Proceedings of the American Committee for Protection of the Foreign Born, Constitution, March 2–3, 1940, Washington, DC, p. 2, copy in the National Jewish Historical Society, Brandeis University, Waltham, MA.

2. Ibid., p. 3.

3. *Ibid.*, pp. 14–17.

4. Confidential memorandum on a National Committee on Postwar Immigration Policy, February 10, 1944, Interim Committee Memoranda Folder, Papers of the National Committee on Postwar Immigration Policy, Container 1, American Jewish Historical Society.

5. Memorandum of April 12, 1944, National Committee on Postwar Immigration Policy, Interim Committee Memoranda Folder, Papers of the National Committee on Postwar Immigration Policy, Container 1, American Jewish Historical Society.

6. Undated memorandum, ibid.

7. Eric Goldman, *The Crucial Decade—and After* (New York: Alfred Knopf, 1966), p. 119.

8. Arthur Schlesinger, Jr., *The Vital Center* (Boston: Houghton-Mifflin, 1949), pp. 9–10.

9. John K. White, *Still Seeing Red* (Boulder, CO: Westview, 1997), p. 149.

10. Fred Greenstein, "Toward a Modern Presidency," in *Leadership in the Modern Presidency* (Cambridge: Harvard University Press, 1988).

11. White, *Still Seeing Red*, p. 9.

12. James Morone, *The Democratic Wish: Popular Participation and the Limits of American Government* (New York: Basic Books, 1990), pp. 196–97.

13. See draft copy of the statement of Secretary of State Dean Rusk to House Immigration and Nationality Subcommittee, Judiciary Committee, July 2, 1964, Immigration Files, Executive Collection, Box 1, Lyndon B. Johnson Library, Austin, Texas.

14. Hugh Davis Graham, *The Civil Rights Era: Origins and Development of National Policy, 1960–1972* (New York: Oxford University Press, 1990), p. 14.

15. See, for example, Elazar Barkan, *The Retreat of Scientific Racism* (New York: Cambridge University Press, 1992), pp. 344–45.

16. Senator Philip A. Hart's remarks to organizations interested in immigration and refugee matters, White House press release, January 13, 1964, Statements of Lyndon Baines Johnson, Container 93, Johnson Library.

17. Gil Loescher and John Scanlan, *Calculated Kindness: Refugees and America's Half-Open Door, 1945 to the Present* (New York: Free Press, 1986), p. 1.

18. Report of Earl G. Harrison, quoted in Loescher and Scanlan, *Calculated Kindness*, pp. 3–5.

19. Undated Confidential Memorandum on Immigration Reform, Interim Committee Memoranda Folder, Papers of the National Committee on Postwar Immigration Policy, Container 1, American Jewish Historical Society.

20. "How Many Europeans to Let In," January 14, 1946, in *The Gallup Poll: Public Opinion, 1935–1971* (New York: Random House, 1972), 1:555.

21. Ibid.

22. Barkan, *Retreat of Scientific Racism*, pp. 344–45.

23. American Federation of Labor, *Proceedings of the Annual Conventions*, 1946 bound volume, p. 598, Resolution 85, George Meany Memorial Archives, Silver Spring, MD.

24. Ibid., Resolution 85, p. 250.

25. Harry S Truman, "State of the Union Address to Congress, January 6, 1947," *Public Papers of the Presidents of the United States: Harry S. Truman, 1947* (Washington, DC: Government Printing Office, 1963), p. 10.

26. Loescher and Scanlan, *Calculated Kindness*, p. 10.

27. *Saturday Evening Post*, February 1, 1947; quoted in *Memo to America: The DP Story: The Final Report of the Displaced Persons Commission* (Washington, DC: Government Printing Office, 1952), p. 12.

28. *Christian Science Monitor*, March 29, 1947.

29. Paul Griffith, national commander of the American Legion, Address before the 56th Congress of the Daughters of the American Revolution, Washington, DC, May 22, 1947, draft copy in the Celler Papers, Container 15.

30. The American Forum of the Air, "Should We Restrict Immigration?" February 11, 1947, transcript in Celler Papers, Container 17.

31. Ed Gossett, "A New Fifth Column or the Refugee Racket," Speech of July 2, 1947, copy in Celler Papers, Container 17.

32. Loescher and Scanlan, *Calculated Kindness*, pp. 13–14.

33. Celler to the editor of the *New York Herald Tribune*, May 19, 1947, Celler Papers, Box 15.

34. Emanuel Celler to Earl C. Michener, chairman of the House Judiciary Committee, May 2, 1947, Celler Papers.

35. *Washington Post*, May 20, 1947.

36. Resolution of the Federal Council of Churches, April 8, 1948, Celler Papers.

37. Statement of the National Executive Committee of the American Legion, November 1947, Celler Papers.

38. Loescher and Scanlan, *Calculated Kindness*, p. 17.

39. *New York Times*, June 26, 1948.

40. Loescher and Scanlan, *Calculated Kindness*, p. 24.

41. Emanuel Celler, "Isolationism Lingers in Our Foreign Policy," speech delivered at the Annual Dinner of the Association of Immigration and Naturalization Lawyers, New York City, December 5, 1950, Celler Papers.

42. Loescher and Scanlan, *Calculated Kindness*, p. 28.

43. John Higham, "American Immigration in Historical Perspective," *Law and Contemporary Problems* 21 (Spring 1956): 124.

44. Ibid., p. 126.

45. Herbert Lehman, "Immigration and Freedom," speech at the National Democratic Club of New York City, April 5, 1952, Celler Papers, Box #110.

46. From the start, Celler struggled to make an opening statement at the hearings. Consider this telling exchange:

Celler: I would like to be heard, Mr. Chairman.
McCarran: I want to hear you, Mr. Celler. . . . We have, however, an agenda of people who come here from a distance.
Celler: You had 10 minutes, and Mr. Walter had 8.
McCarran: I am the chairman of this committee, however.

A copy of this excerpt of the hearings is found in the *Joint Hearings before the Subcommittees of the Committees on the Judiciary*, 82d Congress, 1st Session (Washington, DC: Government Printing Office, 1951), Celler Papers, Box 110.

47. Ibid.

48. Notes of the Legislative Department of the American Federation of Labor on Immigration, 1952, AFL, AFL-CIO Legislative Dept. Papers, George Meany Memoreial Archives, Silver Springs, MD.

49. Walter J. Mason to W. C. Hushing, Memorandum on Immigration and Naturalization, March 20, 1952, AFL Dept. of Legislation, Box 84, File 74.

50. Mike Masaoka of the Japanese American Citizens League is quoted in Ellis Cose, *A Nation of Strangers* (New York: William Morrow, 1992), pp. 82–93.

51. *Congressional Record*, May 15, 1952, p. 5217; June 27, 1952, p. 8261.

52. *Congressional Record*, May 15, 1952, p. 5230.

53. Lehman, "Immigration and Freedom."

54. *Congressional Record*, May 15, 1952, pp. 5234–35.

55. Quoted in Robert Divine, *American Immigration Policy, 1924–1954* (New York: Da Capo Press, 1972), p. 181.

56. White, *Still Seeing Red*, pp. 93 and 97.

57. Quoted in Divine, *American Immigration Policy*, pp. 177, 191.

58. David Reimers, *Still the Golden Door: The Third World Comes to America* (New York: Columbia University Press, 1992), p. 54.

59. Ibid.

60. Harry S. Truman, "Veto of Bill to Revise the Laws Relating to Immigration, June 25, 1952," *Public Papers of the Presidents of the United States: Harry S. Truman, 1952–1953* (Washington, DC: Government Printing Office, 1966), pp. 441–47.

61. "Truman Assails Eisenhower as Supporting Isolationists," *New York Times*, October 18, 1952; "Eisenhower Accepts 'Nazi' Racial Views, Truman Declares," *Washington Evening Star*, October 17, 1952; see other newspaper clippings from the Harry N. Rosenfield Papers, Harry S. Truman Library, Independence, MO.

62. Herbert Lehman, Remarks at the Brooklyn Skating Rink, October 19, 1952, Rosenfield Papers, Box 32, President's Commission on Immigration and Naturalization.

63. Quoted in White, *Still Seeing Red*, p. 87.

64. *New York Times*, October 18, 1952.

65. Dwight D. Eisenhower, "Eisenhower's Talk—Cleveland," September 8, 1952, Rosenfield Papers, Box 35, President's Commission on Immigration and Naturalization.

66. Eisenhower's statement was made in Newark, New Jersey, on October 18, 1952; he is quoted in Jules Cohen, "Revise the McCarran Act," *New Leader*, December 15, 1952, copy of text found in the Papers of the AFL, AFL-CIO Dept. of Legislation, Box 27, Folder 14.

67. "Outline: Major Items for Consideration of the President's Commission on Immigration and Naturalization," undated, Commission Members' Transmittal Memos, President's Commission on Immigration and Naturalization, Rosenfield Papers, Box 30.

68. Commission on Immigration and Naturalization, *Whom We Shall Welcome* (Washington, DC: Government Printing Office, 1953), pp. 91–97, 285–301. In addition, see the memo prepared by Oscar Handlin for the commission refuting the methods and findings of the Dillingham Commission. Handlin, "National Origins System—Concepts and Justifications, Analysis and Critique," in Rosenfield Papers.

69. Commission on Immigration and Nationalization, *Whom We Shall Welcome*, pp. xii–xiii. Truman's statement on civil rights and "world politics" is quoted in Morone, *Democratic Wish*, pp. 196–97.

70. *New York Times*, January 2, 1953.

71. On the "extraconstitutional status of exclusion," see the superb article by Peter H. Schuck, "The Transformation of Immigration Law," *Columbia Law Review* 84, no. 1 (January, 1984): 18–21.

72. *United States ex rel. Knauff v Shaughnessy*, 338 U.S. 537 (1950), p. 544.

73. *Shaughnessy v United States ex rel. Mezei*, 345 U.S. 206 (1953), p. 220.

74. Edward Corsi's statement can be found in "Let's Talk about Immigration," *Reporter*, March 1955.

75. Loescher and Scanlan, *Calculated Kindness*, p. 41.

76. John McCormick to Emanuel Celler, September 25, 1953, Celler Papers.

77. For more on Eisenhower's "hidden-hand" leadership, see Fred I. Greenstein, *The Hidden-Hand Presidency: Eisenhower as Leader* (New York: Basic Books, 1982).

78. *INS Statistical Yearbook, 1995* (Washington, DC: Government Printing Office, 1996).

79. Report of the Executive Council of the American Federation of Labor for 1954, n.d. 1954 File, AFL-CIO Legislative Department Papers, George Meany Memorial Archives.

80. Attorney General Herbert Brownell, undated talk, Papers of the AFL, AFL-CIO Dept. of Legislation, Box 27, Folder 14.

81. *Annual Report of the Immigration and Naturalization Service, 1955* (Washington, DC: Government Printing Office, 1956).

82. Executive Council of the American Federation of Labor to President Dwight D. Eisenhower, February 4, 1954, AFL-CIO Legislative Department Papers.

83. The most incisive account of this iron triangle or subgovernment is provided by Kitty Calavita, *Inside the State* (New York: Routledge, 1992).

84. Loescher and Scanlan, *Calculated Kindness*, p. 49.

85. Gwendolyn Mink, *Old Labor and New Immigrants in American Political Development* (Ithaca: Cornell University Press, 1986).

86. Walter Reuther, CIO representative, statement before the Senate Judiciary Subcommittee on Immigration and Naturalization, November 21, 1955, Papers of the AFL, AFL-CIO Legislative Dept., Box 27, Folder 16.

87. Ibid.

88. Interview with Andrew Biemiller, May 22, 1979, conducted by Alice M. Hoffman, 1980, George Meany Center for Labor Studies Oral History Project, AFL-CIO Merger (Collection 15), Box 1, Folder 4, Meany Archives.

89. Ibid.

90. Hyman Bookbinder, "The Whole Country Benefits," *American Federationist*, copy in Box 27, Folder 20, Celler Papers.

91. Hubert Humphrey, Jr., "The Stranger at Our Gate," pamphlet, distributed by the Public Affairs Committee of the American Jewish Committee, January 1954, copy found in Papers of the AFL, AFL-CIO Dept. of Legislation, Box 27, Folder 14.

92. Author's interview with Myer Feldman, Washington, DC.

93. In addition to the pro-immigration expertise gathered by Truman's immigration commission, see also the fresh study coordinated by William S. Bernard, *American Immigration Policy—a Reappraisal* (New York: National Committee on Immigration Policy, 1950). The latter study challenged the Dillingham's distinctions between older and newer European immigrants in terms of regional origin, and pointed to demographic evidence that robust immigration might offset projected decline in U.S. population growth in coming years. The study also emphasized the economic, social, and political contributions of new immigrants.

94. John Gerring, *Party Ideologies in America, 1828–1996* (New York: Columbia University Press, 1998), p. 18.

95. Message from the Coordinating Council for Amending the McCarren-Walter Act to Congressmen, June 24, 1955, Celler Papers, Box 106.

96. Senator Theodore Green, Remarks at the 1953 Conference of the Democratic National Conference on the work of the Nationalities Division, September 15, 1953, Celler Papers, Box 106.

97. See the memos and fact sheets series of the Democratic Study Group, Papers of the Democratic Study Group of the House of Representatives, Boxes 1–6 Manuscript Division, Library of Congress, Washington, DC; see also Mark Feber, "The Formation of the Democratic Study Group," in Nelson Polsby, ed., *Congressional Behavior* (New York: Random House, 1971); Roger Davidson and Walter Oleszek, *Congress against Itself* (Bloomington: Indiana University Press, 1977); Leroy Rieselbach, *Congressional Reform* (Washington, DC: Congressional Quarterly Press, 1986); and Lawrence Dodd, "The Rise of the Technocratic Congress," in Richard Harris and Sidney Milkis, *Remaking American Politics* (Boulder, CO: Westview Press, 1989), pp. 89–111.

98. John F. Kennedy to Lyndon B. Johnson, June 29, 1955, Senate Files, Pre-Presidential Papers of John F. Kennedy, John F. Kennedy Library, Boston, Massachusetts.

99. John F. Kennedy, Opening speech of the 1960 campaign to the National Press Club, Kennedy Papers.

100. "The Real Power in Congress—A 23-Year-Old Coalition," *AFL-CIO American Federationist* 67 (April 1960).

101. "Immigration," Democratic Study Group Fact Sheet no. 15, copy found in the Papers of the Democratic Study Group of the House of Representatives, Box 6 Manuscript Division, Library of Congress, Washington, DC.

102. Ibid.

103. For example, see George Meany's interview of John F. Kennedy, *AFL-CIO News*, October 1, 1960, Papers of the Democratic Study Group, Box 42.

104. Various brochures from the Kennedy campaign in Italian, German, Spanish, and other languagues can be found in the Papers of the Democratic Study Group, Box 42.

105. Hyman Bookbinder, "The World's Refugees—A Challenge to America," March 30, 1960, copy in the Papers of the AFL, AFL-CIO Department of Legislation, Box 27, Folder 28.

106. Francis Walter to Chester Bowles, August 8, 1960, quoted in Stephen Wagner, "The Lingering Death of the National Origins Quota System: A Political History of U.S. Immigration Policy, 1952–1965" (Ph.D. diss., History Department, Harvard University, October 1986), pp. 360–61.

107. Hyman Bookbinder to Ruth Murphy, February 13, 1961, Papers of the AFL, AFL-CIO Dept. of Legislation, Box 27, Folder 26.

108. Ibid.

109. See Edward Kennedy, "The Immigration Act of 1965," *Annals of the American Academy of Political and Social Science* 367 (September 1966): pp. 137–38.

110. Abba Schwartz to Theodore Sorenson, November 6, 1963, Theodore Sorenson Papers, Legislative Files, Legislation 1963 folder, May 21–November 13, 1963, John F. Kennedy Library.

111. Abba Schwartz, *The Open Society* (New York: William Morrow, 1968), p. 116.

112. H. L. Mitchell and Ernesto Galarzo, Natiional Agricultural Workers Union, to Members of Congress, February 17, 1958, Papers of the AFL, AFL-CIO Department of Legislation, Box 27, Folder 34.

113. Calavita, *Inside the State*, p. 163.

114. Ibid., p. 169.

115. Ibid.

116. Gonzalez's impassioned speech appears in the *Congressional Record*, September 18, 1963, pp. 16438–39.

117. Author's interview with Henry B. Gonzalez, March 1996.

118. Ibid.

119. Michael LeMay, *From Open Door to Dutch Door* (New York: Praeger, 1987), p. 111.

120. Paul Douglas Oral History Interview, by Mike Gillette, November 1, 1974, Washington, DC, for the LBJ Library, p. 4.

121. See Sidney Milkis and Michael Nelson, *The American Presidency* (Washington, DC: Congressional Quarterly Press, 1999), pp. 308–9.

122. Sidney Milkis, *The Presidents and the Parties* (New York: Oxford University Press, 1993), p. 171.

123. William Leuchtenberg, *In the Shadow of FDR* (Ithaca: Cornell University Press, 1985), p. 132; Lyndon Johnson, *The Vantage Point* (New York: Holt, Rinehart, and Winston, 1971), p. 160.

124. Author's interview with Myer Feldman, December 1994.

125. Author's telephone interview with Jack Valenti, December 19, 1993.

126. Author's interview with Feldman.

127. Schwartz, *Open Society*, p. 117.

128. Author's interviews with Feldman and Valenti; and Schwartz, *Open Society.*Johnson's pledge to attack racial discrimination was made in a speech on November 27, 1963, in Johnson, *Public Papers of the Presidents of the United States: Lyndon B. Johnson, 1963–1964* (Washington, DC: Government Printing Office, 1965).

129. Author's interview with Valenti.

130. Lyndon B. Johnson, "State of the Union Address," *Public Papers*, 1:116.

131. "Remarks of the President to Representatives of Organizations Interested in Immigration and Refugee Matters," January 13, 1964, transcript found in Presidential Statements Files, Container 93, LBJ Library.

132. "Remarks of the President and Congressional Leaders to Representatives of Organizations Interested in Immigration and Refugee Matters," January 13, 1964, Press Release, Office of the White House Press Secretary, Celler Papers, Box 110.

133. Lawrence O'Brien Oral History Interview, LBJ Library.

134. Author's interview with Valenti.

135. O'Brien Oral History Interview.

136. "Building for the Great Society," Democratic Study Group 1964 Campaign Cards, Papers of the Democratic Study Group, Box 54.

137. Schwartz, *Open Society*, pp. 120–21; see also the Republican platform of 1964 with respect to reauthorizing the Bracero Program.

138. See the Immigration and Nationality Act File, 1964 Campaign, Robert F. Kennedy Senate Papers, Box 7, John F. Kennedy Library.

139. "Building for the Great Society."

140. *Congressional Report of the National Committee for an Effective Congress* 14, no. 1 (April 19 1965), copy found in the Celler Papers, Box 107.

141. The phrase "politics of haste" is borrowed from Doris Kearns Goodwin, *Lyndon Johnson and the American Dream* (New York: Harper and Row, 1976), p. 216.

142. Nicholas deB. Katzenbach, Testimony on Immigration Reform, Hearings before the Subcommittee on Immigration and Naturalization, Senate Judiciary Committee, 89th Congress, 1st session, pt. 1 (Washington, DC: Government Printing Office, 1965), p. 8.

143. Hubert Humphrey, speech delivered on immigration legislation at Williamsburg, Virginia, April 29, 1965 (passage drafted by Abba Schwartz), the Abba Schwartz Papers, John F. Kennedy Library. Attorney General Nicholas deB. Katzenbach also spoke publicly about what he described as the many areas included under the Johnson administration's civil rights program, including immigration reform; see Katzenbach, Address at the Annual Dinner of the American Justice Committee, New Jersey Area, Morristown, NJ, June 2, 1965, Schwartz Papers, Box 7, Immigration and Legislation Files.

144. Schwartz, *Open Society*; author's interviews with Valenti and Feldman. Johnson was adamant that "no quid pro quo" be offered to Feighan, largely because liberal control of the subcommittee eliminated "the need for and value of an agreement" with him. See Johnson's handwritten notes on memorandum from Jack Valenti, July 1, 1964, Container #3, Handwriting Files; and Norbert Schlei to Johnson, May 7, 1965, Container 73, Legislation-Immigration Files, LBJ Library.

145. O'Brien Oral History Interview.

146. Lyndon Johnson, *Public Papers*, vol. 2.

147. See Reimers, *Still the Golden Door*.

148. On the effects of global pressures on internal politics, see Bartholomew Sparrow, *From the Outside In* (Princeton: Princeton University Press, 1996); and White, *Still Seeing Red*.

149. Jeff Fishel, *Presidents and Promises* (Wasington, DC: Congressional Quarterly Press, 1985), p. 201.

150. Author's interviews with executive and congressional officials, 1994–99; see app. at the end of this volume.

151. Kennedy is quoted in Vernon Briggs, *Mass Immigration and the National Interest* (Armonk, NY: M. E. Sharpe, 1992), p. 75.

152. Lyndon Johnson, "Remarks on the Immigration Law," *Congressional Quarterly* (October 1965), pp. 2063–64.

CHAPTER EIGHT: THE REBIRTH OF AMERICAN IMMIGRATION

1. Immigration and Naturalization Service, *INS Statistical Yearbook, 1980* (Washington, DC: Government Printing Office, 1981), pp. 1–33.

2. Peter Schuck and Rogers Smith, *Citizenship without Consent* (New Haven: Yale University Press, 1995), pp. 104–9; Peter Skerry, "Borders and Quotas," *Public Interest* (1989): 86–87.

3. Schuck and Smith, *Citizenship without Consent*, pp. 106–8.

4. There is considerable confusion concerning the distinctions between "refugees" and "asylees" or "asylum seekers." In legal terms, U.S. understandings of "refugee" once meant those fleeing communist regimes but since 1980 has followed an internationally agreed-upon definition. The difference between a refugee and an asylum seeker is based on location: a refugee lives outside both her homeland and the United States while an asylum seeker resides within American borders.

5. Gil Loescher and John Scanlan, *Calculated Kindness: Refugees and America's Half-Open Door, 1945 to the Present* (New York: Free Press, 1986), pp. 73–74.

6. Lawrence O'Brien Oral History Interview, Lyndon Baines Johnson Library, Austin, TX.

7. Loescher and Scanlan, *Calculated Kindness*, p. 92.

8. Michael Teitelbaum, "U.S. Responses to Refugees and Asylum Seekers," in Myron Weiner and Tadashi Hanami, *Temporary Workers or Future Citizens?* (New York: New York University Press, 1998), pp. 456–62.

9. "Black Americans Urge Admission of the Indochinese Refugees," *New York Times*, March 19, 1978.

10. George Meany to President Jimmy Carter, February 24, 1978, quoted in "To Save Lives of Those Fleeing Oppression," *American Federationist* 86 (August 1979): 6–8.

11. Ibid., p. 88.

12. Ibid.

13. Immigration and Naturalization Service, Department of Justice, *Statistical Yearbook of the Immigration and Naturalization Service, 1994* (Washington, DC: Government Printing Office, 1995).

14. *Proceedings of the American Federation of Labor National Convention*, 1950, copies available at the George Meany Memorial Archives, Silver Springs, MD.

15. Immigration and Naturalization Service, *Statistical Yearbook of the Immigration and Naturalization Service, 1993* (Washington, DC: Government Printing Office, 1994).

16. Quoted in David Reimers, *Still the Golden Door: The Third World Comes to America* (New York: Columbia University Press), p. 202.

17. Alice Ogle, "Revolution in the Vineyards," *America* (December 11, 1965): 747–48; and Andrew Kopkind, "The Grape Pickers' Strike," *New Republic*, January 29, 1966.

18. Cesar E. Chavez to Robert F. Kennedy, Western Union Telegram, August 11, 1968, Robert F. Kennedy Papers, Container #71, Senate Legislative Subject Files, John F. Kennedy Presidential Library, Boston.

19. See *El Malcriado: The Voice of the Farm Worker* (newsletter of the United Farm Workers Organizing Committee) 11 (March 15, 1968); and the unpublished testimony of Chavez before the Senate Judiciary Committee's Subcommittee on Immigration and Naturalization, quoted in Kitty Calavita, *Inside the State: The Bracero Program, Immigration, and the INS* (New York: Routledge, 1992), p. 155.

20. Andrew Biemiller to Peter Rodino, September 8, 1972; Biemiller to

Rodino, March 23, 1973; Biemiller to Rodino, May 1, 1973; Rodino to Biemiller, May 15, 1973, Papers of the Legislative Dept. of the AFL-CIO, Box 71, Folder #28. George Meany Archives, Silver Spring, MD.

21. Author's interviews with lobbyists, lawmakers, and congressional staffers (see appendix); concerning entrepreneurs and the promotion of policy ideas over time, see John Kingdon, *Agendas, Alternatives, and Public Choices* (New York: HarperCollins, 1995), pp. 125–44.

22. *Report of the Select Commission on Immigration and Refugee Policy* (Washington, DC: Government Printing Office, 1981), pt. 1, p. 255.

23. Ibid., pt. 2, p. 594. The testimony of the representative from the U.S. Catholic Conference is found on pp. 567–70.

24. Ibid.

25. For example, see the opening statement of Representative Peter Rodino, "Illegal Aliens," Hearings on Illegal Aliens before Subcommittee no. 1 of the Committee on the Judiciary, House of Representatives, 92d Congress, 1st Session, May 5, June 3, 19, and 21, 1971, pt. 1, (Washington, DC, Government Printing Office, 1971), pt. 1 pp. 2–4.

26. Demands of the Mexican-American Political Association to Senator George McGovern, candidate for the Democratic party nomination for president of the United States in 1972, presented at Los Angeles, at the Holiday Inn, on April 4 1971, reprinted in the *Report of the Select Commission on Immigration and Refugee Policy*, pt. 1, pp. 272–73.

27. *Congressional Record*, September 12, 1972, pp. 30164, 30182–83.

28. Ibid., p. 30182.

29. See, for example, the *New York Times*, December 31, 1974.

30. *Washington Post*, February 3, 1975; *Washington Star-News*, November 19, 1974; and the *New York Times*, December 29, 1974.

31. John Crewdson, *The Tarnished Door: The New Immigrants and the Transformation of America* (New York: Times Books, 1983), p. 126. For the fullest account of the so-called revolving-door between the INS and Eastland's staff, see Calavita, *Inside the State*, pp. 159–62.

32. Roybal is quoted in the *Los Angeles Times*, February 4, 1973.

33. Andrew Biemiller to Peter Rodino, May 1, 1973, Papers of the AFL, AFL-CIO Legislative Dept. Box 71, Folder 28.

34. *Congressional Record*, May 3, 1973, pp. 14193–207.

35. Ibid., pp. 14208–209.

36. "Statement by the AFL-CIO Executive Council on Illegal Aliens," February 18, 1974, Papers of the AFL, AFL-CIO Legislative Dept.

37. Author's anonymous interviews with committee members and staffers (see appendix).

38. Author's interview with Jerry Tinker, assistant to Senator Edward Kennedy (D-MA) on immigration and refugee matters from 1970 to 1994, Hart Senate Office Building, Washington, DC, December 8, 1993.

39. See Raymond Farrell to Richard M. Nixon, January 31, 1973; as well as 1972 newspaper clippings on INS corruption in "Immigration and Naturalization Service," Department of Justice, White House Subject Files, Box 5, Nixon Presidential Materials, the Nixon Project.

40. Webster Todd, Jr., to George Bush and Henry Kissinger, September 25, 1973, ibid.

41. Leonard Chapman, "Illegal Aliens: Time to Call a Halt," *Reader's Digest*, October 1977, pp. 188–92.

42. Ibid.

43. Author's interview with Doris Meissner, former executive director of the Domestic Council Committee on Illegal Immigration and current commissioner of the INS, December 20, 1993.

44. Preliminary Report of the Domestic Council Committee on Illegal Immigration, December, 1976, p. 185.

45. Ibid., pp. 212–13.

46. Ibid., p. 241.

47. Ibid., pp. 240–44.

48. "Illegal Aliens," Hearings before the Subcommittee of Immigration, Citizenship, and International Law of the Committee on the Judiciary, February 4, 26, March 5, 12, 13, and 19, 1975, House of Representatives, 94th Congress, 1st Session (Washington, DC: Government Printing Office, 1975), pp. 34–35.

49. See table 2 in Rodolfo O. de la Garza, "'And then there were some . . .': Chicanos as National Political Actors, 1967–1980," *Aztlan* 15, no. 1 (Spring 1984): 15.

50. Benjamin Marquez, "The Politics of Race and Class: The League of United Latin American Citizens in the Post–World War II Period, *Social Science Quarterly* 68 (March 1987): 84–85, 93–94. LULAC's founding constitution of 1927 in fact restricted membership "exclusively to citizens of the United States . . . either native or naturalized." It also participated in Americanization efforts during the interwar years, and adopted English as its official language. See O. Douglass Weeks, "The League of United Latin-American Citizens: A Texas-Mexican Civic Organization," *Southwestern Political and Social Science Quarterly* 10, no. 3 (December 1929): 257–63. Finally, the assimilationist approach of LULAC's old guard is especially evident in its endorsement of Operation Wetback in 1954; "Wetback Roundup Needs Support of LULAC," *LULAC News* 22 (July 1954): 4.

51. For example, see Jeffrey Berry, *Lobbying for the People* (Princeton: Princeton University Press, 1977); and Kay Schlozman and John Tierney, *Organized Interests and American Democracy* (New York: Harper and Row, 1986).

52. de la Garza, "And then there were some . . . ," p. 14.

53. Karen O'Connor and Lee Epstein, "A Legal Voice for the Chicano Community: The Activities of the Mexican-American Legal Defense and Education Fund, 1968–1982," *Social Science Quarterly* 65 (June, 1984): 248–49.

54. Theodore Hesburgh, chair of the United States Commission on Civil Rights, to Daniel P. Moynihan, April 27, 1970, President's Office Files, Container 4, Nixon Project.

55. *San Antonio v Rodriguez* 1973.

56. Copies of National Council of La Raza documents made available by the NCLR Washington office to the author.

57. Marquez, "Politics of Race and Class," pp. 93–94; and Weeks, "The League of United Latin-American Citizens," p. 257.

58. "Chavez Shifts View of Illegals," reprinted in "Illegal Aliens," Hearings before the Subcommittee on Immigration, Citizenship, and International Law, February 4, 26, March 5, 12, 13, and 19, 1975, pp. 82–83.

59. *Los Angeles Times*, January 30, 1975.

60. Frederick Douglass is quoted in Lawrence Fuchs, "The Reactions of Black Americans to Immigration," in Virginia Yans-McLaughlin, ed., *Immigration Reconsidered: History, Sociology, and Politics* (New York: Oxford University Press, 1990), p. 295.

61. Stanley Lieberson, *A Piece of the Pie: Blacks and White Immigrants since 1880* (Berkeley and Los Angeles: University of California Press, 1980).

62. See the thorough examination of this subject provided by Arnold Shankman, *Ambivalent Friends: Afro-Americans View the Immigrant* (Westport, CT: Greenwood Press, 1982), p. 156.

63. Ibid., p. 73.

64. See, for example, Jacquelyn Jackson, "Illegal Aliens: A Big Threat to Black Workers," *Ebony*, April 1979 p. 34; and William Raspberry, "Their Tired, Their Poor—Our Jobs," *Washington Post*, July 4, 1980; and Raspberry, "Hiring American," *Washington Post*, September 8, 1980.

65. *Washington Post*, December 26, 1974.

66. David Ushio, national executive director of the Japanese American Citizens League, to Marvin Caplan, director of the Washington Office of the Leadership Conference on Civil Rights, January 7, 1975, Leadership Conference on Civil Rights Papers, Container #76, Organization Files.

67. For example, see "Hispanics and Blacks Reach Accords," February 26, 1979, Leadership Conference on Civil Rights Papers, Container 24, Black-Hispanic Relations Files.

68. See "Perspectives on Undocumented Workers: Black and Hispanic Viewpoints," report of the National Council of La Raza, Washington, DC, September, 1980, copy in author's possession.

69. "Perspectives on Undocumented Workers," NCLR report, pp. 8–9, 19, and 32.

70. Ibid., pp. 30–31.

71. Author's anonymous interviews with congressional members and staffers (see appendix); for a discussion of the origins of the Congressional Hispanic Caucus, see Paul Wieck, "Different Interests, Personalities Hurt Unity of Hispanic Caucus," in F. Chris Garcia, *Latinos and the Political System* (South Bend, IN: University of Notre Dame Press, 1988), pp. 300–305.

72. For example, see memorandum from Charles B. Knapp, special assistant to the secretary of Labor, undated [April 1977], to secretary of Labor, Raymond Marshall Papers, Record Group 174, Miscellaneous Cross References, Immigration Files.

73. White House statement, August 4, 1977, Patricia Roberts Harris Papers.

74. The heated battle between Eastland and Bell over the Carter bill and judgeships is recounted by Meissner in interview with the author.

75. "Memorandum on Public Policy and Legislative Priorities," October 17, 1977, National Council of La Raza, copy found in the Papers of the Leadership Conference on Civil Rights, Container 24, "National Council of La Raza" Folder. Manuscripts Division, Library of Congress.

76. "The Legislative Program of the National Council of La Raza: A Progress Report," submitted by Raul Yzaguirre, national director, National Council of La Raza, October 7, 1977, "Organizations: Papers of the Leadership Conference on Civil Rights, Container 80, National Council of La Raza" Folder.

77. "Memorandum to Interested Parties from the Mexican-American Legal Defense and Education Fund: Statement of Position Regarding the Administration's Undocumented Alien Legislative Proposal," November 11, 1977, Papers of the Leadership Conference on Civil Rights, Container #23, "Issues: Alien Civil Rights" Folder.

78. Ibid.

79. Author's interview with Jerry Tinker, December 8, 1993.

80. "Amendments to the Immigration Laws," Hearings before Subcommittee no. 1 of the Committee on the Judiciary, House of Representatives, 91st Congress, 1st Session, December 10, 1969 (Washington, DC: Government Printing Office, 1970), pp. 11–25.

81. The bills are summarized ibid., pp. 1–2; see also "Immigration," Hearings before Subcommittee no. 1 of the Committee on the Judiciary, July 16, 22, and 29, August 5 and 6, 1970. House of Representatives, 91st Congress, 2d Session.

82. Andrew Biemiller to George Meany, July 19, 1968, Papers of the Legislative Department of the AFL-CIO, Box 27, Folder 33.

83. Regarding the original impetus for the Commission on Population Control and the American Future, see Daniel P. Moynihan to President Richard M. Nixon, December 17, 1969, President's Office Files, Box 4; and *The New York Times*, December 17, 1969.

In terms of the influence of the commission's report on environmental and population control advocates, see John H. Tanton, Oral History, interviewed by Otis Graham, April 20, 1989, transcript made available to the author at the Washington office of the Federation of American Immigration Reform. See also Leslie Aldridge Westoff, "Should We Pull Up the Gangplank?" *New York Times Magazine*, September 16, 1973, pp. 15, 78–86.

84. Westoff, "Should We Pull Up the Gangplank?" p. 15.

85. Testimony of Howard D. Samuel, former member of the Commission on Population Growth and the American Future, in "Western Hemisphere Immigration," Hearings before Subcommittee no. 1 of the Committee on the Judiciary, House of Representatives, 93rd Congress, 1st Session, (Washington, DC: Government Printing Office, 1973), pp. 75–82.

86. Ibid., p. 76.

87. Westoff, "Should We Pull Up the Gangplank?" p. 86.

88. Ibid., p. 15.

89. *National Parks and Conservation Magazine*, December 1977, pp. 13–16.

90. Oral History of John H. Tanton, pp. 72–73.

91. "The FAIR Way," pamphlet distributed by FAIR in 1979, copy found in SCIRP Papers, Record Group 220, Box 7, National Archives, Washington, DC.

92. Otis Graham, Jr., interviewed by John H. Tanton, February 19, 1990, p. 34.

93. Ibid.

94. Ellis Cose, *A Nation of Strangers* (New York: William Morrow, 1992), p. 127.

95. Ibid., p. 39.

96. In fact, these statistics can be quite deceptive, given that INS enforcement resources and efforts have varied over time and that the "revolving door" at the United States–Mexican border means undocumented aliens can be apprehended more than once a year.

97. *Christian Science Monitor*, April 28, 1980.

98. For an excellent summary of public opinion polls of this period, see Rita Simon and Susan Alexander, *The Ambivalent Welcome: Print Media, Public Opinion, and Immigration* (Westport, CT: Praeger, 1993).

99. Author's anonymous interview with long-time Senate staffer (see appendix).

100. Author's anonymous interview with House member.

101. Author's interview with senior Senate staffer; see also Lawrence H. Fuchs, "The Immigration Reform and Control Act of 1986: A Case Study in Legislative Leadership and Pluralistic Politics," paper presented at the American Political Science Association Meeting, September 3, 1987.

102. Reimers, *Still the Golden Door*.

103. Schuck and Smith, *Citizenship without Consent*, p. 106–10.

104. *Graham v Richardson*, 204 U.S. 365 (1971).

105. Anthony King, "The American Polity in the 1970s: Building Coalitions in the Sand," in *New American Political System* (Washington, DC: American Enterprise Institute, 1978), p. 391.

106. Theodore Lowi, *The End of Liberalism* (New York: W. W. Norton, 1979).

CHAPTER NINE: TWO FACES OF EXPANSION

1. Author's anonymous interview with House leader (see appendix).

2. See Rita Simon, "Immigration and American Attitudes," 10 *Public Opinion* (1987): 47–50; and Edwin Harwood, "American Public Opinion and U.S. Immigration Policy," *Annals of the American Academy of Political and Social Science* 487 (1986): pp. 201–12; and Rita Simon and Susan Alexander, *The Ambivalent Welcome: Print Media, Public Opinions, and Immigration* (Westport, CT: Praeger, 1993).

3. Elizabeth Hull, *Without Justice for All* (Westport, CT: Greenwood Press, 1985), p. 4.

4. See SCIRP Newsletter interview with Garner J. Cline, staff director of the House Committee on the Judiciary, Records of the Select Commission on Immigration and Refugee Policy, Record Group 240, Box 28, National Archives, Washington, DC.

5. Transcript of the Closed Meeting of the Select Commission on Immigration and Refugee Policy, December 7, 1980, Records of Commission Meetings Files, Record Group 240, Box 29, National Archives, Washington, DC, p. 232.

6. Author's interviews with House, Senate, and White House officials (see appendix).

7. Peter Schuck, "The Politics of Rapid Legal Change: Immigration Policy in the 1980s," in Marc Landy and Martin Levin, eds., *The New Politics of Public Policy* (Baltimore: Johns Hopkins University Press, 1995), pp. 49–50.

8. See Simon, "Immigration and American Attitudes," p. 48.

9. For example, see the essays in Juan Perea, *Immigrants Out! The New Nativism and the Anti-Immigrant Impulse in America* (New York: New York University Press, 1997).

10. Peter Schuck, *Citizens, Strangers, and In-Betweens* (Boulder, CO: Westview, 1998), p. 139.

11. Author's interviews with Republican House and Senate members (see appendix).

12. Abraham is quoted in Dan Carney, "GOP Casts a Kinder Eye on 'Huddled Masses,'" *Congressional Quarterly Weekly*, May 15, 1999, p. 1128.

13. Gary Freeman, "Modes of Immigration Politics in Liberal Democratic States," *International Migration Review* 29 no. 4: 882.

14. *1998 INS Statistical Yearbook* (Washington, DC: Government Printing Office, 1999).

15. Author's interviews with lawmakers, congressional staffers, and White House officials (see appendix).

16. Refugee Act of 1980, March 17, 1980 (Public Law 96–212).

17. Gil Loescher and John Scanlan, *Calculated Kindness: Refugees and America's Half-Open Door* (New York: Free Press, 1986), p. 155.

18. James Gimpel and James Edwards, *The Congressional Politics of Immigration Reform* (Boston: Allyn and Bacon, 1998), pp. 131–33.

19. Michael Teitelbaum, "U.S. Responses to Refugees and Asylum Seekers," in Myron Weiner and Tadashi Hanami, eds., *Temporary Worker or Future Citizens?* (New York: New York University Press, 1998), pp. 456–57.

20. Congressional Research Service, *U.S. Immigration Law and Policy, 1952–1979* (Washington, DC: Government Printing Office, 1979), p. 68.

21. Harris made this statement during a SCIRP meeting of October 9, 1979, Records of the Select Commission. Box 26.

22. Author's interviews with SCIRP members and staff; Draft of the Supplemental Statement of Father Theodore Hesburgh, January 30, 1981, Correspondence Files, Record Group 240, Box 1.

23. Transcripts of SCIRP meeting, May 22, 1979, pp. 17–18; and October 9, 1979, p. 30, Record Group 240, Box 26.

24. Transcript of SCIRP meeting, May 7, 1980, p. 34, Record Group 240, Box 26.

25. Lawrence H. Fuchs, *The American Kaleidoscope* (Hanover, NH: University Press of New England, 1990), p. 252.

26. Ibid.

27. Transcript of SCIRP meeting, May 7, 1980, p. 34, Record Group 240, Box 26.

28. On the "front door" and "back door" metaphor, see the *New York Times*, August 24, 1981.

29. Ibid.

30. Hesburgh, "Opening Remarks at the Wingspread Conference," p. 5, Record Group 240.

31. Author's interview with Simpson and congressional staffers (see appendix).

32. James Q. Wilson, "New Politics, New Elites, Old Publics," in Marc Landy

and Martin Levin, eds., *The New Politics of Public Policy*, (Baltimore: Johns Hopkins University Press, 1995), p. 261.

33. Author's interview with House member.

34. *Christian Science Monitor*, March 18, 1982.

35. Quoted in Ellis Cose, *A Nation of Strangers* (New York: William Morrow, 1992), p. 156.

36. Author's anonymous interview with ethnic group lobbyist.

37. Author's interviews with working group participants (see appendix).

38. Transcript of SCIRP meeting, December 7, 1980, p. 232, Record Group 240, Box 29.

39. Author's interviews with House members and staffers (see appendix).

40. John Gerring, *Party Ideologies in America, 1828–1996* (New York: Columbia University Press, 1998), p. 233.

41. Author's interview with House member (see appendix).

42. Author's interviews with Reagan officials; Martin Anderson, *Revolution* (New York: Harcourt Brace Jovanovich, 1988), p. 273.

43. George Gilder, *Wealth and Poverty* (New York: Basic Books, 1981), p. 67; and George Gilder, *Spirit of Enterprise* (New York: Simon and Schuster, 1984), p. 54.

44. William French Smith discusses these issues in his memoirs, *Law and Justice in the Reagan Administration* (Stanford, CA: Hoover Institution, 1991), pp. 194–95.

45. On the SCIRP report's connection to the Reagan task force, see Robert McClory to Theodore Hesburgh, December 19, 1980, Record Group 240, Box 4. and *New York Times*, February 26, 1981.

46. Gray was quoted in the *New York Times*, February 26, 1981.

47. "Illegal Immigration," April 21, 1981, President's Interagency Task Force on Immigration and Refugee Policy, Papers of Treasury Secretary Raymond Donovan, Container E-2–4, Record Group 174. National Archives, Washington, DC.

48. Meeting transcript, April 22, 1981, Donovan Papers, Container E-2–4, Record Group 174.

49. Memorandum of April 20, 1981, Donovan Papers, Container E-2–4, Record Group 174.

50. Anderson, *Revolution*, pp. 272–77.

51. See Raymond Donovan to William French Smith, July 10, 1981; and Lane Kirkland to Raymond Donovan, March 26, 1981, Donovan Papers, Container E-2-4 Record Group 174.

52. Author's interviews with Reagan officials (see Appendix).

53. "Illegal Immigration," Donovan Papers, Container E-2-4, Record Group 174.

54. *Plyler v Doe*, 457 U.S. 202 (1982), p. 215.

55. Full Committee Markup of HR 1510, Committee on Education and Labor, June 23, 1983, Rayburn Office Building, Washington, DC. p. 4, unpublished transcript.

56. Smith, *Law and Justice in the Reagan Administration*, pp. 215–16.

57. *New York Times*, September 23, 1982.

58. See the *New York Times*, October 2, 10, and 12, 1983.

59. *New York Times*, October 5, 1983.

60. Author's interviews with House Democratic members and staffers.

61. Burdett Loomis, *The New American Politician* (New York: Basic Books, 1988), p. 234. On the diffusion of power in Congress, see Steven Smith, *Call to Order: Floor Politics in the House and Senate* (Washington, DC: Brookings Institution Press, 1989); and Barbara Sinclair, *The Transformation of the U.S. Senate* (Baltimore: Johns Hopkins University Press, 1989).

62. Roger Davidson, "The Emergence of the Postreform Congress," in Davidson ed., *The Postreform Congress* (New York: St. Martin's, 1992), pp. 1–23; and David Rohde, *Parties and Leaders in the Postreform House* (Chicago: University of Chicago Press, 1992).

63. Author's interview with House member (see appendix).

64. On the role of closed-door negotiations and the Social Security reform of 1983 and the Tax Reform Act of 1986, see Paul Light, *Still Artful Work* (New York: McGraw-Hill, 1995); Timothy Conlan, Margaret Wrightson, and David Beam, *Taxing Choices* (Washington, DC: Congressional Quarterly Press, 1990).

65. Author's interviews with Reagan officials and Senate staffers; see also Lawrence Fuchs, "The Immigration Reform and Control Act of 1986," Paper presented at the 1987 Annual Meeting of the American Political Science Association, Chicago, September, 1987, pp. 26–27.

66. Simpson is quoted in the Senate Judiciary Committee Markup, July 18, 1985, unpublished transcript of the Senate Judiciary Committee, p. 60.

67. Business Roundtable statement to Congress on immigration reform, 1985, copy in author's possession; author's interviews with business lobbyists.

68. Author's anonymous interview with grower lobbyist (see appendix).

69. See Fuchs, "Immigration Reform and Control Act," pp. 31–32.

70. *Congressional Record*, September 17, 1985, p. S11600. The farmworker amendment passed 51 to 44. The Simpson bill won by a 69 to 30 vote.

71. Author's interviews with ethnic and immigrant rights lobbyists.

72. *New York Times*, July 18, 1985.

73. Author's interview with congressional staffer.

74. Quoted in Schuck, "The Politics of Rapid Legal Change," p. 39.

75. Jason Juffras, "IRCA and the Enforcement Mission of the Immigration and Naturalization Service," in Michael Fix, ed., *The Paper Curtain* (Washington, DC: Urban Institute, 1991), p. 56.

76. Author's interview with Reagan official (see appendix).

77. Author's interview with immigration lawyer and lobbyist.

78. Information, including budgetary material, was provided to the author by various officials during anonymous interviews. See also the U.S. Commission on Immigration Reform, *U.S. Immigration Policy: Restoring Credibility* (Washington, DC: Government Printing Office, 1994), p. 95.

79. Alan Simpson to Lawrence Fuchs, January 24, 1991, Correspondence Files of Lawrence Fuchs, made available to the author by Fuchs.

80. U.S. General Accounting Office, *Immigration Reform: Employer Sanctions and the Question of Discrimination* (Washington, DC: Government Printing Office, 1990).

81. Lane Kirkland to Lawrence Siskind, February 16, 1989, Addition: Papers

of the Coalition on Civil Rights, Container 46. Manuscript Division, Library of Congress.

82. Frank Bean, Barry Edmonston, and Jeffrey Passel, eds., *Undocumented Migration to the United States* (Washington, DC: Rand, 1990).

83. David Heller, associate deputy attorney general, to Robert McConnell, assistant attorney general of legislative affairs, January 12, 1984, copy in author's files.

84. *H.R. Report 682*, 99th Congress, 2nd Session, pt. 1 (Washington, DC: Government Printing Office, 1986), pp. 72–74.

85. Author's interviews with ethnic, immigrant rights, and civil liberties lobbyists.

86. *Doe and Roe v. Nelson* No. 88–C-6987 (N.D.Ill 1988).

87. Final Rule, *Federal Register* 52, no. 84 (May 1, 1987), 16206.

88. Susan Gonzalez Baker, *The Cautious Welcome* (Washington, DC: Urban Institute, 1990), p. 85.

89. *Farzad v Chandler*, 670 F.Supp. 690 (N.D.Tex. 1988); *Immigration Assistance Project v INS*, no.C88–379 (W.D.Wash. 1988); and *Ayudha, Inc. v Meese* 687 F.Supp. 650, 700 F.Supp. 49 (D.D.C. 1988).

90. *Catholic Services v Meese*, no.S-86-1343-LKK (E.D.Calif., 9th Cir. 1987, 1988).

91. Baker, *Cautious Welcome*, p. 86.

92. *Congressional Quarterly Weekly Review*, July 19, 1980, p. 2066.

93. Letter from Joe Moakley to the author, and author's interviews with conference committee participants.

94. Norman Zucker and Naomi Zucker, *The Guarded Gate* (New York: Harcourt Brace Jovanovich, 1987), p. 143.

95. Lawyer's Committee for Human Rights, Refugee Project, "A Survey and Report," September 1992, copy in author's files.

96. See, for example, Department of State, *World Refugee Report* (June 1992).

97. Among setbacks for asylum-seekers and refugees in the 1980s, see *Jean v Nelson* 727 F.2d 957 (11th Cir. 1984); *Orantes-Hernandez v Meese*, 685 F. Supp. 1488 (C.D. Cal. 1988); and *Haitian Refugee Center v Gracey*, 809 F.2d (D.C. Cir. 1987). Notable legal gains included *Dias v INS* 648 F. Supp. 638 (E.D. Cal. 1986); *INS v Cardoza-Fonseca*, 480 U.S. 421 (1987); and *American Baptist Churches v Thornburgh*, Civ. No. C-85–3255 RFP (N.D. Cal. December 19, 1990).

98. Samuel Maury, president of the U.S. Business Roundtable, to Alan Simpson, August 11, 1982, copy provided to the author by Maury; and anonymous interviews with business group lobbyists.

99. Author's anonymous interview with House staffer.

100. Author's interview with Warren Leiden of AILA.

101. Ibid.

102. Senate Judiciary Committee Markup of S.358, June 8, 1989, transcript, p. 4, Senate Judiciary Committee files, Dirksen Senate Office Building, Washington, DC.

103. Ibid., p. 15.

104. Ibid., p. 36.

105. Ibid., pp. 34, 53–54.

106. William Johnston and Arnold Packer, *Workforce 2000* (Indianapolis, IN: Hudson Institute, 1987).

107. Alan Simpson, Edward Kennedy, and Paul Simon letter to colleagues, May 30, 1989, Immigration Files of Lawrence Fuchs, copy provided to the author.

108. Wilson, "New Politics, New Elites, Old Publics," p. 252.

109. Author's interviews with House members, staffers, and lobbyists (see appendix).

110. Elizabeth Dole to Richard Darman, August 25, 1989, Immigration Files of Lawrence Fuchs.

111. *Wall Street Journal*, October 1 and 12, 1990.

112. General Accounting Office Report to Chair, Senate Subcommittee on Immigration and Refugee Affairs, November 1989, p. 1.

113. See, for example, *Wall Street Journal*, October 16, 1990.

114. Dole to Darman letter.

115. Author's anonymous interviews with Bush White House officials.

116. Author's anonymous interviews with conferees and their staff.

117. *Congressional Record*, October 26, 1990, pp. H12984–85.

118. See FAIR, *Immigrant Report*, September 1993.

119. Author's interview with FAIR staff and local activists (see appendix).

120. Author's interview with Harold Ezell and anonymous interview with SOS staffer.

121. *Los Angeles Times*, October 29, 1994.

122. Simon and Alexander, *The Ambivalent Welcome*; see also Thomas Espenshade on intriguing regional differences. *Keys to Successful Immigration* (Washington, DC: Urban Institute, 1997), pp. 89–118.

123. One can track the steady increase in restrictionist sentiment in Gallup Poll, *Public Opinion*(Wilmington, DE: Scholarly Resources, 1994), pp. 250–51 and the American National Election Studies, (Ann Arbor: University of Michigan, 1994).

124. NBC News/*Wall Street Journal* poll, October 14, 1994.

125. Gallup/Chicago Council on Foreign Relations Poll, October 7, 1994, in John Reilly, ed., *American Public Opinion and U.S. Foreign Relations, 1995* (Chicago: Chicago Council on Foreign Relations, 1995), p. 32.

126. Jack Citrin, Donald Green, Christopher Muste, and Cara Wong, "Public Opinion toward Immigration Reform," *Journal of Politics* 59, no. 3 (1997): 858–81.

127. Author's interviews with Republican House members; see also Dan Carney, "GOP Casts a Kinder Eye on 'Huddled Masses,' *Congressional Quarterly Weekly*, May 15, 1999, pp. 1127–1129.

128. Quoted in David Reimers, *Unwelcome Strangers: American Identity and the Turn against Immigration* (New York: Columbia University Press, 1999), p. 134.

129. U.S. Commission on Immigration Reform, *U.S. Immigration Policy: Restoring Credibility* (Washington, DC: Government Printing Office, 1994).

130. U.S. Commission on Immigration Reform, *Legal Immigration: Setting Priorities* (Washington, DC: Government Printing Office, 1995).

131. *New York Times*, May 25, 1995.

132. Vernon Briggs, Jr., *Mass Immigration and the National Interest* (Armonk, NY: M. E. Sharpe, 1992); and Donald Huddle, *The Net Costs of Immigration* (Washington, DC: Carrying Capacity, 1996).

133. Chilton Williamson, Jr., *The Immigration Mystique* (New York: Basic Books, 1996), p. 9.

134. Peter Brimelow, *Alien Nation* (New York: Random House, 1995); and Roy Beck, *The Case Against Immigration* (New York: W. W. Norton, 1996).

135. See the comments of Chris Smith and Mark Souter, *Washington Times*, March 20, 1996.

136. Author's anonymous interviews with group leaders and lobbyists; see also John Juddis, "Huddled Elites," *New Republic*, December 23, 1996, pp. 23–26.

137. *Wall Street Journal*, June 9, 1995; and *Congressional Quarterly*, November 25, 1995, p. 3600.

138. Reimers, *Still the Golden Door*, p. 133.

139. *Congressional Quarterly Almanac, 1995*, (Washington, DC: Congressional Quarterly Press, 1996).

140. Kenneth Lee, *Huddled Masses, Muddled Laws: Why Contemporary Immigration Policy Fails to Reflect Public Opinion* (Westport, CT: Greenwood Press, 1998), pp. 108–9.

141. *New York Times*, December 8, 1994.

142. *Congressional Quarterly Report*, March 23, 1996, p. 798.

143. *Congressional Quarterly Report*, April 15, 1995, p. 1071.

144. Fuchs memorandum, 1994, Fuchs immigration files, copy provided to the author.

145. Quoted in Reimers, *Unwelcome Strangers*, p. 143.

146. See FAIR advertisement, *Washington Times*, August 25, 1996.

147. Freeman, "Modes of Immigration Politics," p. 885.

148. Quoted in *Congressional Quarterly Report*, May 17, 1997, p. 1133.

149. Author's interviews with congressional members; see also 1996 Republican visions of immigration as "a wedge issue" in *Congressional Quarterly Report*, May 15, 1999, pp. 1127–29.

150. *Congressional Quarterly Report*, May 15, 1999, p. 1127.

151. *INS Statistical Report of 1997* (Washington, DC: Government Printing Office, 1998), p. 135.

152. *Congressional Quarterly Weekly*, May 17, 1997, p. 11132.

153. For an especially rich discussion of Mexican-American opinion on immigration, see Peter Skerry, *Mexican-Americans: The Ambivalent Minority* (New York: Free Press, 1993); regarding polling of Latinos on curbing immigration, see *Investor's Business Daily*, September 9, 1997.

154. *Investor's Business Daily*, September 9, 1997.

155. *Congressional Quarterly Weekly*, p. 1133.

156. Ibid.

157. Quoted in Scott Laidlaw, "Bush Provides Good News for GOP as It Courts Hispanics," Associated Press Story, November 29, 1999.

158. *Washington Post*, May 6, 2000.

CHAPTER TEN: CONCLUSION

1. For example, see Donald Horowitz and Gerard Noiriel, eds., *Immigrants in Two Democracies: French and American Experience* (New York: New York University Press, 1992).

2. David Jacobson, "Introduction: An American Journey," in David Jacobson, ed., *The Immigration Reader: America in a Multidisciplinary Perspective* (Oxford: Blackwell Publishers, 1998), pp. 1–2.

3. Ibid., pp. 3–4.

4. Joseph Carens, "Aliens and Citizens: The Case for Open Borders," in Ronald Beiner, ed., *Theorizing Citizenship* (Albany: State University of New York Press, 1995), pp. 229–55; see also Linda Bosniak, "Universal Citizenship and the Problem of Alienage," *Northwestern University Law Review* 84, no. 3 (Spring 2000): 963–82.

5. For example, see Michael Walzer, *Spheres of Justice: A Defense of Pluralism and Equality* (New York: Basic Books, 1983).

6. John Rawls, *The Law of Peoples* (Cambridge: Harvard University Press, 1999), pp. 38–39.

7. Roger Daniels, *Coming to America* (New York: HarperCollins, 1990); Desmond King, *In the Name of Liberalism: Illiberal Social Policy in the United States and Britain* (New York: Oxford University Press, 1999); Gwendolyn Mink, *Old Labor and New Immigrants in American Political Development: Union, Party, and the State, 1875–1920* (Ithaca: Cornell University Press, 1986); Juan Perea, "'Am I an American or Not?' Reflections on Citizenship, Americanization, and Race," in Noah Pickus, ed., *Immigration and Citizenship in the Twenty-First Century* (New York: Rowman and Littlefield, 1998), pp. 49–76; Juan Perea, ed., *Immigrants Out! The New Nativism and the Anti-Immigrant Impulse in the United States* (New York: New York University Press, 1997); Rogers Smith, *Civic Ideals: Conflicting Visions of Citizenship in U.S. History* (New Haven: Yale University Press, 1997); Ronald Takaki, *From Different Shores: Perspectives on Race and Ethnicity in America* (New York: Oxford University Press, 1994); and Ronald Takaki, *Iron Cages: Race and Culture in Nineteenth-Century America* (New York: Oxford University Press, 1990).

8. Smith, *Civic Ideals*, p. 9.

9. Peter Brimelow, *Alien Nation: Common Sense about America's Immigration Disaster* (New York: Random House, 1994), p. 13.

10. Ibid., p. 3.

11. David Moore, "Americans Ambivalent about Immigration," *Poll Analyses*, May 3, 2001, The Gallup Organization Website.

12. Gallup Poll on Immigration, June 11–17, 2001, "Gallup Poll Topics, A–Z," The Gallup Organization Website.

13. Theda Skocpol, *Protecting Soldiers and Mothers: The Origins of Social Policy in the United States* (Cambridge: Harvard University Press, 1992), p. 486.

14. John Higham, *Strangers in the Land: Patterns of American Nativism, 1860–1925* (New York: Atheneum, 1974), p. 330.

15. Paul Pierson, "Not Just What, but When: Timing and Sequencing in Political Processes," *Studies in American Political Development* 14 (Spring 2000): 72–92.

16. For an excellent account of the "second reconstruction," see Manning Marable, *Race, Reform and Rebellion* (Jackson: University Press of Mississippi, 1991).

17. See Kathleen Thelen, "Timing and Temporality in the Analysis of Institutional Evolution and Change," *Studies in American Political Development* 14 (Spring 2000): 101–8; and Mary Douglas and Steven Ney, *Missing Persons* (Berkeley and Los Angeles: University of California Press, 1998), pp. 169–73.

18. For an incisive treatment of critical junctures, see Ruth Berins Collier and David Collier, *Shaping the Political Arena* (Princeton: Princeton University Press, 1991).

19. Albert Hirschman, "Rival Interpretations of Market Society," *Journal of Economic Literature*, 20 (December 1982): 1483.

20. Thelen, "Timing and Temporality," p. 104.

21. Ibid., p. 106.

22. E. E. Schattschneider, *Politics, Pressures, and the Tariff* (New York: Prentice-Hall, 1935), p. 288; Theodore Lowi, "American Business, Public Policy, Case Studies, and Political Theory," *World Politics* (1964): 677–715.

23. Susanne Jonas, Suzie Dod Thomas, and John Ibister, "Introduction," in Jonas and Thomas, eds., *Immigration: A Civil Rights Issue for the Americas* (Wilmington, DE: Scholarly Resources, 1999), p. viii.

24. See, for example, Peter Salins, *Assimilation, American Style* (New York: Basic Books, 1997).

APPENDIX: THE SAMPLE OF INTERVIEWEES

1. The interview strategies and methods used to strengthen the case study research in chapter 8 were richly informed by Richard Fenno, *Home Style: House Members in Their Districts* (Boston: Little, Brown, and Co., 1978); Joseph Pika, "Interviewing Presidential Aides: A Political Scientist's Perspective," in George Edwards II and Stephen Wayne, eds. *Studying the Presidency* (Knoxville: University of Tennessee Press, 1983), pp. 272–300; and Mark Peterson, *Legislating Together: The White House and Capitol Hill from Eisenhower to Reagan* (Cambridge: Harvard University Press, 1990), pp. 299–301.

2. There is some disagreement among scholars about the quality of telephone versus in-person interviews. My in-person interviews were typically longer and more in-depth than were the telephone interviews. See Paul Light, "Interviewing the President's Staff: A Comparison of Telephone and Face-to-Face Techniques," *Presidential Studies Quarterly* 12 (Summer 1982): 428–33; and Pika, "Interviewing Presidential Aides," p. 295.

Index

Page references to tables and figures are in italics.

eracy tests and, 82, 84, 124–25; Mexican immigrants and, 193; national origins quotas and, 143; visa allocations and, 24

Business Roundtable, 253, 260, 268, *276*

Butler, Pierce, 51

California: Chinese exclusion in, 21, 89–99, 102–3, 106–7; Japanese exclusion in, 123; Proposition 187 in, 15, 21, 35, 245, 275–78, 283–85, 287, 296; as racial frontier, 89–90; voting blocs in, 286–87

Calivita, Kitty, 59

Canadian immigrants, 167, 170

Cannon, Joseph Gurney, 31, 116–17, *121*, 124–27, 132, 148

Carens, Joseph, 289

Carey, James B., 176

Carnegie, Andrew, *36*, 37

Carnegie Institution, 160

Carr, Wilbur J., 154, 157

Carribbean immigration, 2, 219, 238, 252

carriers of contagious diseases. *See* categories, exclusionary

Carter, Jimmy, 22, 223–24, 234–35, 238, 248

Carter, Leonard, 226

Castells, Manuel, 23

Castle Garden, 46, 67, 69–70

Castro, Fidel, 248

categories, exclusionary, 49, 57–58, 67, 69–70, 99, 141, 156, 158, 179, 190, 196, 243, 272–73

Cather, Willa, 140

Catholic Conference, U. S., 227

Catholic immigration. *See* anti-Catholicism

CATO Institute, *36*, *276*, 282

Celler, Emanuel, 163–64, 181–82, 185, 188, 191, 201, 207, 209, 213–14, 216, 227

Center for Immigration Studies (CIS), 279

Central Intelligence Agency Act (1949), 188

Central Pacific Anti-Coolie Association, 91, 94

Central Pacific Railroad, 97

Century Magazine, 72

Chae Chan Ping, 109

Chamber of Commerce (N.Y.), 160

Chamber of Commerce (U.S.), *121*, 139, 253, 281

Chandler, William, 76, 81–82, 153

Chapman, Leonard, 229–30

Chase, Salmon P., 66, 92

Chavez, Cesar, 226, 232

Cherne, Leo, 223

children, 163–65

Children's Bureau, 164

China. *See* Burlingame Treaty (1868)

Chinese Bureau, 110

Chinese Equal Rights League, 103, 108

Chinese Exclusion Acts, 2, *3*, 21, *32*, 90, 99, 106–10, 115

Chinese Exclusion Case (1889), 109

Chinese Exclusion Leagues, *104*, 124

Chinese immigrants, 11–12, 87–113, 147–48; agricultural interests and, 169; Burlingame Treaty and, 67, 88, 92–94, 102, 105, 108–9; business interests and, 24, 103, 112; civil disobedience and, 24; contract labor and, 88, 94, 103; court challenges and, 24, 40; Democratic party and, 92–94, 98–100, 102, 104–7, 136; marginalization of, 40, 108; missionaries and, 103; national origins quotas and, 166; nation-building and, 98; organized labor and, 90–92, 94, 103, 112, 118, 203; racism/racial exclusion and, 88–89, 99, 111–13, 115, 166; Republican party and, 92–100, 102, 104–7; states' regulation of, 88, 98; statistics on, 89, *90*, 97, 111, 115; visas for, 166, 177; voting rights for, 96, 103; as war brides, 189; Workingmen's party and, 102–3, 105. *See also* Chinese Exclusion Acts; Joint Special Committee to Investigate Chinese Immigration

Chinese Police Tax, 92

Chisholm, Shirley, 224, 233

Christian Coalition, 283

Christian Science Monitor, 184, 238

Chrysler, Dick, 283

Citizens Committee on Displaced Persons (CCDP), 183–88

Citizen's Committee on Indochinese Refugees, 223

citizenship rights. *See* naturalization

Citizenship USA initiative, 285

Citrin, Jack, 277

Civil Rights Acts, 96, 212, 215

Costain, Anne, 39
Craighead, E. B., 315n.177
Crevocoeur, Michael-Guillaume-Jean de, 305n.12
Crewdson, John, 228
criminals. *See* categories, exclusionary
Crocker, Charles, 100, *104*
Cuban Adjustment Act (1966), 222
Cuban Americans, 286
Cuban Refugee Act (1960), *4*
Cuban refugees, 218, 222, 244, 246–49, 278–79
cultural protectionists, 35, 221, 241
Customs Office, 110
Cuyler, Rev. T. W., 71
Czechoslovakian refugees, 222

Dahl, Robert, 24
Dana, Charles, 63
Daniels, Roger, 290, 305n.12
Darwin, Charles, 79, 140
Daughters of the American Revolution, 121, 139, 164
Davidson, Roger, 31
Davis, Gray, 287
Davis, James, 155
DeConcini, Dennis, 271
Democratic National Committee, 205–6
Democratic party: American Protective Association and, 72; anti-Catholicism and, 99; Chinese exclusion and, 92–95, 98–100, 102, 104–7; contract labor and, 69–70; divisions in, 61, 63, 65, 235; electoral statistics of, *96, 101–2, 106*; employer sanctions and, 226, 228, 235, 255; European immigration and, 48, 55, 59–60, 67–69, 99, 136; expansionist stance of, 11, 205–7, 214, 217; family reunification and, 270; Irish immigrants and, 48, 55, 65; Jewish refugee immigration and, 157, 159; Know-Nothings and, 64; literacy tests and, 82–83, 121, 135, 137; McCarran-Walter Act and, 197; Mexican immigrants and, 173; nationalization of immigration control and, 68; national security concerns and, 179; organized labor alignment and, 41, 69, 94–95; "partisan speakership" and, 132; preference system and, 189; racism/racial exclusion and, 94–95, 99
Democratic-Republican party, 53–56

Democratic Study Group (DSG), 206–8, 211, 214
democratization, 59–60, 76
deportations, 70, 142, 159, 173–74, 189, 195, 221
depressions, economic, 20–21, 74, 97, 155–56, 158, 160, 172–73
Derthick, Martha, 41
Dickstein, Samuel, 163–65
Dictionary of Races (Dillingham Commission), 130–31
Dies, Martin, 160
Dillingham, William P., 124, 127–28, 141, 143
Dillingham Commission, 42–43, 128–33, 138, 143, 168–69, 198, 249–50
"direct democracy," 76, 132–33, 148–49
Dirksen, Everett, 212, 215
disabled, mentally or physically. *See* categories, exclusionary
displaced persons, 181–88
Displaced Persons Acts, *4*, 187–89, 200
Dole, Elizabeth, 272
Dole, Robert, 278, 285–86
Domestic Council Committee on Illegal Immigration, 229–30
Dornan, Robert, 286
Douglas, Paul, 194, 201–2, 225
Douglas, Stephen A., 61
Douglass, Frederick, *36*, 37, 97, 232
Drinan, Robert, 224
Dutch immigrants, 65, 130

Eastern Panic (1873), 97
Eastland, James, 181, 189, 193–94, 197, 199, 201, 203, 208–9, 213–14, 225, 227–29, 234, 240
Eaves, Lucille, 91
economic causation models, 19–23
Education and Labor Committee (House), 257
Education Bureau, 140
Edwards, James, 303n.44
egalitarian nationalists, 36–37, *50*, 88, 103, *121*
Ehrlich, Paul, 236
Eilberg, Joshua, 223, 237
Eisenhower, Dwight, 34, 197–98, 200–201, 203, 207, 240
elective offices, 51–52
"electoral realignments," 6–7, 27–28

PRINCETON STUDIES IN AMERICAN POLITICS: HISTORICAL, INTERNATIONAL, AND COMPARATIVE PERSPECTIVES